THE
TEXAS GUN OWNER'S Guide

Who can bear arms?

❖

Where are guns forbidden?

❖

When can you shoot?

by *Alan Korwin*
and *Georgene Lockwood*
illustrations by Gregg Myers and Ralph Richardson

BLOOMFIELD PRESS
Scottsdale, Arizona

BLOOMFIELD PRESS
4848 E. Cactus #505-440
Scottsdale, AZ 85254
(602) 996-4020 Offices
(602) 494-0679 Fax
1-800-707-4020 Sales Hotline

GunLaws.com

ISBN-13: 978-1-889632-38-4
Library of Congress Catalog Card Number: 95-77340
Photo of Mr. Korwin by Jeremy Voas

ATTENTION
Firearm Training Instructors, Clubs, Organizations,
Educators and all interested parties:
Call us for deep quantity discounts!

To Order: For single copies or for wholesale shipments, call
1-800-707-4020, or write to us at the address above.
For Updates: sign up for free email updates at our website!

Every gun owner needs this book—
"It doesn't make sense to own a gun and not know the rules."

Printed and bound in the United States of America
at McNaughton & Gunn, Saline, Michigan

8th Edition

TABLE OF CONTENTS

ACKNOWLEDGMENTS

This book is really the result of all the help we received, great and small, from the good people who shared their thoughts and resources with us. Thank you.

And with apologies to the countless friends, fans, officials and others whose continued involvement, support and input has made a difference, yet whose names do not appear on this list made in 1995 for the first edition.

Ron Bertsch, Deputy, National Forests and Grasslands
Dr. James T. "Doc" Brown, Texas State Rifle Association
Susan Carley, Research and Support
Bill Clede, Sysop, Firearms Forum, CompuServe, along with
    Jeff Halapin, M. Scott Hammon, Kelley Hughes, John Rich
    and Mark Thompson
Larry Cooper, Marksman Indoor Range, Inc.
James Dark, Executive Director, Texas State Rifle Association
Candice M. DeBarr, Research and Support
Diane Eisele
Randy Gibson, Exec. Dir., Texas State Rifle Association
Tom Gresham, Contributing Editor, Sports Afield
Steve Hall, Conservation Ed. Dir., Texas Parks & Wildlife Dept.
Sean P. Healy, Healy Law Offices, P.C.
Gary Kansteiner, Attorney, Texas Legislative Council
Fred D. Knot, Research and Support
Marshall Kummel, Research and Support
Cheryl and Tyler Korwin
Jim Lockwood
Jeff Long, Information Coordinator, Texas General Land Office
Joe McBride, President, McBride's Guns, Inc.
Tara Mica, Texas State Rifle Association
John Molleston, Texas General Land Office
Harold D. Oates, Captain, Texas Parks & Wildlife Dept.
Karl N. Olson, Security Officer, Texas Parks & Wildlife Dept.

The Honorable Senator Jerry Patterson
Linda Paulson, CompuServe Journalism Forum
Terrence Plas, The Pensus Group
E.B. Reddoch, III, Exec. Dir., Texas State Rifle Association
Albert C. Ross, General Counsel, Texas State Rifle Assn.
Richard Shaw, The Pensus Group
David Smith, Alpine Range
Ralph Talbot, Texas State Rifle Association
Texas Arms Rights Coalition, Neil Atkins
Texas Gun Dealers Association
Charles H. "Chuck" Thompson,
    American Defensive Firearms Institute
Gabriel Torre, Sportsman Shooting Center
Alice Tripp, Legislative Director, Texas State Rifle Association
Carlos Vaca, Asst. Commander, Texas Parks & Wildlife Dept.
Paul Velte IV, Attorney at Law
Lt. Dan H. Walker, Texas DPS (Retired)
Charles Wallace, Coordinator, TSRA Grass Roots
W.L. Don Welch, Chief Ranger, Lower Colorado River Authority
James C. "Jimmy" Williams, Attorney
Karen Ziegler, Red's Indoor Range

The Texas State Rifle Association
allowed the use of information in their pamphlet,
"Know Your Texas Firearm Laws."

The National Rifle Association Institute
allowed the use of material in their pamphlet,
"Your State Firearms Laws."

In their dealings with us we found the Texas Dept. of Public Safety
to be cooperative, professional, hard-working and dedicated to fair
implementation of the complex 1995 Right-to-Carry law.

The Texas River Authorities' cooperation was greatly appreciated.
Special thanks to Phoenix trial lawyer Michael P. Anthony
Cover design by Ralph Richardson

PREFACE

Texas has strict gun laws. You have to obey the laws.
There are serious penalties for breaking the rules.

Many gun owners don't know all the rules.
Some have the wrong idea of what the rules are.
It doesn't make sense to own a gun and not know the rules.

Here at last is a comprehensive book, in plain English,
about the laws and regulations that control firearms in Texas.

This book is published under the full protection of the
First Amendment with the expressed understanding that you,
not we, are completely responsible for your own actions.

The One-Glaring-Error theory says there's at least
one glaring error hidden in any complex piece of work.
This book is no different. Watch out for it.

"It will be of little avail to the people that the laws are made by men of
their own choice, if the laws be so voluminous that they cannot be
read, or so incoherent that they cannot be understood; if they be
repealed or revised before they are promulgated, or undergo such
incessant changes that no man who knows what the law is to-day can
guess what it will be to-morrow."
–James Madison, Federalist Papers, #62

"Do you really think that we want those laws to be observed? We
want them broken. We're after power and we mean it. There's no way
to rule innocent men. The only power any government has is the
power to crack down on criminals. Well, when there aren't enough
criminals, one makes them. One declares so many things to be a crime
that it becomes impossible for men to live without breaking laws. Who
wants a nation of law-abiding citizens? What's there in that for
anyone? But just pass the kind of laws that can neither be observed nor
enforced nor objectively interpreted, and you create a nation of law
breakers—and then you cash in on guilt."
–Ayn Rand (*Atlas Shrugged*)

FOREWORD • WARNING! • DON'T MISS THIS!

This book is not "the law," and is not a substitute for the law. The law includes all the legal obligations imposed on you, a much greater volume of work than the mere firearms statutes contained in this book. You are fully accountable under the exact wording and current official interpretations of all applicable laws, regulations, court precedents, executive orders and more, when you deal with firearms under any circumstances.

Many people find laws hard to understand, and gathering all the relevant ones is a lot of work. This book helps you with these chores. Collected in one volume are copies, reporduced with great care, of the main state laws controlling gun use in Texas.

In addition, the laws and other regulations are expressed in regular conversational terms for your convenience, and cross referenced to the statutes. While great care has been taken to accomplish this with a high degree of accuracy, **no guarantee of accuracy is expressed or implied, and the explanatory sections of this book are not to be considered as legal advice or a restatement of law.** In explaining the general meanings of the laws, using plain English, differences inevitably arise, so **you must always check the actual laws.** Only edited pieces of the laws are included here. The authors and publisher expressly disclaim any liability whatsoever arising out of reliance on information found in this book. New laws and regulations may be enacted at any time by the authorities. **The authors and publisher make no representation that this book includes all requirements and prohibitions which may exist.** Local ordinances, rules, regulations and policies are not covered.

This book concerns the gun laws as they apply to law-abiding private residents in the state of Texas only. It is not intended to and does not describe most situations relating to licensed gun dealers, museums or educational institutions, local or federal military personnel, American Indians, foreign nationals, the police or other peace officers, any person summoned by a peace officer to help in the performance of official duties, persons with special licenses (including collectors), posse members, non-residents, persons with special authorizations or permits, bequests or intestate succession, persons under indictment, felons, prisoners, escapees, dangerous or repetitive offenders, criminal street gang members, delinquent, incorrigible or unsupervised juveniles, judicial officers, government employees, any other people restricted or prohibited from firearm possession and more.

While this book discusses possible criminal consequences of improper gun use, it avoids most issues related to deliberate gun crimes. This means that certain laws are excluded, or not explained in the text. Some examples are: criminally negligent homicide and capital murder; manslaughter; concealment of stolen firearms; enhanced penalties for commission of crimes with firearms, including armed robbery, burglary, theft, kidnapping, drug offenses and assault; smuggling firearms into public aircraft; threatening flight attendants with firearms; taking a weapon from a peace officer; possession of contraband; possession of a firearm in a prison by a prisoner; false application for a firearm; removal of a body after a shooting; drive by shootings; retaliation; and this is only a partial list.

The main relevant parts of Texas statutes that relate to private gun ownership and use are reproduced in Appendix D. These are formally known as *Texas Revised Statutes,* and includes the *Penal Code* and *Code of Criminal Procedure.* Other state laws which may apply, such as Hunting Laws and official agency regulations, are discussed, but these laws are *not* reproduced. Key federal laws are discussed, but the laws themselves are *not* reproduced. Case law decisions, which affect the interpretation of the statutes, are *not* included.

FIREARMS LAWS ARE SUBJECT TO CHANGE WITHOUT NOTICE. You are strongly urged to consult with a qualified attorney and local authorities to determine the current status and applicability of the law to specific situations which you may encounter. The proper authorities are in Appendix C.

Guns are deadly serious business and require the highest level of responsibility from you. Firearm ownership, possession and use are rights that carry awesome responsibility. Unfortunately, **what the law says and what the authorities and courts do aren't always an exact match.** You must remember that each legal case is different and may lack prior court precedents. A decision to prosecute a case and the charges brought may involve a degree of discretion from the authorities involved. Sometimes, there just isn't a plain, clear-cut answer you can rely upon. Abuses, ignorance, carelessness, human frailties and plain fate subject you to legal risks, which can be exacerbated when firearms are involved. Take nothing for granted, recognize that legal risk is attached to everything you do, and **ALWAYS ERR ON THE SIDE OF SAFETY.**

Special Note on Pending Legislation

Bills have been proposed by law makers nationally who would:

- Outlaw specific or classes of firearms by price range, melting point, design, operating characteristics, accuracy, type of safety mechanism, type of sights, point of origin, appearance and by name.
- Restrict the amount of ammunition a gun can hold, devices for feeding ammunition, allowable types of ammunition or reduce ammo shelf life
- Restrict the number of firearms and the amount of ammunition a person may buy or own, and implement burdensome storage requirements
- Require proficiency testing and periodic licensing with expiration dates
- Register firearms and owners nationally
- Use taxation as a way to limit firearm and ammunition ownership
- Create new liabilities for firearm owners, manufacturers, dealers, parents and persons involved in firearms accidents
- Require firearms to be unloaded, locked away or otherwise inoperable
- Censor classified ads for firearms, eliminate firearms publications and outlaw any dangerous speech or publication
- Melt down firearms that are confiscated by police
- Prohibit gun shows and abolish hunting
- Deny or criminalize civil rights for government-promised security
- Adopt standards from countries that don't recognize the right to arms
- Require technologies that don't exist or cannot be economically used
- Repeal or flatly ignore the Second Amendment to the U.S. Constitution

In contrast, less attention has been paid to laws that would:

- Mandate school-based safety training
- Provide general self-defense awareness and training
- Encourage personal responsibility in resisting crime
- Protect people who stand up and act against crime
- Guarantee people's right to travel legally armed for personal safety
- Fix the conditions which generate hard-core criminals
- Assure sentencing of serious criminals, increase the percentage of sentences actually served, provide more prison space and permanently remove habitual criminals from society
- Improve rehabilitation and reduce repeat offenses
- Reduce plea bargaining and parole abuses
- Close legal loopholes and reform criminal justice malpractice
- Reform the juvenile justice system
- Improve law enforcement quality and efficiency
- Establish and strengthen victims' rights and protection
- Hold the rights of all American citizens in unassailable esteem
- Provide for the common defense and buttress the Constitution

Some experts believe that easy-to-enact but ineffectual "feel good" laws are being pursued instead of the much tougher course of laws and social changes that would reduce crime and its root causes. Many laws aim at disarming citizens while ignoring the fact that gun possession by criminals is already strictly illegal and largely unenforced. Increasing attacks on the Constitution and civil liberties are threatening freedoms Americans have always had. You are advised to become aware of any new laws which may be enacted. Contact your legislators to express your views on proposed legislation.

To our patient and supportive families

THE RIGHT TO
KEEP AND BEAR ARMS
1

In the United States of America, people have always had the right to keep arms, and the right to bear arms. The Second Amendment to the United States Constitution is the national guarantee for this preexisting human right to have and use guns. The Second Amendment is referred to as The Right To Keep And Bear Arms. This is what it says:

> "A well regulated Militia, being necessary to the security of a free State, the right of the people to keep and bear Arms, shall not be infringed."

The intentions of the revolutionaries who drafted the Constitution were clear at the time. It was this right to bear arms that allowed those people more than two centuries ago to break away from British rule. An armed populace was a precondition for independence and freedom from oppressive government. The founders of the United States of America were unambiguous and unequivocal in their intent:

No free man shall be debarred the use of arms.
–Thomas Jefferson

The Constitution shall never be construed to authorize Congress to prevent the people of the United States, who are peaceable citizens, from keeping their own arms.
–Samuel Adams

Little more can reasonably be aimed at with respect to the people at large than to have them properly armed.
–Alexander Hamilton

Americans have the right and advantage of being armed.
–James Madison

15

> The great object is that every man be armed.
> Everyone who is able may have a gun.
> **–Patrick Henry**

Today the issue is controversial and emotionally charged. There are powerful and vocal groups on all sides of the topic of guns. Some people have taken to saying that the Second Amendment doesn't mean what it always used to mean, and there have been calls to repeal it. The U.S. Supreme Court has heard more than 100 gun cases, and contrary to news reports, has recognized an individual right to arms consistently for two centuries. In the 2008 landmark *Heller* case, the Court unequivocally recognized it as a "specific enumerated right" of individuals, on a par with the right to counsel and free speech, and discarded the revisionist "collective rights" theory invented to attack this fundamental liberty. Importantly, all 50 states recognize a person's right to act in self defense, completely apart from firearms debates.

The Second Amendment of course means what it always used to mean, which explains the armed populace we observe today. This is also seen in the fact that 43 states have the right to keep arms and the right to bear arms imbedded in their own Constitutions, often in terms more direct than the wording in the Bill of Rights itself. If our Second Amendment guarantee was ever torn asunder, the state constitutions would still be in place. This is what Texas says:

Excerpt from the Constitution of the State of Texas
Article 1, Section 23: Right To Keep And Bear Arms

> "Every citizen shall have the right to keep and bear arms in the lawful defense of himself or the State; but the Legislature shall have power, by law, to regulate the wearing of arms, with a view to prevent crime."

Nothing in Texas law may conflict with our fundamental creed, the U.S. Constitution, and so the right to arms is passed down to Texans, as it is to the people of all the states in the union. The states, however, have passed laws to regulate arms people keep and bear within their borders. That's what this book is about.

The state of Texas has a *rule of preemption* about gun laws, found in §1.08 of the Penal Code. This means that, with limited exceptions, local authorities within the state cannot pass laws or regulations that conflict with the state's laws and regulations. Power is delegated only to the state to regulate firearms, which provides uniform rules statewide.

The Dreaded "§" Section Symbol:
Texas Penal Code §46.15

The character "§" means "section." You read it aloud (or to yourself) as "section" whenever it appears. Every individually named chunk of law in America is called a section and has a section number, so you see this symbol a lot. It's an integral part of the written name for every statute on the books. A section may be just a few words or extremely long, and it may be amended by new laws. Penal Code section forty six fifteen, the law shown above, is one of the main Texas gun laws.

The section "§" symbol intimidates many people and as such, is valuable for keeping the law mysterious and somehow unknowable to the general public. Don't let it scare you. Just think "section" whenever you see "§." To write a section symbol, make a capital "S" on top of another capital "S."

To make a "section" symbol
draw an "S" over another "S"

A Word About Federal Law

The TEXAS Gun Owner's Guide covers the federal laws that relate to the right of the people to keep and bear arms.

Federal law generally does not control the day-to-day details of how you can carry a firearm in any given state, or the rules for self defense and crime resistance, or where you can go for target practice. The individual states control these things. Federal law focuses on commercial aspects, interstate transportation, certain prohibited weapons, crimes against the nation and other specifically defined areas.

It's a common mistake to think that federal laws are "higher" than state laws, or that they somehow come first. They control different things, and the states and the feds each have full jurisdiction over their respective areas. They may also disagree on where those lines are drawn.

WELCOME TO THE STATE GUN LAWS

The majority of Texas "gun laws" (they are never actually called that) can be found in the *Texas Penal Code* and the *Code of Criminal Procedure*. The complete Penal Code and Code of Criminal Procedure are both contained in an 800-page book called *Texas Criminal Laws*. It is widely available in libraries, online, and a copy may be obtained inexpensively from the Texas Dept. of Public Safety.

You'll find the main relevant sections of state gun law printed in *The Texas Gun Owner's Guide* in Appendix D. Many of the fine details concerning guns come from other sources, listed in Appendix C. Texas gun laws appear in at least 15 titles of the state code:

Agriculture Code (AC)
Alcoholic Beverage Code (ABC)
Civil Practice and Remedies Code (CPRC)
Code of Criminal Procedure (CCP)
Education Code (EC)
Family Code (FC)
Government Code (GC)
Health and Safety Code (HSC)
Labor Code (LC)
Local Government Code (LGC)
Occupational Code (OC)
Parks and Wildlife Code (PWC)
Penal Code (PC)
Property Code
Transportation Code (TC)

Reasons for the Texas Gun Laws

Texas criminal law begins with a list of reasons for its existence (see Penal Code §1.02), all of which have direct impact on the right to keep and bear arms:

1–To safeguard conduct that isn't criminal;

2–To define what the state can and can't do in criminal matters;

3–To guide and limit official discretion in law enforcement;

4–To insure public safety by banning conduct that might harm people;

5–To give people fair warning of what is considered prohibited behavior and the consequences of violating the law;

6–To discourage crimes by providing penalties;

7–To provide punishment that discourages future criminal activity;

8–To rehabilitate people who are convicted.

WHAT IS A FIREARM?

In Texas, a firearm is defined in §1.07 of the Penal Code as a *deadly weapon*, a term that includes anything that is either designed for lethal use (like a gun or a bayonet), or can be used lethally (like a kitchen knife or a baseball bat). Specifically, state law says that *firearm* means:

> "any device designed, made, or adapted to expel a projectile through a barrel by using the energy generated by an explosion or burning substance or any device readily convertible to that use."

Antique or curio firearms made before 1899 are excluded, including those having a folding knife blade as part of their design. Also excluded are replicas of pre-1899 arms that don't use rimfire or centerfire ammo. Guns that have been thoroughly disabled and are only for show are not regarded as guns under federal law. Questions about how to make a gun unserviceable can be directed to the Firearms Technology Branch of the Bureau of Alcohol, Tobacco, Firearms and Explosives (BATFE).

A zip gun is anything that was not originally a firearm, but has been adapted to work like a firearm. These fall into the Prohibited Weapons category, described in Chapter 3.

Air Guns

Air guns got defined for the first time in **2013** in LGC §229.001 as any gun that discharges a pellet, BB or paintball by means of compressed air, gas propellant or spring. Some types of BB gun designed for hunting are quite powerful and the safest course is to always treat them with the respect due regular firearms, though they don't meet that technical definition. The fairly new category of *toy gaming guns*, such as airsoft and paintball, sometimes used for playing "tag," should always be used with protective gear. Adult supervision is advisable.

Air guns are included in city preemption and shooting-range statutes so they are regulated in a manner similar to firearms. See also LGC §§235.022, 235.023, 236.002, 236.003 dealing with powers your county has and limitations it may have placed on possession, ownership, transport, discharge, registration and more for air guns. Minors carrying air guns on public property or private property without consent of the property owner can be regulated by cities under LGC §229.001. Check with your own city and county about air gun rules where you live. This lack of preemption for uniform air gun rules at the city and county level demonstrates the problems gun owners would face without such protection at the state level for firearms.

These various *nearly guns* typically use compressed air or CO_2, or battery or hand-powered piston action to compress air or springs. The nearly-gun issue continues to grow, with the introduction of the TASER-brand electronic-control device for consumer use. Some states have begun regulating those as a special category of arms. BATFE in at least two rulings has said they are not guns. Rumors that a Class 3 Officer's Phaser will be on the market soon are unsubstantiated.

Airsoft and other designs are often precise replicas of popular firearms and virtually identical at a quick glance, so care must be taken to avoid giving the impression they are real. Don't panic the neighbors. And remember, people have been shot for brandishing nearly guns.

For the letter of the law and the strict legal wording of the various weapons definitions, see §46.01 of the Penal Code.

In this book, the words *gun, firearm* and *arms* are used to refer to all handguns or long guns. When you see the terms *handgun, rifle, shotgun, long gun, semiautomatic pistol* or *semiauto,* or *revolver,* the reference is to that specific type of firearm only.

Toy Guns

Federal toy-gun laws since 1988 have required a blaze orange plug of at least 6mm in the muzzle of certain toys, except for theater, movie and TV use, or as modified by the Secretary of Commerce. Toy, look-alike and imitation guns, including water guns, as federally defined, specifically exclude traditional BB, paintball or pellet air guns. The sale of BB-type air guns or certain non-firing replicas have federal protection that even real firearms don't presently enjoy—states are specifically prohibited from banning sales, under 15 USC §5001. The government is authorized to study the criminal misuse of toy guns and the effectiveness of the marking systems in police combat situations. The initial study was due in 1989.

Non-Guns

No consistent legal status for non-guns has surfaced in the state. These include gun drawings, pointed-finger guns, gun-T-shirts, gun photos, gun bumper stickers and slogans, twig guns, gun speech, the notorious brandished chicken leg and half-eaten toaster cakes. These are used primarily by schools to threaten, harass and intimidate students, and also for expulsions, suspensions, reprimands, derision, scorn, and in some cases, anti-rights bigotry directed at the public and letters to parents. Up until the 1970s, many high schools had shooting ranges on campus and kids brought guns to school for competition, got varsity letters in marksmanship, went to ROTC or hunting after class, and even brought guns and ammo for show and tell. Today we find a system that has vilified these vital exemplars of freedom out of the school experience.

WHO CAN BEAR ARMS IN TEXAS?

An adult resident of Texas may have a gun unless:

1–You have been convicted of a felony. A felon may not possess a gun until five years after release from prison (or from parole, community supervision, etc., whichever is later) and then, only at the premises where the person lives (see Penal Code §46.04). A violation is a third degree felony;

2–You have been convicted of a misdemeanor domestic violence charge as defined under Penal Code §22.01 and it is less than five years since your release;

3–You are under certain domestic violence court orders as defined under Penal Code §46.04, except for full time peace officers, for the duration of the order;

4–You are subject to a court order concerning sexual assault specified in Penal Code §38.112;

5–You are serving a term of imprisonment in any correctional or detention facility;

6–You suffer from any of a long list of disqualifying mental impairments specified in Government Code §411.052;

7–You are prohibited by federal law, as described below.

Having a firearm under items 2 or 3 is a class A misdemeanor, see Penal Code § 22.01 and §46.04. An offense under item 4 is a class 3 felony, see Penal Code §46.10. Federal sentencing guidelines (item 7) were 1,200 pages long last time we looked.

Under Penal Code §46.06, it's a class A misdemeanor to transfer a handgun to a person you know will use it unlawfully, or to a person you know is subject to an active protective order (sometimes referred to as a court restraining order). The same penalty applies to knowingly selling a firearm or ammunition to anyone who is intoxicated, or to a person who has been convicted of a felony in less than five years from their release date (under state law; federal law would prohibit such a transfer unless the person had somehow had their federal firearms rights restored, which would be lost because of the felony). In 1999, Health and Safety Code §247.065 introduced a "right" of assisted-living facilities operators to maintain an environment free of weapons.

The Federal Prohibited Possessor List

In addition, you may also be prohibited from firearm possession under federal laws designed to keep weapons out of the hands of criminals and others. These overriding restrictions are listed in Section 8 of the Firearms Transaction Record, Form #4473, which must be completed when you buy a gun from a federally licensed dealer. Federal law prohibits having, shipping, transporting or receiving a gun by anyone who:

- Is charged with or has been convicted of a crime that carries more than a one-year sentence (except two-year state misdemeanors);
- Is a fugitive from justice;
- Unlawfully uses or is addicted to marijuana, a depressant, a stimulant or a narcotic drug;
- Is mentally defective;
- Is mentally incompetent;

- Is committed to a mental institution;
- Has been dishonorably discharged from the armed forces;
- Has renounced U.S. citizenship;
- Is an illegal alien;
- Is under a court order restraining harassment, stalking or threatening of an intimate partner or partner's child. (Note that state law requires protective orders to include language about this restriction, see Family Code §85.026.)
- Has been convicted of a domestic violence misdemeanor as described by federal law (for more on this new addition to federal law see Chapter 7).

When filling out a Firearm Transaction Record form you're required to state that you are not in any of these categories. It's a five-year federal felony to make false statements on a Firearms Transaction Record form, and it's illegal to knowingly provide a firearm to a prohibited possessor.

DPS must send relevant mental health and other disqualification records to the FBI, for inclusion in the NICS background-check database. Courts must send this confidential info to DPS, only such info as is needed may be sent, and you are guaranteed access to your info, with a process in place to correct any errors and send those to the FBI, as described in Government Code §411.052 and .0521, and Health and Safety Code §574.088.

JUVENILES

The law for a law-abiding parent to remember nowadays is that, any time your child goes shooting with or without you, your kid needs to carry written permission from you, even if you're with your child, to receive or have a gun or go shooting. That's the net effect of a Clinton-era federal law (18 USC §922x) regulating children.

Texas law sets no legal minimum age at which a child can have or use a firearm. This is a choice made by parents or legal guardians of the minor, who have a legal obligation to act in a responsible manner.

However, transferring a firearm to a child under 18 is a class A misdemeanor (Penal Code §46.06), unless the transfer is with the permission of the child's parent or legal guardian. If the transfer is a sale, the permission must be in writing according to state law, and federal law forbids a dealer to sell to a person under 18; a child may have possession of a gun under proper circumstances, or even own guns through gifts or inheritance, but cannot buy one at retail.

A child alleged to have acted delinquently with a firearm must be detained until released by the proper authorities, as defined in Family Code §53.02. Under Family Code §54.0406, a child convicted of specified firearms offenses must tell authorities how the firearm was acquired, in order to receive probation.

Federal Regulation of Juveniles

Federal rules now generally prohibit people under 18 from having handguns or matching ammunition, or providing these to juveniles, unless they meet some additional requirements, under 18 USC §922(x). While carrying written consent from a parent or guardian (who must not be prohibited from possessing a firearm themselves), a minor may have a handgun:

1–in the course of employment;
2–in legitimate ranching or farming;
3–for target practice;
4–for hunting;
5–for a class in the safe and lawful use of a handgun;
6–for transport, unloaded in a locked case, directly to and from such activities.

Also allowed is a minor who uses a handgun against an intruder, at home or in another home where the minor is an invited guest. If a handgun or ammunition is legally transferred to a minor, who then commits an offense with the firearm, the firearm must be returned to its lawful owner after due process. Minors may inherit title (but not possession) of a handgun. Violation of this law carries fines and a one-year jail term.

Child Safety Law

If a child under 17 years old gains access to an unsecured and loaded firearm (whether a round is in the chamber or not) because it was left where an adult knew or should have known the child could get it, the adult can be charged with a class C misdemeanor. If the child fires the gun and hurts or kills anyone the adult can be charged with a class A misdemeanor. See Penal Code §46.13 for the letter of the law.

A firearm is secured, for the purposes of this law, when you've taken the steps a reasonable person would take to prevent child access, including (but not limited to) putting it in a locked container, using a trigger lock, or by other means.

There is a defense to prosecution under this law if:

1–someone older than 18 is supervising the child in hunting, sporting or other lawful purpose;
2–the child uses a firearm lawfully to defend people or property;
3–the child was in an agricultural enterprise at the time; or
4–the child got the weapon through illegal entry.

Law enforcement officials must wait seven days before arresting the adult who made the gun available if the child is a member of that family and the child self-inflicted death or serious injury.

Firearms dealers must post a sign in block letters at least one inch high stating:

> "It is unlawful to store, transport, or abandon an unsecured firearm in a place where children are likely to be and can obtain access to the firearm."

If a court allows community supervision for an adult who has violated this law, it may require the person to give public service at the court's discretion, or to pay for and attend a firearms safety course, for as long as 17 hours, that meets or exceeds National Rifle Association requirements (see Code of Criminal Procedure Article 42.12 §13B).

HOW DO YOU OBTAIN FIREARMS?

Guns and ammunition may be bought or sold between private residents of this state under the same conditions as any other private sale of merchandise, provided you comply with all other laws (you can't sell to prohibited possessors or to minors, etc.).

Sale *and delivery* of firearms by a private resident to any non-resident is prohibited by federal law. Such sales are allowed, but delivery must take place through licensed dealers in the two people's states—it's a violation to transport the firearm interstate yourself. For details see *Transport and Shipping* in this chapter.

As long as all other laws are complied with, a non-resident may temporarily borrow or rent a firearm for any lawful sporting purposes from a dealer or a resident. You are free to own any number of firearms and any amount of ammunition.

If you are going to deal in guns (or import, manufacture or ship firearms in interstate or foreign commerce), you need a license from BATFE. Federal and state authorities may exercise a degree of judgment in determining when multiple firearm sales by a private individual constitute "dealing" in firearms, which is a felony without a license. Federal regulations provide some guidance on the matter. A dealer is:

> "A person who devotes time, attention, and labor to dealing in firearms as a regular course of trade or business with the principle objective of livelihood and profit through the repetitive purchase and resale of firearms, but such a term shall not include a person who makes occasional sales, exchanges, or purchases of firearms for the enhancement of a personal collection or for a hobby, or who sells all or part of his personal collection of firearms." (CFR §178.11)

In-State Purchase

Federally licensed dealers of firearms and ammunition are spread across the state. Residents need no special license or permit to walk in and buy a regular firearm from a regular dealer. Firearms may be paid for in the same ways as any other retail merchandise. You may sell guns you own to any dealers in the state willing to buy them from you.

To purchase a handgun and matching ammunition you must be at least 21 years old. Your request to purchase a handgun from a dealer, if you don't have a CHL, is sent by the dealer to the FBI in Clarksburg, W. Va. They then conduct an instant criminal-history background check (referred to as a "NICS" check) required by both state and federal law. However, a waiting period of up to three business days may apply if the FBI decides it needs more time to make a determination (see Chapter 7 for more on the Brady law). Once issued, the federal NICS approval is good for 30 days, but only for a single business transaction, which may include more than one firearm. For another transaction (that is, to make another purchase at another time), another check is required. The NICS check went active on Nov. 30, 1998, effectively federalizing all retail gun sales in America.

To purchase a rifle or shotgun and matching ammunition you must be at least 18 years old, and the same NICS process applies (The Brady handgun law, it turns out, controls all long guns too). Some ammunition may be used in either a handgun or a rifle. This type of ammo can only be sold to a person between the ages of 18 and 21 if the dealer is satisfied that it will be used only in a rifle.

Government-issued photo ID with your name, address, date of birth and signature, must be shown to the dealer. A driver's license (or state ID card issued in place of a driver's license) is the usual form of ID expected by most dealers.

When you buy firearms from a licensed dealer you must fill out a federal Firearms Transaction Record, form 4473. There are no duplicate copies made of this form, and the original is permanently filed by the dealer. The form requires personal identification information, identification of the gun and its serial number, and your signature, stating that you are not ineligible to obtain firearms under federal or state law. Licensed dealers keep copies of this form available.

The purchase of more than one handgun from the same dealer in a 5-day period is reported to BATFE and, under the Brady law, to local authorities as well, before the close of business on the day of the sale.

At the end of 2004, the NICS Index had 3,664,827 names in it, triple what it began with, growing to 5.6 million by May 2009 and 10.3 million by **2013**. Illegal aliens were 51% of the total, felons 15.3%, fugitives 3.8%, mental cases 27.7% and other types below 1% each. Instant responses in 2004 were about 92%, system uptime was at 99%, and NICS referred more than 7,200 firearm retrieval cases to BATFE. Total NICS checks through June 2009 was 103,019,294. This rose to 174,623,643 by August of **2013**. Over less than a 15-year period this suggests that privately held firearms nationally of only 200 million, a commonly cited figure, may be quite low.

Out-of-State Purchases

Texas residents, including businesses and corporations, can buy guns anywhere in the U.S. (PC §46.07). The old "contiguous states" rule was repealed in 2009. Such purchases must conform to local laws at the place of purchase. However, the overlapping local, state and federal gun laws in the nation are frequently incompatible, and can sometimes make this difficult.

When you buy a long gun in person from a licensed dealer out of state you may take delivery immediately if the laws of that state allow it. Such a purchase may be shipped directly to your home (one of the rare times when direct interstate shipments are permissible). Federal law 18 USC §922 requires that handguns bought out of state must be shipped to you through a licensed dealer in your home state—you cannot legally take possession of a handgun directly from a dealer outside your home state.

Since an out-of-state dealer may not be able to check your credentials as they would for residents of their own state, you may find that the system in the dealer's state, or some other procedure, will be used. Some dealers, concerned with overlapping and often conflicting state and federal gun laws, and reluctant to jeopardize their licenses, have been known to refuse sales to residents of other states, even when those sales would be perfectly legal.

In any case, to purchase a firearm from an out-of-state dealer, you can always have that dealer transfer the firearm (sidearm or long gun) to a Texas dealer, from whom you can legally make the purchase and take possession with few concerns about the perplexing proprieties of interstate purchases.

Gun Shows

Gun shows are periodically sponsored by national, state and local organizations devoted to the collection, competitive use or other sporting use of firearms. You may buy firearms from an in-state dealer at a gun show the same as you could on their regular retail premises. Out-of-state dealers can display their wares and take orders, but cannot make deliveries to non-licensees at the show. Purchases made from an out-of-state dealer must be transferred to a licensee within this state, from the out-of-state dealer's licensed premises.

CARRYING FIREARMS

Dating back to 1871, during Reconstruction in the days after the War Between the States, a severe handgun "traveling" ban was inconsistently imposed on Texans. It began as a ploy to prevent newly freed slaves and former confederates from bearing arms, and just continued. That finally changed in 1995 with the shall-issue **Right-To-Carry** licensing law, and improved in 1997 with amendments. In 2005 the onerous, confusing "traveling" law for non-licensees began to unravel for the first time in 135 years. The next leap forward was in 2007, supporting freedom and our right to keep and bear arms, with the **Motorist Protection Act**. This moved us away from "where are your papers?" so-called "right-to-carry" and toward true *Freedom To Carry* without burdensome government dictates, taxes, tests and conditions.

It is still basically against the law in Texas to *carry* a handgun intentionally, knowingly or recklessly "on or about yourself," unless you have a concealed-handgun license. It is a class A misdemeanor under Penal Code §46.02, but if an offense occurs in a place licensed or permitted to sell alcoholic beverages, it's a third degree felony. During training DPS has said a firearm is "on or about you" if you can reach it without materially changing your position. The limited exceptions to the carry ban are discussed in this and the next chapter.

The apparent conflicts between the U.S. Constitution and the carry bans, on the books for so long, bewilders many Texas residents, though we have come to live with it. Texas is not the Wild West many outsiders (and Hollywood) believe it to be.

Freedom To Carry

The old "traveler" rules (summarized for history's sake later in this chapter) were replaced in 2007 with much clearer rules for handgun possession (or knives or clubs), without licenses or any prior government involvement, on your own premises and to a motor vehicle you control (Penal Code §46.02). Now you can have a handgun, knife or club on or about you if you are:

1–On your own premises or premises under your control;

2–Inside or directly enroute to a motor vehicle or watercraft you own or that is under your control, as long as the handgun is concealed from plain view. Possession remains illegal if you're engaged in criminal activity (other than Class C misdemeanor traffic or law violations), or if you are a prohibited possessor or a member of a criminal street gang.

Premises includes *real property,* the legal term for land, and generally anything erected, growing on or affixed to the land. The law has no requirement for concealment on *premises,* so you're free to carry openly. Premises includes a **recreational vehicle**, whether motorized or designed to be towed, being used as temporary or permanent living quarters (the RV change first began in 2003). A travel trailer, camping trailer, truck camper, motor home and horse trailer with living quarters are included. Since an RV is both a premises and a motor vehicle, it's most likely wise to maintain concealment when aboard.

Long guns are unaffected by the handgun restriction, and it's not uncommon to see pickup trucks with rifle racks statewide. The obvious temptations for theft though have curtailed this form of open carry. Texas carrying laws make no distinction between loaded and unloaded firearms (but LEO students must transport unloaded to and from class). Some firearm trainers note that an empty gun is unsafe, because it can't provide the protection it is designed to provide. See *Guns In Vehicles* later in this chapter.

Limits of the Handgun Carrying Law

For the longest time, the carry bans were detailed under Penal Code §46.02 and many Texans thought of this as the "main" gun law. As rewritten in 2007, §46.02 now *protects* carry as outlined above (and it includes the main penalties for violators). The main exceptions have been moved to §46.03, §46.035 and §46.15. The old *affirmative defense*—an abusive standard that subjected people to arrest for mere possession of a handgun, and then gave them a narrow window of opportunity to prove their innocence after the fact—has been abolished.

Under Penal Code §46.15(a), the handgun-carry limitations in §46.02, as well as prohibited places in §46.03 (described later), don't apply to "proper authorities," who are "above these laws," including peace officers, special investigators, active and retired law-enforcement officers, parole officers, community supervision or corrections department officers, federal and state judges and justices, bailiffs, district and county attorneys and more.

In §46.15(b), carry prohibitions of §46.02 don't apply if you're:

1–Engaged in official duties as a member of the armed forces or state military forces (as defined under Government Code §431.001), or as a guard employed by a penal institution;

2–Traveling (see court cases and explanations in this chapter, but note that the old ambiguous "traveling" requirement for possession has been generally abandoned);

3–Engaging in and at the site of legal hunting, fishing or other sporting activity, if the weapon is a type commonly used in the activity, or enroute between the site and your residence or motor vehicle;

4–A commissioned and uniformed security officer on duty or traveling to or from a place of assignment with the weapon in plain view;

5–A commissioned personal protection officer (bodyguard) carrying proper papers while on duty or traveling to or from a place of assignment; if in uniform carrying openly, or if not in uniform properly carrying concealed;

6–The holder of a valid concealed-handgun license;

7–A liquor-license holder (or employee of the holder) while supervising the licensed premises;

8–A law-enforcement student carrying a weapon specifically for a class where the class is held, or to or from the class and the person's residence if the weapon is unloaded;

9–A public security officer employed by the adjutant general (under GC §431.029) while on or traveling to or from duty;

10–Participating in a proper historical reenactment as defined.

In addition to the statutory exceptions listed above, having a handgun in your possession is permissible in an instance of self defense or other justifiable use such as crime prevention (see

Chapter 5). The generic defense against a weapons charge is known as the defense of *necessity* (see Penal Code §9.22).

The bottom line is that, as of 2007, if you legally have a sidearm in Texas, and you're not in a prohibited place, you can carry it in your own home or business, or on your own land, openly or discreetly, and to and in your own watercraft or motor vehicle including an RV, just keep it concealed. DPS in its classes says *concealed* means its presence cannot be discerned.

Inadvertent Display

In **2013**, PC §46.035 was amended so that a brief inadvertent display in public, not intended to cause a disturbance, would not lead to mandatory criminal charges as it had previously—when general "open carry" was inexcusable. Law now makes it clear the offense is *intentional* display in plain view of a person in public, without justification. A sidearm "printing" through clothing or briefly visible should be avoided but is no longer an automatic offense. Traditional open carry while hunting, fishing or during proper sporting activities remains legal as before.

National Police Concealed Carry

Federal law enacted in 2004 (Law Enforcement Officers Safety Act, "LEOSA," HR218, now 18 USC §926B and C) paved the way for specified active duty and retired local, state and federal law enforcement officers to carry concealed nationwide, despite any state laws to the contrary. People who can carry under this law must qualify periodically and meet other requirements. Texas enacted several laws to facilitate this program, which requires periodic proficiency testing, suitable ID, and other details, described mainly in OC §1701.357 and GC §614.121. Check your department for details, and know the rules for states you visit, since they all differ. Some of the exemptions for such people are found in Penal Code §46.02, §46.03, and §46.15.

Additional Carry Restrictions and Exemptions

Penal Code §46.03 makes it a third-degree felony for a person, even with a valid concealed-handgun license, to intentionally, knowingly or recklessly bring or have a firearm:

1–On the premises (defined in §46.035 as a building or part of a building) of a public or private school or of an educational institution, any building or grounds while they are sponsoring an activity there, or a passenger vehicle of such an establishment, without written permission from them or under their written regulations;

2–On the premises of a public polling place on the day of an election or while early voting is in progress;

3–On the premises of any government court or offices used by the court, unless by written regulations or with written authorization from the court;

4–To a racetrack;

5–To the secured area of an airport;

6–Within 1,000 feet of a place of execution on the day of an execution if you had notice that such possession is banned.

There is a defense to prosecution in this statute, against the first four of the prohibitions, for anyone with a firearm who is actively engaged as:

1–A member of the armed forces;

2–A member of the National Guard;

3–A guard employed by a penal institution;

4–An officer of the court.

The law also includes a separate (and, it would seem, at least partially redundant) defense to prosecution from all six of the restrictions listed above to anyone who has a firearm while traveling to or from or actually discharging duties as a member of the armed forces, National Guard, a guard employed by a penal institution, a properly commissioned and outfitted security guard (see separate section in this chapter for details), or a properly commissioned bodyguard as covered under Chapter 1702 of the Occupations Code.

An additional defense to prosecution is included in this law for a person who has properly checked all firearms as baggage before entering the secured area of an airport.

The law is clear that a concealed handgun license offers no exemption or protection from the restrictions in this statute. An extensive list of prohibited places, which also impacts the carrying of firearms, appears with the illustration in Chapter 2.

Security Guards and Bodyguards

A person can only work as a security guard or a bodyguard with proper credentials and training as a commissioned security officer, from the Texas Private Security Board, as described beginning at Occupations Code §1702.001.

The certification process for applicants include:

1–At least 30 hours basic training approved by the Board;

2–Minimum marksmanship competency demonstrated to the satisfaction of an approved firearm training instructor;

3–Between 10 to 15 hours of classroom instruction on handgun proficiency, which must include laws related to weapons and deadly force, handgun use, proficiency and safety, nonviolent dispute resolution, and proper storage of handguns to eliminate accidents with children;

4–Range instruction on handgun proficiency with at least 9mm or .38 caliber handguns;

5–Satisfactory scores on examinations;

6–Field note taking, report writing, general security issues and any other topics the Board considers necessary.

Many other conditions apply to commissioned security officer status, and the Board has a training manual and broad authority to manage the program. Disqualifications for these people are found in §1702.163. A Personal Protection Officer, commonly known as a bodyguard, must have a commission and meet additional requirements that begin at §1702.201.

To carry a firearm, a commissioned security officer must:

1–Be engaged in the performance of official duties, or enroute to the place of assignment;

2–Be wearing a distinctive uniform indicating the person's role as a security officer;

3–Carry in plain view. Special rules allow a bodyguard to carry concealed while on duty (§1702.206).

School Marshals

Responding to attacks in schools, Texas passed the Protection of Texas Children Act in **2013**, establishing the position of School Marshal. In Education Code §37.0811, certain school boards can designate specially trained employees who are CHL holders for armed protection of the schools. A complex set of rules applies to qualifying for and operating as a School Marshal, found in the statute, and only frangible ammunition is allowed. The Marshals may make arrests and have other peace-officer authority, but only in connection with their specified duties on school premises. Identity of School Marshals is confidential. Only one Marshall per 400 students may be appointed. Special training requirements for the position are found in Chapter 2.

The History of the Old Texas Traveling Laws

For almost 125 years, the limited right to carry a handgun in Texas while "traveling" caused massive confusion and lead to the arrest of countless innocent people. The widely held belief that crossing several county lines or staying overnight would amount to traveling was never true, leading to convictions of many unfortunate individuals.

In 2005, House Bill 823, which changed Penal Code §2.05 and §46.15, attempted to correct this, but unfortunately created its own new complications and left risks in place for the average handgun owner. Legal analysts at the NRA, along with the Texas State Rifle Association's Legislative Committee described those amendments this way:

> Texas HB 823 prevents the police from routinely arresting a law-abiding person who is transporting a concealed handgun in a private motor vehicle. This is accomplished by clothing a law-abiding person with the presumption of being a traveler. The traveler presumption may be rebutted by the state by presenting proof beyond a reasonable doubt. In plain terms, a law-abiding person should have no problem transporting a handgun in a private motor vehicle provided the handgun is concealed.

The NRA's short version is: "Legalizes the carrying of concealed handguns in private vehicles without a CHL." If only it was that simple. An eight-page legal analysis posted as an Update at gunlaws.com goes into more detail than most people will ever want to know. Car carry was not properly legal in Texas until 2007 with passage of HB1815, the Motorist Protection Act.

Background: Since 1871, carrying a handgun in Texas, despite Hollywood's version of history, had been nearly totally banned for the public (long guns are unaffected by all this). A person "traveling" with a handgun though had been one of the very limited exemptions under the law. However, under this arrangement, mere possession of a handgun was presumed to be guilt of illegal carry, and it was up to you to prove your innocence after arrest, by proving you were traveling.

"Traveling" however was not defined. Scores of county and state court cases generated numerous opinions of what constitutes "traveling," many not even similar, many conflicting with each other. See 60 of these summarized in this chapter. Gun owners had no way of knowing if they were legal or not, abuse was rampant, it was a mess.

A primary function of written law is to give fair warning of what behavior is subject to punishment. The law therefore must give a clear, understandable, unambiguous description of what the law is. When it fails to do so, it is invalid in court. That's the principle at least, but it was not sufficient to save Texans from over a century of guessing whether they were legally traveling when they did so armed. Arrests and convictions were all too common for simple possession of their private property.

Some Texans regained the ability to bear arms in 1995, when the CHL law was passed and signed by then Governor (and then President) George Bush. It provided much needed relief from the long denial of rights. About 1% of all Texans have obtained a government license and can carry as they travel around the state. The other 99% remained under the ban from 1871.

A 2005 law almost defined traveling at last, for carrying a handgun in a private motor vehicle only. Actually, it defined a "presumption" of traveling, which the state would have to rebut (disprove) in order to go after you for possession of a concealed handgun in your vehicle. This was a roundabout way of decriminalizing a law-abiding person's carry of a concealed handgun in a vehicle without a permit. Technically, it left the offense intact, and made it harder for the state to come after you for possession.

It helped partially restore the right to keep and bear arms. But when the courts got a hold of a few people in their vehicles under this law the results were mixed, people remained at legal risk, and who wants to be a test case. At least one Texas county attorney went after people in their vehicles, publicly bragging about ignoring the protections the new law was supposed to provide.

Under that now-replaced halfway step, a person was presumed to be traveling if the person was: 1–in a private motor vehicle; 2–not engaged in criminal activity other than a Class C misdemeanor law or traffic violation; 3–not otherwise prohibited by law from possessing a firearm; 4–not a member of a criminal street gang under §71.01; and 5–not carrying a handgun in plain view, quite similar to the law finally enacted in 2007. The difference is the old version created a legal presumption for courts to wrestle with; the new law says there's no violation if you obey the rules.

Further confusion came from the old law's complicated jury instructions, burdens of proof, and presumptions about whether the person charged was in fact traveling at the time. It did put the burden of proof on the state, where it belongs and which is proper, so you would be innocent unless proven guilty.

The prior model was the opposite—you were guilty unless you could prove your innocence as an indefinable traveler—a horrendous, un-American festering wound on the justice system. The euphemistically named *affirmative defense* procedure was so contrary to everything America stands for it deserved to be abolished. The laughably long line of legal logic that had attached to the traveling definition was:

> If charged with illegal carry, and there's a presumption you're a traveler, the jury must be told of the traveler exemption, unless the judge decides the evidence can't reasonably support it; if the jury gets the traveler evidence it's presumed good unless the state can disprove it beyond a reasonable doubt; if the state fails to disprove it the jury gets it as a fact; if the jury decides it is not fact the state still must prove each other element of the complaint. It's actually even more complicated than this simplified version, and there is not universal agreement on its meaning.

Finally, note this protection in Penal Code §2.01:

"All persons are presumed to be innocent and no person may be convicted of an offense unless each element of the offense is proved beyond a reasonable doubt. The fact that he has been arrested, confined, or indicted for, or otherwise charged with, the offense gives rise to no inference of guilt at his trial." This was conveniently ignored under old traveling laws.

Here is a review of some of the hundreds of "traveling" cases that had been decided over the years, to help provide perspective. These short summaries do not provide full details and in that sense may be misleading. *For the whole story you must study the entire court decision—often many pages of involved legal text. Do not rely on these brief gists for any legal purposes whatsoever.* You'll also note that the decisions are sometimes in complete disagreement with each other, adding another element of risk and uncertainty.

IN GENERAL: Driving a herd of cattle across a county to Kansas is traveling. (Rice vs. State 1881); Fugitives are not travelers. (Shelton vs. State 1889); Borrowing a handgun to see your brothers in another county does not make you a traveler several days later in your own county. (Brownlee vs. State, 1895); An auditor collecting tickets and fares from railroad passengers is a traveler. (Barker vs. Satterfield, 1908); Taking the most direct route to a permanent boarding house from a hotel is traveling. (Ward vs. State 1911); A merchant going to see customers who owe money is not a traveler. (Hickman vs. State, 1913); Riding around a neighborhood, working and looking for work, is not traveling, even if you intend to go out of the county if you can't find work. (Younger vs. State, 1915); Coming to a city as a traveler does not allow you to carry a handgun around for several days after you've arrived. Also, the right to carry a handgun as a traveler is lost if you suspend your travel to burglarize a house. (Smith vs. State, 1915); Carrying a pistol in your car is not, by itself, traveling. (Welch vs. State, 1924); Carrying a gun in a car while traveling is not a violation of carrying on your person. (Christian vs. State, 1927); Using a gun illegally doesn't necessarily make you guilty of unlawful carry. (Grant vs. State 1929); Moving from one home to another is traveling. (Senters vs. State, 1983)

PURPOSE: If you are a traveler, the reason you are traveling is not relevant. (Evers vs. State, 1978)

TIME AND DISTANCE: Going to the county seat of your own county and returning the next day is not traveling. (Darby vs. State, 1887); Taking a trip by wagon for two or three days is traveling. (Smith vs. State, 1875); Taking a handgun 60 miles away for repairs and then boarding a train with it bound for home is traveling. (Impson vs. State, 1892); Traveling 25 miles and then preparing to camp out is traveling (Price vs. State, 1895); Going 15 miles from home is not traveling. (Stanfield vs. State, 1896); Going 18 miles from home is not traveling. (Creswell vs. State, 1897); Going 35 miles from home to another county, and then returning home immediately is traveling. (Bain vs. State, 1898); Returning 150 miles to get home is traveling. (Thomas vs. State, 1897); A railroad porter going 150 miles on a daily run is traveling. (Williams vs. State, 1903); Going from one county to another, or planning to, and boarding a train, is traveling. (Campbell vs. State, 1910); Driving a car 40 miles and back on the same day in daylight is not traveling. (George vs. State, 1921); Going 35 miles to a place in another county is not traveling. (Wortham vs. State, 1923); Taking paying passengers 37 miles in a car is not traveling, even if you claim you were told you might have to go much further. (Paulk vs. State, 1924); The mode of travel must be considered when determining traveling, not just distance alone. (Kemp vs. State, 1930); Leaving at 5 p.m. and returning before midnight is not traveling. (Vogt vs. State, 1953); Leaving your air force base to go 120 miles to spend a weekend with your family is traveling. (Allen vs. State, 1968)

INTERRUPTION OF TRAVELING: Stopping your travel for business or pleasure removes your protection as a traveler. (Stilly vs. State, 1889); Going out of your way to bring a doctor home while traveling, is still traveling. A mere delay does not remove the travel protection. (Irvin vs. State, 1907); Stopping momentarily on a business trip to discuss a debt with a creditor at the creditor's request, does not remove the travel protection. (Hunt vs. State, 1908); Stopping a journey for business relevant to the journey is traveling. (Campbell vs. State, 1910) (Kemp vs. State, 1930); Going directly from a hotel to a boarding house and stopping along the way to eat with a friend is traveling. (Ward vs. State, 1911); Turning aside from a journey that was traveling, for business not related to the original journey, is not traveling. (Pecht vs. State, 1918) (Tadlock vs. State, 1934)

TERMINATION OF TRAVEL: Traveler status ends when you arrive at your destination (U.S. vs. Pozos, 1983); Going from one county to another is traveling, but after arriving and staying overnight, you are not a traveler while going around town the next morning. (Ballard vs. State, 1914); Returning to your home from an out-of-state trip, changing your clothes, and taking your wife for a ride in the country is not traveling. (Kiles vs. State, 1966)

TEMPORARY RESIDENCE: Going from your temporary home to your permanent home in another county is traveling. (Campbell vs. State, 1889); For the purpose of determining travel, a person may have both permanent and temporary legal residences. A girl friend's home is not necessarily legal temporary residence, and so carrying a gun from your place of work to her house, after a fishing trip, is not traveling. (Smith vs. State, 1982)

HUNTING: You cannot carry a pistol while hunting hogs on the range, or hunting anything off your own premises. (Baird vs. State, 1873) (Titus vs. State, 1875); You cannot take a pistol out on the range to kill a beef, even if you have no other means available. (Reynolds vs. State, 1877); Government employees may carry handguns while hunting predators and rodents, if the guns are a type typically used for this. (Atty. Gen. Opinion, 1980)

SECURITY OFFICERS: Night watchmen cannot carry while not on duty. (Robison vs. State, 1926)

PEACE OFFICERS: Peace officers and people legally acting as peace officers may carry handguns while actually on duty (Atty. Gen. Opinions, 1941, 1946, 1973, 1975, 1980). Whether a person is truly a peace officer, except for those specifically spelled out in the law, and whether the person is actually acting in an official capacity is subject to question and has numerous court precedents. A peace officer in one location does not automatically have rights in another location. Being deputized, being appointed or acting under another person's authority does not automatically make you a peace officer, as the following examples show, and as is frequently the case, not all the precedents agree with each other.; Being appointed a deputy constable in good faith by a constable who has no authority to make such an appointment is not a defense. (Johnson vs. State 1914); A sheriff who can appoint one deputy in a precinct but actually appoints two does not protect both appointees. (Ranson vs. State, 1914); An appointment by an adjutant general but without taking an oath, etc., is insufficient as a defense for carrying a handgun. (Ringer vs. State, 1894); Being commissioned as a deputy sheriff and allowed to carry is not a defense while you are not acting in an official capacity and are carrying for personal protection. (Gandara vs. State, 1924); Although you can be criminally prosecuted for failing to assist a peace officer if requested, a private security officer who requests such assistance and arms you is not a peace officer under the law, cannot appoint you a peace officer and provides no defense. (Bohn vs. State, 1983); A person properly deputized by a magistrate to make an arrest may carry. (Jenkins vs. State, 1904); A magistrate can name a suitable person who is not a peace officer to make an arrest in an arrest warrant, and that person may carry a gun. (Stephenson vs. State 1923) (Hawkins vs. State 1988)

REASONABLE BELIEF: If a person honestly believes to be an appointed officer and therefore carries, the person is not guilty. (Carroll vs. State 1900) (Barnett vs. State 1921) (Franklin vs. State 1944)

These are just a fraction of the cases that had come to the courts on the issue of carrying a handgun in Texas. The law was complex and subject to unusual interpretation and inconsistent results. In addition, numerous cases had a tendency to presume you had no exception or defense against having been found carrying a handgun on or about your person. It was then up to you as a defendant to prove conclusively that an exception existed at the time of the arrest and that you were innocent. You had to exonerate yourself from guilt. Based on the old *affirmative defense*, those days were more like Napoleonic Code than the American standard of innocent unless proven guilty.

Motorist Protection Act—Guns In Vehicles

Starting in Sep., 2007, it is legal to travel with a handgun in a motor vehicle, and from a premises you control to a motor vehicle,* as along as the gun stays concealed from plain view. To be legal, you can't be in any criminal activity (except for Class C misdemeanor traffic or law violations), and cannot be a prohibited possessor or a member of a criminal street gang. A premises includes real property and a recreational vehicle being used as temporary or permanent living quarters, whether it is motorized or designed to be towed. A travel trailer, camping trailer, truck camper, motor home and horse trailer with living quarters are included. The prohibited places in §46.03, §46.035 and §46.15, described in Chapters 1 and 2 of this book, apply.

*An oversight in the law only mentions carry *from* a premises *to* a vehicle; authorities agree you should be protected from the vehicle to the premises too.

Routine travel rarely involves encounters with authorities, and since the sidearm must be concealed from sight, difficulties which used to be common are now unlikely. In the event of an encounter, there is no obligation in the law to mention the presence of a personal sidearm or any other private property, and quiet attention to business is probably wise. Ironically, that's a small liberty over CHLs, who *are* required to advise an officer if they are armed. DPS currently advises CHLs to operate under the disclosure requirement that general motorists are not. During traffic stops, DPS recommends you keep your hands in plain sight (like on the wheel) and at night, turn on the dome light, and they note different localities have different policies.

Most drivers have been stopped by police at some point in their lives, and know that questions about firearms (or other probing questions for that matter) are rare. If you are a victim of what is often called a "fishing expedition," with unprovoked questions about firearms or subtle requests for consent to search you or your vehicle without cause, be cautious. It is a red flag. Lawyers typically advise against palaver or granting consent to a search without articulable probable cause or reasonable suspicion.

Some people are not comfortable in politely refusing an officer's interest in conducting an unwarranted search, and officers can be touchy about that, but it may be best not to consent, or to request the assistance of a lawyer before answering probing questions. Experts disagree on what your best course of action in such a volatile situation should be.

The trunk is sometimes mentioned as the best place to carry any firearm, unloaded, with the ammunition apart from the firearm. This method of transportation is federally guaranteed under 18 USC §926A, but not uniformly accepted by all authorities, and not required at all in Texas. Trunk carry defeats the value of a gun for personal safety, but does greatly reduce your chance of problems with authorities. The 2007 Texas Motorist Protection Act provides broad protection for discreet vehicle possession.

Because long guns have long been legal in vehicles, many people find it easier to keep a rifle or shotgun available and not worry about it. If you have a valid Texas concealed-handgun license, you may carry a loaded handgun concealed in your car under most circumstances with few worries. Check chapter 4 for a note on travel with Texas State Rifle Association license plates.

Parking-Lot Protection Law

This law enacted in 2011 prevents public or private employers from stopping employees who want to transport or store lawfully possessed firearms or ammunition in their locked private motor vehicles while parked in any parking lot, garage or other parking area provided for employees. See Labor Code §52.061.

This law doesn't authorize people to go armed anywhere that's prohibited under federal or state law. It does not apply to vehicles owned or leased by the employer, unless the employer allows it as part of the job. It also does not include a school district, open-enrollment charter school or private school, as defined, or certain properties with oil, gas or mineral leases that prohibit firearms. On certain properties that deal with hazardous materials (chemical makers or oil and gas refiners), only CHL employees may leave arms in locked vehicles if specially secured, constantly monitored, non-public parking space is provided. Employers who must obey parking-lot rules can still keep arms off their business premises, as defined. LC §52.062.

Except for gross negligence, employers who must comply with these rules, and their staffs, are not liable civilly for personal injury, death, property or other damage from firearms or ammo they are required to allow in locked vehicles on their property. The law specifies that the presence of those guns and ammo do not create an unsafe workplace (protection from a possible OSHA assault against the guns). Employers and staff have no duty to patrol, inspect or secure parking spaces, vehicles in them, or to determine employees' compliance. LC §52.063.

This law doesn't change the liability of anyone causing harm or injury using a gun or ammo, or anyone who aids or encourages such harm or injury, or an employee who fails to comply with this law, per LC §52.064. The parking-lot law doesn't change the existing power of private and public employers to ban CHLs from their business premises. GC §411.203

Transport and Shipping

You may ship and transport firearms around the country, but it's illegal to use the U.S. Postal Service to ship handguns, under one of the oldest federal firearms statutes on the books, dating from Feb. 8, 1927. (The oldest federal law still in effect—except for constitutional provisions—appears to be a firearm forfeiture law for illegal hunting in Yellowstone National Park, passed on May 7, 1894. It's interesting to note that no federal gun laws from the country's first 128 years are still on the books. The very first federal gun law, in 1792, actually *required* gun possession.) The Post Office says to use registered mail and not identify the package as containing a firearm (long gun). Check with your local Post Office yourself before shipment.

You may ship a weapon to a licensed dealer, manufacturer or repair shop and back. However, depending upon the reason for the shipment and the shipper used, the weapon may have to go from and back to someone with an FFL. You should check with the intended recipient and you must inform the shipping agent in writing before shipping firearms or ammunition.

A handgun obtained outside Texas, if shipped to you in Texas, must go from a licensed dealer where you got it to a licensed dealer here. Many dealers will act as a "receiving station" for a weapon you get elsewhere, sometimes for a fee. Taking *any* gun with you, from a *private transfer out of state*, if it's coming back to your home state, is generally prohibited by federal law, and must be transferred between licensed dealers.

The only times when you may directly receive an interstate shipment of a gun are:

1–the return of a gun that you sent for repairs, modification or replacement to a licensee in another state, and,

2–a long gun legally obtained in person from out-of-state dealer.

Interstate Travel

Personal possession of firearms in other states is subject to the laws of each state you are in. The authorities have been known to hassle, detain or arrest people who are legally traveling with weapons, due to confusion, ignorance, personal bias and for other reasons, even when those reasons are strictly illegal.

Federal law guarantees the right to transport (not the same as carry) a gun in a private vehicle, if you are entitled to have the gun in your home state and at your destination. The gun must be unloaded and locked in the trunk, or in a locked compartment other than the glove compartment or the console, if the vehicle has no trunk. Some states have openly challenged or defied this law, creating a degree of risk for anyone transporting a firearm interstate.

Carrying a firearm (armed and ready) is practically impossible unless you're willing to face misdemeanor or felony criminal charges as you pass through each state. A very helpful book, *The Traveler's Guide to the Firearm Laws of the Fifty States* summarizes the requirements and restrictions on keeping a gun with you on the road, and is listed in the back of this book.

Article IV of the U.S. Constitution requires the states to respect the laws of all other states. In addition, the 14th Amendment to the Constitution forbids the states from denying any rights that you have as an American citizen. These fundamental requirements are unfortunately frequently ignored by some states. Your constitutional guarantees may be little comfort when a state trooper has you spread eagled for possession of a firearm that was perfectly legal when you were at home.

The bottom line is that the civil right and historical record of law-abiding Americans traveling with firearms for their own safety has evaporated due to laws and policies at the state level.

People often have no idea what the gun laws are in any state but their own (and rarely enough that), a complete set of the relevant laws is hard to get, understanding the statutes ranges from difficult to nearly impossible, and you can be arrested for making a simple mistake.

The legal risk created by our own government for a family traveling interstate with a personal firearm may be greater than the actual risk of a criminal confrontation. Because of this, the days of traveling armed and being responsible for your own safety and protection have all but ended for people who leave their home state. The proper authorities are generally exempt from these restrictions.

The chilling conclusion is that the Constitution no longer constrains law making as it used to, and the government has rights to travel that the people do not.

You don't fix a major national problem like this by writing a book—even though those books would be valuable and ought to exist. You fix it by restoring the Lost National Right to Carry, also known as the Second Amendment, to the position it always held in America until the last few decades, during which its erosion has been nearly total for interstate travelers.

Readers who purchased this book hoping it would somehow enable or empower them to travel interstate with a loaded personal firearm must contact elected representatives and begin to ask about the Lost National Right to Carry. It has quietly disappeared through incremental attrition at the local level.

Common or Contract Carriers

You may transport firearms and ammunition interstate by "common carriers" (scheduled and chartered airlines, buses, trains, ships, etc.), but you must notify them in writing and meet their requirements. Note that it must also be legal for you to possess the firearms and ammunition at your destination.

Federal law requires written notice from you and a signed receipt from the carrier when you pick up the firearm, but verbal communication is often accepted. Call in advance and get precise details and the names of the people you speak with— you wouldn't be the first traveler to miss a departure because of unforeseen technicalities and bureaucratic run-arounds.

For air travel, firearms must be unloaded, cased in a way deemed appropriate by the airline, and may not be possessed by or accessible to you in the "sterile" area anywhere on the gate side of the passenger security checkpoint, including on the aircraft. You may ship your firearms as baggage, which is the usual method, and it is also legal to give custody of them to the pilot, captain, conductor or operator for the duration of the trip (though they're not required to take custody).

Airlines must comply with firearms rules found primarily in the Code of Federal Regulations, Title 14, Sections 107 and 108, and other laws. A little-known provision of the Brady law bans carriers from identifying the outside of your baggage to indicate that it contains a firearm, a prime cause for theft in the past.

New rules posted on the Internet by the Transportation Security Administration say that when in airport sterile areas, or onboard an aircraft for which screening is conducted, passengers may not carry these items as accessible property or on their person: BB guns, compressed air guns, guns and firearms, flare pistols, gun lighters, parts of guns and firearms, pellet guns, realistic replicas of firearms, spear guns, starter pistols, stun guns/cattle prods/shocking devices. The rules for private aircraft that are not subject to screening are ambiguous.

Local Ordinances and Preemption

Texas law generally prohibits local authorities from passing air gun or firearms laws that conflict with state statutes. This is called *preemption*, and is generally found in Penal Code §1.08. Despite this rule, you may find some localities that have enacted laws that appear to conflict with state law. LGC §229.004, in 2011, limited certain cities from controlling shooting ranges.

An amendment made by the Right-to-Carry law, now in Local Government Code §229.001, says cities do not have authority to regulate carrying of concealed handguns by concealed-handgun licensees at public parks, public meetings of a city, county or other governmental body, a political rally, parade or official political meeting, or nonfirearms-related school, college, or professional athletic events. It also limits cities from regulating transfer, private ownership, keeping, transportation, licensing, or registration of firearms, ammunition, or firearm supplies. This was amended in **2013** to include air guns as well.

Cities *can* substantially regulate certain other aspects of firearms and air guns, from *requiring* residents or public employees to arm themselves for personal or national defense, law enforcement, or other lawful purpose, to prohibiting shooting in city limits, controlling their lands for hunting or other sporting use, and more. These are described in Chapter 4 under *The Land of Texas*.

Most local firearm ordinances merely reiterate state statutes, giving local courts jurisdiction in some areas. This typically has no direct effect on law-abiding gun owners, but conflicting laws might. Even an "illegal" law can be enforced, and it is not technically illegal until a proper court says it is, no matter how flagrantly it seems to flout the rules. Some cities, for example, have toyed with the idea of making their own gun laws about buses and public transportation, which they have no apparent authority to enact.

To stop this and other blatant abuse by local bureaucrats LGC §229.001 and §236.002 were amended in **2013** to give the state attorney general direct authority to obtain temporary and permanent injunctions against municipalities and counties that adopt regulations violating broad specific rights of gun owners.

Note that The Texas Gun Owner's Guide does not cover local ordinances, whether they agree or conflict with state law. The liability to people who obey state laws that conflict with local laws is uncertain and creates a degree of legal risk.

Prohibited Places

Always keep in mind that some places are strictly off limits to people with firearms, even if you are otherwise legally in possession of arms. The list of places where guns are not allowed at all, including restrictions for CHL holders, appears at the end of Chapter 2.

Product Liability Limit

Texas has a law that discourages nuisance lawsuits against manufacturers and sellers of firearms and ammunition (Civil Practice and Remedies Code §82.006). Under this law, a suit cannot be brought because a gun is inherently dangerous and causes damage. Rather, a suit has to prove a bona fide design defect that results directly in the alleged damage. If a gun functions in the way it is normally expected to function, there is no grounds for legal action.

Also, as of 1999, Civil Practice and Remedies Code §128.001 creates unique standards for bringing a government lawsuit against gun and ammunition manufacturers and suppliers.

Frivolous Lawsuits

In an effort to disarm the public, various groups, including in some cases tax-funded government officials, have initiated enormously expensive junk lawsuits against gun manufacturers, distributors and related businesses — for the non-criminal manufacture and lawful proper sale of firearms. Destroying the domestic firearms industry is quite a clever tactic, and would have a devastating impact on the civil and human right of gun ownership. The Defense Dept. testified to Congress on the severe national security threat a weakened or eliminated gun-making industry would have on the nation as a whole. Federal law was amended in 2005 (P.L. 109-92), to prohibit such frivolous lawsuits, and Congress noted among many things:

"The Second Amendment to the United States Constitution protects the rights of individuals, including those who are not members of a militia or engaged in military service or training, to keep and bear arms." They refer to it as, "a basic constitutional right and civil liberty," and that they are enacting this law, "To preserve a citizen's access to a supply of firearms and ammunition for all lawful purposes, including hunting, self-defense, collecting, and competitive or recreational shooting."

Congress notes that the lawsuits are, "an abuse of the legal system," and, "based on theories without foundation in hundreds of years of the common law and jurisprudence of the United States," and an, "attempt to use the judicial system to circumvent the Legislative branch of government." And finally, they are enacting this law, "To guarantee a citizen's rights, privileges, and immunities, as applied to the States, under the Fourteenth Amendment to the United States Constitution, pursuant to section 5 of that Amendment."

Congress has specifically recognized the Second Amendment as an individual right in enacted legislation six times now:

The Freedman's Bureau Act of 1866
The Property Requisition Act of 1941
The Firearm Owner's Protection Act of 1986
The Protection of Lawful Commerce in Arms Act of 2005
Disaster Recovery Personal Protection Act of 2006
Protecting Americans From Violent Crime (P.L. 111-24, Sec. 512) 2009

Congress also required dealers to provide locks with every gun sold, and included immunity for anyone who uses them, from a "qualified civil liability action." They used the same name for this immunity as for the industry immunity, even though they are quite different. If your gun is locked up and useless you are protected from a certain type of liability, from a thief who steals it and criminally misuses it. If your gun is not locked up and is available for immediate use, you have whatever protections you had before the law passed, from a thief's victims. Language was also added to help prevent courts from creatively "finding" any new liabilities.

LOSS OF RIGHTS

The right to bear arms is not absolute. Gun control—in the true sense—means disarming criminals and is a good idea, a point on which everyone but the criminals agree. The list of people who may not bear arms at all appears earlier in this chapter. A person whose rights are whole may lose those rights, mainly for conviction of a felony.

Forfeiture of Rights

Your right to bear arms can be lost. Conviction of any felony removes your civil right to bear firearms under state and federal law. The right to bear arms is forbidden to anyone who is or becomes a prohibited possessor under federal law, as described earlier, or as defined under Penal Code §46.04. State law, under narrow conditions and after five years, allows a felon to possess a firearm at home only, but federal law still applies. A law put forth in 2009 requires you to be fully informed that if you plead or are convicted of a minor domestic violence offense you lose your right to arms. Code of Criminal Procedure §14.06

Forfeiture of Weapons

The authorities can take your weapons if they have just cause. Firearms may be seized by a peace officer during an arrest or search, and if convicted of an offense involving the use of the weapon, or if the weapon is prohibited according to Chapter 46 (the weapons section) of the Penal Code, or if it is alleged to be stolen property (in Chapter 47 of the Penal Code), the court can either order that the weapon be turned over to the state for use by the law enforcement agency that seized it or sold. In **2013** courts got the option to sell any legal weapons to licensed dealers. Courts and police are incentivized to sell the weapons, since they get their costs and money from the sales. See Code of Criminal Procedure Article 18.19.

If you *are not* convicted, you have 60 days after being notified by the magistrate that the weapon was seized to make a written request to have it returned. Otherwise, it will be destroyed, sold or turned over for use by law enforcement. See CCP Art. 18.19.

If you *are* convicted you may request and get the weapon back provided: 1–You ask within 60 days; 2–you have no prior convictions under state weapons laws; 3–it is not a prohibited weapon; 4–the offense wasn't committed at a playground, video arcade, youth center or school; and 5–in the court's opinion, based on your record, returning the weapon poses no threat to the community. Otherwise, the weapon is destroyed or given to the authorities that seized it.

Certain weapons are contraband if unregistered and are subject to seizure by the authorities. Included are weapons identified under the National Firearms Act (see Chapter 3), or identified as prohibited weapons under state law.

Personal property, including firearms and ammunition, may be seized by BATFE when used or intended to be used or involved in violation of any U.S. laws the agents can enforce. Acquittal or dismissal of charges allows you to regain any confiscated property, but this may be more difficult than it sounds.

Police can disarm CHLs temporarily at non-public secure police facilities and put their firearms in a locker for the duration of the visit. Signs must be posted in English and Spanish. A non-public secure police facility and the type of sign required is defined in Government Code §411.207.

Reveal and Relinquish

Texas is now a "reveal and relinquish" state for CHLs, under GC §411.207. CHLs, unlike other residents, must reveal they are armed during an encounter with law enforcement officers. If an officer deems it needed for your protection, or for protection of the officer or other individuals, the officer may disarm you, and return your firearm at the scene when the danger has subsided (provided you have broken no rules yourself). There is some controversy around this rule, because handling loaded firearms in public instead of leaving them safely holstered is dangerous.

The Katrina Confiscation Ban

Responding to arbitrary and unlawful firearm confiscations in Louisiana after the 2005 Hurricane Katrina emergency, states enacted statutes to protect the public against such abuse. In Texas, GC §418.003, §418.184, §433.002 and §433.0045, and LGC §229.001 prevent authorities from seizing or confiscating firearms or ammunition from the public during an emergency. A peace officer may *temporarily* disarm you during an encounter for safety, but must *immediately* return the firearm and any ammunition as the encounter ends, unless you're under arrest or the firearm is seized as evidence in a criminal investigation.

Foster Homes

Anyone who chooses to take in foster children, or a foster home of any type, forfeits the right to keep loaded accessible firearms or ammunition, under powers given to the Dept. of Family and Protective Services. The Dept. cannot ban possession, which it had tried to do, but can issue regulations to require guns and ammunition to be stored separately and locked up (see HRC §42.042). Requirements to lock up firearms, which might help reduce accidents or unauthorized use, significantly reduces their value in stopping crime and saving lives in an emergency.

No other statute in Texas gives such broad power to anyone, let alone bureaucrats, to discriminate against fundamental civil rights and selectively disarm a portion of the general public. Foster parents must undergo extensive background checks and inspections in order to take on that role. Discriminating against them in this way is highly controversial. In 2011, this law was amended to allow foster parents with a CHL to transport foster children in a vehicle where a handgun is present as long as the firearm is in the possession and control of the parent.

State Restoration of Rights

To restore your rights you can petition in court for the needed orders, and the court must consider evidence to ensure you are qualified to have your rights restored, including circumstances that led to the disability, your mental history, criminal history and reputation. The court must officially state that you are no longer likely to act in a manner dangerous to public safety, and removing your disability to purchase a firearm is in the public interest. Courts are required to provide relevant mental-health dispositions to DPS, including disqualifying and relief-from-disabilities findings, within 30 days of determination with copies of the relevant court orders. Health and Safety Code §574.088.

Federal Restoration of Rights

A person with a truly compelling reason, and sufficient time, money and luck, can conceivably pursue a relief from federal firearms prohibition through the federal courts. Successful examples of this are few. Complete restoration of rights requires clearing both federal and state disabilities. The book *Brady Denial* describes the processes for appealing, updating old records, correcting errors (quite common) and other federal rights restoration issues, and is listed in the back of this book.

Federal law (18 USC §925) also provides a method for restoring a person's right to bear arms if it has been lost. This has been useful to people who are responsible community members and whose restrictions were based on decades-old convictions of youth, or other circumstances that pose little threat. The Justice Dept., responsible for implementing this law, has claimed since 1992 that it has no budget with which to do this, Congress has refused to provide any, and the federal restoration of rights process has effectively ground to a halt for anyone whose disability is based on federal requirements.

Some local courts have been responsive in re-examining and mitigating domestic-violence misdemeanors (which are sometimes little more than routine pleas in divorce cases) and easing that gun-rights disability when circumstances warrant.

A presidential pardon also restores gun rights, and though rare, at least one of the many people pardoned by Bill Clinton on his last day in office used that to obtain a CCW permit in Arizona.

Firearms Safety and Training

Enacted in 2001, school districts in Texas may choose, at least annually, to work with police officials to provide firearm accident-prevention programs for public elementary schools. Such programs must include the message, "Stop! Don't touch. Leave the area. Tell an adult," and may include safety-training materials from the Eddie Eagle GunSafe Program. See Occupational Code §1701.603. Texas offers a variety of hunter education classes, and federal law guarantees the public's right to train with firearms and encourages the public to do so:

Federal Laws Promote Civilian Firearm Proficiency

Reflecting attitudes and public sentiment that has been eroded in recent years, federal law has typically supported and worked toward keeping the public prepared and well trained to arms.

10 USC §4309:   Public access to federally funded rifle ranges.

10 USC §4312:   Public national shooting matches and small arms school, with subsidies for youngsters.

18 USC §922(q): Firearms OK at approved school programs.

18 USC §922(x): Handguns and ammunition can be transferred temporarily to juveniles for target practice. Juveniles can have handguns and ammunition for a course of instruction in safe and lawful use of a handgun.

36 USC §40701:   Civilian marksmanship programs, with special programs for youngsters, discounted firearms for citizens.

WHAT DO YOU NEED TO GET A FIREARM?

WHAT DO YOU NEED TO GET A FIREARM FROM A FEDERALLY LICENSED DEALER?

• You must be at least 18 years old for a long gun or 21 years old for a handgun, and not be a "prohibited possessor" under state or federal law;

• You need a government-issued photo ID that establishes your name, address, date of birth and signature;

• You must fill out and give the dealer federal form 4473, identifying yourself, the firearm you are buying, and certifying that you are not a prohibited possessor;

• You must wait while the dealer conducts an "instant" NICS background check, by phone or electronically directly with the FBI, required by the Brady law;

• If there is a delay in the NICS check the FBI has up to three business days to clear it up, during which you must wait, but after which your sale can take place automatically;

• If you have a valid Texas CHL license you may present it and be excluded from the background check and possible delay (since you're already on file in the criminal databases and monitored for violations);

• If you are not a Texas resident:

　–It must be legal for you to have the gun in your home state;

　–The transaction must comply with your state's laws;

　–You may take possession of a long gun over the counter if that's allowed in your home state;

　–You may not purchase and take possession of a handgun out of your home state (federal law) but you may have a licensed dealer ship a handgun to your home state for purchase there, if dealers in both states are willing to arrange such a transaction; and

• You must be able to pay for your purchase.

WHAT DOES IT ALL MEAN?

Law books don't use the word *crime*. They divide offenses into *felony* and *misdemeanor* categories to help match the punishment to the crime. Felonies are extremely serious; misdemeanors are less serious.

Felonies are divided into five categories (Penal Code §12.31 through §12.35), starting with the most serious: Capital felony, then 1st degree, 2nd degree and 3rd degree felonies, and a final category called state jail felonies. Generally, a felony conviction revokes your civil rights, including your right to keep and bear arms, to hold public office and to vote, and may include limits on your right to travel, work, associate with designated people and other conditions at court discretion.

Misdemeanors are grouped into three *classes* (see Penal Code §12.21 through 12.23). Class A is the most serious charge, followed by class B and class C.

The punishments are matched to the seriousness of the crime. This ranges from a capital felony, which can be punishable by death or life imprisonment, to a class C misdemeanor, which carries a fine of under $500 and no jail sentence. See the Crime and Punishment Chart in Appendix B for the basic penalties for each type of crime.

THE RIGHT TO CARRY LAW 2

In the closing days of the 1995 Texas legislative session, Senate Bill 60, The Right-to-Carry law, made it through conference committee and was passed by both houses. A tense few days later the governor signed it, and a new era had dawned. More than a century of severe handgun restrictions were relaxed for residents of the state. Gov. George W. Bush signed the bill on May 26, 1995. Its effective date was Sep. 1, 1995.

In Texas, it's generally against the law to be *carrying* a handgun personally on yourself, openly or concealed, without a license under the Right-to-Carry law. Carrying a handgun if you have no license and aren't otherwise exempt is a class A misdemeanor or higher. In 2005, the limits on *traveling* with a handgun—to or in a private vehicle—were relaxed, and in 2007 those limits were virtually eliminated, described in Chapter 1. The difference between *carry* and *travel* is subtle but crucial to understand.

The ability to legally *carry* a handgun "on or about yourself" in Texas is so heavily restricted that the only practical way to carry one legally for personal safety is with a valid license, issued by the Dept. of Public Safety (DPS). The requirements are rigorous, but the license grants broad immunity from the restrictions that infringe upon unlicensed people.

Under certain conditions, active and retired local, state and federal employees, certain special investigators and out-of-state peace officers may be authorized to carry weapons. Texas peace officers may carry statewide, on or off duty. As of Jan. 1, 1996, Texas residents and others may also obtain a license for carrying a concealed handgun, under the 1995 Right-to-Carry law.

The Concealed-Handgun License (CHL)

A license to Carry a Concealed Weapon is called a CCW license in various parts of the country. In Texas this is actually a Concealed Handgun License or CHL, since no other weapon may be carried. It is available to any person who is qualified as described below. Qualified license holders are exempt from most but not all the restrictions that normally prohibit carrying sidearms in Texas, and a few new limitations have been created. After 124 years without this fundamental human right, Texans have a way to legally carry personal sidearms for self defense.

Unlike some states, the Texas concealed-carry law is a "must issue" law. The statute prohibits DPS, which administers the CHL program, from denying a license "on the basis of a capricious or arbitrary decision," and says that DPS "shall issue" a license to anyone who qualifies. Basically, it means that if you meet the qualifications, you get the license.

This is an awesome responsibility. Legal battles to establish this law were long and hard-fought, and the law is not perfect. It is now up to the citizens to demonstrate intelligent use of this law, to exhibit restraint in all but the most life-threatening situations, and to work hard to make Texas a better place to live.

The words of the law (which license applicants must certify they have read *and* understand), were originally found in the 1995 *Senate Bill 60.* This received numerous amendments in 1997, and was codified, first as *Article 4413(29ee) Revised Statutes,* then, as Government Code Chapter 411, which is where most of it is today, and appears in Appendix D of this book. DPS now prepares an "informational sheet" you must certify you've read.

General Conditions

- You're supposed to carry the license with you whenever you carry a concealed handgun and show the license, along with your driver's license (or DPS ID card), to any peace officer or magistrate who asks you for ID, if you are armed (§411.205). However, the penalty for failing to have the license with you was dropped in 2009 (it is after all redundant, since DPS has you in their computers, and non-licensed citizens now have no duty to disclose when legally in possession), but good etiquette suggests showing it when necessary.

- You must keep your concealed handgun fully concealed. Intentionally, knowingly or recklessly letting it show is a class A misdemeanor under Penal Code §46.035, unless you are using it in a situation that legally justifies the use of force or deadly force (sometimes called "the defense of *necessity*"). Letting it show in a manner calculated to cause alarm is also a class A misdemeanor, under Penal Code §42.01.

   In **2013** the law was amended slightly to tolerate momentary inadvertent display while carrying, for example, if the gun "prints" through clothing or is briefly visible. The law makes clear the offense is intentional display of a handgun in plain view of another person in a public place without justification.

- Nothing prevents you from carrying more than one firearm; (the semi-auto/non-semi-auto category was dropped in **2013**).

- It's a class A misdemeanor for a CHL to carry if intoxicated.

- If you are arrested or indicted for an offense that would disqualify you for a CHL after you have obtained one, the license is suspended until the matter is resolved. If you are convicted, your license is revoked.

- If you are found carrying without a *valid* license (expired, revoked, suspended, unreported change of name, address or status, an arrest is possible. You may get officer discretion similar to driving without your driver's license—a deep sweat you won't soon forget and definite potential for arrest.

- As of 2007, licenses include your *residence* address (but for specified judges (per §411.171) or their spouses, a courthouse address is used for security). The license also indicates your "status" (§411.179) as an instructor, judge, prosecutor or other specified officials. If you move, change your name or if your status changes you must notify DPS within 30 days and get a new license (§411.181) for your license to remain valid.

- DPS must keep CHL-incident statistics, including arrests for carrying in prohibited places, and records about handgun discharges. That includes accidental, unjustified or criminal shots, and justified uses of deadly force (crime prevention). A reasonable person would take care not to be a statistic in any of those categories. DPS must adopt procedures to gather reports from local authorities. Under rules enacted in 2001 (§411.047), DPS posts extensive CHL statistics on its website.

The CHL program goes through regular changes over time.
Many changes are made by DPS using regulation, not legislation.
Get current information on the program by phone or online:
512-424-7293 • www.txdps.state.tx.us

QUALIFICATIONS FOR A CONCEALED-HANDGUN LICENSE

Texas DPS is required by Government Code §411.171 et seq. to issue your concealed-handgun license (CHL) if you:

1–Are a legal Texas resident for six months before your date of application, are a permanent resident alien (green card), or you are an eligible legal citizen of the United States as determined by DPS upon application. This means you:

2–Are at least 21 years of age, or between 18 and 21 years old if a member of or honorably discharged from designated armed forces (note that a CHL if you're under 21 does not override the federal ban on retail handgun sales to people under 21, and some states (see *Reciprocity*) will not honor your license);

3–Have not been convicted of a crime* that was a felony (unless expunged, pardoned, vacated, set aside, voided, annulled, invalidated or sealed under any state or federal law) as the terms *convicted* and *felony* are specially defined in CHL law);

4–Are not *charged* with a class A or B misdemeanor, disorderly conduct or a felony (note this restriction does not require a guilty judgment, just that an unsettled charge has been filed)*;

5–Are not a fugitive from justice for a felony or class A or class B misdemeanor*;

6–Are not a chemically dependent person;

7–Are not incapable of exercising sound judgment with respect to proper use and storage of a firearm—the complex mental impairment category; you are considered incapable if you:

A–Have been diagnosed by a licensed physician as having a psychiatric disorder or condition that may cause substantial impairment in judgment, mood, perception, impulse control or intellectual ability;

B–Have the disorder or condition listed in A above and it is in remission but likely to reoccur, or if you need continuous medical treatment to avoid reoccurrence; evidence of such a disorder or condition includes:

–involuntary psychiatric hospitalization;

–psychiatric hospitalization;

–inpatient or residential substance abuse treatment in the preceding five-year period;

–diagnosis by a licensed physician in the preceding five-year period that you are dependent on alcohol or a controlled or similar substance; or

–diagnosis at any time by a licensed physician that you suffer or have suffered from a psychiatric disorder or condition consisting of or relating to:

-schizophrenia or delusional disorder;
-bipolar disorder;
-chronic dementia caused by illness, brain defect, or brain injury;
-dissociative identity disorder;
-intermittent explosive disorder; or
-antisocial personality disorder;

C–Have been diagnosed by a licensed physician or declared by a court to be incompetent to manage your own affairs;

D–Ever entered a plea of "not guilty by reason of insanity" to a criminal proceeding;

If you have been previously diagnosed as suffering from a psychiatric disorder or condition described above, in order to no longer be considered incapable of exercising sound judgment, you may provide the department with a certificate from a licensed physician, whose primary practice is in the field of psychiatry, stating that your psychiatric disorder or condition is in remission and is not reasonably likely to develop at a future time (the state Medical Advisory Board is required to cooperate in all these determinations if asked by DPS, under Health and Safety Code §12.092 and §12.095);

8–Have not been convicted of disorderly conduct or a class A or class B misdemeanor in the last five years*;

9–Are qualified under federal and state law to buy a handgun;

10–Have not been judged delinquent on child support payments administered or collected by the state attorney general;

11–Have not been judged delinquent on back taxes in Texas;

12–Are not under a court protective order or restraining order from your spouse, except for one regarding property only;

13–For ten years prior to applying have not had any delinquent conduct violations of a felony grade;

14–Haven't lied or failed to disclose material facts in applying;

15–Have not had two class B misdemeanors or worse in the preceding ten years for alcohol or illegal-drug violations;

16–Pass a DPS-approved handgun-safety-training program to obtain official evidence of handgun proficiency from a DPS-approved instructor;

17–Are cleared through a local, state and federal criminal history background check, and a non-criminal history check if DPS decides it's needed;

18–Pay the fee.

*In 2009, "equivalent offenses" were included to cover crimes in other jurisdictions that are similar but not specific to Texas.

Preliminary CHL Application
From 1995 to 2009 you had to first apply to get a CHL application. This "application for the application" was free, intended to save you from the *non-refundable* $140 fee if it turned out you were ineligible—for anything from back taxes to a prior criminal record. That's been dropped in favor of checking your eligibility on the Internet, or just getting a packet directly from DPS.

CHL Application (§411.174)

The CHL application, available on the DPS website, currently requires your name, place and date of birth, race, sex, hair and eye color, height, weight, driver's license number or DPS identification certificate number, criminal-history information, drug, alcohol and psychiatric treatment history for the past five years, and your residence and business addresses for the preceding five years. DPS may not request and you are not required to provide your social security number to apply for or to renew a CHL. Filling out the form untruthfully is grounds to revoke the license. A completed CHL application packet currently includes:

1–Concealed-handgun license application form;

2–One or more photos that meet DPS standards, which DPS sets by regulation (currently two full-color passport-style pictures; these may become digital images in the future);

3–Birth certificate or other certified proof of age (driver's license or state ID card are both acceptable);

4–Proof of residency (detailed below);

5–Fingerprints in the manner acceptable to DPS (currently taken electronically by MorphoTrust USA with offices statewide);

6–A fee set by statute, currently $140 for the duration of the license, which may be paid by cash or credit card, or personal check, cashier's check or money order, payable to the Texas Dept. of Public Safety. The fee is *non-refundable* and if your payment bounces a $25 fee is charged to reapply (for new, duplicate, modified or renewals), which must then be made in 30 days with cashier's check or money order. Cash payments must be made in person. Fees for seniors (60 or over) or people at or below the federal poverty level is 50% of the full rate. Many groups have special rates. More than three dozen fee variations are listed on the DPS website.

7–Official evidence of handgun proficiency, in the manner DPS sets by regulation, obtained from an approved CHL course;

8–Affidavits, signed by you, stating that you have:

a–read *and* understand the CHL law *and* all statutes of Texas state law regarding the use of deadly force;

b–that you meet the eligibility requirements listed above;

9–authorization for DPS to investigate any of your non-criminal background history as far as they deem necessary.

You should also note that:

• If an application is incomplete, not legible or any parts are missing, the application will not be processed. You have 90 days from the time DPS gets your application to correct any problems, and you can request an additional 90 days. The application is not considered received until it is complete.

• DPS originally required officially printed forms—and advised applicants to keep photocopies for your own records. Forms may now be downloaded from the DPS website, and as with all the paperwork, this is subject to change by DPS, always check their website for details.

Application Background Checks (§411.176)

When DPS receives your completed application, they conduct a background check through their computerized criminal history system, and county mental health records. Within 30 days, DPS must forward your application to officials in your geographic area for a local check to verify the accuracy of your application. Local authorities must respond within 60 days from when DPS received your application. DPS is also required to send your fingerprints to the FBI for a national criminal history check.

The scope of the DPS investigation is at the "sole discretion of the department." The unlimited nature of this investigation may cause some residents to think twice about applying. Juvenile records that are sealed may be opened and inspected.

When done, the local authorities return your application to Austin, with either approval or disapproval recommended. Disapproval must include an affidavit stating personal knowledge or naming people with personal knowledge of information that would make you ineligible for a license.

Issuance or Denial (§411.177)

Within 60 days of your local officials' receipt of your application (which would be within 60 to 90 days of when DPS got your application), DPS must either:

1–Issue your license;

2–Notify you in writing that you've been denied (for reasons described under *Application Denials* below); or

3–Notify you that your application is delayed, stating why and how long the delay is likely to last. They have a total of 180 days from when they first received your materials in which to complete any lingering investigation.

Your county sheriff may be notified if you get a license, and local law-enforcement agencies may request notification too.

Form of License (§411.179)

A license is valid from date of issue, and includes your CHL ID number, expiration date, color photo, full name, date of birth, residence address, hair and eye color, height, weight, signature, driver's license or DPS ID card number, and status (e.g., judge, instructor, DA, etc.).

Residency (§411.173)

Determining residency used to be a major government concern before issuing a license, but with experience those fears and the red tape that went with it have eased. Now, Texas DPS accepts applications for CHLs from all U.S. citizens and permanent alien green-card holders. This is a policy subject to rule making so check with DPS for required proofs and details. As a historical note, the law was first changed in 2003 to allow people from states with no permit system to get a CHL here, and in 2005 to expand that to issuance for all states, as long as people met all requirements except for residency. Statute still retains six-month residency language, and might be cleaned up in a later session.

Application Denials (§411.180)

Instead of notifying you of a final determination of denial, DPS may simply wait 30 days from when they must act (the 180-day point), and their lack of notice constitutes denial. In the worst case, then, you could apply, be notified of a delay within 90 days, wait 210 days altogether, hear nothing, and thus be denied. Typically, however, DPS makes a good-faith effort to process applications as quickly as practical.

If DPS denies your license after the background check and notifies you in writing, there are three reasons they can give:

1–You don't meet all of the qualifications;

2–The local authorities disapproved; or

3–Your certified instructor disapproved, and DPS determined that the disapproval, based on a lack of required handgun proficiency, was made in good faith and based on a preponderance of the evidence (§411.188).

When you receive the denial, you may request a hearing, in writing, if you seek to have it reversed.

The request is made to DPS at its Austin address and must reach them within 29 days of your receipt of the denial. DPS must *schedule* a hearing within 30 days of receiving your request, in your local county justice court. The hearing must be *held* within 60 days of your request. A justice of the peace acts as an administrative hearing officer for the proceeding. DPS may be represented by a district attorney, county attorney, the attorney general or a designated member of the department.

The court will decide if there is a "preponderance of the evidence" or overwhelming evidence to support the denial. You have an opportunity to present evidence as well. If the court decides that there is not enough evidence to support the denial of a CHL, DPS is ordered to immediately issue or return the license. If the judgment goes against you, you are entitled to appeal the ruling within 30 days.

Similar procedures exist for the return or reinstatement of a license that has been suspended or revoked.

Replacing a License (§411.181)

If you have a CHL and change your name, address or status, or if your license is lost, stolen or destroyed you must notify DPS, in the manner they require, within 30 days. The department will issue a modified or duplicate license for a fee of $25 or less (it depends on your status). If your CHL is lost, stolen, or destroyed and was due to be renewed within 60 days, you may renew the license instead and pay only the nonrefundable renewal fee. Expiration dates remain unchanged for modified or replaced licenses. Failure to notify the department as described causes suspension of your license. Your local sheriff (and other agencies if they ask) are notified of license changes.

Duration and Renewal (§411.183 and §411.185)

Initially, a license is valid for four years from the day it is issued plus the time to your next birthday. A renewed license expires on your birthdate, five years from the expiration of your last license (so your birthdate is your renewal date every five years). Duplicate and modified licenses expire when their originals would have expired. States have chosen time frames of five years or less, to comply with Brady-law exemptions for license holders—a license less than five years old exempts you from background check delays on retail gun sales, see Chapter 7.

License renewal is now easy. On or before your expiration date, send an official application to DPS by mail or on the Internet, with the current nonrefundable fee. DPS provides a document with state law regarding use of deadly force and places that are prohibited for carry, which you must sign and return, indicating you've read *and* understand it all. DPS is required to send you the renewal information within 60 days of your expiration date, and issue a renewed license within 45 days if your application is in order and you qualify.

The renewal classes, testing, proof of proficiencies and other bureaucratic elements formerly required for the exercise of your rights were repealed in **2013**. Instructors who relied on those government-mandated classes for students, instead of free-market promotion, will very likely experience a steep drop off in clients and may, as in other states that reduced infringements, grouse about a "shrinking government rice bowl." Savvy outfits that start selling gun-safety training like any other consumer commodity will pick up the slack and profit.

Suspended License (§411.187)

Your license shall be suspended for a first offense (or equivalent first offense committed elsewhere):

1–Until charges are dismissed for class A or B misdemeanors;

2–Until charges are dismissed for disorderly conduct (§42.01);

3–Until charges are dismissed if you are charged with a felony under an information or indictment;

4–For 30 days if you fail to notify DPS within 30 days of a change of name, address or status (judge, instructor, prosecutor, etc.), or of a lost, stolen or destroyed license;

5–For 30 days if you carry a firearm that doesn't match your license category (the revolver and semi-auto distinction, described later);

6–For 30 days if you don't return an old license after a modified one is issued;

7–For a person under an order for emergency protection (Code of Criminal Procedure Art. 17.292);

8–For a person under a protective order who was found to have committed family violence (Family Code §85.022).

Suspension for a second offense can last from one to three years, and a third offense is grounds for revocation. Administrative details are provided in the law to guide law enforcement in the suspension process, and to allow licensees to respond.

Revoked License (§411.186)

Your license shall be revoked if:

1–You were not legally entitled to have it in the first place;

2–You lied on the application;

3–You become ineligible after getting it (for example, you are convicted of a felony; but not, on the other hand, if you were charged and the charges were later satisfactorily resolved);

4–You're convicted of carrying a firearm in a place prohibited under Penal Code §46.035; or

5–Your license is suspended three times for the same reason.

Administrative details are provided in the law to guide law enforcement in the revocation process, and to allow licensees to respond. Details to reapply for a license, two years after one is revoked, are also provided.

License Seizure (§411.206)

If you are arrested and taken into custody while carrying a CHL and handgun, the peace officer must confiscate the license and weapon. The firearm may be returned (per Article 18.19 of the Code of Criminal Procedure) if you're found to be not guilty.

Peace Officer May Disarm License Holder (§411.207)

If a peace officer believes it's necessary for your protection, or for the protection of the peace officer or other individuals, the officer is authorized to disarm you, and to return your firearm at the scene when the danger has subsided (provided you have broken no rules yourself).

Immunity for State Government and Instructors (§411.208)

Courts are prohibited from finding any part of the government, or a qualified handgun instructor (except in cases of fraud or deceptive trade practices), liable for damages for any actions or omissions as a result of the Right-to-Carry law, or any actions an applicant or licensee takes after getting or being denied a license (§411.208). DPS is not responsible for any injury or damage done by a license holder. A case for damages may not even be brought to court with one exception. The only exception to these immunities are actions or omissions by the state that are "capricious or arbitrary."

Records and Privacy (§411.192)

Formerly required to disclose private CHL information to almost anyone who asked, DPS was banned from doing so in 2007. Anti-rights activists were dangerously publishing such info in some states, and such abuse is now prevented here. The data can only be released to a criminal justice agency, or to you on request for a reasonable fee, and you are notified of the agency requesting your records, which can normally only include your name, date of birth, gender, race, and zip code. GC §411.192

MANDATORY CONCEALED-HANDGUN TRAINING

The Dept. of Public Safety (DPS) is required under Government Code Chapter 411 to establish training standards for concealed-handgun instructors and the programs they teach. Any person who seeks a license to carry a concealed handgun must earn an official "evidence of handgun proficiency," by taking and passing an approved course with a qualified instructor, in Texas.

DPS develops and distributes the procedures and materials for the course, testing and recordkeeping. You go to a qualified instructor (not to DPS) to take a course for a license. (The course to become a certified instructor is given only by DPS, and is described later.) DPS maintains files of all test results, and the individual instructors keep records of their own. The course includes both a classroom-type of instruction and firing-range instruction, and DPS officials may sit in and observe a class.

Minimum Course Requirements (§411.188)

The law and subsequent regulations set out minimum training requirements for a license. The classroom portion must be between 4 and 6 hours in length (reduced from 10–15 hours in 2013) and based on lesson plans developed by DPS. It must be conducted in person by certified instructors and recordings are no longer allowed, although handouts, such as this book, can be used. Ranges for shooting tests no longer need an official DPS ID number, which the range operator obtained from DPS. The training program must include at least these four modules:

1–Weapon-related laws (federal and state laws affect weapons), and the laws related to the use of deadly force (state laws regulate the use or threatened use of deadly force);

2–Handgun use and safety;

3–Non-violent dispute resolution;

4–Proper storage practices for handguns, with an emphasis on storage practices that eliminate the possibility of accidental injury to a child.

By regulation, all applicants must pass a written exam based on this material with a minimum 70% score to qualify. More than one attempt to pass may be allowed. You must pass within six months of your application.

5–The fifth component is live demonstration that you can safely and proficiently handle firearms of your choice, of at least .32 caliber at a range; the shooting test is on the back cover. Note that as of 2005, qualified active-duty or honorably-discharged military personnel (§411.1881) may be exempted from the range instruction portion of the training, and as of 2009, certain judicial officers can use a specially sworn statement from a certified instructor, as defined in §411.1882;

Handgun Categories

The new legal concept of handgun *categories*, semiautomatics (SA) and non-semiautomatics (NSA), introduced in the CHL law in 1995, was dropped in **2013**. The minimum caliber allowed for qualifying remains at .32, and successful applicants are now free to carry any legal firearm they choose after qualifying.

Marksmanship Requirements

The minimum requirements set by law to qualify for official evidence of handgun proficiency are:

1–Passing a written exam on the topics covered in the class;

2–Firing your handgun for qualifying scores (see back cover).

DPS is charged with setting minimum standards for the ability to safely and proficiently handle and fire a handgun. The course of fire appears in a chart on the inside back cover of this book, and is subject to change by DPS. The basic requirements include:

- An unmodified official DPS qualification target.

- A 50-round course of fire, using your own handgun, with timed shots fired at 3, 7 and 15 yards.

- 90% of maximum possible score to pass (225 out of 250) for instructors; 70% of maximum score to pass for licensees (175). Instructors and license applicants are given up to three attempts to pass.

- Firearms are to be held at the ready before and between firing strings, finger outside the trigger guard, muzzle pointed 45° ahead of you. No drawing is included in the test. Firing double action or from safety-on or decocked is recommended from a tactical and safety standpoint.

- Turning targets or whistles can be used to time strings. The time between strings is at the range officer's discretion.

- A shot fired late deducts one highest-scoring shot. A shot lost to a malfunction cannot be made up (just as in a real emergency). An accidental discharge, firing out of sequence or unsafe handling of a firearm is grounds for removal from the course of fire or disqualification. Makeups depend on available time and the instructor's discretion.

School Marshal Requirements

In addition to a valid CHL, a proper school employee seeking to qualify for School Marshal status must undergo training outlined in Occupations Code §1701.260. This includes at least 80 hours of instruction on strategies for preventing school shootings and securing the safety of potential victims, legal issues relating to police officer duties and the use of force and deadly force in the protection of others, effective law-enforcement strategies and techniques, improved proficiency with a handgun, and responding to an emergency requiring deadly force, such as a situation involving an active shooter.

The candidate must also undergo and pass a psychological evaluation. A fee for the marshal license and a renewal license will be determined, and the license must be issued to a person who passes the program. The license expires on your birthday, two years after you initially get your license, and then in two-year periods on your birthday. The renewal course is up to 16 hours and includes classroom and simulation training, handgun proficiency, psychological fitness evaluation and an exam. You must keep your CHL valid as well. Procedures for handling all the details are scheduled to be put in place by Jan. 1, 2014, and it would be reasonable to expect a modest period of time as the program comes up to speed and needed adjustments are made.

INSTRUCTOR QUALIFICATIONS

To be eligible to take the DPS instructor's course you needn't have a CHL, but you must meet the qualifications of a regular CHL applicant (no criminal record, etc., described above) and have at least one acceptable certification from (per §411.190):

- TCLEOSE: Texas Commission on Law Enforcement Officer Standards and Education;

- Texas Private Security Board (Occupations Code Ch. 1702);

- National Rifle Association of America handgun instructor; or

- You regularly instruct others in the use of handguns and have graduated from a school that uses a nationally accepted course designed to train handgun instructors.

- In addition DPS can by rule provide extended training for instructor applicants with less intensive training backgrounds.

Eligible instructor applicants must successfully complete a DPS-provided course of instruction to become certified as a CHL instructor. Program length is set by DPS. Shorter programs can be offered to students who have prior certification or can pre-qualify on tests arranged by DPS. See their website for details.

Instructor training was provided solely at DPS HQ in Austin, and applicants made their own arrangements for room and board while attending (five days), before **2013**. Later, provisions began for training at locations around the state on a scheduled basis. Check with DPS for current training, duration and location dates. The non-refundable course fee can vary up to $100, and like all fees is subject to change.

If you pass, the requirement for your own official evidence of handgun proficiency is waived if you decide to apply for a CHL (a fee still applies). Instructors are not required to be licensed to carry, but *certification to instruct is not a license to carry*. If an instructor becomes ineligible for a carry license, DPS will take action against the person's instructor status as well.

Instructor certifications expire after two years. The one-day retraining requires a $100 fee and a class as determined by DPS, which is being reorganized as of **2013**. DPS is now authorized by law to provide training online, though none is available as we go to press. Classes at DPS Austin HQ are now being supplemented with classes staged around the state periodically, so you don't necessarily have to travel. Instructors are asked to qualify each other at a range, rather than assembling at the DPS range as they formerly did. Check with DPS for the latest details, which are subject to change.

Any disruptive or unsafe behavior is grounds for immediate dismissal from training, at the instructor's sole discretion. Use of alcohol or illegal drugs during training is also grounds for immediate removal. Applicants must comply with all Texas laws and Training Academy operational procedures. By law, an instructor must be able to teach, and the DPS training includes:

• The laws concerning weapons and the use of deadly force (state laws regulate the use of deadly force; state and federal laws regulate firearms);

• Handgun use, proficiency, and safety;

• Non-violent dispute resolution;

• Proper storage practices for handguns, especially to prevent accidents involving children.

DPS also provides training in techniques of group instruction and other subjects as deemed necessary. In 2001 they added a section on "pre-incident indicators," that covers awareness and crime avoidance training. The training of instructors is intensive and no matter how much you know you will learn a lot.

If instructor applicants must bring equipment you'll be notified. In the past this has included: A revolver of at least .32 caliber; a semi-automatic handgun of at least .32 caliber; at least 200 rounds of factory-made ammunition per firearm (with approved brands; reloads not allowed); eye and ear protection, and protective clothing; and other gear DPS determines as needed.

Handguns may have no modifications that compromise the safety of the weapon. Handguns are subject to inspection before and during training and may be rejected if the course instructor finds one to be unsafe.

Instructor applications are similar to carry-license applications, except that no photograph was required. An instructor applicant who is denied certification to instruct has similar options to have the decision reversed that a CHL applicant has (described under *Application Denials*). An instructor applicant who fails to qualify is given some preference in reapplying.

Prior notice must be given to DPS for each training session an instructor holds, including date, time, classroom location, range name/location, and the instructor(s) giving the course. Records and reports of all classes held must be securely stored by instructors for three years, are subject to inspection, and include license applicant records, test scores, critiques, course materials, and copies of all reports sent to DPS. Reports on students who've taken a class must be submitted on official forms within five business days.

Note: The old system of sequentially numbered official handgun-proficiency certificates sold to instructors by DPS, for $5 each in lots of ten or more, was dropped in 2009 in favor of an interim online form, while DPS develops "evidence of handgun proficiency" in a form best suited to its needs. Expect new and ongoing streamlined automated processes and procedural changes.

Guest instructors who are not themselves certified and other tools that may have been acceptable in earlier years probably no longer meet DPS standards. Check with the Austin office and password-protected online instructor guidelines for guidance.

School Safety Certification for Instructors

To accommodate changes implemented in **2013**, GC §411.1901 requires DPS to establish a process for CHL instructors to get training and be certified in skills related to the School Marshals program. This must include at least: protection of students, interaction of license holders with "first responders," tactics for denying intruder entry into a classroom or school facility and increasing CHL handgun accuracy under duress. The training is to run between 15 and 20 hours and have its own fee.

A person who qualifies under this program can provide school safety training in the subjects listed above to employees of a school district or an open-enrollment charter school who have a CHL. Check with DPS for details on this program as it develops, and who will be responsible for delivering the program.

Miscellaneous

• DPS has a list of certified handgun instructors on its website, and keeps track of scheduled classes (which instructors must report to DPS prior to beginning). Detailed statistical reports on CHLs issued, denied, revoked or suspended for instructors and licensees, with breakouts by age, gender, race and zip code are also on the DPS website.

• The taxes (called "fees") collected under the CHL program are used exclusively to run the program. Excess at the end of the fiscal year goes to the Crime Victims Compensation Fund.

• Written notices required by the Right-to-Carry law must be sent by certified mail. Your official address is the last address you provided to DPS. If a certified letter to you is returned as undeliverable, DPS can give you legal notice by publishing one announcement in a local newspaper.

• Although *The Texas Gun Owner's Guide* doesn't specifically cover gun laws for peace officers or other officials, the Right-to-Carry law has provisions for issuing nationally recognized CHLs to active and honorably retired peace officers who meet federal requirements. The license has the same duration as a civilian license, though some conditions are different (such as a proficiency requirement in LGC §415.035, and definitions in OC §1701.357 and GC §614.121). A set of requirements is also established for active and retired judicial officers. These can be found in the state statutes.

• DPS must provide a copy of the standards, course requirements and examinations to any qualified handgun instructor on request, and issues statistics on offenses of Penal Code §46.035, as required by Government Code §411.047.

RECIPROCITY IN GENERAL

Historical Note: A national movement is afoot to ease the stranglehold that state laws have placed on law-abiding travelers. Introduced at state and federal levels, *reciprocity laws* seek to guarantee that people who may legally carry in their home states cannot be held in violation when in another state. It seems that the Second Amendment is providing no protection for travelers, and a legislative solution is being sought.

Your home state's rules would not apply when you go "abroad." You would be subject to laws, regulations and customs of the state you are in at the time.

Most proposals seek this relief for people with government-issued permits only. Supporters cite the portion of Article IV of the Constitution, known as the *full faith and credit clause*, which says, in part, "Full Faith and Credit shall be given in each State to the public Acts, Records, and judicial Proceedings of every other state". This sets a model similar to marriage and driver licenses.

Other efforts seek to allow people not acting criminally to be free from harassment or arrest for simple possession of a legally owned firearm, independent of the state involved or the method of carry. A distinction would then exist between so-called *"right to carry"* (which requires government taxes and papers) and *"freedom to carry"* (which simply leaves government out of your personal affairs). This is sometimes referred to as Vermont- or Alaska-style carry, where such systems exist. Efforts to establish this level of freedom for simple possession of private property has been called **"Constitutional Carry."**

Some states take the approach that, if your permit is similar to ours, and your state formally honors ours, then we'll honor yours. A method is then set up to determine if the states' requirements are a rough match. Such comparisons are problematic because they again subject your rights to bureaucratic review, as in the days before "shall issue" permits, and indeed, states have experienced difficulty in agreeing if their "standards" match. When officials decide there is no match, they remove the right to carry between those states. To link all 50 states to each other this way and thus restore rights to properly government-licensed individuals would require 1,225 pacts (49 + 48 + 47... etc.).

Each state's requirements are of course different. Studying the laws of your home state (a common requirement) hardly prepares you and is certainly not a match for the laws in any other state. Florida requires no shooting test for its permit, Virginia seeks proof of demonstrated competence with a gun but does not define it further, Texas requires 50 shots at three distances with all shots timed, Arizona requires seven hits out of ten, and so it goes, state to state.

Some states honor anyone who has a state-issued permit. Some will issue a permit to anyone qualified, resident or not, getting around the problem in yet another way. A handful of states have no permit system, leaving them out of the picture when their residents are on the road, or for you when you visit. A few have introduced laws that would allow you to drive through their states on a "continuous journey," or to enter the state but only for a competition or designated event. You *should* have rights. You have a mess.

Federal bills have so far unsuccessfully sought to require all states to honor the permits of all other states. Residents in Vermont are excluded because they need no permit to carry in the first place (and you need none while there; possession of personal property, absent some overt criminal act, has simply not been outlawed). The 98% of Americans who bear arms but have refused to sign up for a government carry-rights permit are also left out completely.

Rumors swirl about which state has adopted what policy, and relying on a rumor where no rule exists can get you arrested. Viewing the statute yourself is a good way to avoid rumors. Laws offer less protection when new, before on-the-street police policy is established and well known in the law enforcement community. As noted earlier, a state can revoke a deal without notice.

Do not assume from the information below or any other listings you may be able to find that reciprocity or recognition exists, only that the states are looking into the possibilities, and you might want to too.

It would be nice if there was a rock-solid reliable place to call to find out exactly where reciprocity exists, but there is none at the present time, and none is expected. Besides, a complete answer with precisely all the do's and don'ts is more than you can possibly get over the phone. The job of telling you is not the role of the police, the sheriff, the DA, the AG, the library or anyone else. Why, you'd need a book the size of this one for every state you visited.

One solution that addresses these problems is the proposed American Historical Rights Protection Act. This basically says that if a person has a gun, the person isn't a criminal, and the gun isn't illegal, then that is not a crime, based on the 14th Amendment. For a copy of this draft statute contact Bloomfield Press or go to Position Papers on our website, gunlaws.com.

TEXAS RECIPROCITY

This has gone through a bewildering set of changes since the idea of reciprocity was first introduced. The original scheme was so awkward that from 1997 to 2000, deals had been cut with only seven states. Under rules as of 2010, 29 states recognized us, and we recognized 40. By **2013**, we recognized 41 and 31 recognized us. See the DPS website, linked at the National Directory at gunlaws.com, for details.

Under current law the governor must negotiate agreements with states that have their own concealed-carry license procedure, and recognize those licenses, or simply proclaim recognition if the Texas Attorney General determines that:

The other state requires a background check for a license applicant, conducted by authority of state or local officials, which includes a search of the federal National Crime Information Center and the Interstate identification Index.

The Attorney General issues an annual report of the states that qualify for recognition, and changes for laws of the states that do not qualify, which would make them eligible for recognition.

The Reciprocity Lists

Be very cautious here, because other states are very different from Texas, with no official way for finding out how they work. Some states may only recognize a Texas CHL if you are a Texas resident. The *Traveler's Guide to the Firearm Laws of the 50 States*, in the back of this book, provides an overview. *One of the main reasons reciprocity works is that you remain incognito.*

These lists change rapidly and are available through private, commercial and government websites. Most rights organizations have a version posted, all linked from our National Directory at gunlaws.com. The accuracy, timeliness, and what it actually means to be on such a list can be hard to tell, and is usually undercut by disclaimers accompanying the lists. Info below is from sources believed to be reliable as of September **2013**, but **states may be added or removed without notice**.

Texas Reciprocal States, from the DPS website: (we recognized each other's permits when the list was posted)**:** Alabama, Alaska, Arizona, Arkansas, Colorado, Delaware, Florida, Georgia, Idaho, Indiana, Kansas, Kentucky, Louisiana, Michigan, Mississippi, Missouri, Montana, Nebraska, New Mexico, North Carolina, North Dakota, Oklahoma, Pennsylvania, South Carolina, South Dakota, Tennessee, Utah, Virginia, West Virginia, Wyoming.

Texas "Unilateral Proclamation" States: (Governor proclaims we'll recognize them regardless that they do not recognize us): California, Connecticut, Hawaii, Iowa, Maryland, Massachusetts, Nevada, New Jersey, New York, Rhode Island, Washington.

No agreement: (We have no agreement with these): Illinois, Maine, Minnesota, New Hampshire, Ohio, Oregon, Vermont, Wisconsin.

Get Another State's License: (these states may issue licenses to qualified non-residents) Arizona, Connecticut, Florida, Idaho, Indiana, Iowa, Maine, Maryland, Massachusetts, Minnesota, Nevada, New Hampshire, New Jersey, North Dakota, Oregon, Pennsylvania, Rhode island, Tennessee, Texas, Utah, Washington.

These states have passed laws that would allow some bureau within the state (indicated in parenthesis) to cut deals with a bureau in another state, or they have set up other conditions that might lead them to recognize each other's permits—check with them for details: Arkansas (State Police), Connecticut (Commissioner of State Police), Georgia (County Probate Judge), Kentucky (Sheriff), Louisiana (Deputy Secretary of Public Safety Services), Massachusetts (Chief of Police), Mississippi (Dept. of Public Safety), Missouri (residents currently prohibited from concealed carry), Montana (Governor), New Hampshire (Chief of Police), North Dakota (Chief of the Bureau of Criminal Investigation), Oklahoma (State Bureau of Investigation), Pennsylvania (Attorney General), Rhode Island (Attorney General), South Carolina (Law Enforcement Division), Texas (Dept. of Public Safety), Utah (Dept. of Public Safety), Virginia (Circuit Court), West Virginia (Sheriff). The different authorities named in this list are a measure of the inconsistency of the laws from state to state. If, after reading these lists, you get the sense that reciprocity schemes don't solve the problem and unshackle honest citizens, well, you're not alone.

In place of an uninfringed civil right to keep and bear arms, and innocence unless you are proven guilty, your human rights as an American have been reduced to a list of government-approved states for licensees only, under the infringement of reciprocity schemes. The 98% of the public that refuses to jump through the hoops, be taxed, get on the criminal database and get a "rights" permission slip is left out in the cold. *Enormous police effort that could be going directly toward reducing crime is instead being diverted into registering, regulating and tracking the innocent.*

In 2005, Texas had 247,345 active CHL holders, and 1,613 licensed CHL instructors. With a population then of 22,859,968, about 1.1% of Texans had the carry license. By the end of 2008 this was 314,574 CHLs and 1,511 instructors. With 24,326,974 in population that's 1.3% of all Texans. By 2012 this had swelled to 584,850 CHLs and 3,017 instructors. With a population of 26,059,203 that brought CHLs to 2.24% of all Texans, or about one out of 45.

PROHIBITED PLACES

Many of the restrictions on possession of firearms are found in the Texas Penal Code. Others are found in federal statutes and regulations, and land office and agency regulations, codes and laws. The prohibited places listed generally do not apply to the proper authorities (peace officers, commissioned security guards and bodyguards, members of the military and prison guards, judges and other special exempt agents of the government).

See Chapter 4 for information on where *shooting* firearms is prohibited. This section deals with places where *bearing* arms is prohibited. CHL holders are required to certify that they know where firearms are prohibited to obtain a renewal license by mail, and the subject is included in training classes.

> Keep in mind that the Parking Lot Protection Act of 2011 may allow discreet possession of guns and ammo in locked private vehicles for employees at parking facilities in some of the situations listed below, check carefully before proceeding. See LC §52.061 et seq.—and don't be surprised by disagreements.

Under §46.03 of the Penal Code it's a third degree felony for a person, even with a valid concealed-handgun license, to intentionally, knowingly or recklessly bring or have a firearm:

1–On the premises (defined in §46.035, next page) of a public or private **school** or educational institution, any building or grounds while they are sponsoring an activity there, or a passenger vehicle of such an establishment, without written permission from them or under their written regulations;

2–On the premises of a public **polling place** on the day of an election or while early voting is in progress;

3–On the premises of any government **court** or offices used by the court, unless by written regulations or with written authorization from the court;

4–To a **racetrack** (and possibly its on-site parking area if any; since this isn't fully settled, it is a risk you may want to avoid);

5–To the secured area of an **airport** (with an exception for properly checked baggage);

6–Within 1,000 feet of a **place of execution** on the day of an execution, if you received notice that it is prohibited. Exceptions include driving on a public road or while at home or at work.

There are limited exceptions for military and proper authorities, listed in Chapter 1 under *Who Can Bear Arms*.

Under Penal Code §46.035, established by the Right-to-Carry law, CHL holders are prohibited from carrying:

1–On the premises of establishments that get 51% or more of their income from **servicing or serving alcoholic beverages** for on-premises consumption (typically known as *bars* though other places might qualify). The Texas Alcoholic Beverage Commission is required to determine which establishments meet the 51% rule, and those places must post a sign that gives you effective notice, see *Bars* in this chapter;

2–On the premises where a high school, collegiate or professional **sporting event**, or an interscholastic event, is taking place (unless you're using the handgun in the event);

3–On the premises of a **correctional facility**;

4–On the premises of **hospitals** or **nursing homes** (without written authorization), if proper notice is given (see below);

5–In an **amusement park**, if proper notice is given;

6–On the premises of a **church**, synagogue or other established place of worship, if proper notice is given;

7–At any **meeting of a government entity** (with proper notice).

The 'proper notice' that hospitals, nursing homes, amusement parks, places of worship, government meetings and watering holes must provide includes verbal or written communication, or posted signs (§30.06), described in detail under *No-Guns-Allowed Signs* later in this chapter. A lengthy list of judges and judicial officers have a defense to prosecution from these bans.

The word *premises* as used here means a building or part of a building. It does not include a public or private driveway, street, sidewalk or walkway, parking lot, garage, or other parking area. This allows you to disarm before entering a prohibited place, and allows foot and vehicle travel in the vicinity of those places.

Carrying a firearm at the places listed in §46.035 is a class A misdemeanor, except for bars and correctional facilities, where it is a third degree felony. An overall exception is made for the justified use of deadly force (self defense, etc.) under chapter 9 of the Penal Code.

Under Penal Code §46.11, a violation of any of the state weapons laws (found in Penal Code chapter 46, except for §46.03-a-1 concerning schools) carries the next higher penalty if it's proven that you knew you were:

1–Within 300 feet of a school;

2–On the premises where an official school function took place;

3–At a University Interscholastic League sponsored event.

See Chapter 7 for additional school restrictions under the federal Gun-Free School Zones Act.

Also note that:

• Individual municipalities have some regulatory control over firearms within municipal limits (see Chapter 4) but may not make regulations that affect concealed-handgun licensees.

• Commissioned security officers are subject to the same CHL requirements as regular residents, in addition to their own requirements as commissioned guards.

• A separate law (Education Code §4.31) makes it a five-year felony to interfere with the normal activities of any type of school, or a school bus carrying children, by showing or using a firearm, or by threatening to show or use one.

• The Texas Parks and Wildlife Dept. is authorized to close areas to firearm possession, use, or to possession or use of specific types of firearms, under a number of different laws and regulations in the Parks and Wildlife Code.

• Under Parks and Wildlife Code §62.081, it's illegal to possess firearms on Lower Colorado River Authority land, except at official non-profit target ranges, by members of the boy scouts, girl scouts, or other non-profit public service groups, under the supervision of an authorized instructor.

• Possession of firearms on Lavaca-Navidad River Authority property is prohibited. See Chapter 4 for CHL exceptions.

Private Property and Trespass

All property owners have explicit rights and control the terms by which others may enter their property. Private-property rights are a fundamental element of American freedom and deserve utmost respect. Access to a private residence is legally under near-total control of the resident, with no need for posting signs or other regulations.

Places open to the public however may not discriminate and are generally subject to the notification requirements in Penal Code §30.05 and §30.06. Most private property can be posted to exclude people from entering.

Any person who enters or remains on someone else's property, including an aircraft or vehicle, without permission, or enters or remains in a building without permission and got notice that entry was forbidden, or was asked to leave but does not, faces a trespassing charge under §30.05. Notice may be oral or written, and may include a wide variety of signs, fencing, vertical purple paint marks, cultivated crops, livestock enclosures and more, that would give reasonable notice to exclude intruders.

Criminal trespass under §30.05 is a class C misdemeanor if it occurs on agricultural land. In other cases, it is a class B misdemeanor, unless it's committed in a home, a shelter center, a Superfund site, a critical infrastructure facility, or with a deadly weapon, in which case it's a class A misdemeanor.

A CHL holder cannot be kept out simply on the basis of firearm possession under §30.05. The exclusion of CHLs requires the special sign and other requirements under §30.06.

Added in 1997, Penal Code §30.06 establishes special trespass offenses and sign requirements to legally exclude concealed-handgun-license holders from private property. It is illegal for a CHL holder to carry a handgun, without effective consent, if the person receives *valid notice* that:

1-Entry on the property by a CHL who is carrying a concealed handgun is forbidden; or

2–You are notified that remaining on the premises with a concealed handgun is forbidden and you do not leave.

Valid notice requires a specially worded and lettered sign at each entrance, described below. The sign language can also be handed to you, or you can be told orally that you must leave. Failure to leave when asked is a class A misdemeanor. This law was amended in 2003 to make it clear that most government buildings *cannot* ban CHL holders.

No-Guns-Allowed Signs

Four laws passed in 1997 define three no-guns-allowed signs, what they must look like, and how to give "proper notice" that guns are prohibited at different kinds of public places.

1–For the purpose of the CHL trespassing law (§30.06 described above) and for the CHL restrictions in §46.035, you have "received notice" when the owner (or someone with apparent

authority to act for the owner) gives you notice either orally
or in writing. If it's in writing it may be handed to you, or
prominently posted in English and Spanish on the property, in
contrasting-color block letters at least one inch high, with this
precise message:

> "Pursuant to Section 30.06, Penal Code (trespass by holder of license
> to carry a concealed handgun), a person licensed under Subchapter
> H, Chapter 411, Government Code (concealed handgun law), may
> not enter this property with a concealed handgun"

Any place open to the public could post a 'thirty-ought-six'
sign to restrict CHLs. If a hospital, nursing home, amusement
park, place of worship or government meeting does not post
such a sign (or give written or oral notice), then properly
licensed CHLs are not prohibited from entering.

2–A business with a liquor license or permit, which gets 51% or
more of its income from the sale of alcohol for consumption
on the premises, must conspicuously post a sign at each
entrance, in English and Spanish, that it is unlawful for a CHL
to carry a handgun on the premises. The sign must be in
contrasting colors with block letters at least one inch high,
with the number "51" in solid red at least five inches high.
(Government Code §411.204). PC §46.035 adds a defense to
prosecution in 2009 if the sign doesn't give effective notice.

3–Any place with a liquor license or permit that doesn't have to
post a "51" sign (in other words, they get less than 51% of
their income from providing drinks) must post a sign that says
it is unlawful to carry a weapon on the premises *unless* you
have a valid CHL license. The basic idea here is to make bars
off limits to everyone, but to allow CHLs to enjoy a restaurant
even if it serves alcohol (and it's illegal for a CHL to get drunk
while armed). The sign must be at least six inches high and
14 inches wide, in contrasting colors, and conspicuously
displayed. The liquor authorities can require a language in
addition to English if they deem it necessary. (Alcoholic
Beverage Code §11.041 and §61.11).

To summarize, there are three possible signs: 1–The thirty-
ought-six sign to exclude CHLs based on trespass law, 2–The big
red "51" sign that prohibits all guns in bars, and 3–A sign that
allows CHLs into places that service (bring your own bottle) or

serve alcohol but get less than 51% of their revenue from drinks. Private property owners can post their own signs to say "no trespassing" and exclude anyone, regardless of gun possession.

Bars

Intentionally, knowingly or recklessly carrying a handgun into a place that serves or services alcoholic drinks is a third degree felony (see Penal Code §46.02). A concealed-handgun license only exempts you from this requirement if the place gets less than 51% of its revenue from alcohol sales. Places licensed or permitted to provide alcohol drinks are required to post certain signs, defined by law, concerning firearms on the premises.

A bar (in the over 51% category) that knowingly allows a person to have a firearm on the premises can have its liquor license revoked, and their signs must give "effective notice" to be valid. These restrictions do not apply to the liquor-license holder (or the holder's employee) while supervising the licensed premises.

The Texas Alcoholic Beverage Commission can adopt certain rules related to firearms, and must determine which places are under and over the 51% threshold. They may allow a gun show on the premises of a liquor-license holder, if the premises is a government entity or a non-profit civic, religious, charitable, fraternal or veterans' organization. They may allow an off-premises-consumption license holder to hold a gun show if the license holder also has a federal firearms license. Finally, they may allow the ceremonial display of firearms at a licensed establishment, and historical reenactments provided no live ammunition is allowed. The reenactment provision required changes to the Alcoholic Beverage Code §11.61 and §61.71, and Penal Code §46.035 and §46.15.

Federal Facilities

• Guns are generally prohibited in federal facilities (18 USC §930). Knowingly having a gun or other dangerous weapon (except a pocket knife with a blade under 2-1/2 inches) in a federal facility is punishable by a fine and up to one year imprisonment. Exceptions are made for the proper authorities and lawful carrying, "incident to hunting or other lawful purposes." There has been no definitive test case on whether a CHL (or other routine legal carry) will qualify, and federal authorities routinely post this rights restriction without posting the exception, a deplorable practice. The statute says you cannot be convicted of this offense unless notice of the law is posted at each public entrance or if you had actual notice of the law (which, it could be argued, you now do). A federal facility is a building (or part), federally leased or owned, where federal employees regularly work.

- Except for limited hunting privileges, there is a fine of up to $500 for carrying a gun in the **National Parks**. This was set to expire in Feb. 2010, check gunlaws.com to see if it does.

- Possession of firearms on any **military base** is subject to control by the commanding officer.

- Firearm possession is prohibited by federal law on the gate side of **airport** passenger-security checkpoints. You are allowed to check firearms as baggage if you do it in accordance with federal rules (see *Common and Contract Carriers* in Chapter 1).

Texas Gun-Free School-Zone Laws

It is a felony, punishable by up to five years in state penitentiary for a first offense, to interfere in any way with the normal operation of any type of school (public, private, vocational, technical, at any grade or degree level), or any portion of its campus, or a school bus transporting children, by exhibiting, using, or threatening to exhibit or use a firearm. See Education Code §4.31. A student must be expelled for using, showing or having a firearm or other weapon while on school property or at school events even if off school property. An exception was passed in 2009 for properly sponsored approved events like target practice and school sports, EC §37.007.

Penal Code §46.03 makes it a third-degree felony for a person, even with a concealed-handgun license, to intentionally, knowingly or recklessly bring or have a firearm on the premises of a public or private school or educational institution, or a passenger vehicle of such an establishment, without written permission from them or under their written regulations.

CHL holders are prohibited under PC §46.035 from carrying a handgun where high school, collegiate or professional sporting events, or interscholastic events, are taking place (unless they're using the handgun in the event). EC §37.125 makes it illegal to intentionally use, exhibit, or threaten to use or exhibit a firearm in a manner intended to cause alarm, harm, or damage to school property, parking areas or a school bus transporting children. The federal gun-free-school-zone law is in Chapter 7.

Under PC §46.11 (and except for the felony in 46.03 above, which doesn't change), the penalties for all Penal Code firearm offenses increase to the next highest category if they were committed in a place you knew was within 300 feet of a school, or where an official school function was taking place, or were done at an event sponsored or sanctioned by the University Interscholastic League.

Texas School-Zone Laws Exception

Beginning in **2013**, institutions of higher education, as defined by law, may not adopt or enforce any rules or take any actions, including posting signs, to prohibit or restrict the storage or transportation of a firearm or ammunition in a locked, privately owned or leased motor vehicle by a person, including a student enrolled at that institution. The person must hold a valid CHL and lawfully possesses the firearm or ammunition, and be on a street or driveway located on the campus of the institution, or in a parking lot, garage, or other parking area on the campus.

Hotels

Some hotels have a policy of prohibiting or restricting firearms possession, transportation or storage by their hotel guests, and although this might seem like blatant denial of or discrimination against your fundamental civil rights, they do it anyway and have not been charged with any crime, yet. Occupational Code §2155.102 was enacted in **2013** to require such hotels to post such policies on their Internet reservation sites. If the hotel provides written confirmation of phone reservations the firearms policy must be included. Failure to do so carries a misdemeanor penalty with a fine of up to $100.

Open Carry

Texas is among a handful of states that require hiding sidearms in public, so concealed ("discreet") carry is the basic rule, and open carry is generally banned (only six other states completely ban open carry). A growing call for relaxing this ban has been heard here lately.

While some people see open carry as threatening and politically intimidating, polarizing an already misinformed public, others consider the ban a severe limit on freedom and a handicap in "inoculating" the public on the decent and normative values of an armed populace. The tactical pros and cons of open carry are heated talks that proceed without end.

Notably, in **2013**, state law was amended so brief inadvertent public display is no longer an offense. This means a CHL who "prints" through clothing or otherwise accidentally reveals in public has no longer automatically committed a crime, solving a problem that has caused some serious grief in the past. Texas also enjoys some open carry in its legal structure, including:

1–On your premises or premises you control;

2–On your business premises;

3–At your place of employment (only with owner's permission);

4–On land ("real property") controlled by you;

5–On a recreational vehicle used as living quarters;

6–While engaging in lawful sporting activity with arms of the type normally used in that activity, such as at gun shows or while hunting or fishing.

7–During properly sanctioned reenactments or theatrical events.

Gun-Free-Zone Liability Act

Places where a law or policy requires you to disarm, and that provide no adequate alternative protection from criminal assault, are *make-believe gun-free zones* and have been the preferred locations for homicidal maniacs. Like the Luby's event in Kileen, Texas, these zones, whether private or government sanctioned, are known to be dangerous, reckless and negligent. Efforts are underway to mitigate them, or hold those who create them responsible for any harm they cause. See The Gun-Free-Zone Liability Act model language at GunLaws.com.

Does a place that bans guns and restricts your ability to respond in an emergency take on a liability to protect you? Are you more safe or less safe at a place that has a no-guns-allowed sign on the door? Will insurance companies refuse to pay for damages if a store doesn't ban guns—or if it does? Are you really easier pickins when you're in a so-called "gun-free" zone? Will foot traffic go up or down at a store with no-guns-allowed signs? These are unanswered questions of law and practice. Some pro-rights groups are posting lists and only patronizing outfits that respect the right to keep and bear arms.

One thing to keep in mind is that boisterous arguments with store managers in public will serve little purpose, and creating too much commotion, especially if armed, can have decidedly negative repercussions. It is true that banning legally armed people defeats the whole purpose of the Right-to-Carry law and the right to arms in general—to allow the people to respond in a dire emergency.

A WORD TO THE WISE

Expect changes to all the rules covering the concealed-handgun license. Anticipate new regs, with old ones adjusted, dropped or interpreted differently. Everyone may not agree on everything, and **elements of this book will undoubtedly change.** Remember that you face serious risks for what may seem like minor infractions. *The TEXAS Gun Owner's Guide* is **just one tool for helping you on a long road to knowledge.** That road has turns and pitfalls—don't rely on any one tool for such a complex route, and be very cautious as you travel its course. Take steps to stay current.

DPS and Texas law requires you to read *and* **understand the statutes**. You are not the first person to find out that the statutes—which is what DPS hands out—are written in a way that is hard to understand, and that's putting it mildly.

Bloomfield Press will be preparing **updates** periodically. To receive a copy send us a stamped, self-addressed envelope, check our website, or simply sign up for periodic email updates on our website home page. The addresses are on page two of this book.

WHEN CAN YOU CONCEAL A FIREARM?

WHEN CAN YOU CONCEAL A FIREARM?

Without a Concealed Handgun License (CHL) valid in Texas, the eight *instances* where you may legally have a completely concealed handgun (and hence have it "on or about" you) are:

1–On your premises or premises you control;

2–On your business premises;

3–At your place of employment (only with owner's permission);

4–On land ("real property") controlled by you;

5–Inside or directly enroute to a motor vehicle or watercraft you own or that is under your control;

6–On a recreational vehicle, whether motorized or designed to be towed, being used as temporary or permanent living quarters, including a travel trailer, camping trailer, truck camper, motor home and horse trailer with living quarters;

7–While "traveling" according to old legal definitions discussed in Chapter 1, still on the books but becoming obsolete;

8–While engaging in lawful hunting, fishing, or other sporting activity, or directly enroute between your premises and such activity, with a weapon of the type normally used in that activity (concealment is not required but is prudent).

In many states, unlike Texas, *open* carry of firearms is legal and somewhat unrestricted, and it is *concealed* carry that is banned, heavily regulated, or requires government permission slips often called CCW permits. In Texas it's just the opposite—*open* carry is generally a violation and *concealed* carry is usually *required.*

However, to *carry* a sidearm "on or about" you, you need a valid CHL license, and the gun must basically remain concealed at all times. Intentionally letting a gun show or even threatening to let it show can be charged as several offenses.

Allowing a sidearm to be plainly visible is generally only legal in justified self defense, or hunting and sporting events if the firearm is one typically used in that pursuit. In public, sidearms must be concealed from plain view if they are to be possessed legally, with a narrow exception for brief inadvertent display (passed in **2013**) not intended to cause a public disturbance.

TYPES OF WEAPONS 3

There are weapons and there are weapons. If a gun has been modified in certain ways, it can become a *prohibited weapon* and it may be a crime to have it at all. In the years from 1994 to 2004, certain firearms and accessories, under the so-called assault-weapon ban, could only be owned if they were made before Sep. 13, 1994 (that ban has ended). The definitions of legal firearms are a moving target, as politicians tinker with our right to keep and bear arms, just like the gun laws themselves.

Weapons include *dangerous instruments,* things that can be deadly depending on their use, like fireplace tools or a baseball bat. The term *deadly weapons* specifically refers to things designed for lethal use. Guns are only one kind of deadly weapon.

A responsible gun owner needs an understanding of the different types of firearms, their methods of operation, selections for personal defense, holstering options, ammunition types, loading and unloading, cleaning and maintenance, accessories, safe storage and more. Many fine books cover these areas. This chapter of *The Texas Gun Owner's Guide* only covers weapons from the standpoint of those that are illegal, restricted or otherwise specially regulated.

PROHIBITED WEAPONS

In 1934, responding to mob violence spawned by Prohibition, Congress passed the National Firearms Act (NFA), the first major federal law concerning guns since the Constitution. This was an attempt to control what Congress called "gangster-type weapons." Items like machine guns, silencers, short rifles and sawed-off shotguns were put under strict government control and registration. These became known as "NFA weapons."

This was supposed to give authorities an edge in the fight against crime. Criminals never registered their weapons, and now simple possession of an unregistered "gangster gun" was a federal offense. Failure to pay the required transfer tax on the weapon compounded the charge. Regular types of personal firearms were completely unaffected.

Political assassinations in the 1960s led to a public outcry for greater gun controls. In 1968, the federal Gun Control Act was passed, which absorbed the provisions of earlier statutes and added bombs and other destructive devices to the list of strictly controlled weapons. Texas calls these *prohibited weapons* (see Penal Code §46.05 for the letter of the law), though a more accurate title might be *controlled weapons,* as you'll see under Machine Guns. It is generally illegal to make, have, transport, sell or transfer any prohibited weapon without prior approval and registration. Violation of this is generally a third degree felony under state law (see Penal Code §46.05), and carries federal penalties of up to 10 years in jail and up to a $10,000 fine.

Defaced Deadly Weapons

Removing, altering or destroying the manufacturer's serial number on a gun is a federal felony. Knowingly having a defaced gun is a federal felony.

State Prohibited Weapons

Penal Code §46.05 makes it illegal to intentionally or knowingly have, make, transport, repair or sell:

1–An explosive weapon;

2–A machine gun;

3–A short-barrel firearm;

4–A firearm silencer;

5–Knuckles;

6–Armor-piercing ammunition;

7–A chemical dispensing device (not including small personal self-defense sprays available commercially, and properly trained commissioned security officers are exempt);

8–A zip gun;

9-A tire deflation device (2013).

Violations are a third degree felony, except for number 5, a class A misdemeanor, and number 9, a state jail felony. All but 5, 7 and 9 also carry federal penalties. State law was changed in 2009 to distinguish between popular knives that can be opened easily with one hand and are not switchblades, and those which spring open automatically by using a release button or similar device and are switchblades, see Penal Code §46.01. In 2013, switchblades were eliminated from the state ban completely.

Prohibited Weapon Exceptions

It is legal to intentionally or knowingly have, make, transport, repair or sell those prohibited weapons if:

1–You are performing official duties as a member of the armed forces, national guard, a governmental law enforcement agency or a penal institution;

2–You are acting within boundaries of the NFA weapons laws;

3–Regarding a short-barrel firearm or tire deflation device, you are dealing with it solely as an antique or curio;

4–In the case of armor-piercing ammunition, you are only acting to make it available to the armed forces, the national guard, a governmental law enforcement agency, or a penal institution.

ILLEGAL GUNS

(Sometimes also referred to as NFA weapons,
prohibited weapons or destructive devices)

Frequently but inaccurately termed illegal, these weapons and
destructive devices are among those that are legal only if they
are pre-registered with the Bureau of Alcohol, Tobacco,
Firearms and Explosives.

1–A rifle with a barrel less than 16 inches long;

2–A shotgun with a barrel less than 18 inches long;

3–A modified rifle or shotgun less than 26 inches overall;

4–Machine guns;

5–Silencers of any kind;

6–Firearms over .50 caliber;

7–Street Sweeper, Striker-12 and USAS-12 shotguns.

Guns with a bore of greater than one-half inch (except regular
shotguns) are technically known as destructive devices. Some
antique and black powder firearms have such large bores but
are not prohibited, as determined on a case-by-case basis by the
Bureau of Alcohol, Tobacco, Firearms and Explosives.

AFFECTED WEAPONS

Historical Note: The federal Public Safety and Recreational Firearms Use Protection Act
(also called the Crime Bill, also called the assault-weapons ban, which expired on Sep.
13, 2004), allowed citizens to possess certain firearms and accessories only if they were
made before Sep. 13, 1994. New products required a date stamp and were off-limits for
the public. Having an affected weapon or accessory that had no date stamp was
presumption that the item was not affected (that is, it was a pre-crime-bill version) and
was OK. This law has now expired, none of these conditions apply any longer, and we
can see the value of laws with expiration dates. For the record, these weapons (there
were about 200) included all firearms, copies or duplicates, in any caliber, known as:

Norinco, Mitchell, and Poly Technologies (Avtomat Kalashnikovs (all models); Action
Arms Israeli Military Industries Uzi and Galil; Beretta AR-70 (SC-70); Colt AR-15;
Fabrique National FN/FAL, FN/LAR, and FNC; SWD M-10, -11, -11/9, and -12; Steyr
AUG; Intratec TEC-9, -DC9 and -22; and revolving cylinder shotguns, such as (or similar
to) the Street Sweeper and Striker 12, and, any **rifle** that can accept a detachable
magazine and has at least 2 of these features: a folding or telescoping stock; a pistol grip

that protrudes conspicuously beneath the action; a bayonet mount; a flash suppressor or threaded barrel for one; and a grenade launcher, and, any **semiautomatic pistol** that can accept a detachable magazine and has at least 2 of these features: a magazine that attaches outside of the pistol grip; a threaded barrel that can accept a barrel extender, flash suppressor, forward handgrip, or silencer; a shroud that is attached to, or partially or completely encircles, the barrel and permits the shooter to hold the firearm with the nontrigger hand without being burned; a manufactured weight of 50 ounces (3-1/8 lbs.) or more when unloaded; and a semiautomatic version of an automatic firearm, and, any **semiautomatic shotgun** that has at least 2 of these features: a folding or telescoping stock; a pistol grip that protrudes conspicuously beneath the action; a fixed magazine capacity in excess of 5 rounds; and an ability to accept a detachable magazine, and, any **magazines**, belts, drums, feed strips and similar devices if they can accept more than 10 rounds of ammo (fixed tubular devices for .22 caliber rimfire ammo are not included).

OTHER ILLEGAL DEADLY WEAPONS

(Also called destructive devices)

A number of other deadly weapons that are not guns are also prohibited under federal law and often state law as well. Possession of these devices is a third degree felony, except for knuckles, which is a class A misdemeanor. (See Penal Code §46.05 for the letter of the law, §46.01 for definitions.)

1–Explosive, incendiary or poison gas bombs;

2–Explosive, incendiary or poison gas grenades;

3–Explosive, incendiary or poison gas rockets with more than 4 ounces of propellant (includes bazooka);

4–Explosive, incendiary or poison gas mines;

5–Mortars;

6–Molotov cocktails;

7–Armor piercing ammunition (a handgun bullet with at least a core of steel, iron, brass, bronze, beryllium, copper, depleted uranium, or one or a combination of tungsten alloys. Excluded are nontoxic shotgun shot, frangible projectiles designed for target shooting, projectiles intended for industrial purposes, oil- and gas-well perforating devices, and ammunition that is intended for sporting purposes);

8–Missiles with an explosive or incendiary charge greater than 1/4 ounce;

9–An unregistered machine gun;

10–A short-barrel firearm (rifle with a barrel length of less than 16 inches or a shotgun with a barrel length of less than 18 inches, or any weapon made from a shotgun or rifle if, as altered, it has an overall length of less than 26 inches);

11–A firearm silencer;

12–A club, which includes but isn't limited to a blackjack, nightstick, mace or a tomahawk;

13–Knuckles;

14–A chemical dispensing device ("a small chemical dispenser sold commercially for personal protection" is *not* prohibited);

15–A zip gun.

NOTE: Effective Mar. 1, 1994, Street Sweeper, Striker-12 and USAS-12 shotguns are classified as destructive devices, subject to NFA regulations (similar to machine guns), and *must now be registered even if you acquired it before that date.* The tax is waived for all such weapons owned before the effective date. If you own and do not wish to register such a weapon, or wish to transfer ownership without filing federal transfer papers, you could transfer the weapon to a properly qualified dealer, manufacturer or importer (with their permission), or to a law enforcement agency, during a pre-arranged grace period.

MACHINE GUNS

Under strictly regulated conditions, most private citizens who can own regular firearms can own certain other weapons that would otherwise be prohibited. An example is the machine gun.

Unlike normal firearm possession, the cloak of privacy afforded gun ownership is removed in the case of so-called "NFA weapons" (technically, Title II devices), including full autos, suppressors, "sawed off" long guns, and more—those originally restricted by the National Firearms Act of 1934. The list has grown since that time, through subsequent legislation. For a law-abiding private citizen to obtain an NFA weapon, five conditions must be met. These requirements are designed to keep the weapons out of criminal hands, or to prosecute criminals for possession.

1–The weapon itself must be "available,"—registered in the National Firearms Registry and Transfer Records of the Treasury Dept. This list of arms includes about 193,000 machine guns.

> The registry was closed to full autos on 5/19/86. New registrations since then can only include the other Title II devices. Any full autos made after that date may now only be transferred to proper government agents.

2–Permission to transfer the weapon must be obtained in advance, by filing "ATF Form 4 (5320.4)" available from the BATFE.

3–An FBI background check is performed to locate any criminal record that would disqualify you from possessing the weapon. This is done with a recent 2" x 2" photo of yourself, fingerprints (FBI FD-258 Fingerprint Card) submitted with the application, and signature approval of your local chief law enforcement officer, typically the sheriff or police chief. Corporations are exempt from the photo, fingerprint and CLEO signature requirements.

4–You must pay a $200 transfer tax to the Internal Revenue Service. For some NFA weapons, the transfer tax is $5.00.

5–The previous owner's name in the National Registry is changed to the new owner's name, and a new tax stamp, showing the weapon's serial number, is issued. The original or a copy of this stamp must always accompany the weapon, and permission to take the weapon across state lines must be obtained in advance.

The three ways to legally obtain a machine gun include:

1–A properly licensed dealer (a Class III FFL) can sell a registered machine gun to a qualified private buyer; 2–A legal owner can obtain permission from BATFE to transfer the firearm to a qualified recipient in the same state, and 3-You can inherit one. Any inherited NFA weapon can be transferred interstate directly to the heir, after the registration papers are approved. Special rules for executors of estates that contain NFA weapons are available from BATFE.

With prior approval you can make NFA weapons (except machine guns), such as short rifles, sawed-off shotguns, suppressors, "gadget guns" (technically, "any other weapons" such as pen, cane or wallet guns), etc. The application process is similar to the process for buying such weapons. Unregistered NFA weapons are contraband, and are subject to seizure. Having the unassembled parts needed to make an NFA weapon counts as having one.

The authorities are generally exempt from these provisions. Open trade in automatic weapons in Texas is allowed between manufacturers and dealers, and includes state and city police, prisons, the state and federal military, the National Guard, museums, educational institutions, and people with special licenses and permits.

The official trade in machine guns is specifically prohibited from becoming a source of commercial supply. Only those machine guns that were in the National Firearms Registry and Transfer Records as of May 19, 1986 may be privately held. This includes about 15,500 machine guns in Texas. The number available nationally will likely drop, since no new full-autos are being added to the registry, and the existing supply will decrease through attrition. Texans own about 30,000 NFA weapons in total.

CURIOS, RELICS AND ANTIQUES

Curios and relics are guns that have special value as antiquities, for historical purposes, or other reasons that make it unlikely they will be used currently as weapons. The Curio and Relic List is a 60-page document available from the Bureau of Alcohol, Tobacco, Firearms and Explosives. They can also tell you how to apply to obtain curio or relic status for a particular weapon.

Antique firearms, defined as firearms with matchlock, flintlock, percussion cap or similar ignition systems, manufactured in or before 1898, and replicas meeting specific guidelines, are exempt from certain federal laws. For complete details contact the Bureau of Alcohol, Tobacco, Firearms and Explosives. Remember, though, if it can fire or readily be made to fire it is a firearm under state law.

New Legislation

Congress has been considering a variety of selective and categorical firearms bans. Citizens are advised to follow developments and remain keenly aware of any firearms or accessories that were formerly legal and then declared illegal or subject to new regulations. One such example is the Striker-12 shotgun, described earlier.

WHAT'S WRONG WITH THIS PICTURE?

These weapons and destructive devices are illegal unless they are pre-registered with the federal Bureau of Alcohol, Tobacco, Firearms and Explosives.

• A rifle with a barrel less than 16 inches long
• A shotgun with a barrel less than 18 inches long
• A modified rifle or shotgun less than 26 inches overall
• Street Sweeper, Striker-12 or USAS-12 shotguns
• Machine guns or machine pistols
• Silencers of any kind
• Firearms using fixed ammunition over .50 caliber
• Armor-piercing ammunition
• Explosive, incendiary or poison gas bombs
• Explosive, incendiary or poison gas grenades
• Explosive, incendiary or poison gas mines
• Explosive, incendiary or poison gas rockets with more than 4 ounces of propellant (includes bazooka)
• Missiles with an explosive or incendiary charge greater than 1/4 ounce
• Mortars

Keep in mind that additional weapons may be added to this list in the future.

WHERE CAN YOU SHOOT? 4

Once you own a gun, it's natural to want to go out and fire it. In fact, it makes good sense. If you've decided to keep a gun, you should learn how it works and be able to handle it with confidence. Most hunting and shooting in Texas takes place on private land, although there is some limited access to national and state land for these purposes. Public ranges, both indoor and outdoor, provide an excellent and safe opportunity.

Ninety-six percent of the 267,338 square miles of Texas is in private hands. The remainder is regulated by many different authorities, and it's important to know the laws if you're contemplating hunting or shooting outdoors.

In order to understand where you can shoot outdoors in this state, you must first know where you cannot shoot. The restrictions come first when determining if shooting in an area is permissible.

Certain legal justifications may allow shooting, even if it would otherwise be illegal. An example is self-defense. A list of justifications is in Chapter 5.

GENERAL RESTRICTIONS

These are restrictions that apply whether you are on private land or land owned by the federal, state or local government. Special exceptions may apply in justified cases, such as self defense.

Illegal Trajectory

It's illegal to shoot in such a manner that bullets will travel anywhere they may create a hazard to life or property. In National Forests, you may not shoot from or across a body of water adjacent to a road.

Aside from being a violation of several laws, there is a general rule of gun safety here: Be sure of your backstop. Take this a step further: Be sure of your line of fire. Never fire if you are unaware of (or not in full control of) the complete possible trajectory of the bullet, and are sure that the shot poses no threat to life or property.

In 2005, Parks and Wildlife Code §62.0121 was added to ban knowingly shooting across property lines unless you own the property on both sides of the line, or have specific written permission to do so, as described in the statute.

Discharge in City Limits or in Public

It is a class A misdemeanor (Penal Code §46.12) to recklessly fire a gun in a municipality with a population of 100,000 or more. This is sometimes called the accidental discharge law. It is illegal to shoot a gun on or across a public road (class C misdemeanor) or in a public place other than a road or shooting range (class B misdemeanor), under Penal Code §42.01, with an exception for defense from a wild-animal attack. Under Local Government Code §229.003 and other laws, certain cities can exercise some controls over shooting within their boundaries.

From Vehicles or Boats

It is illegal to shoot from a vehicle on or across a public road or from a boat on public water while hunting. The only exception is that migratory waterfowl (ducks, geese, brant and coot) may be hunted from a boat or any floating craft (except a sink box) that is beached, anchored or tied (see Parks & Wildlife Code §62.003). Chapter 6 discusses the laws and regulations governing hunting in Texas in more detail.

It's also illegal to knowingly shoot upon, from, across or into a public road or railway while hunting, including roads in the National Forests. Authorities frown on "road shooting" of any kind, and it's extremely unsafe. Shooting from vehicles or on public roads carries a heavy penalty and is just not a good idea.

Posted Areas

Under certain circumstances signs can be posted that restrict firearms use, possession or access to land or premises.

- *Private Land* may be posted by authority of the landowner or lessee. (See Penal Code §30.05; special signs related to concealed carry are described in Penal Code §30.05 and §30.06, the CHL law found in Government Code chapter 411, and the Alcoholic Beverage Code §11.041 and §61.11.)

- *State Land* controlled by the Texas Parks and Wildlife Dept. may be posted to restrict hunting and/or shooting.

- *National Forests* may have areas posted by the authorities for a number of reasons.

Most private, local, tribal, state and federal authorities may legally post an area under their control. The penalty for a violation varies widely, depending upon who posted what area. The conditions for posting private property open to the public, such as a store, or a place with a liquor license, are described in Chapter 2.

Common Nuisance

Under Civil Practice & Remedies Code §125.0015, maintaining a public place that is not a sanctioned shooting range, where people habitually go shooting in violation of the Penal Code, is a common nuisance. A person who maintains a multiunit residential property where people habitually carry a weapon in violation of Penal Code §46.02 is maintaining a common nuisance. Tolerating or failing to take reasonable steps to stop such activity is evidence of maintaining a common nuisance. Various legal remedies exist to abate such nuisance.

THE LAND OF TEXAS

The land of Texas is divided up several different ways. The General Land Office divides the state into 34 Land Districts, and there are 254 counties in Texas.

Texas General Land Office

The Texas General Land Office has preserved and maintained records about Texas lands since 1836. Their collection, dating from the middle 1700s, includes land grants issued by the Spanish Crown, the Mexican Government and the Republic and State of Texas, and documents land distribution through original surveys, titles, registers, patents, reports, clerk returns, contracts, legislative acts, deeds of acquittance and other records. The GLO has no authority to regulate firearms, but they can tell you about the background for any ground in Texas.

Cities, Towns and Villages

In general, a municipality can't adopt regulations concerning private ownership, keeping, transportation, transfer, licensing, or registration of firearms, ammunition, or firearm supplies, spelled out in Local Government Code §215.001.

Cities cannot regulate shooting on lands annexed after Sep. 1, 1981, or on lands where they have extraterritorial jurisdiction, if shots can reasonably be expected to remain within a tract: They cannot regulate firing a shotgun, air rifle or pistol, BB gun or bow and arrow on a 10-acre or larger tract more than 1,000 feet from a residence or occupied building on another property; and they cannot regulate centerfire or rimfire rifles or pistols of any caliber on at least 50 acres, more than 300 feet from a residence or occupied building on another property. See Agriculture Code §251.005 and Local Government Code §43.002 and §229.002. Complex new formulas for shooting on specified tracts in certain cities were added in 2009 under LGC §229.003.

However, a municipality may require or regulate:

- Citizens or public employees to be armed for personal or national defense, law enforcement, or other lawful purpose;

- Certain discharges of firearms within city or town limits;
- The use of property or the locations of businesses under the city's fire code, zoning ordinances, or land use regulations;
- The use of firearms in the event of an insurrection, riot, or natural disaster where the city finds such measures necessary to protect public health and safety;
- The storage or transportation of explosives to protect public safety (up to 25 lbs. of black powder for each private resident and up to 50 lbs. of black powder for each retail dealer are not subject to regulation);
- Carrying of firearms at public parks or public governmental meetings, political rallies, parades or official political meetings, or at non-firearms related school, college or professional athletic event. Exempt from this are any areas designated for hunting, fishing or firearms sporting event and the weapon is the type commonly used in that activity.

Under an amendment to Local Government Code §215.001 provided by the Right to Carry law, municipalities do not have authority to regulate the carrying of concealed handguns by license holders at the locations mentioned in the paragraph above (public parks, etc.).

Special Cases
- *Air Guns*—These were first defined and became specifically regulated in **2013** under Local Government Code §229.001 and §235 et seq. Individual cities and counties can have their own rules about air guns (which are not firearms under state law). You may be able to set up an air gun range indoors or outdoors within city boundaries if proper safety measures are taken. Check with local authorities for exact details at your location. Air guns are prohibited for hunting game.
- *Control of Nuisance Wildlife*—A required permit is available for this purpose from the Texas Parks & Wildlife Dept. (in Parks and Wildlife Code §43.154 through §43.157) or from the United States Fish and Wildlife Service. Problems with nuisance wildlife can often be handled best by contacting an exterminator who has the proper permits.
- *Special Permits*—The chief of police of a municipality may issue a special permit for firing guns within city limits

(typically related to celebrations, parades, etc.).

* *Legally Justified Cases*—The law allows shooting within city limits under certain narrow circumstances called *justification*. An example is self-defense. For details, see Chapter 5. In 2001, a special exception was made in the disorderly conduct law for defense against wild-animal attacks

County Land

The state of Texas is divided into 254 counties. County land may contain authorized shooting ranges, and information about these can be best obtained from the county sheriff's department where you want to shoot. You may notice that each county sheriff has a "style" to how they run their counties.

To promote public safety, the commissioners court of a county may regulate or prohibit the shooting (but no other aspects) of firearms on lots that are ten acres or smaller, in certain unincorporated areas of a county (see Local Government Code §240.021). Check with your county for any special air-gun rules.

In counties with a population of 2,000,000 or more, you must have written consent of the landowner (or the landowner's legal representative) in order to hunt or target shoot (see Parks and Wildlife Code §62.012). You must have the consent with you and to be valid it must contain your name, identify the land involved, be signed by the owner or the owner's representative, and have the address and phone number of the person signing.

Indian Country

There are three Indian reservations in Texas, belonging to the Alabama-Coushatta, the Tigua (Ysleta del Sur Pueblo) and the Kickapoo Traditional Tribe of Texas. The tribes do not allow public hunting or shooting on tribal lands at this time.

Generally, those who live on Indian lands in Texas are under the same regulations that apply to other residents of the state. However, overlapping federal, state, tribal and local authority creates confusion when laws are violated in Indian country. Enforcement of laws on Indian reservations can cause a fundamental conflict over jurisdiction. Actual penalties for violations may be the subject of dispute.

National Forests

Approximately 673,000 acres in Texas are made up of National Forests and National Grasslands operated by the Forest Service of the U.S. Dept. of Agriculture. You may carry firearms at anytime and anywhere in the National Forests, as long as you and your gun are in compliance with the law. Call the local National Forest office (listed in Appendix C) for details before venturing out. Don't confuse the National Forests with the National Parks, where for recent decades you could not even carry a loaded gun (see that listing below).

Hunting is allowed in the National Forests, but requires proper licenses. Contact the Texas Parks and Wildlife Dept. for details, and see Chapter 6 on Hunting Regulations. You cannot shoot inside a designated recreation area, at a crossroads, near a trail or in a posted area. Special conditions may apply in Wildlife Management Areas. It's best to call first if you're not sure about a particular location.

Target shooters are required to use removable targets in designated areas only. Clay pigeons, bottles, trash and other targets that leave debris are prohibited. Your choice of a target site should be against an embankment that will prevent bullets from causing a hazard. Your location should be *remote* from populated sites.

The laws controlling the National Forests are in a book called *Code of Federal Regulations, Title 36*, available online and at larger libraries. These federal rules prohibit shooting:

• Within 150 yards of a residence, building, campsite, developed recreation site or occupied area;

• Across or on a Forest Development road;

• Across or on a body of water adjacent to a Forest Development road;

• In any way that puts people at risk of injury or puts property at risk of damage;

• Which kills or injures any timber, tree or forest product;

• Which makes unreasonable noise;

• Which damages any natural feature or property of the U.S.

Violation of these restrictions carries a possible $500 fine and a maximum prison sentence of 6 months under federal law.

The Forest Supervisor or other proper authority may issue special restrictions on firearm possession or use, or close a section to access if it seems necessary to protect public safety, or for other good reason.

It's always recommended to check with a representative of the Forest Service about any piece of National Forest land you're planning on using. National Forests and their offices within the state of Texas are listed in Appendix C.

National Park Service Land

The National Park Service of the U.S. Dept. of the Interior manages six national sites in Texas including National Parks, National Monuments, National Historic Sites, National Seashore and National Recreation Areas.

Limited hunting privileges exist in National Recreation Areas by special agreement of the Dept. of the Interior and the Texas Parks and Wildlife Dept. The unconstitutional federal ban on mere firearm possession in our National Parks Services Lands, implemented by federal bureaucrats without an act of Congress, was lifted on Feb. 22, 2010, and now, state rules for carry apply on these federal lands, a nice return to federalism. A list of Texas' National Park Service sites is in Appendix C.

Private Land

Most hunting and shooting in Texas occurs on the 96% of the state that is in private hands. Land owners may grant permission for others to shoot on their land. To shoot on someone else's private land, you must first obtain permission from the owner. This can be an informal arrangement between you and the landowner, or you may pay for entry to the property as part of a leasing arrangement.

In counties with more than 2,000,000 people, you need *written* consent to shoot on private land (see *County Land*). Under Parks and Wildlife Code §62.0121, you need either special written permission to shoot across a person's property line, or own the land on both sides of the line you're shooting across.

If you have a simple agreement with a landowner and are granted permission, it's important to remember that this is not "for life." Just because you were allowed to hunt or shoot one time, doesn't mean you're automatically allowed the next time. You would do well to ask each time, it's just common courtesy and good neighborly relations. Plus, if you enter someone else's property for shooting or any other purpose, without permission, you can be charged with trespassing.

Owners of private land may allow access to the public for hunting, fishing, wildlife watching, photography, and other outdoor activities, through a lease arrangement. A list of the many Texas landowners who participate in this program can be found in a brochure called the *Hunter's Clearinghouse Directory*. Updated annually, it's published by the Texas Parks & Wildlife Dept. It's divided into seven areas or geographic regions–the Panhandle, Rolling Plains, West, Central, East, Gulf Coast and South–and then is arranged alphabetically by county within those regions. All arrangements relating to private land leased to the public should be made with the landowner, *not* the Parks & Wildlife Dept.

The private lands that are leased to the Texas Parks and Wildlife Dept. become part of Texas' Public Hunting Lands, totaling about 1,400,000 acres, including land owned by the Parks & Wildlife Dept. and land leased to them by the U.S. Forest Service, the Army Corps of Engineers, Texas Utilities, the Sabine River Authority, timber companies and private citizens.

For more information on leasing your land for public hunting, contact Texas Parks and Wildlife, listed in Appendix C.

River Authorities

At least 14 agencies govern Texas waterways: we have 12 River Authorities, the International Boundary and Water Commission, and the U.S. Army Corps of Engineers. Five River Authorities allow at least some kind of recreation on the land and waters under their jurisdiction:

The Brazos River Authority

The waters under the authority of the BRA are Lake Granbury, Lake Limestone and Possum Kingdom Lake. There are designated target ranges where firearms are permitted. Hunting of waterfowl is permitted in season, and special hunting privileges may be authorized by the Board of Directors of the Authority.

The Lavaca-Navidad River Authority

The possession or use of firearms on L-NRA property is prohibited, because "all project lands and water are a wildlife preserve." This includes BB or pellet guns, rifles, sidearms, and shotguns. An exception to this, however, is in some limited areas designated by the Authority for hunting small game and water fowl, and then only by written permission issued by the Authority.

The Lower Colorado River Authority

Possession of firearms, hunting or shooting on or across the land of the Lower Colorado River Authority is prohibited, unless the LCRA decides to lease land for a nonprofit target rifle range. Violation is a PWC class C misdemeanor (PWC §62.081) with an exception made for possession or justified use by a valid CHL licensee (see PWC §62.082). Nonprofit public service groups like the boy scouts or girl scouts may bring in a qualified instructor that has been registered with and approved by the LCRA on designated ranges. This is for target shooting only. No hunting is allowed. A map showing designated ranges and a list of approved and registered instructors is maintained at the LCRA's Austin office, listed in Appendix C.

The Sabine River Authority

The waters of the SRA are actually controlled by the Texas Parks & Wildlife Dept. when it comes to hunting and shooting. Areas may be posted by the SRA in places close to facilities or on lands or waters where the SRA has deemed it hazardous to allow hunting or shooting.

The Trinity River Authority

Other than at Lake Livingston, where hunting is allowed, the discharge of a firearm on TRA land is prohibited. Law enforcement officials in the course of their duties are the only exception.

The Nine-County Navigable-River Rule

Special rules passed in 2005 prohibit discharging firearms from, in or on the bed or bank of a navigable river or stream in Dimmit, Edwards, Frio, Kenedy, Llano, Maverick, Real, Uvalde or Zavala counties, if any portion of the ammunition could contact the bed or bank. An exception is made for the proper authorities, or a shotgun that releases only shot when fired.

Shooting Ranges

Officially-approved and commercially operating shooting ranges may be the best place to learn and practice the shooting sports. Ranges may be legally set up within city limits as long as they conform to local requirements and ordinances. State regulations for operating outdoor shooting ranges are found beginning at HSC §756.041. LGC §250.001 protects ranges from lawsuits and government, civil or criminal charges due to noise. This was expanded in 2001 to protect private clubs or associations. Protections and nuisance-lawsuit limits were enhanced in 2011 in a series of laws, including LGC §229.001, §236.001, .002, .003, §250.001; and CPRC §128.001, §128.051, .052, and .053.

The list of fine shooting ranges in Texas is a long list, and there's no way to fairly represent a portion of them in *The Texas Gun Owner's Guide*. Each county sheriff's office is usually familiar with the ranges in their county, and the yellow pages include lists of indoor and outdoor ranges. The Texas State Rifle Association, listed in Appendix C, can help you locate ranges in your area, and it organizes shooting events and competitions statewide. With passage of the concealed-handgun law, DPS had issued ID numbers to ranges that met their standards and were authorized to conduct handgun tests for CHL applicants. Copies of those lists, which DPS made public, still exist.

Anyone who keeps a gun for personal safety or any other reason would be wise to visit a range regularly and practice. A range finder is linked from our website, gunlaws.com, where you can just enter a zip code and get details on local shooting facilities.

State and Federal Military Land

Land reserved for military use, whether under the jurisdiction of the National Guard or a branch of the federal armed forces such as the Army or the Air Force, is controlled by a military commander. What a commander says, goes. As a practical matter, possession or use of firearms on a military base is subject to control by the commanding officer, though no statute specifically prohibits arms.

You can't do much of anything on military land without prior approval. Anyone on military land is subject to a search. For details concerning a specific military installation, contact the base provost Marshall or the base commander's office.

Military ranges are frequently made available to the public or to organized groups on a controlled basis. Federal law actually says that a range built with any federal funds may be used by the military "and by persons capable of bearing arms." The rules for use are set by whoever controls the range, and the military has first call on use of the range (10 USC §4309).

Under the federal Civilian Marksmanship Program the Army cooperates with civilians to provide practice and instruction in firearms for citizens and for youths in the Boy Scouts, 4-H and similar clubs. For details see the entry in Chapter 7. This program is part of the historical record of cooperation between the government and the citizens in keeping the population trained in the use of small arms.

Carrying firearms while traveling on a public road that passes through military land is subject to standard state rules.

Certain State Lands

The Texas Parks and Wildlife Dept. can restrict shooting on land under its jurisdiction. By the general authority granted to the Dept. under the Parks & Wildlife Code §13.101 and §13.102, it can make regulations governing the health, safety, and protection of people and property in:

• State parks;

• State property adjacent to state parks and within 200 yards of their boundaries (see Parks & Wildlife Code §13.201);

• Historic sites;

• Scientific areas;

• Forts under its control;

• Public water within the above areas.

For example, discharging a firearm in, on, along, or across Lake Lavon in Collin County is a misdemeanor and is punishable by a fine of not less than $10 and not more than $200 plus costs, or confinement in the county jail for not more than one year, or both. This doesn't apply if you're hunting with a shotgun during a lawful hunting season (Parks & Wildlife Code §143.023).

At the very least, you can be ejected from an area. In addition, a court order can be issued to prevent you from returning for any period the court determines (Parks & Wildlife Code §13.108).

As you can see, shooting outdoors in this day and age is not just a matter of leaning off your back porch (well, not for most of us). You may ask, "How am I supposed to know all that?" The answer is, it's always best to call ahead and be sure before going hunting or setting up target practice on any land not your own. Even on your own land, depending on where your property is located, there may be subtle or total restrictions (especially true in or near cities). Call your local authorities to be sure, and recognize that nothing in life is completely free from risk.

Transporting Firearms for Shooting

Texas law protects your right to have a handgun on or near yourself while you are directly enroute to or from, or engaged in hunting or a sporting activity where it can be lawfully used (see Penal Code §46.15). Under the 2007 Motorist Protection Act, any legal handgun possession in a vehicle is now protected as long as the firearm is concealed from plain view. Open or concealed possession of rifles and shotguns is also protected, as it always has been.

Technically, while you are directly on the way to a range, a visible handgun, at your side or even holstered, is as legal as it is at the range. Because it's difficult to demonstrate that legality convincingly if you're stopped, it may be best to keep sidearms concealed, and if you have a concealed-handgun license, you're required to maintain concealment. Ironically, a non-CHL going directly to a range or hunting actually has a small latitude here that CHLs may not; however, to avoid tense encounters with law enforcement at the side of a road, concealed carry now seems to be the preferred method of possession. See Chapters 1 and 2 for more detail on "traveling" and the laws that affect CHL holders and the general public.

Texas State Rifle Association License Plates

While you're traveling to go shooting, or for any other reason, you can sport Texas State Rifle Association license plates. It's a good way to show the world where you stand. Check with the Dept. of Transportation to get yours. Half of the fees for the specialty plates go to the Tubb Scholarship fund at Texas A&M University, and half go to support 4H shooting sports.

WHAT'S WRONG WITH THIS PICTURE?

WHAT'S WRONG WITH THIS PICTURE?

1–Shooting within city limits is normally prohibited.

2–It's illegal to deface signs.

3–Trespassing is illegal.

4–You can't use targets that leave debris.

5–Shooting at wildlife requires a permit or license.

6–The target has no backstop. The shooter is not controlling the entire trajectory of the bullet.

7–The shooter isn't wearing eye or ear protection.

8–The saguaro cactus grows in Arizona.

THERE'S NOTHING WRONG WITH THIS PICTURE!

THERE'S NOTHING WRONG
WITH THIS PICTURE!

Practicing marksmanship and the shooting sports outdoors is a natural and wholesome pursuit as long as you comply with the laws.

- The shooters are at a remote location, on land that isn't restricted;
- The target leaves no debris;
- The target has a backstop that prevents bullets from causing a potential hazard;
- No wildlife or protected plants are in the line of fire;
- The shooters are not firing across any property lines;
- The shooters are using eye and ear protection.

DEADLY FORCE and SELF DEFENSE 5

"I got my questionnaire baby,
You know I'm headed off for war,
Well now I'm gonna kill somebody
Don't have to break no kind of law."

- from a traditional blues song

There are times when you may shoot and kill another person and be guilty of no crime under Texas law. The law calls this *justification*, and says justification is a complete defense against any criminal charges (see Penal Code Chapter 9 for the letter of the law). The specific circumstances of a shooting determine whether the shooting is justified, and if not, which crime has been committed.

Whenever a shooting occurs, a crime has been committed. Either the shooting is legal as a defense against a crime or attempted crime, or else the shooting is not justified, in which case the shooting itself is the crime.

Your civil liability (getting sued) after a shooting can be a greater risk than criminal charges. You can be charged both ways, and your legal protections are lower in civil cases than in criminal ones. With narrow limits, overcoming criminal charges does not protect you from a civil lawsuit—you can be tried twice.

Justification in killing someone does not provide criminal or civil protection for recklessly killing an innocent third person in the process. A stray shot you make can be as dangerous to you legally as committing a homicide. Using lethal force is so risky legally it is yet another reason to avoid it if at all possible—for your own safety.

121

USE OF DEADLY PHYSICAL FORCE

A reasonable person hopes it will never be necessary to raise a weapon in self defense. It's smart to always avoid such confrontations. In the unlikely event that you must resort to force to defend yourself, **you are generally required to use as little force as necessary to control a situation. Deadly force can only be used in the most narrowly defined circumstances, and it is highly unlikely that you will ever encounter such circumstances in your life.** You have probably never been near such an event in your life so far. Your own life is permanently changed if you ever kill a person, intentionally or otherwise.

People often wonder, "When can you shoot to kill," and not be guilty of a crime? When the authorities or a jury, *after the fact*, determine that your actions were justifiable. *You never know beforehand.* As a strategic matter, the Dept. of Public Safety teaches you to "shoot to stop" or "shoot to control or neutralize the threat," *never* shoot to kill. In self-defense cases, your goal— your intention and mental state—is not to kill, but to protect.

No matter how well you know the law, or how justified you may feel you are in a shooting incident, everyone's perceptions are different, and your fate will probably be determined much later, in a court of law. Establishing all the facts precisely is basically an impossible task and adds to your legal risks.

What were the exact circumstances during the moments of greatest stress, as best you remember them? Were there witnesses, who are they, what will they remember and what will they say to the authorities—each time they're asked—and in a courtroom? What was your relationship to the deceased person? How did you feel at the moment you fired? Did you have any options besides pulling the trigger? Can you look at it differently after the fact? Has there been even one case recently affecting how the law is now interpreted? Was a new law put into place yesterday? How good is your lawyer? How tough is the prosecutor? How convincing are you? Are the police on your side? Does the judge like your face? What will the jury think?

Be smart and never shoot at anyone if there is any way at all to avoid it. Avoiding the use of deadly force is usually a much safer course of action, at least from a legal point of view. You could be on much safer ground if you use a gun to protect yourself *without* actually firing a shot. Even though it's highly unlikely you'll ever need to draw a gun in self defense, the number of crimes prevented by the presence of a citizen's gun— *that isn't fired*—are estimated to be in the millions. And yet, just pulling a gun can subject you to serious penalties. Think of it in reverse—if someone pulled a gun on you, would you want to press charges because they put your life in danger? You must be careful about opening yourself up to such charges.

Still, the law recognizes your right to protect yourself, your loved ones and other people from certain severe criminal acts. In the most extreme incident you may decide it is immediately necessary to use lethal force to survive and deal with the repercussions later. Shooting at another human being is a last resort, reserved for only if and when innocent life truly depends on it. If it doesn't, don't shoot. If it does, don't miss.

You are urged to read the actual language of the law about this critical subject, and even then, to avoid using deadly force if at all possible. Get the annotated criminal statutes in a library and read some case law to get a deeper understanding of the ramifications of using deadly force—and dealing with the legal system after the fact.

***The Texas Gun Owner's Guide* is intended to help you on a long journey to competence. Do not rely solely on the information in this book or on any other single source, and recognize that by deciding to prepare to use deadly physical force if it ever becomes necessary you are accepting substantial degrees of risk.**

Even with a good understanding of the rules, there may be more to it than meets the eye. As an example, shooting a criminal who is fleeing a crime is very different than shooting a criminal who's committing a crime. You may be justified in shooting in a circumstance, and you might miss and only wound, but if you ever shoot to intentionally wound you'll have an uphill battle in court. The law is strict, complex and not something to take chances with in the heat of the moment if you don't have to.

It's natural to want to know, beforehand, just when it's OK to shoot and be able to claim self defense later. Unfortunately, you will never know for sure until *after* a situation arises. You make your moves whatever they are, and the authorities or a jury decides. The law doesn't physically control what you can or can't do—it gives the authorities guidelines on how to evaluate what you did after it occurs. **There are extreme legal risks when you choose to use force of any kind.**

Because cases of murder outnumber cases of justifiable homicide, the authorities have a distinct tendency to think of the person holding a smoking gun as the perpetrator, later as the suspect, and finally as the defendant, while the person who gets shot, or was merely threatened with a gun, is the victim and in need of protection. If you ever come close to pulling the trigger, remember there is a likelihood you will face charges when it's all over. The effects of the shot last long after the ringing in your ears stops.

"The quotations below are plain, conversational expressions of the gist of the law." These are followed by a more precise description of the law. Finally, each subject is cross-referenced to the actual section ("§") of the law. *Be sure to review the Precautionary Note at the end of this section.*

Public Duty

"The use of deadly force is justified if it is required by law."

This includes circumstances such as combat during a war, executions, actions of peace officers, required assistance to a public servant, and other situations required by statute. You must reasonably believe your actions are justified by law in such circumstances. This instance of legal justification has little direct effect on the average citizen. See Penal Code §9.21 for the letter of the law.

Necessity

"This justification, called *the defense 'of necessity,'* applies to an immediate need to act to prevent harm, regardless of laws that might otherwise prohibit your actions."

When you believe that action is immediately necessary to avoid imminent harm, and the harm you seek to avoid is urgent and clearly greater than the harm your actions would cause (and that is otherwise usually prohibited by law, such as carrying a handgun), and no specific exclusion for your actions have been established by law, your actions may be justified, if the authorities or a jury agree, after the fact, that you were justified.

The "defense of necessity" is frequently what allows a proper case of self defense to exclude charges of illegal possession of a handgun. See Penal Code §9.22 for the letter of the law.

Deadly Force in Self Defense
"Only when someone is about to kill or maim you unlawfully, can you shoot at them."

Except for the special cases below, you are justified in using deadly force against another person only if you reasonably believe it is immediately necessary to protect yourself against the other person's use or attempted use of unlawful deadly force, if the authorities or a jury agree, after the fact, that you were justified.

You cannot use deadly force:

• In response to insults or "verbal provocation" alone;

• To resist arrest or search by a peace officer (or someone acting for the officer), even if it's an unlawful arrest or search, unless the officer (or the person acting for the officer) is using undue force, you haven't offered any resistance up to that point, and only when and only to the degree you reasonably believe it's immediately necessary to use force to protect yourself from the undue force being used or threatened against you;

• If you've agreed to the force of another person against you— the "let's step outside and settle this" scenario, sometimes referred to as *dueling* (or in old West terms, a *showdown*);

• If you've provoked the force of another person against you. However, if you then back down and the other person refuses to back down, you may be justified;

• If you seek to discuss your differences with someone and have a prohibited weapon (under Penal Code §46.05) with you, or a handgun in violation of the carrying restrictions (Penal Code §46.02).

See Penal Code §9.31 and §9.32 for the letter of the law.

The Castle Doctrine and Standing Your Ground

"Your legal protections in self defense are stronger under certain circumstances in your home, vehicle or place of business."

Your belief in your need to immediately act in self defense is presumed to be reasonable, and hence legal, if you knew or had reason to believe that the person you acted against:

1–unlawfully and forcefully entered or unlawfully and forcefully attempted to enter your home, vehicle, or place of business or employment;

2–unlawfully and forcefully removed or unlawfully and forcefully attempted to remove you from your home, vehicle or place of business or employment;

3–was committing or attempting to commit murder, aggravated kidnapping, aggravated sexual assault, aggravated robbery, sexual assault or robbery.

This holds true as long as you did not provoke the person you acted against, and only if you are not engaged in any criminal activity yourself except for a Class C misdemeanor law or traffic ordinance. See Penal Code §9.31 and §9.32.

If these conditions are met and you have a right to be where you are when you act in self defense you are not required to retreat, and a court may not consider whether you failed to retreat. If you are found to be justified under the law you are immune from civil liability for personal injury or death that results from your actions. See Civil Practice and Remedies Code §83.001.

Defense of a Third Person

"You can protect someone else the same as you can protect yourself."

You are justified in threatening or using deadly force to protect a third person under similar circumstances as you would to protect yourself: if you reasonably believe your actions are immediately necessary to protect the third person against the use of unlawful deadly force, if the authorities or a jury agree, after the fact, that you were justified. See Penal Code §9.33 for the letter of the law.

Crime Prevention and No Duty to Retreat

"Deadly force is justified to prevent certain crimes."

Texas law says you are justified in using deadly physical force when and to the degree you reasonably believe it is immediately necessary to prevent someone's use or attempted use of force on you, and a reasonable person in your situation wouldn't retreat, and to prevent someone from committing:

1–Aggravated kidnapping,

2–Murder,

3–Sexual assault,

4–Aggravated sexual assault,

5–Robbery, or

6–Aggravated robbery,

if the authorities or a jury agree, after the fact, that you were justified. See Penal Code §9.32 for the letter of the law.

Law Enforcement

"Deadly force is justified to control certain criminal activities related to arrest and escape."

If you are a peace officer or acting in an officer's presence and at the officer's direction, you may use or threaten deadly force to assist in making an arrest or search, or to prevent an escape after arrest, if the authorities or a jury agree, after the fact, that you were justified. See Penal Code §9.51 thru §9.53 for the letter of the law. There are certain things you must be sure of in this tense situation, including:

• Whether the arrest or search is lawful;

• If there's a warrant, that the warrant is valid;

• That the person directing you is indeed a peace officer, and has the legal authority to empower your actions.

If you believe you're being directed by a peace officer, who later turns out not to be one, you may have a difficult defense. The same is true if it turns out after the fact that the officer acted improperly. In some cases, a person believing they were duly authorized was enough, in other cases that belief was not valid as a defense against prosecution.

Protection of Life or Health

"You are justified in using deadly force against a person when and only to the degree you reasonably believe it is immediately necessary to protect that person's life in an emergency, if the authorities or a jury agree, after the fact, that you were justified."

See Penal Code §9.34 for the letter of the law.

Protecting Property

<See the Precautionary Note at the end of this section>

"Deadly force is justified to prevent another person from committing certain property crimes or to keep them from fleeing after committing these crimes."

Texas law says that you can use deadly force to protect land or tangible movable property if you reasonably believe it is immediately necessary to stop another person from committing:

• Arson;
• Burglary;
• Robbery;
• Aggravated robbery;
• Theft during the nighttime; and
• Criminal mischief during the nighttime;

if the authorities or a jury agree, after the fact, that you were justified.

The law adds that you can shoot to prevent a person from fleeing after committing burglary, robbery, aggravated robbery or theft during the nighttime, and from escaping with the property, if you reasonably believe you can't protect or recover the property any other way. It also says you are justified if using less than deadly force would expose you or another to a substantial risk of death or serious bodily injury. (See Penal Code §9.42)

Included is protecting property for a third person if the other person would do the same (under the law) themselves, and you have been asked by the third person to protect the property or have a legal duty to do so. You may also protect a third person's property if the third person is your spouse, parent, child, lives with you or is in your care. (See Penal Code §9.43)

PRECAUTIONARY NOTE

"Sometimes guilty people go free, sometimes innocent people do not."

Many factors make reliance on justification laws quite risky. Yes, the laws support the use of physical or deadly physical force in life-threatening emergencies, and yes, your right to self defense is an invaluable and fundamental right. People are indeed often acquitted under justification, but remember that justice is not always served, and some people may wonder forever if you were really guilty and walked. Remember that you are only justified if the authorities or a jury agree, *after the fact,* that you were justified. You get to sweat it out the whole time the case is pursued, which can take years.

Some experts feel that use of deadly force in a property crime, which doesn't involve a threat to life or limb, could be difficult or impossible to defend in court (and in some states has no legal protection as it does here). As you might imagine, shooting an escaping thief in the back (per §9.42) does create a risky legal defense (and a media circus).

Many of the precedent-setting cases are old and may not reflect the current state of jurisprudence. Some U.S. Supreme Court decisions suggest that the use of deadly force in property-only crimes, or to stop a criminal who is fleeing once the crime has ended, may not be justifiable. Your civil liability is only removed if you are cleared of any possible criminal charges (you run the risk of a lawsuit by the perpetrator's kin). Also note that "theft or criminal mischief in the nighttime" is not defined by statute.

These and other factors make reliance on justification quite risky and hard to recommend. Yes, it is the law, and Texans are perhaps rightly proud that their statutes are very tough on criminals and help serve as a deterrent to crime. Remember too that a prosecutor's role is to work hard to convict, regardless of your guilt or innocence, and conviction rates can approach 100%.

You might hope that's because they only pursue bad apples. Many convictions though come from plea bargains, where regardless of guilt or innocence, you plead to a lesser charge to avoid the huge cost, humiliation, inconveniences—and risk—of a lengthy trial. Plea bargains help manage the huge case loads and have been called everything from wise to pragmatic, from expedient to extortion. The pursuit of high conviction rates may lead to what some would consider dirty lawyer tricks, with your future on the line. There's an old saying that has some merit here, "Better a criminal goes free than a lien on your home." It is admittedly a very tough and risky choice.

RELATED LAWS

Aggravated Assault

"You can't shoot or threaten to shoot someone without a legal reason."

Intentionally, knowingly or recklessly shooting a person (or causing serious bodily injury in any other way, for that matter), without legal justification, is aggravated assault, a second degree felony. Threatening to shoot someone or just exhibiting a weapon during an assault is considered aggravated assault. See Penal Code §22.02 and §22.021 for the letter of the law.

Disorderly Conduct

"You must act seriously with guns."

It's illegal to discharge a firearm in a public place other than a sport shooting range, to display a gun in a public place with the purpose of creating alarm, or to shoot a gun on or across a public road. An exception exists for defense against a wild-animal attack. See Penal Code §42.01 for the letter of the law.

Deadly Conduct

"It's illegal to endanger the life of another person through the use of firearms."

You must not discharge or even point a firearm near people, in the direction of a house, building or vehicle where people might be inside, whether or not you believe the firearm is loaded. This can range from a class A misdemeanor to a third degree felony. See Penal Code §22.05 for the letter of the law.

Reporting Gunshot Wounds

"It's a crime to treat a gunshot wound and not report it."

A physician, administrator, superintendent, or other person in charge of a medical facility who is called on to treat a gunshot wound, regardless of the activity that may have caused it, must immediately notify the authorities and report the circumstances. Failure to make a report is a misdemeanor and carries a six month jail sentence or a fine of up to $100. See Health and Safety Code §161.041 and §161.043 for the letter of the law.

Responsibility
"Everyone is not equally criminally responsible for their acts."

A person under the age of 15 when an offense occurs can't be charged criminally for a shooting. No one can be given the death penalty for a crime committed when under the age of 17. (See Penal Code §8.07 for the letter of the law.) Certain mental states may have an affect on your legal responsibility for your actions.

Booby Traps
It's illegal to rig a gun as a booby trap (see Penal Code §9.44).

Firing a Warning Shot
"There is no justification for firing a warning shot."

There is no statute that allows for warning shots. Any such shot in a city could result in a charge of misdemeanor disorderly conduct, and other charges could be brought. Because warning shots are dangerous to bystanders (even a mile away when the round comes down) they are ill advised, and causing an injury could be a felony.

The justification to shoot in self defense or in resisting certain crimes does not in any way allow using a firearm as an audible warning device, and it can attract more police attention to you (since the bad guys will have long since split) than you ever wanted. The firearm used may be subject to confiscation, and you really don't want to have to explain your innocence to uniformed officers at your door.

If the situation isn't immediately life or death, don't fire. If you really are locked in mortal combat, don't waste a potentially life-saving shot making scary noises. Firing a warning may serve as evidence that you didn't believe the situation presented an immediately deadly threat, and that you really did fire without justification. Warning shots are an instrument of Hollywood, that have little place in the real world.

Bullet-Proof Vests

There is no law against owning or wearing bullet-proof vests (or as the trade refers to them, bullet-resistant vests, ballistic vests or body armor). A felon cannot possess metal or body armor, see Penal Code §46.041.

Keeping Control of Your Firearms
"You could be liable for damage others cause with your guns."

You could face civil lawsuits for negligently letting a minor or other incompetent person get possession of a firearm you own, if it is used to cause injury or damage. This is a volatile area of law controlled more by lawyerly zeal and precedent than by statute. Some legal arguments attempt to spread blame to people other than those who commit criminal acts. It points to the wisdom in controlling access to your firearms at all times.

Disarming a Peace Officer
"It's generally illegal to take or try to take an officer's weapon."

It is a state jail felony to intentionally or knowingly, and with force, try to take a weapon from a peace officer, parole officer, or community supervision and corrections department officer. It is a third degree felony to take such a weapon (including a stun gun). However, there is a defense to prosecution if the officer was using greater force than allowed by law. See Penal Code §38.14 for the letter of the law.

Criminal Mischief
"It's illegal to use a gun to cause property damage."

It is a state jail felony to damage or destroy a home with a firearm or explosive weapon. Many other penalties apply depending on the amount and nature of the damage. See Penal Code §28.03 for details.

Appointing and Arming Deputies

"Appointed deputies may only be armed as allowed by law."

The Commissioners Court of a county may authorize the sheriff to appoint reserve deputy sheriffs. The sheriff may authorize all reserve deputies to carry firearms when on official duty, and in the case of a reserve deputy who is already a peace officer as defined by law, may authorize carry when not on duty. Similar conditions apply to reserve deputy constables and reserve police officers, as defined in Local Government Code §85.004.

Ballistics Testing and Recordkeeping

"DPS must conduct ballistics tests of bullets and firearms."

Although the federal government is specifically banned from creating or maintaining centralized firearm registries of innocent people (under the Federal Firearm Owners Protection Act of 1986 and other laws), state officials are required to conduct tests of guns and ammo for law enforcement purposes. Broad power to conduct such tests, and presumably to maintain records of results is found in Government Code §411.042.

Defensive Display

"Presenting a firearm to thwart a crime may be justifiable."

Prior to amendment in **2013**, a CHL who allowed a carry gun to show faced a charge for failure to conceal. The change made to PC §46.035, that provides some latitude for brief inadvertent display, such as "printing" through clothing, apparently also may protect a CHL who uses a firearm without discharging it to deter certain criminal activity, as use of force but not deadly force, under PC §9.04, *Threats as Justifiable Force*. Because this is a new and untested element of law, caution and discretion is advised. Non CHLs, protected by the necessity defense and §9.04, were not encumbered by the conceal requirement of the CHL laws, and are unaffected.

IF YOU SHOOT A CROOK OUTSIDE YOUR HOUSE DO YOU HAVE TO DRAG HIM INSIDE?

No! Acting on this wide-spread myth is a completely terrible idea. You're talking about tampering with evidence, obstructing justice, interfering with public duties, false reporting and more. If you're involved in a shooting, leave everything at the scene just the way it is and tell your attorney to call the police and an ambulance right away. You do have an attorney, right?

Don't think for a minute that modern forensics won't detect an altered scene of a crime. At any shooting a crime has been committed. Either the shooting is justified, which means you were in your rights and the person shot was acting illegally, or you exceeded your rights in the shooting, regardless of the circumstance. The situation will be investigated to determine the facts, and believe it, the facts will come out. Police tell time-worn jokes about finding "black heel marks on the linoleum." And once you're caught in a lie, your credibility is shot.

If you tamper with the evidence, you have to lie to all the authorities to back it up. Then you have to commit perjury to follow through. Can you pull it off?

If the guy with the mask was shot from the front, armed as he is, the homeowner has a good case for self defense. If the masked man was shot from behind, the homeowner has a case for acting to prevent aggravated burglary. Either way, he's better off leaving the body where it falls.

Suppose you shoot an armed intruder coming through your window, and the body falls outside the house. You'll have a better time convincing a jury that you were scared to death, than trying to explain how the dead crook in your living room got blood stains on your lawn.

The reason this fable gets so much play is because there is a big difference between a homeowner shooting a crook in the kitchen, and one person shooting another outdoors. Shooting at a stranger outside your house can be murder.

CAN YOU POINT A GUN AT SOMEONE?

CAN YOU POINT A GUN AT SOMEONE?

No matter how many aces a person is holding, you can't settle the matter with a gun. This also shows how the law can be interpreted in more than one way.

Using a gun to put a person in reasonable fear of imminent physical injury is *aggravated assault*—a second degree felony. A more lenient view would be to say that this is reckless display of a gun, which is *disorderly conduct,* a class B misdemeanor.

When you go to court, it could be argued that this is actually *attempted murder,* a felony. And if the guy with the gun is angry enough to take back his money, it becomes *aggravated robbery,* also a first degree felony.

By drawing your gun, the other guy may be able to shoot you dead and legally claim self defense. You may never pull a gun to leverage an argument. Merely having the gun with you may violate a handgun-carrying prohibition of Texas law, and if the scene is taking place in a bar, the crime goes from a misdemeanor to a felony.

If someone pointed a gun at you, would you get angry and want to see them arrested? Consider how someone would feel if roles were reversed and it was you who pulled the gun when it wasn't absolutely necessary to prevent a life-threatening situation.

Despite all this, the law recognizes your right to defend yourself, your loved ones, and other people. The law also recognizes a citizen's right to act to prevent certain crimes. These cases, when you *can* point a gun at another person, are described in Chapter 5.

HUNTING REQUIREMENTS 6

Texas hunting regulations are complex, highly-detailed and mandatory requirements issued for the most part by the Texas Parks and Wildlife Dept. This chapter is intended to point you in the right direction. Hunters need more information than just the firearms details provided here. For more detailed information and complete hunting regulations and procedures, contact the Texas Parks and Wildlife Dept.

A hunting license is required for any person, of any age, who hunts in the state of Texas. The Texas Parks and Wildlife Dept. requires every hunter whose date of birth is on or after September 2, 1971 to take and pass a Hunter Education Course through a program administered by Parks & Wildlife. Those who wish to hunt and are aged 12 through 16 can either successfully complete the course or they must be accompanied by a licensed hunter 17 years of age or older. Children under 12 must be accompanied by a licensed hunter 17 or older. You must carry proof of certification of completing the course on your person (called Hunter Safety Certification) while you are hunting. Failure to carry this certification is a class C misdemeanor under the Parks & Wildlife Code and carries a fine of $25 to $500.

The Hunter Education Training Course costs five dollars. To get information on a course near you, contact your local Texas Parks and Wildlife Dept. Law Enforcement office (see Appendix C for contact information). You may be exempted from the course if you have been certified in the voluntary Texas Hunter Safety Education Program, or if you have been certified through another state. To find out if you qualify call the Texas Parks and

Wildlife Hunter Education Section to see if your prior training is acceptable.

The Hunter Education Program is governed by §62.014 of the Parks & Wildlife Code. The course must cover at least:

- Safe handling and use of firearms and archery equipment;
- Wildlife conservation and management;
- Hunting laws and applicable rules and regulations;
- Hunting safety and ethics, including landowners' rights;

A certificate is issued by the department upon completion of the course.

A Texas hunting license is valid only from Sep. 1 or the date it's issued, whichever comes later, to Aug. 31 of the following year. It must be renewed each year. To be considered a resident, you must have lived in the state continuously for six months immediately before applying for your license, or be an active duty member of the U.S. armed forces. Dependents of active members of the armed forces are included. This does not, however, apply to the National Guard.

Hunting on Leased Land

The annual *Hunter's Clearinghouse Directory* gives detailed information from the nearly 300 private landowners who lease their land for hunting and other outdoor activities. It divides these lands into seven geographic areas. Information for each area is then arranged alphabetically by county and is presented in chart form. Charts include such information as types of game available, acreage, lodging and amenities.

Anyone who leases hunting rights and charges a fee for hunting on their property or property they control must have a Hunting Lease License and must keep detailed records in a Hunting Lease Record Book provided by the Texas Parks and Wildlife Dept.

Hunting on U.S. Army Corps of Engineers Land

The U.S. Army Corps of Engineers manages certain lands around the state, and allows hunting at many of these locations in accordance with local, state and federal laws. Prohibited areas include lands around dams, outlet facilities, project offices and areas leased for recreational purposes. Since each area has its own unique environment that might affect hunting and firearms safety, you must contact the local authorities to be sure. You can also get a guide published by the Southwestern Division of the U.S. Army Corps of Engineers. Their address is in Appendix C.

Public Lands Regulated by Texas Parks and Wildlife Dept.

A booklet describing certain public hunting lands in Texas is issued to purchasers of an annual hunting permit. It's called the *Public Hunting Lands Map Booklet*, and contains detailed maps and instructions for hunting on land owned or controlled by the Texas Parks & Wildlife Dept. or leased from the U.S. Forest Service, Army Corps of Engineers, Texas Utilities, Sabine River Authority, timber companies or private landowners. The tracts range from 500 acres to 400 square miles.

Loaded firearms are not allowed in or on a motor vehicle or in a designated campsite on these lands and buckshot is prohibited altogether. Muzzleloading firearms are legal for taking deer, provided they are .45 caliber or larger. It is illegal to discharge a firearm (or bow and arrow) from, onto, along or across a road or campsite. Using or displaying a firearm in an unsafe or threatening manner is also illegal.

Only certain areas are designated for target practice, so be sure to check the map booklet for the appropriate information. Also be aware that certain areas have their own specific regulations and you're responsible for following these. As an example, on Unit #747, the Alazan Bayou WMA in Nacogdoches County it's illegal to have a rifle or handgun greater than .22 caliber rimfire during squirrel hunting season, and taking feral hogs during the general season is prohibited with anything other than a muzzleloader.

Some Key Hunting Regulations

Below you'll find the main rules about the use of firearms while hunting (Parks & Wildlife Code). Remember, hunting regulations are not limited to guns and include archery and falconry. A free booklet called the *Texas Hunting Guide* is available from the Texas Parks & Wildlife Dept. and is updated annually.

• A valid hunting license is required to hunt any animal (terrestrial vertebrates) or bird.

• It's illegal to use another person's license, stamp or game tags to hunt or fish.

• Generally, you can't hunt from a motor vehicle, aircraft or any airborne device, powerboat, sailboat or other floating device. However, you may hunt non-migratory animals and birds from a motor vehicle or boat if you are within the boundaries of private property or on private water and you stay clear of the state road system (see P&WC §62.003).

• You must carry your driver's license or personal ID certificate (issued by the Texas Dept. of Public Safety) on yourself while hunting, if you're 17 years old or older. Non-residents must carry similar documents issued by their state or country of residence.

• It's Illegal to hunt at night or to use artificial light to "blind" prey, and you can't use artificial light to help you take game animals and game birds, but battery-powered scoping devices that project a light or dot only inside the scope are OK.

• Sight-impaired hunters (with doctor note) may use laser sights if accompanied by a sighted hunter at least 13 years old.

• It's illegal to let any edible portion of an animal you take go to waste.

• Many hunting regulations concern the types of firearms allowed depending on the game and the season. Some examples are listed below:

   Only muzzleloading weapons (includes handguns) of .45 caliber or larger are legal for hunting deer during a muzzleloader-only deer season.

   There's no restriction on the number of shells a shotgun or rifle may hold when hunting birds or animals, with the exception of migratory game birds where the limit is two in the magazine, one in the chamber.

It's illegal to take game animals or game birds with fully automatic weapons or using silencers.

It's illegal to use rimfire ammunition for taking deer, pronghorn or elk anywhere in the state, or for taking aoudad sheep in certain Panhandle counties.

It's illegal to shoot migratory game birds with any gun other than a shotgun that's not larger than 10 gauge.

• It's illegal to shoot any mammal, reptile, amphibian or bird listed by the state or federal authorities as an endangered species or threatened species.

• Residents are requested to report sightings of mountain lions dead or alive, and to report the shooting of a mountain lion (which may be legally hunted). The state is trying to gather information on the number and distribution of these animals.

• Poaching (hunting in violation of any of the regulations) is a serious crime. Hunters (and others) are encouraged to report poaching incidents, by calling Operation Game Thief (see Appendix C).

• It's illegal to take otter with firearms.

• It's illegal to shoot at, take or attempt to take any fur-bearing animal, from a boat on public waters in Texas.

• It's illegal to discharge a firearm on, along or across a public road.

• It's illegal to possess a firearm or be accompanied by a person possessing a firearm while taking game animals, game birds and fur-bearing animals by falconry.

• It's illegal to use smoke, explosives or chemicals of any kind to kill or flush fur-bearing animals in the wild.

• A firearm (and other things) may be confiscated if you are charged with using it in a Parks and Wildlife violation. Upon conviction, anything confiscated may be auctioned off or kept by the department. Upon acquittal the goods are returned to the owner.

A Hunter's Pledge

Responsible hunting provides unique challenges and rewards. However, the future of the sport depends on each hunter's behavior and ethics. Therefore, as a hunter, I pledge to:

• Respect the environment and wildlife;
• Respect property and landowners;
• Show consideration for nonhunters;
• Hunt safely;
• Know and obey the law;
• Support wildlife and habitat conservation;
• Pass on an ethical hunting tradition;
• Strive to improve my outdoor skills and understanding of wildlife;
• Hunt only with ethical hunters.

By following these principles of conduct each time I go afield, I will give my best to the sport, the public, the environment and myself. The responsibility to hunt ethically is mine; the future of hunting depends on me.

The Hunter's Pledge was created cooperatively by:

International Association of Fish and Wildlife Agencies
Izaak Walton League of America
National Rifle Association
Rocky Mountain Elk Foundation
Tread Lightly! Inc.
Sport Fishing Institute
Times Mirror Magazines Conservation Council
U.S. Dept. of Agriculture Extension Service
Wildlife Management Institute

NOTES ON FEDERAL LAW 7

Although federal laws regulate firearms to a great degree, the same laws prohibit the federal and local government from encroaching on the right to bear arms. This is seen in the 2nd, 4th, 9th and 14th Amendments to the Constitution, and in federal statutory laws, which number about 270.

Dealers of firearms must be licensed by the Bureau of Alcohol, Tobacco, Firearms and Explosives (BATFE). Federal law requires licensed dealers to keep records of each sale, but prohibits using this information in any sort of national registration plan. The information is permanently saved by the dealer and is not centrally recorded by the federal authorities. If a dealer goes out of business the records are sent to a central federal depository for storage (or a state site if approved by the Treasury Dept.). Although federal law prohibits using these records to establish a national firearms registration system, violations of that ban are increasingly common and efforts to prevent bureaucratic work in this area have been of limited effect. Reportedly, fingerprints submitted for background checks to the FBI are stored by that agency until the individual reaches 99 years of age.

Paperwork required by the Brady law is collected by local authorities, but must be destroyed shortly after it is used to conduct background checks, and by law, no records of the checks may be kept. Local authorities are required to certify their compliance with record destruction to the U.S. Attorney General every six months. The Justice Department reports that compliance with this requirement has been quite low. National records of innocent gun owners is an increasing concern.

In theory, there's no central place for anyone to go and see if a given individual owns a firearm (except perhaps in the case of those people who have registered for a concealed-handgun license, if you assume they all own guns). Firearm ownership in America is traditionally a very private matter, the last thing government should know, it defeats the basic principles of the Second Amendment. For someone to find out if you have a gun they would have to check all the records of all the dealers in the country, a daunting task, and only BATFE is authorized to check the records of manufacture, importation and sale of firearms. As a practical matter, however, the authorities are increasingly able to easily determine which people have chosen to own firearms. Local authorities occasionally ask to see a dealer's records, and dealers may feel it's in their best interests to cooperate, even if it isn't required by law.

The dealer's records allow guns to be *traced,* a very different and important matter. When a gun is involved in a crime, BATFE can find out, from the manufacturer's serial number, which licensed dealer originally received the gun. The dealer can then look through the records and see who purchased the weapon. It's a one-way street—a gun can be linked to a purchaser but owners can't be traced to their guns. One study of successful traces showed that four out of five were of some value to law enforcement authorities.

When President Reagan was shot by John Hinckley Jr., the weapon was traced and in fourteen minutes time, a retail sale to Hinckley was confirmed.

Buying, selling, having, making, transferring and transporting guns is in many cases regulated by federal laws. These rules are covered in *The Texas Gun Owner's Guide,* but for the most part, only the state penalties are noted. There may be federal penalties as well.

Under the Assimilative Crimes Act, state law controls if there is no federal law covering a situation. It is important to recognize that there can be a question of jurisdiction in some cases.

A long history of federal regulation exists with regard to firearms and other weapons. For a detailed examination of the historical record, read Stephen Halbrook's book, *That Every Man Be Armed.*

The main federal gun laws in effect today include:

- 2nd, 4th and 9th Amendments to the Constitution (1791)
- Fourteenth Amendment to the Constitution (1868)
- National Firearms Act (1934)
- Federal Firearms Act (1938)
- Omnibus Crime Control and Safe Streets Act (1968)
- Gun Control Act (1968)
- Organized Crime Control Act (1970)
- Omnibus Crime Control Act (1986)
- Firearms Owners' Protection Act (1986)
- Brady Handgun Violence Prevention Act (1993)
- Public Safety & Recreational Firearms Use Protection Act (The Crime Bill) (1994)
- Promotion of Rifle Practice and Firearms Safety Act (1996)
- Antiterrorism and Effective Death Penalty Act (1996)
- Omnibus Consolidated Appropriations Act for FY 1997 (Domestic Violence Gun Ban, Gun Free School Zones)
- Omnibus Consolidated & Emergency Supplemental Appropriations Act, 1999 (numerous requirements detailed later in this chapter)
- Smith & Wesson-preference ban (P.L. 106-398, 10/30/00, DOD FY 2001); The Patriot Act: Anti-terrorism measures (P.L. 107-56, 10/26/01); Aviation Security Act: Arm the pilots (P.L. 107-71, 11/19/01); Homeland Security Act: Arm the government measures (P.L. 107-296, 11/25/02)
- Vision 100--Century of Aviation Reauthorization Act (2003) (Deputize Cargo Pilots so they may be armed)
- Reauthorization of the ban on undetectable firearms. (2003)
- Consolidated Appropriations Resolution (2003)
- Law Enforcement Officers Safety Act, LEOSA (2004)
- Protection of Lawful Commerce In Arms Act (2005)
- Disaster Recovery Personal Protection Act (2006)
- NICS Improvements Amendments Act (2008)

Additional federal requirements may be found in the Code of Federal Regulations (CFR) and the United States Code (USC).

FEDERAL FIREARMS TRANSPORTATION GUARANTEE

Passed on July 8, 1986 as part of the Firearms Owners' Protection Act, federal law guarantees that a person may legally transport a firearm from one place where its possession is legal to another place where possession is legal, provided it is unloaded and the firearm and ammunition are not readily accessible from the passenger compartment of the vehicle. The law doesn't say it in so many words, but the only non-accessible spot in the average passenger car is the trunk. If a vehicle has no separate compartment for storage, the firearm and ammunition may be in a locked container other than the glove compartment or console.

There have been cases, especially in Eastern states, where local authorities have not complied with this law, creating a degree of risk for people otherwise legally transporting firearms. To avoid any confusion, the text of the federal guarantee is printed here word for word:

Federal Law Number 18 USC §926A
Interstate transportation of firearms

Notwithstanding any other provision of any law or any rule or regulation of a State or any political subdivision thereof, any person who is not otherwise prohibited by this chapter from transporting, shipping, or receiving a firearm shall be entitled to transport a firearm for any lawful purpose from any place where he may lawfully possess and carry such firearm to any other place where he may lawfully possess and carry such firearm if, during such transportation the firearm is unloaded, and neither the firearm nor any ammunition being transported is readily accessible or is directly accessible from the passenger compartment of such transporting vehicle: Provided, That in the case of a vehicle without a compartment separate from the driver's compartment the firearm or ammunition shall be contained in a locked container other than the glove compartment or console.

Anyone interested in a complete copy of the federal gun laws, with plain English summaries of every law, can get a copy of *Gun Laws of America*, published by Bloomfield Press. See the back section of this book for details.

The Brady Law

Enacted in 1993 as the Brady Handgun Violence Prevention Act, the Brady law in reality turned out to be five things:

1–Centralized federal control over all handgun and long gun retail sales;

2–A $200 million funding mechanism for a national computer system capable of checking out any individual from a single FBI location;

3–The establishment of a national ID card infrastructure (based on drivers' licenses and social security numbers) for all original firearm purchases;

4–The most thorough commerce tracking system on Earth, initially only for retail sales of firearms in America; and

5–A mechanism for preventing known criminals from directly purchasing firearms at retail and paying sales tax.

The widely publicized five-day waiting period was largely a myth, and never existed in most states (in Texas the "wait" ranged from zero to nine days as a local check was conducted, and there is no routine wait today). The effect of the Brady law on crime reduction is essentially unknown, since the hundreds of thousands of criminals reportedly identified by the system (the number is hotly disputed) are on the loose—virtually no effort to track or apprehend them has been made. It is a five-year federal felony for criminals and other disqualified persons to attempt to purchase a firearm.

Part 1 of the law, the handgun part, set to expire 60 months after enactment, is described below in small type (it expired Nov. 30, 1998). Brady Part 2, the National Instant Background Check (dubbed NICS by the FBI, who has replaced BATFE to operate the system), controls rifles, shotguns and handguns, and is described as it appears in the federal statute. Complex regulations to implement the new law, which are basically transparent in this state, are not covered (available in their entirety on the FBI and BATFE Internet sites).

The FBI's use of the Brady NICS computer system to record the name and address of every retail gun buyer in America, in apparent violation of long-standing law (strictly forbidden in both the McClure Volkmer Act, 1986, and the Brady law itself), has prompted outcries from the public and Congress, but continued unabated throughout and then after the Clinton administration. In addition, the Justice Dept. tried to levy a tax on the sale of firearms, to benefit the FBI, without apparent authority (taxes are supposed to originate in Congress). The Bush administration appeared intent on fixing such abuses, but it is distressing to see how politicized administration of the laws has become. States that cooperate with the FBI, as Texas has done, would avoid the proposed tax on its dealers. For updates on the complex Brady scheme, check our website, gunlaws.com.

The Brady Law, Part 1 (First Five Years, Expired 11/30/98)

The Brady Handgun Violence Prevention Act was signed into law on Nov. 30, 1993. Its provisions for common carriers, reporting multiple handgun sales and license fee increases are among the rules affecting private citizens that took effect immediately. The waiting-period provisions took effect on Feb. 28, 1994, and were set to expire on Nov. 30, 1998.

In addition to the regulation of private citizens described below, the Brady law: places special requirements on dealers, sets timetables and budgets for the U.S. Attorney General to implement the law, provides funding, sets basic computer system requirements, mandates criminal-history record sharing among authorities, enhances penalties for gun thieves and more. Your federal legislators can send you the full 12-page Brady law.

The Brady law refers to a "chief law enforcement officer," defined as the chief of police, the sheriff, an equivalent officer or their designee. The description below refers to such persons as "the authorities." Where the law refers to an individual who is unlicensed under §923 of USC Title 18, this description says "private citizen" or "you." Federally licensed dealers, manufacturers and importers are referred to as "dealers." The act of selling, delivering or transferring is called "transferring." The law defines *handgun* as, "a firearm that has a short stock and is designed to be held and fired by the use of a single hand." A combination of parts that can be assembled into a handgun counts as a handgun.

Under the Brady law, to legally obtain a handgun from a dealer you must provide:

- A valid picture ID for the dealer to examine;

- A written statement with only the date the statement was made, notice of your intent to obtain a handgun from the dealer, your name, address, date of birth, the type of ID you used and a statement that you are not: 1–under indictment and haven't been convicted of a crime that carries a prison term of more than one year, 2–a fugitive from justice, 3–an unlawful user of or addicted to any controlled substance, 4–an adjudicated mental defective, 5–a person who has been committed to a mental institution, 6–an illegal alien, 7–dishonorably discharged from the armed forces, 8–a person who has renounced U.S. citizenship.

Then, before transferring the handgun to you, the dealer must:

- Within one day, provide notice of the content and send a copy of the statement to the authorities where you live;

- Keep a copy of your statement and evidence that it was sent to the authorities;

- Wait five days during which state offices are open, from the day the dealer gave the authorities notice, and during that time,

- Receive no information from the authorities that your possession of the handgun would violate federal, state or local laws.

The waiting period ends early if the authorities notify the dealer early that you're eligible. The federal mandate that local authorities "shall make a reasonable effort" to check your background in local, state and federal records, was declared unconstitutional by the U.S. Supreme Court in 1997. Long guns are unaffected by the Brady law until the National Instant Check described below comes on line.

You are excluded from the Brady waiting-period process:

1–If you have a written statement from the authorities, valid for 10 days, that you need a handgun because of a threat to your life or a member of your household's life; or

2–With a handgun permit, in the state that issued it, if the permit is less than five years old and required a background check (the Texas concealed-handgun license qualifies, eliminating the need for license holders to wait for handgun purchases or to do additional paperwork or background checks); or

3–In states that have their own handgun background check (Texas does not presently have one); or

4–If the transfer is already regulated by the National Firearms Act of 1934, as with Class III weapons; or

5–If the dealer has been certified as being in an extremely remote location of a sparsely populated state and there are no telecommunications near the dealer's business premises (written for Alaska, but other localities may qualify).

If a dealer is notified after a transfer that your possession of the handgun is illegal, the dealer must, within one business day, provide any information they have about you to the authorities at the dealer's place of business and at your residence. The information a dealer receives may only be communicated to you, the authorities or by court order. If you are denied a handgun, you may ask the authorities why, and they are required to provide the reason in writing within 20 business days of your request.

Unless the authorities determine that the handgun transfer to you would be illegal, they must, within 20 days of the date of your statement, destroy all records of the process. The authorities are expressly forbidden to convey or use the information in your statement for anything other than what's needed to carry out the Brady process.

The authorities may not be held liable for damages for either allowing an illegal handgun transfer or preventing a legal one. If you are denied a firearm unjustly, you may sue the political entity responsible and get the information corrected or have the transfer approved, and you may collect reasonable attorney's fees.

The Brady Law Part 2—National Instant Check: The Brady law requires the U.S. Attorney General (AG) to establish a National Instant Criminal Background Check system (NICS) before Nov. 30, 1998 (which they did). With NICS now in effect, the previous process (above, in small type) is eliminated. In order to transfer *any firearm, not just handguns,* with the NICS system up, a dealer must verify your identity from a government-issued photo-ID card, contact the system (in Clarksburg, W. Va., run by the FBI, and a contract call center), identify you and either:

• get a unique transfer number back from the system, or

• wait three days during which state offices are open and during which the system provides no notice that the transfer would violate relevant laws.

Some states have been designated "Point of Contact" states by the FBI. This means dealers there contact the State Police for all gun sales. The State Police include a check of the FBI's NICS system, and the process is transparent to the customers. In Texas, as in most states, the dealer must contact the FBI directly, which conducts both the federal and state checks.

The NICS system is required to issue the transfer number if the transfer would violate no relevant laws, and it is supposed to destroy all records of approved inquiries except for the identifying number and the date it was issued. The FBI, however, has indicated they are recording the name and address of everyone who buys a gun now that the system is running, and Congress has been unable to stop them so far. If the transfer is approved, the dealer includes the transfer number in the record of the transaction (on a redesigned version of the 4473 form). The NICS system is bypassed under conditions similar to 2, 4 and 5 listed above (in small type) as exceptions to the Brady process (with number 2 broadened to include a "firearms" permit).

A licensed dealer who violates these requirements is subject to a civil fine of up to $5,000 and suspension or revocation of their license, but, according to the statute, only if the system is operating and would have shown that the customer would have been ineligible to make a purchase.

It's important to note that the NICS law plainly says you only have to use NICS if it exists and it's running (18 USC §922 (t)(5)), a clause specifically put there by lobbyists who were afraid the system might never be built, ending gun sales altogether. But BATFE and the FBI have re-interpreted that clause to mean you can't sell a gun when NICS is down—rewriting the statute from their bureau desks.

Licensed dealers, fearing federal reprisals against their licenses and livelihoods, have generally been unwilling to do business when NICS is down, which occurs frequently through technical glitches and from planned "maintenance periods" during regular business hours. State police insta-check departments nationwide haven't been willing to stand up for states' rights and force the issue either. So when NICS is off, retail gun sales grind to a halt. This has occurred scores of times, and even on a regional basis.

Essentially, as of late 1998, federal forces have gained control of all retail gun sales in America. The only sales not controlled by federal agents are lawful private transfers among the people. This basic American freedom is now being attacked as a "loophole," ironically, by officials we elect who take an oath to preserve, protect and defend the Constitution.

If you are denied a firearm under NICS, the law says you may request the reason directly from NICS and it must present you with a written answer within five business days. You may also request the reason from the AG, who must respond "immediately," according to the law. You may provide information to fix any errors in the system, and the AG must immediately consider the information, investigate further, correct any erroneous federal records and notify any federal or state agency that was the source of the errors.

Multiple sales of handguns (two or more from the same dealer in a five day period) have long been reported to BATFE, and must now be reported to local authorities as well. Local authorities may not disclose the information, must destroy the records within 20 days from receipt if the transfer is not illegal and must certify every six months to the AG that they are complying with these provisions.

Common or contract carriers (airlines, buses, trains, etc.) may not label your luggage or packages to indicate that they contain firearms. Federal law requires you to notify the carrier in writing if you are transporting firearms or ammunition, but verbal notice is frequently accepted. The long-time labeling practice had been responsible for the frequent theft of luggage containing firearms.

Licensing fees for obtaining a new federal firearms license are increased to $200 for three years. The fee for renewing a currently valid license is $90 for three years.

Public Safety and Recreational Firearms Use Protection Act

This law, popularized as the 1994 Crime Bill, affected three areas of existing firearms law: 1–Possession and use of firearms by juveniles; 2–Possession of firearms by people under domestic violence restraining orders, and 3–it created a new class of regulated firearms and accessories. The information on juveniles is found in Chapter 1 since it relates to who can bear arms. The new class of prohibited purchasers (for domestic violence cases) is also in Chapter 1, as part of the list for federal form 4473—the form dealers use with all sales.

Historical Note: The portion of the law that created the legal *assault-weapons* category expired on Sep. 13, 2004. Nothing was actually banned—Americans could still buy, own, sell, trade, have and use any of the millions of affected firearms and accessories.

What the law actually did was to prohibit *manufacturers and importers* from selling newly made goods of that type to the public (and it was a crime for the public to get them). Maybe that is a ban, but not in the sense that was reported. Ten years later, after the end of the ban, there was widespread recognition that it had no effect on crime. The list of affected weapons is preserved for history in Chapter 3. Perhaps more laws should be enacted with expiration dates.

The net effect of the law was to motivate manufacturers to create stockpiles before the law took affect, then to introduce new products that were not affected, and to step up marketing efforts overseas for affected products. Demand and prices skyrocketed for the fixed supply of goods domestically, and then adjusted downward when it became obvious that supplies were still available. When it was over, a normal 15-round magazine for a sidearm dropped from more than $100 to around twenty bucks. If all this is news to you, it's time to question you're source of news.

Rifle Practice and Firearms Safety Act (1996)

The Civilian Marksmanship Program, run by the U.S. Army, has served as the federal government's official firearms training, supply and competitions program for U.S. citizens, since 1956. Its history traces back to the late 1800s, when programs were first established to help ensure that the populace could shoot straight, in the event an army had to be raised to defend the country. The program is privatized by this act.

The federal government transfers the responsibility and facilities for training civilians in the use of small arms to a 501(c)(3) non-profit corporation created for this purpose. All law-abiding people are eligible to participate, and priority is given to reaching and training youth in the safe, lawful and accurate use of firearms.

Functions formerly performed for this program by the Army are now the responsibility of this new corporation. The Army is required to provide direct support and to take whatever action is necessary to make the program work in its privatized form.

Official federal policy, as stated in the program goals, is to:

1–Promote safety in the use of firearms;

2–Teach marksmanship to U.S. citizens;

3–Promote practice in the use of firearms;

4–Conduct matches and competitions;

5–Award trophies and prizes;

6–Procure supplies and services needed for the program;

7–Secure and account for all firearms, ammunition and supplies used in the program;

8–Give, lend or sell firearms, ammunition and supplies under the program. Priority must be given to training youths, and reaching as many youths as possible.

Any person who is not a felon, hasn't violated the main federal gun laws, and does not belong to a group that advocates violent overthrow of the U.S. government, is free to participate in the Civilian Marksmanship Program.

What do you think would happen if Americans everywhere knew of this fine new law, and enrolled their children in programs that teach responsible use of firearms and gun safety? It would build understanding and self-esteem, replacing the gun ignorance fostered by wildly violent senseless TV shows, with knowledge and respect for the power and proper use of firearms. The Civilian Marksmanship Program is listed in Appendix C.

Antiterrorism Act of 1996

A wide variety of gun-law changes were introduced in this 48,728-word act. Eight sections introduce new law, and other sections make 17 amendments to existing federal law. Much of it deals with intentional criminal acts, and so falls outside the scope of *The Texas Gun Owner's Guide*. Other sections could give rise to unexpected results and are included.

Section 702. Using a firearm in an assault on any person in the U.S. is a federal crime if:

1–the assault involves "conduct transcending national boundaries" (described below) and
2–if any of the following also exist:

   A–any perpetrator uses the mail or interstate or foreign commerce in committing the crime;
   B–the offense in any way affects interstate or foreign commerce;
   C–the victim is anyone in the federal government or the military;
   D–any structure or property damaged is owned in any part by the federal government, or
   E–the offense occurs in special U.S. territorial jurisdictions.

The maximum penalty in a non-lethal assault with a firearm is 30 years in a federal prison.

Causing a serious risk of injury to anyone, by damaging any structure or property in the U.S., is a federal crime if the conditions described in 1 and 2 above exist. The maximum penalty is 25 years.

Threatening, attempting or conspiring to commit the above acts is a crime, and various penalties are defined.

The phrase "conduct transcending national boundaries" means "conduct occurring outside of the United States in addition to the conduct occurring in the United States." It is not clear what this might include.

The Attorney General investigates "federal crimes of terrorism." Such crimes occur when any of a long list of felonies is committed to influence the government by intimidation or coercion, or to retaliate against government actions. An assault involving conduct transcending national boundaries, described in the first part of this law, is one of the felonies.

Section 727. Using or attempting to use deadly force against anyone in the federal government or the military, if the attack is because of the person's government role, is a federal crime (in addition to existing assault and homicide laws). All former personnel are included. Federal penalties for an attack on anyone in this protected class are defined. In the case of such an assault, a gun is considered a gun, even if it jams due to a defective part.

Omnibus Consolidated Appropriation Act for Fiscal Year 1997 Section 657, Gun-Free School Zone.

Congress was stopped in its attempt to exercise police powers at the state level by the U.S. Supreme Court, when the court declared in 1995 (U.S. v. Lopez), that the 1991 Gun-Free School Zone law was unconstitutional. That law was reenacted by Congress, to the surprise of many observers, as an unnoticed add-on to a 2,000-page federal spending bill in 1996, in a form essentially identical to the one the Supreme Court overturned.

The law makes it a federal crime to knowingly have a firearm at a place that you know, or should reasonably believe, is a school zone. A school zone means in or on the grounds of an elementary or secondary public, private or parochial school, and the area within 1,000 feet from the grounds of the school.

An exemption is granted to anyone willing to register with the government for a license to carry the firearm (if the license required the state's authorities to verify that you were qualified under law to receive the license; the Texas CHL qualifies). In addition, the ban does not apply to:

1–Firearms while on private property that is not part of the school grounds;

2–Any firearm that is unloaded and in a locked container;

3–Any firearm unloaded and locked in a firearms rack on a motor vehicle;

4–Possession for use in an approved school program;

5–Possession under a contract with the school;

6–Possession by law enforcement in an official capacity; and

7–An unloaded firearm, while crossing school premises to public or private land open to hunting, if crossing the grounds is authorized by the school.

It is also illegal to fire a gun (or attempt to fire a gun), knowingly or with reckless disregard for safety, in a place you know is a school zone, with the following exceptions:

1–On private property that is not part of the school grounds;

2–As part of a program approved by the school;

3–Under contract with the school;

4–By law enforcement acting in an official capacity.

An exemption for self defense is conspicuously absent, creating a shocking suggestion that self defense or defense of a third person within 1,000 feet of a school could be a federal crime (two actually, for possession and for discharge). An offense is designated as a misdemeanor, but carries a five year federal prison term. States are not prohibited from passing their own laws.

America had 121,855 public and private schools as of 1994. In effect, this law criminalizes the actions of nearly anyone who travels in a populated area with a legally possessed firearm, creating millions of federal offenses every day (see maps and details at gunlaws.com). As with its overturned predecessor, its affect on the very real problem of youth violence is unclear, and of course, any firearm used illegally in America, whether it is near a school or not, is already a serious crime with penalties.

Section 658.
Misdemeanor Gun Ban for Domestic Violence Offense.

Anyone convicted of a state or federal misdemeanor involving the use or attempted use of physical force, or the threatened use of a deadly weapon, among family members (spouse, parent, guardian, cohabiter or similar) is prohibited from possessing a firearm under federal law. This marks the first time that a misdemeanor offense serves as grounds for denial of the constitutional right to keep and bear arms. The number of people affected is unknown, and no provision is made for the firearms such men and women might already possess. Firearms possession by a prohibited possessor is a five-year federal felony.

A number of narrow conditions may exempt a person from this law, including whether they were represented by an attorney, the type of trial and plea, an expungement or set aside, or a pardon or other restoration of civil rights. Because such offenses are often handled in courts-not-of-record, such a determination may not be possible.

The current congressional practice of placing unrelated laws in larger acts, in order to get them passed without debate (or even unnoticed), has raised concerns among many observers. This law, sometimes referred to as the Lautenberg amendment, is an extreme example of such a practice, and caught both firearms-rights advocates and adversaries by surprise.

The law is drafted broadly, affecting sworn police officers nationwide, the armed forces, and agencies such as the FBI, CIA, Secret Service, Forest Service and others, most of whom are accustomed to being exempted from such laws. Many of these groups are currently battling to get themselves exempted from the law. They don't believe they should be prevented from defending themselves or others because of prior minor infractions. Some police departments have begun laying off officers who are in violation.

So many problems exist with respect to this legislation that it has raised concerns unlike any recent act of Congress. Indeed, some members reportedly were told before voting that this language had been deleted from the final version, and the vote was held before copies of the 2,000-page act were available for review. Experts close to the issues cite numerous constitutional conflicts, including:

1–It is *ex post facto*—a law passed after the fact to affect your former actions (prohibited by Art. 1, Sec. 9);

2–It impacts the right to keep and bear arms (2nd Amendment);

3–Legally owned property becomes subject to automatic seizure (prohibited by the 4th Amendment);

4–It holds people accountable to a felony without a Grand Jury indictment, represents a second punishment for a single offense creating a double jeopardy, and it requires dispossession of personal property without compensation or due process (all prohibited by the 5th Amendment);

5–It denies your right to be informed of an accusation, and to counsel and a public jury trial because an existing misdemeanor now automatically creates a federal felony (prohibited by the 6th Amendment);

6–Using a misdemeanor (a minor infraction) instead of a felony (a serious crime) to deny civil rights may be cruel and unusual punishment (8th Amendment);

7–Family conflicts, historically an issue at the state level, become federalized (prohibited by the 10th Amendment); and

8–It denies due process, abridges the rights of U.S. citizens by state law, and denies equal protection under the law (violates 14th Amendment guarantees).

Domestic violence does not have a single definition at the state level. Some states' laws require the arrest of at least one party if the police respond to an apparent domestic-violence report. This raises all the issues of judicial process and plea-bargaining after an arrest. A parent who pays a small fine rather than endure a long expensive trial can now be charged with a federal felony; domestic violence pleas have been a standard ploy in divorce proceedings for decades; these charges now deny your right to keep and bear arms, to vote, to hold office and more.

An analogy to cars crystallizes this law's affects. It is as if a former speeding ticket were now grounds for felony arrest if you own a car or gasoline. When a law is scrutinized for constitutionality it is typically held up to a single constitutional provision. The eight constitutional issues in this short piece of legislation may set a record.

Omnibus Consolidated & Emergency Supplemental Appropriations Act, 1999. This 4,000-page budget bill was secretly drafted in committee, rushed to the floor of Congress, voted on two days later, and enacted in October 1998 without any of your representatives actually reading it. It increased federal gun law by almost 6%, with provisions for NICS funding, gun-law enforcement funding, gun safety devices sold at retail, public gun safety training funding, restrictions on aliens, NICS record-keeping and taxing prohibitions, shotguns and certain antiques redefined, undetectable gun law reenactment, relief for importers, a pawn shop NICS glitch fix, the Arms Control and Disarmament Agency disbanded with duties moved to the State Dept., and a special ban on using the U.S. global arms control and disarmament agenda against the public. Go to gunlaws.com for detailed analysis of these and other federal requirements.

The USA Patriot Act and the "Arm the Pilots" Law (2001). Hurriedly enacted as a response to the September 11 attacks, a small part of the huge Patriot Act introduces definitions of terrorism and various gun provisions related to terrorism. Also rushed into law, the Aviation & Transportation Security Act allows pilots to be deputized, so those deputies, whose jurisdiction is solely the flight deck, can be armed. Curiously, there is nothing in current law that prevents pilots from being armed without this bill, it's come down to a plain issue of political pressure, and not law. Pilots are even authorized under existing law to take custody of *your* gun while enroute (though they are not required to do so) in 18 USC §922(e).

Undetectable Firearms Ban Extension, 2003: The ban on these guns, none of which are publicly known to exist, was extended for another ten years, to Dec. 10, **2013.**

Arming Cargo Pilots, 2003: Air-cargo pilots, omitted from efforts to arm passenger-plane pilots, may now also be deputized and, as federal officers, be armed against terrorism. Bureaucratic foot-dragging has plagued this effort, the same as passenger pilots.

Consolidated Appropriations, 2003: Many items, including: Dept. of Agriculture may selectively arm its employees; Judiciary may not tax or add fees to the Brady NICS check and must destroy certain records related to retail gun sales; Federal officers get funding for firearm competitions and awards; reiteration of ban on centralizing certain firearms records; no changes to *Curios or Relics* list; continued denial of relief for people with federal firearms disability except for corporations; no electronic retrieval allowed for out-of-business dealer records; safeguards on using dealer records in police work; $45 million for prosecutions to reduce gun violence; and a renewed ban against advocating or promoting gun control by the Centers for Disease Control.

Congress continues to churn out gun measures, issuing a national concealed-carry law for active and retired police in 2004 (enacted as HR 218, now 18 USC §926B and C, known as LEOSA). The 1994 Crime Bill, with its list of hundreds of restricted weapons, expired in 2004, and frivolous lawsuit protection for the firearms industry passed in 2005 with many civilian conditions attached. In 2006, responding to abusive firearm confiscations in New Orleans following the Katrina hurricane disaster, they passed the Disaster Recovery Personal Protection Act to help ban further abuses. The Protection of Lawful Commerce in Arms Act protects manufacturers from frivolous lawsuits by people seeking to hold gun makers liable for the acts of criminals. The NICS Improvement Act in 2008 cleaned up record-keeping requirements and enhanced the process for getting old records corrected or removed. Other smaller changes have also been made. Check gunlaws.com update pages for details.

Infringement Creep: Judicial and legislative activity are underway with regard to federal firearms issues on a practically non-stop basis. Despite pronouncements in 1996 about a moratorium on new gun laws, federal gun law grew by more than 13% that year. That's more new federal law in one year than we've seen in almost any *decade*.

Multiple Long Gun Sales: BATFE now registers anyone buying two or more long guns over .22 caliber with a detachable magazine, in a five-day period from the same dealer, in the Mexico-border states, AZ, CA, NM, TX. Federal law specifically bans such a registry, and it's under challenge in court. The agency decided to do this without congressional approval after getting caught smuggling guns into Mexico, under the guise of stopping gun smugglers, in the Fast and Furious debacle.

Quarterly Excise Tax on Arms: HR 5552, The Firearms Excise Tax Improvement Act, became law on Aug. 16, 2010, P.L. 111-237, removing the burden on firearms and ammo makers to pay excise tax every two weeks, an enormous and costly burden. They now pay it quarterly like other conservation industries.

HealthCare: Broadly framed and undefined "injury control," "health promotion" and "wellness programs" woven into the federal takeover of the medical industry has caused concern among some industry observers that these could be used to place gun owners in more expensive insurance brackets, or identify "unhealthy" behavior (firearm possession) for treatment. The national health database will allow data mining for past or current use of red-flagged drugs, such as anti-depressants, for special attention, as government advances the argument that "the government has the authority to control private behavior" and enforce compliance with "applicable standards."

LEOSA Improvements: A new bill (SB1132, P.L. 111-272) adds federal agents to the carry-anywhere privilege LEOs have, protects carrying hollowpoint ammo for LEOs, reduces the years of service needed to qualify from 15 to 10, and makes getting the needed ID cards easier. The public, originally promised to be "next," is still left out of these plans, only former government agents are granted the power to carry nationally.

National Parks and National Wildlife Refuges: The bans in place for mere possession of firearms in National Parks and National Wildlife Refuges were repealed by HR627 (P.L. 111-024) in 2009, effective in 2010. The bill describes in exquisite detail how these bans violated the right to keep and bear arms, entrapped unwary people, and stood out against the laws of the states the places are located. "Congress needs to weigh in on the new regulations to ensure that unelected bureaucrats and judges cannot again override the Second Amendment rights of law-abiding citizens..." Almost more important than the lifting of the rights bans in 83.6 million acres of NP and 90.8 million acres of NWR, the law makes these places subject to the state laws they are in. In other words, federal authority over this land is overridden by the states, an excellent development in the quest for increased federalism, an end to federal usurpation, and greater recognition of the Tenth Amendment.

Gun rights in the military: The 2011 National Defense Authorization Act has an amendment championed by the NRA: "Section 1062 of the Act prohibits the Secretary of Defense from issuing any requirement, or collecting or recording any information, 'relating to the otherwise lawful acquisition, possession, ownership, carrying, or other use of a privately owned firearm, privately owned ammunition, or another privately owned weapon by a member of the Armed Forces or civilian employee of the Department of Defense' on property not owned or operated by the DOD. It also requires the destruction of any information of the type prohibited by the Act, within 90 days."

Fort Riley in Kansas started the fiasco with regulations requiring, "troops stationed there to register privately owned firearms kept off-base and firearms owned by their family members residing anywhere in Kansas. It prohibited soldiers who have carry permits from carrying for protection off-base. And, it authorized unit commanders to set arbitrary limits on the caliber of firearms and ammunition their troops may privately own," according to the NRA. There is no end to the attacks the Second Amendment faces, even from our own military.

The bill also includes an improvement on previous attempts to make military surplus available to the public who funds it all. Section 346 requires, "Small arms ammunition and ammunition components in excess of military requirements, including fired cartridge cases, which are not otherwise prohibited from commercial sale or certified by the Secretary of Defense as unserviceable or unsafe, may not be demilitarized or destroyed and shall be made available for commercial sale." It applies to loaded ammo and other components as well as fired brass. The military is also encouraged to continue granting access to its vast lands for hunting and fishing.

Spring-Assisted Knives: An attempt by U.S. Customs and the Dept. of Homeland Security to ban importation of spring-assisted knives, or knives that can be opened with one hand, which constitute the vast majority of knives sold in America today, was defeated in 2009. This power grab and attack on the right to arms and on free enterprise was beaten back, and Customs dropped the effort after massive public outcry and some inside lobbying that never made the news.

The federal Switchblade Knife Act of Aug. 12, 1958 (P.L. 85–623, now 15 U.S.C. §§1241–1245), says whoever knowingly introduces, or manufactures for introduction, into interstate commerce, or transports or distributes in interstate commerce, any switchblade knife, shall be fined or imprisoned, or both. Notably, possession or use of the knives is not covered. And of course, use of any knife in the commission of a crime is a serious crime with commensurate penalties.

Switchblades are defined in 19 CFR §12(a) as "any imported knife... including "balisong", "butterfly"... knives, which has one or more of the following characteristics or identities: (1) A blade which opens automatically by hand pressure applied to a button or device in the handle of the knife, or any knife with a blade which opens automatically by operation of inertia, gravity, or both..." including kits or knives that can be easily converted to such operation, and knives with a spring-powered blade that shoots out of the handle, known as ballistic knives.

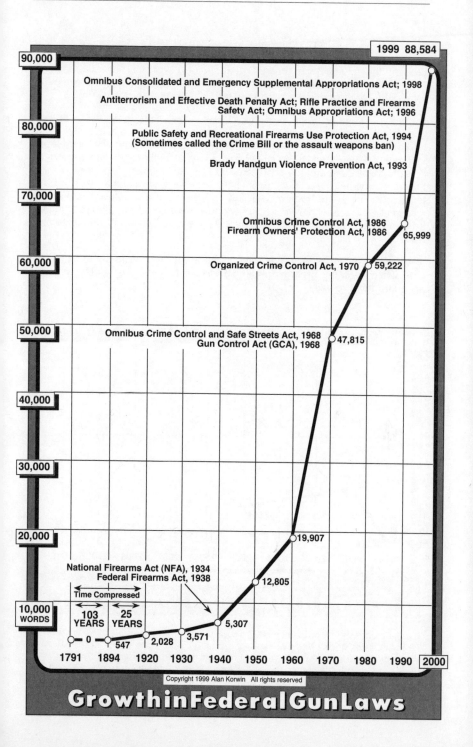

GrowthinFederalGunLaws

Only two decades in U.S. history—the 1960s and 1970s—saw more gun law enacted by Congress than in 1996 alone. Nearly 10,000 new words of gun law brought the federal total to more than 83,000 words. This represented a 13.43% increase for the year, which, measured by percentage or word count, set records for the federal regulation of the right to keep and bear arms.

Failure to comply with new laws and regulations can have serious consequences to you personally, even if you believe your constitutional rights have been compromised. In fact, many experts have noted that increasing latitudes are being taken by some governmental authorities with respect to constitutional guarantees. Legislative and regulatory changes present serious risks to currently law-abiding people, since what is legal today may not be tomorrow. The entire body of U.S. law is growing at a significant rate and it represents some potential threats to freedoms Americans have always enjoyed. It is prudent to take whatever steps you feel are reasonable to minimize any risks.

New laws may be passed at any time, and it is your responsibility to be up-to-date when handling firearms under all circumstances. *This book's contents are guaranteed to age.*

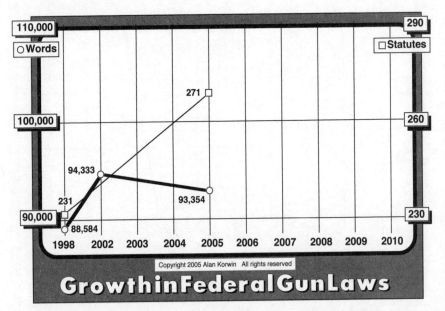

The net reduction in words since 2002 results mainly from losses due to codification of the Public Laws since 1995, plus repeals, expirations and amendments. In several cases amendments expanded a law's scope but reduced its word count (e.g., 610 words less in 18 USC §1114). Expiration of the assault-weapon law removed 1,105 words, and the 3,710-word list of approved guns. The increase in numbered statutes is a net gain, accounting for repeals and new enactments. New statutes since 2002 added 4,339 words.

The Changing Federal Landscape

Court challenges are actively underway with regard to the Brady law and other federal firearms issues. Despite pronouncements in 1996 about a moratorium on new gun laws, federal gun law grew by more than 13% that year. That's more new federal law in one year than we've seen in almost any *decade*.

Failure to comply with new laws and regulations can have serious consequences to you personally, even if you believe your constitutional rights have been compromised. In fact, many experts have noted that increasing latitudes are being taken by some governmental authorities with respect to constitutional guarantees. Legislative and regulatory changes present serious risks to currently law-abiding people, since what is legal today may not be tomorrow. The entire body of U.S. law is growing at a significant rate and it represents some potential for threats to freedoms Americans have always enjoyed. It is prudent to take whatever steps you feel are reasonable to minimize any risks.

<u>New laws may be passed at any time, and it is your responsibility to be fully up-to-date when handling firearms under all circumstances. The information contained in this book is guaranteed to age.</u>

GUN SAFETY and Concealed-Handgun Training 8

Many fine books and classes exist that teach the current wisdom on gun safety and use. In Texas, some of the best public classes are given by the Texas Parks and Wildlife Dept. and the Texas State Rifle Association, both listed in Appendix C. There are also firearms proficiency and safety trainers spread across the state, with thousands of hunting instructors for Parks and Wildlife. The list of certified CHL trainers is available on request from the Dept. of Public Safety and posted on their website.

When studying firearm safety (and every American should), you will likely come across the Ten Commandments of Gun Safety. These well-intentioned lists have serious drawbacks—no two lists are ever the same and there are many more than ten rules to follow for safe gun use. In addition, hunters must learn many rules that don't apply to other shooters. For instance, a hunter should never openly carry game—it makes you an unwitting target of other hunters.

The Commandments of Safety are actually a way of saying, "Here's how people have accidents with guns." Each rule implies a kind of mishap. It's good exercise to look at each rule and read between the lines to find its counterpart—the potential disaster the rule will help you avoid. For example, Rule 1 translates into, "People have accidents with guns that they think are empty." Always keep in mind the prime directive: Take time to be safe instead of forever being sorry.

THE GUN OWNER'S COMMANDMENTS OF SAFETY

1–Treat every gun as if it is loaded until you have personally proven otherwise.

2–Always keep a gun pointed in a safe direction.

3–Don't touch the trigger until you're ready to fire.

4–Be certain of your target and what is beyond it before pulling the trigger.

5–Keep a gun you carry discretely holstered or otherwise concealed unless you're ready to use it.

6–Use but never rely on the safety.

7–Never load a gun until ready to use. Unload a gun immediately after use.

8–Only use ammunition that exactly matches the markings on your gun.

9–Always read and follow manufacturers' instructions carefully.

10–At a shooting range, always keep a gun pointed downrange.

11–Always obey a range officer's commands immediately.

12–Always wear adequate eye and ear protection when shooting.

13–If a gun fails to fire: a) keep it pointed in a safe direction; b) wait thirty seconds in case of a delayed firing; c) unload the gun carefully, avoiding exposure to the breech.

14–Don't climb fences or trees, or jump logs or ditches with a chambered round.

15–Be able to control the direction of the muzzle even if you stumble.

16–Keep the barrel and action clear of obstructions.

17–Avoid carrying ammunition that doesn't match the gun you are carrying.

18–Be aware that customized guns may require ammunition that doesn't match the gun's original markings.

19–Store guns with the action open.

20–Store ammunition and guns separately, and out of reach of children and careless adults.

21–Never pull a gun toward you by the muzzle.

22–Never horseplay with a firearm.

23–Never shoot at a hard flat surface, or at water, to prevent ricochets.

24–Be sure you have an adequate backstop for target shooting.

25–On open terrain with other people present, keep guns pointed upwards, or downwards and away from the people.

26–Never handle a gun you are not familiar with.

27–Learn to operate a gun empty before attempting to load and shoot it.

28–Be cautious transporting a loaded firearm in a vehicle.

29–Never lean a firearm where it may slip and fall.

30–Do not use alcohol or mood-altering drugs when you are handling firearms.

31–When loading or unloading a firearm, always keep the muzzle pointed in a safe direction.

32–Never use a rifle scope instead of a pair of binoculars.

33–Always remember that removing the magazine (sometimes called the clip) from semi-automatic and automatic weapons may still leave a live round, ready to fire, in the chamber.

34–Never rely on one empty cylinder next to the barrel of a revolver as a guarantee of safety, since different revolvers rotate in opposite directions.

35–Never step into a boat holding a loaded firearm.

36–It's difficult to use a gun safely until you become a marksman.

37–It's difficult to handle a gun safely if you need corrective lenses and are not wearing them.

38–Know the effective range and the maximum range of a firearm and the ammunition you are using.

39–Be sure that anyone with access to a firearm kept in a home understands its safe use.

40–Don't fire a large caliber weapon if you cannot control the recoil.

41–Never put your finger in the trigger guard when drawing a gun from a holster.

42–Never put your hand in front of the cylinder of a revolver when firing.

43–Never put your hand in back of the slide of a semiautomatic pistol when firing.

44–Always leave the hammer of a revolver resting over an empty chamber.

45–Never leave ammunition around when cleaning a gun.

46–Clean firearms after they have been used. A dirty gun is not as safe as a clean one.

47–Never fire a blank round directly at a person. Blanks can blind, maim, and at close range, they can kill.

48–Only use modern firearms in good working condition, and ammunition that is fresh.

49–Accidents don't happen, they are caused, and it's up to you and you alone to prevent them in all cases. Every "accident" that ever happened could have been avoided. Where there are firearms there is a need for caution.

50–Always think first and shoot second.

It is the responsibility of every American to prevent firearms from being instruments of tragedy.

TEACH YOUR CHILDREN WELL

School Firearms Safety Program

Texas school districts are authorized and "strongly encouraged," under Education Code §21.118, to provide firearms safety programs for students in grades Kindergarten through 12. The districts must consult with a certified firearms instructor before implementing a program, and the program must meet the standards set by the National Rifle Association Eddie Eagle Children's Gun Safety Course.

Parents may give written notice to deny firearm safety training for their children, and the school district must comply. At no time may a student on school property be allowed to handle a readily dischargeable firearm.

Keeping Children Safe

Choosing to own a firearm—or choosing not to—has serious implications for the safety of your children and family. Your ability to respond in an emergency or not, and a child's dangerous access to a loaded firearm without your approval, should motivate you to take serious precautions for safety where firearms are concerned.

Firearms are dangerous; they're supposed to be dangerous; they wouldn't be very valuable if they weren't dangerous. The same as with power tools, automobiles, medicines, kitchen knives, balconies, swimming pools, electricity and everything else, it is up to responsible adults and their actions to help ensure the safety of those they love and the rest of the community.

In Texas these are not just good ideas, it's the law. A firearm owner has a direct responsibility to control a child's access to a loaded firearm (see Penal Code §46.13). Knowing about child safety and guns is required by DPS as part of the instruction needed to qualify for a CHL.

It is your responsibility to see that your own children, children who might visit you and careless adults are prevented from unauthorized access to any firearms you possess.

A delicate balance exists between keeping a gun immediately ready for response in an emergency, and protecting it from careless adults and children. This is the paradox of home-defense firearms. The more out-of-reach a gun is for safety's sake, the less accessible it is for self-defense (also for safety's sake).

Secured Storage

Leaving a loaded gun *out in the open* where careless adults or children could get at it is not being responsible and subjects you to criminal charges if an accident occurs.

Putting a loaded gun in *a hard-to-find spot* may fool some kids (and it's better than doing nothing), but remember how easily you found your folks' stuff when you were a kid.

Putting a gun in *a hard-to-get-to spot* (like the top of a closet) has advantages over hard-to-find spots when small children (like toddlers) are involved. Remember that kids reach an age where they like to climb. And you really have no idea what goes on when the baby-sitter is around.

Hinged *false picture frames*, when done well, provide a readily available firearm that most people will simply never notice. The frame must be in a spot that can't be bumped, and if ever the frame is detected its value is completely and immediately compromised.

Flexible plastic trigger tags warn that a gun is loaded, but they provide a low level of child-proofing since they are typically designed to be removed easily.

Combination gun locks eliminate the key problem, but mustn't be forgotten. If written down somewhere handy they too may be discovered. Many are difficult or impossible to operate in the dark. A number of push-button lock designs have been introduced which are made to fit directly into a handgun's mechanism. Trigger locks on loaded guns are highly dangerous.

Gun locks can be effective in preventing accidents but are completely compromised if a child can get at the key. The location of the key then becomes the paradox factor in keeping the gun at-the-ready yet safe. The closer together you keep the gun and its key the less safety the lock provides.

Gun safes used properly can prevent accidents and provide reasonable access to personal firearms, but it is an expensive option. Many people with gun collections keep their firearms in a floor-standing safe, for theft and fire protection, simultaneously providing a high degree of accident proofing. Single-gun handgun safes are made for floor or wall mounting and use finger touch buttons that can be operated quickly in the dark. This is an excellent option for keeping a gun available yet highly protected from unauthorized use. Keep batteries fresh. Safes work best when you're away. If you're present, a home invasion makes a gun safe an obvious target and almost useless.

A home that doesn't have many visitors and never has kids around faces different challenges than a home with four kids growing up, when it comes to staying safe. Be sure your home is safe for your kids—safe from those who would do you harm, and safe from the potential for harm your own home holds.

Disabling

Disabling a gun provides a safety margin. The more disabled a gun is the greater the safety, but the more difficult it becomes to bring the gun to bear if it should be needed.

The least disabled condition, and hence the least safe (though better than nothing), is a safety lever engaged on a semi-automatic or an appropriate empty cylinder on a revolver.

An unloaded firearm is disabled in a sense, and incapable of firing, though that reverses completely upon the presence of ammunition. The margin of safety here, for both preventing accidents and providing defense, is as wide as the distance between the gun and its ammunition.

Removing a firing pin or otherwise disassembling a firearm represents a high degree of disabling, essentially lowering chances of accidents to zero, and removing the possibility of putting the weapon to use in an emergency.

Keeping no firearm at home eliminates the ability to respond for safety if necessary, and still leaves a child at risk when visiting friends (especially if the child is not firearms aware).

The bottom line is that there are no perfect solutions, and life has risks. You trade some for others, and make personal choices that affect everything you do. Be sure you make the hard choices necessary to keep your family safe in your own home.

One Man's Approach

Internationally recognized firearms instructor and author Massad Ayoob believes it's wiser to educate your children than attempting to childproof your gun. For a detailed discussion of his approach to guns and child safety, read his booklet, *Gun-Proof Your Children,* available from Bloomfield Press.

The Eddie Eagle Program

If you look behind all the hot political rhetoric, you'll notice that the main provider of firearms safety training in America is the National Rifle Association, fulfilling a century-old historic tradition that is actually embodied in federal law. Handgun Control, Inc. and the NRA agree that child accidents are tragic and that responsible citizens must take steps to protect youngsters. In response to this well perceived need, the NRA developed its highly acclaimed and widely used Eddie Eagle Safety Program. For teacher lesson plans, class materials, parent kits, video tapes, coloring books, posters and more, contact the NRA, listed in the Appendix.

THE EDDIE EAGLE
SAFETY RULES FOR KIDS —
If you find a gun:
STOP!
Don't touch.
Leave the area.
Tell an adult.

HOW WELL DO YOU KNOW YOUR GUN?

Safe and effective use of firearms demands that you understand your weapon thoroughly. This knowledge is best gained through a combination of reading, classes and practice with a qualified instructor. The simple test below will help tell you if you are properly trained in the use of firearms. If you're not sure what all the terms mean, can you be absolutely sure that you're qualified to handle firearms safely?

☐ Action
☐ Ammunition
☐ Automatic
☐ Ballistics
☐ Barrel
☐ Black powder
☐ Bolt
☐ Bore
☐ Break action
☐ Breech
☐ Buckshot
☐ Bullet
☐ Butt
☐ Caliber
☐ Cartridge
☐ Case
☐ Casing
☐ Centerfire
☐ Chamber
☐ Checkering
☐ Choke
☐ Clip
☐ Cock
☐ Comb
☐ Cylinder
☐ Discharge
☐ Dominant eye
☐ Effective range
☐ Firearm
☐ Firing Pin
☐ Firing Line

☐ Forearm
☐ Fouling
☐ Frame
☐ Gauge
☐ Grip
☐ Grip panels
☐ Grooves
☐ Gunpowder
☐ Half cock
☐ Hammer
☐ Handgun
☐ Hangfire
☐ Hunter orange
☐ Ignition
☐ Kneeling
☐ Lands
☐ Lever action
☐ Magazine
☐ Mainspring
☐ Maximum range
☐ Misfire
☐ Muzzle
☐ Muzzleloader
☐ Pattern
☐ Pistol
☐ Powder
☐ Primer
☐ Projectile
☐ Prone
☐ Pump action
☐ Receiver

☐ Repeater
☐ Revolver
☐ Rifle
☐ Rifling
☐ Rimfire
☐ Safety
☐ Sear
☐ Semi-automatic
☐ Shell
☐ Shooting positions
☐ Shot
☐ Shotgun
☐ Sights
☐ Sighting-in
☐ Sitting
☐ Smokeless powder
☐ Smoothbore
☐ Standing
☐ Stock
☐ Trigger
☐ Trigger guard
☐ Unplugged shotgun

CONCEALED-HANDGUN TRAINING

Texas requires its Concealed-Handgun-License (CHL) holders to study legal issues related to firearms, use of deadly force and more (see Chapter 2 for details), and to pass written and handgun proficiency tests in order to qualify for the license. The law as of **2013** requires the course to be 4 to 6 hours in length. The written test is based on a set of questions created by DPS and provided to instructors. Instructors administer the test at the end of the class. Handgun proficiency standards are developed by DPS and appear in Chapter 2 and on the inside back cover. The details are subject to change. Check our website or with DPS for news. The subjects you must study in the CHL course are based on the statutory requirements and regulations issued by DPS. Here are some sample test questions CHL applicants—and all responsible gun owners—probably should know:

Areas of Study

1–Where are firearms prohibited in Texas?
   (At least 10 places, study chapter 2)
2–What are the penalties for improper display of a handgun?
   (It depends on the charges that are filed, study chapter 5)
3–What risks exist in drawing a firearm in public?
   (Could be used to justify a self-defense claim by another party, accidental discharge, discharge in prohibited area, more, study chapter 5)
4–When does state law justify the use of deadly force?
   (The circumstances are described, study chapter 5)
5–What factors mitigate the strict legal definitions for justifiable use of deadly force?
   (This is a complex issue frequently subject to debate and interpretation, fact-intensive and very specific to the given circumstances, study chapters 5, 8, and other books, such as In The Gravest Extreme, *by Massad Ayoob)*
6–What responsibility does a shooter have for shots fired that miss the intended target?
   (Severe liabilities and penalties can result from the effect of stray bullets, study chapters 4 and 5)
7–Can you bring a firearm into a bar?
   (Usually prohibited, but certain exceptions apply, study chapter 2)
8–What types of weapons are illegal?
   (For federal- and state-law restrictions, study chapter 3)
9–Who can legally bear arms in Texas?

(Age, background, mental condition, residency and more are taken into account, study chapter 1)

10–Under what circumstances can minors bear arms?
(Study chapters 1 and 6)

11–How can firearms be carried throughout the state?
(Different rules apply depending on what you're doing, for minors and for a person with a concealed handgun license, study chapters 1, 2 and 5)

12–What are the requirements for getting a carry license?
(Personal background, training, testing and a fee are involved, study chapters 2 and 8)

13–What do you have to do to ship firearms or carry them with you on a train, plane, or as you travel by car?
(Federal regulations control shipping, study chapter 1, state laws control "reciprocity," see chapter 2)

14–Under what circumstances can you practice target shooting outdoors?
(Official shooting ranges are OK, regulations and trespass law applies to most other land, study chapter 4)

15–How much judgment is involved in deciding whether you can use deadly force in a situation?
(No easy answers to this, read everything you can find on the subject, study chapters 5 and 8, and recognize that in using deadly force you accept very definite and substantial legal risks that cannot be fully assessed before the fact.)

16–What are the main rules of firearm safety?
(We've come up with 50, more exist, study chapter 8.)

17–What types of weapons are suitable for self-defense, and what are the best choices for you?
(A very important topic not covered in this book. You should discuss this at length with your instructor and other professionals, read some of the excellent books available.)

18–How do the various types of firearms operate?
(This topic should be covered by your instructor.)

19–What are the options for carrying a concealed handgun?
(This topic should be covered by your instructor.)

20–Have any new laws passed that you should know about?
(This requires ongoing information and vigilance. Send Bloomfield Press a self-addressed stamped envelope for an update when one becomes available, or visit gunlaws.com.)

21–Are you mentally prepared to use deadly force?
(Mental conditioning for the use of deadly force is a critical component in preparing for armed defense if it should ever be needed, and one that is not easily addressed. Until a moment arrives you may never truly know the answer to this question.)

Practice Test Questions

Approved CHL-training programs use test questions that are developed and approved by the Dept. of Public Safety. The questions presented here are designed for study—to challenge your understanding, provoke thought and encourage discussion. Some of these have obvious yes-no or true-false (T or F) answers, while others require a deeper understanding and must be answered with "maybe" or "it depends." *Some questions defy clear answers.* If you have trouble with any of these, ask your firearms safety instructor for assistance.

1–Is it legal to point an empty gun at a person?
2–Is it legal to point an empty gun at anything?
3–Is it legal to put a gun in your pocket?
4–Is home defense with a machine gun legal?
5–Never tell family members that you keep a loaded gun in the house. T or F?
6–Always tell family members that you keep a loaded gun in the house. T or F?
7–Texas requires you to lock your guns in a safe. T or F?
8–Texas requires you to put a trigger lock on your guns. T or F?
9–Does the law say you may kill if your life is in danger?
10–Does the law say you may kill if your friend is in danger?
11–If a peace officer is in danger may you shoot to kill?
12–You may conceal weapons in Texas without a license. T or F?
13–Carrying weapons openly in Texas, unlicensed, is OK. T or F?
14–A CHL prohibits concealing a bayonet. T or F?
15–A CHL prohibits bringing a gun onto a plane. T or F?
16–A CHL prohibits concealing explosives. T or F?
17–It's always illegal to bring a gun into a bar. T or F?
18–A bar owner may carry a handgun in the bar. T or F?
19–A bar owner may allow the employees to be armed. T or F?
20–A bar owner may allow patrons to be armed. T or F?
21–Drawing a gun to settle a severe argument is legal. T or F?
22–Drawing a gun wrongly may lead to criminal charges. T or F?
23–Drawing a gun wrongly is allowed if you don't shoot. T or F?
24–If someone else draws a gun, you may too. T or F?
25–If your life is immediately at risk you may draw a gun. T or F?
26–May you draw a gun to stop a serious crime in progress?
27–May you draw a gun to stop a kidnapping?
28–May you draw a gun to stop a robbery?
29–May you draw a gun to stop an armed robbery?
30–May you draw a gun to stop a sexual assault?
31–May you draw a gun to stop child molestation?

32–May you draw a gun to stop a serious traffic violation?

33–May you draw a gun to stop criminal trespass?

34–May you draw a gun to stop an arsonist?

35–May you draw a gun to stop vandals?

36–May you draw a gun to stop shoplifting?

37–May you draw a gun to stop an escape from the custody of law enforcement?

38–May you shoot in items 24 through 37 above?

39–Do you want to ever have to shoot someone?

40–All states treat self-defense shooting the same way. T or F?

41–Federal law guarantees your rights no matter what. T or F?

42–Shooting criminals is legal if they are "in the act." T or F?

43–You should declare you have a CHL to the police. True of false?

44–Never mention your CCW license unless asked. T or F?

45–It's OK to let a concealed handgun show occasionally. T or F?

46–If you shoot a criminal you don't have to report it. T or F?

47–You should report any shooting incident to authorities. T or F?

48–If you shoot a criminal leave the body where it falls. T or F?

49–If you shoot a criminal outside your home drag him inside. T or F?

50–You're normally aware of everything around you. T or F?

51–When danger lurks, your awareness always goes up. T or F?

52–Even if you're cautious, danger can surprise you. T or F?

53–When you're surprised you're not always predictable. T or F?

54–Acting under stress can lead to surprising responses. T or F?

55–Name the four modes of mental awareness.

56–Describe the four modes of mental awareness.

57–The only official way to shoot is the Weaver stance. T or F?

58–You must grip a firearm with both hands to be legal. T or F?

59–Any shooting position you like is legal for self-defense. T or F?

60–If you pass your CHL exam, you're perfectly qualified. T or F?

61–A CHL increases your personal safety. T or F?

62–A CHL increases your ability to respond. T or F?

63–A CHL will allow you to take back the streets. T or F?

64–With a CHL you may go wherever you want. T or F?

65–If a man charges you with a knife may you shoot him?

66–If a man charges you with a bat may you shoot him?

67–If a woman charges you with a bat may you shoot her?

68–If a man hits your spouse with a bat may you shoot him?

69–If a man threatens you with a bat may you shoot him?

70–If a man enrages you for no reason may you shoot him?

71–If a man won't let you get gasoline may you change his mind by drawing a gun?

72–If someone starts shooting someone else, may you shoot the first person to stop the attack?

73–Methods for controlling a violent confrontation are something that cannot be learned. T or F?

74–Will you need a gun more after you have a CHL than you did before you had a permit?

75–Have you ever witnessed a serious crime that would justify drawing a gun, such as a kidnapping, sexual assault, armed robbery or murder?

76–How much more likely are you to witness a serious crime once you have a CHL?

77–Is it a good idea to qualify in your CHL proficiency test with the same gun you plan on carrying regularly?

78–Unless you need to use it in an emergency, you should never let a concealed handgun show. T or F?

79–If you sell a gun to a person who uses it to commit a crime can you be charged with a crime?

80–What happens if you are found in Texas with an unregistered handgun in your possession?

81–What is the legal maximum distance for a justifiable self-defense shooting in Texas?

82–Texas has preemption, which means that cities and counties may pass their own gun laws. T or F?

83–Many cities in Texas have different gun laws that you must know and follow. T or F?

84–Many locations in Texas interpret the laws differently and are allowed to do so by their courts. T or F?

85–What is a "citizens arrest," how do you make one, and is it a good idea to make one if you witness a crime?

86–If you see a drug deal going down, may you draw your gun and use deadly force to stop it?

87–If you see a prostitute working in your neighborhood, may you threaten deadly force, without using it, to make the person leave?

88–If you use a gun legitimately to defend yourself there is a possibility you will be charged with a serious offense. T or F?

89–Many people who are charged with murder claim self-defense or accidental discharge. T or F?

90–Many people who use deadly force in self-defense are charged with murder. T or F?

91–The person who survives a lethal confrontation is often referred to as the defendant by the authorities. T or F?

92–If someone starts hitting you is that justification for threatening to use deadly force?

93–If someone starts hitting you is that considered justification for using deadly force?

94–If someone says they're going to start hitting you is that justification for threatening to use deadly force?

95–If someone hits you repeatedly in the face until you're bleeding and then stops, you may draw and shoot the attacker. T or F?

96–If someone comes into your place of business and commits a robbery, may you respond with deadly force?

97–A man says he's going to shoot you and sticks his hand in his pocket. May you shoot him first?

98–A woman says she's going to shoot you and sticks her hand in her pocketbook. May you shoot her first?

99–If you are armed may you operate as a free-lance police officer?

100–The police may use or threaten deadly force in certain situations that you may not. T or F?

101–Tactics refers to the steps you take in an emergency. T or F?

102–Strategy refers to the plans you make in the event you are ever in an emergency. T or F?

103–A crime avoidance plan includes tactics and strategy. T or F?

104–"Shoot first and ask questions later," is bad advice for personal self-defense. T or F?

105–It's always better not to shoot at someone if you can safely avoid it. T or F?

106–If you get a CHL, does that change anything with respect to the number and seriousness of the threats you normally face in your daily routine?

107–Why does it make sense for you personally to get a concealed-handgun license?

108–If you own a gun, spending regular practice time on a shooting range is a good idea.

In addition to questions such as the ones presented here, you should study material and be able to answer questions on topics not covered in *The Texas Gun Owner's Guide*, such as:

> What are the various types of firearms, what are their component parts, and how do they operate; what are the various types of ammunition; what are the criteria for selecting a self-defense weapon and ammunition; what are the options for holsters and carrying weapons; how can you reduce the chances of unintentional firing and what are the primary firearm safety rules; what affects aiming and firing accurately; how should guns and ammunition be stored; how are guns cleaned, lubricated and checked, what are the tactics and strategies for personal self-defense and having weapons accessible; what alternatives are there to confrontation; how can threatening situations be managed; how can confrontations be avoided.

JUDGMENTAL SHOOTING
Shoot—Don't-Shoot Decisions

All gun owners, and CHL holders in particular, should study issues related to judgmental shooting. Anyone considering armed response needs an understanding of the issues involved.

The decision to use deadly force is rarely a clear-cut choice. Regardless of your familiarity with the laws, your degree of training, the quality of your judgmental skills and your physical location and condition at the time of a deadly threat, the demands placed on you at the critical moment are as intense as anything you will normally experience in your life, and your actual performance is an unknown.

Every situation is different. Answers to many questions relating to deadly force are subject to debate. To be prepared for armed response you must recognize that such situations are not black or white, and that your actions, no matter how well intentioned, will be evaluated by others, probably long after you act.

The chances that you will come away from a lethal encounter without any scars—legal, physical or psychological—are small, and the legal risks are substantial. That's why it's usually best to practice prevention and avoidance rather than confrontation, whenever possible.

Most people can think about it this way: You've gotten along this far in life without ever having pulled a weapon on someone, much less having fired it. The odds of that changing once you have a CHL are about the same, practically zero. A concealed handgun may make you feel more secure, but it doesn't change how safe your surroundings actually are, in the places you normally travel, one bit. And it certainly isn't safe to think of a firearm as a license (or talisman) for walking through potentially dangerous areas you would otherwise avoid like the plague.

Remember that the person holding a gun after a shooting is frequently thought of as the bad guy—the perpetrator—even if it's you and you acted in self-defense. The person who is shot has a different, more sympathetic name—the victim—and gets the benefit of a prosecutor even if, perhaps, you learn later it's a hardened criminal with a long record. Maybe your defense will improve if it is indeed a serious repeat offender, but you won't know that until after the fact, and don't count on it. If you ever have to raise a gun to a criminal, you'll find out quickly how good they can be at portraying you as the bad guy and themselves as the helpless innocents, at the mercy of a crazed wacko—you.

Situational Analysis

Think about the deadly force encounters described below, and consider discussing them with your firearms-safety trainer:

1–If you are being seriously attacked by a man with a club, is it legal for you to aim for his leg so you can stop the attack without killing him?

2–If you enter your home and find a person looting your possessions are you justified in shooting?

3–If you enter your home and find a person looting your possessions, who runs out the back door as he hears you arrive, can you shoot him to stop him from escaping?

4–If you enter your home and find a person looting your possessions, who turns and whirls toward you when you enter, literally scaring you to death, may you shoot and expect to be justified?

5–If you enter your home and find a stranger in it who charges you with a knife, may you shoot?

6–A stranger in your home has just stabbed your spouse and is about to stab your spouse again. May you shoot the stranger from behind to stop the attack?

7–As you walk past a park at night, you notice a woman tied to a tree and a man tearing off her clothing. May you use deadly force to stop his actions?

8–A police officer is bleeding badly and chasing a man in prison coveralls who runs right past you. May you shoot the fleeing suspect while he is in close range to you?

9–You're in your home at night when a man with a ski mask on comes through an open window in the hallway. May you shoot?

10–You're in your home at night, sleeping, when a noise at the other end of the house awakens you. Taking your revolver you quietly walk over to investigate and notice a short person going through your silverware drawer, 45 feet from where you're standing. The person doesn't notice you. May you shoot?

11–As you approach your parked car in a dark and remote section of a parking lot, three youthful toughs approach you from three separate directions. You probably can't unlock your vehicle and get in before they reach you and you're carrying a gun. What should you do?

12–From outside a convenience store you observe what clearly appears to be an armed robbery—four people are being held at gunpoint while the store clerk is putting money into a paper bag. You're armed. What should you do?

13–You're waiting to cross the street in downtown and a beggar asks you for money. He's insistent and begins to insult you when you refuse to ante up. Finally, he gets loud and belligerent and says he'll kill you if you don't give him ten dollars. May you shoot him?

14–You get in your car, roll down the windows, and before you can drive off a man sticks a knife in the window and orders you to get out. Can you shoot him?

15-You get in your car and before you start it a man points a gun at you and tells you to get out. You have a gun in the pocket on the door, another under the seat, and a gun in a holster in your pants. What should you do?

16–Before you get in your car, a man with a gun comes up from behind, demands your car keys, takes them, and while holding you at gun point, starts your car and drives away. Can you shoot at him while he's escaping?

17–You're walking to your car in the mall parking lot after a movie when two armed hoods jump out of a shadow and demand your money. You've got a gun in your back pocket. What should you do?

18–A masked person with a gun stops you on the street, demands and takes your valuables, then flees down the street on foot. You're carrying a concealed handgun. What should you do?

19–A youngster runs right by you down the street and an old lady shouts, "Stop him, he killed my husband!" May you shoot to stop his getaway?

20–You're at work when two ornery-looking dudes amble in. You can smell trouble, so you walk to a good vantage point behind a showcase. Sure enough, they pull guns and announce a stick-up. You and your four employees are armed and there are several customers in the store. What's your move?

21–Your friend and you have been drinking, and now you're arguing over a football bet. You say the spread was six points, he says four. There's $500 hanging in the balance of a five-point game, and it represents your mortgage payment. He pulls a knife and says, "Pay me or I'll slice you up." You've got a gun in your pocket. What should you do?

22–At a gas station, the lines are long, it's hot, and the guy next in line starts getting surly. You're not done pumping and he hits you in the face and tells you to finish up. He shuts off your pump and says he'll kick your butt if you don't move on. Should you pull your gun to put him in his place?

Observations about the situations presented:

1–It's an unlikely case where the justification to use deadly force would be justification to intentionally wound. Firing and missing is a different story (and you are accountable for every round fired), but it could be argued that if the threat wasn't enough to use deadly force then there was no right to shoot at all. Any shooting is use of lethal force, and has lethal potential regardless of your ability to aim under extreme duress; a person can die from fright, loss of blood, infection. In the desperate seconds where such a shot could be fired, attempting the most difficult shot known—winging a moving limb—is a dubious strategy. It costs critical time and wastes a shot that may be crucial to your survival. The law does not provide for justifiable wounding. Hollywood vigorously promotes the concept of *shoot to wound*, but it's about as valid as most other depictions of things gun in the movies.

2–Not enough information is provided to make an informed choice.

3–Although Texas statutes do justify the use of deadly force in certain property crimes and to prevent escape under certain conditions, acting in such a situation, according to many experts, presents an unacceptable legal risk to the shooter. Once the danger to you is over—and it generally is once the criminal is fleeing—it is probably best to hold your fire.

4–Probably. But do you always enter your home prepared for mortal combat? Does your story have other holes a prosecutor will notice?

5–It's hard to imagine not being justified in this situation, but stranger things have happened.

6–It's hard to imagine not being justified in this situation, but stranger things have happened. Will the bullet exit the attacker and wound your spouse?

7–Not necessarily, since you don't know if the people are consenting adults who like this sort of thing. A seasoned police officer might cautiously approach the couple, weapon drawn, and with words instead of force determine what's happening, and then make further choices depending on the outcome.

8–Not enough information is provided to make an informed choice.

9–Probably, though a well-trained expert might instead confront the intruder from a secure position and succeed in holding the person for arrest, which is no easy task. The longer you must hold the suspect the greater the risk to you. Armed and from good cover, you might just convince the intruder to leave the way he came.

10–Perhaps, but the distance and lack of immediate threat will make for a difficult explanation when the police arrive, and if the perpetrator has an accomplice that you didn't notice, the danger to you is severe. If the perpetrator turns out to be a thief with a long rap sheet, you might not even be charged. If it turns out that the intruder is 11 years old your court defense will be extremely difficult. Remember, you're obligated to not shoot if you don't absolutely have to. A shot would be in conflict with a prime safety rule—clearly identify your target before firing. Has your training prepared you for this?

11–That's a good question, and you should never have parked there in the first place.

12–Call for assistance, go to a defensible position, continue to observe, and recognize that charging into such a volatile situation is incredibly risky for all parties.

13–You are never justified in using deadly force in response to verbal provocation alone, no matter how severe.

14–The prosecutor will make it clear that if you could have stepped on the gas and escaped, the threat to you would have ended, and the need to shoot did not exist. If you were boxed into a parking space, the need to defend yourself would be hard for a prosecutor to refute. These things often come down to the exact circumstances and the quality of the attorneys.

15–Get out quietly and don't provoke someone who has the drop on you. All your guns are no match for a drawn weapon. This is where a real understanding of tactics comes into play.

16–The statutes suggest that you may fire in this case, but the legal risk to you is so severe (as described in #3 above) that it's probably best to hold your fire. Once the threat to you is over, the justification for using lethal force is less reliable.

17–Not enough information is provided to make an informed choice.

18–Anyone crazy enough to rob you at gunpoint must be considered capable of doing anything, and the smart move is to avoid further confrontation and stay alive. You could draw and fire, but the justification for using deadly force on the street is not as reliable if your life is not in immediate danger (even though Texas statutes say it is permissible). If you miss in the adrenaline-filled rush of the moment your shot could pose a threat to a bystander, and it could encourage return fire from the fleeing criminal. You could chase after him, but it's extremely unwise and risky to you. Many experts advise that once the danger to you is over don't escalate the situation by firing.

19–You don't have enough information. When in doubt, don't shoot.

20–This is where strategy and tactics are critical. If you allow your employees to carry and are prepared for armed defense of your premises you better get plenty of advanced training in gunfighting and self-defense. You'll need it to survive, and you'll need it to meet the legal challenges later. If a customer gets shot by one of your own, even if you get the villains, you're in for big time trouble and grief. If no one gets hurt but the criminals, you'll be a hero. Either outcome remains burned in memory. Tough choice.

21–Too many killings occur between people who know each other. Your chance of a successful legal defense in a case like this are remote. Would he really have killed you? Probably not. Did you have any other options besides killing him? Probably so. Have you fought like this before? Maybe. What would the witnesses say? Nothing you could count on, and probably all the wrong things. The fact that you have a firearm and can use it doesn't mean you should, the likelihood of absolutely having to use it is small, and using it to settle a bet with a friend over a point spread may not be the worst thing you can do, but it's close.

22–Cap your tank and move on, you don't need the grief. Or go into the station and tell them what's happened, preparing yourself mentally for further hostilities. Go to a defensible position and call the police. Avoid a confrontation at all costs. See what the other guy does before you do anything. Decide to take another course in how to handle volatile situations and difficult people. And realize that because you have a CHL and some training doesn't solve any problems or reduce your risks in life.

RECOMMENDED READING

Knowledge is power, and the more you have the better off you are. Some trainers will require that you read books on personal safety, crime avoidance, self-defense and the use of deadly force. **Whether your instructor requires it or not, decide to read about this critical subject.** The single best book on the subject is probably *In The Gravest Extreme*, by Massad Ayoob. If you're concerned about preserving your right to keep and bear arms, read up on being effective politically. Don't make the mistake of endlessly studying the Bill of Rights so you can win debates—if you win all your debates you're actually losing. You don't want to win debates, you want to win friends and influence people. Bloomfield Press now carries a line of books with this focus— Getting To Yes, How To Win Friends And Influence People, Confrontational Politics and other titles that supercharge your efforts. See all these fine books online at: http://www.gunlaws.com

THE NOBLE USES OF FIREARMS

THE NOBLE USES OF FIREARMS

In the great din of the national firearms debate it's easy to lose sight of the noble and respectable place firearms hold and have always held in American life. While some gun use in America is criminal and despicable, other applications appeal to the highest ideals our society cherishes, and are enshrined in and ensured by statutes on the books:

- Protecting your family in emergencies
- Personal safety and self defense
- Preventing and deterring crimes
- Detaining criminals for arrest
- Guarding our national borders
- Deterring and resisting terrorism
- Preserving our interests abroad
- Helping defend our allies
- Overcoming tyranny
- International trade
- Emergency preparedness
- Obtaining food by hunting
- Commerce and employment
- Historical preservation and study
- Olympic competition
- Collecting
- Sporting pursuits
- Target practice
- Recreational shooting

News reports, by focusing almost exclusively on criminal misuse of firearms, create the false impression that firearms and crime are directly linked, when in fact almost all guns never have any link to crime whatsoever. The media judiciously ignore stories concerning legitimate self defense, which occur almost daily according to the FBI. There is silence on the effect the industry has on jobs in the manufacturing sector, contributions to the tax base, capital and investments, scientific advances, national trade and balance of payments, ballistics, chemistry, metallurgy, and, of course, the enjoyment of millions of decent people who use firearms righteously. Some people associate guns with crime, fear and danger, and want them to go away. Those who associate guns with liberty, freedom, honor, strength and safety understand the irreplaceable role firearms play in our lives.

It's interesting to note that the top three participant sports in the nation, measured by equipment sales, are exercise, the shooting sports, and golf. People know all about golf tournaments but many don't even know shooting sports exist, an indicator of the massive suppression of real news the media unethically perpetrates on the American public.

APPENDIX A
GLOSSARY OF TERMS

Words, when used in the law, often have special meanings you wouldn't expect from simply knowing the English language. For the complete legal description of these and other important terms, see each chapter of the criminal code and other legal texts dealing with language. The following plain English descriptions are provided for your convenience only.

ACT = A bodily movement, including speech.

ACTION = Single action, revolver, or semi-automatic action.

ACTOR = A person who may be criminally responsible in a criminal action, sometimes referred to as the "suspect."

AIR GUN = Any gun that discharges a pellet, BB or paintball by means of compressed air, gas propellant or spring.

AMUSEMENT PARK = A permanent indoor or outdoor facility with rides, in a county with a population of more than one million, on at least 75 acres, open to the public at least 120 days annually, with full time security guards and controlled access.

ARMOR-PIERCING AMMUNITION = Handgun ammunition designed primarily for penetrating metal or body armor.

BATFE = Bureau of Alcohol, Tobacco, Firearms and Explosives.

BENEFIT = Anything of economic value to a person or someone associated with that person.

BODILY INJURY = Physical pain, illness or impairment.

CHEMICAL DISPENSING DEVICE = A device that can cause an adverse psychological or physiological effect on a person. Small chemical dispensers sold commercially for personal protection are not included.

CHEMICALLY DEPENDENT PERSON = Someone who frequently or repeatedly drinks to excess or is a habitual drug user. SB60 §1-2 A person who has been convicted two times in the 10 years prior to application for a CHL license for a class B misdemeanor or greater involving the use of alcohol or a controlled substance is considered chemically dependent and automatically disqualifies the applicant.

CHL = Concealed Handgun License or Concealed Handgun Licensee.

192

CLUB = An instrument that can inflict serious bodily injury or death by striking a person. This includes, but isn't limited to, a blackjack, nightstick, tomahawk and mace.

CONDUCT = The actions you take or refrain from, and your thoughts about them.

CONCEALED HANDGUN = A handgun that can't be seen through ordinary observation.

CONVICTED = Found guilty of an offense by a court, even if the sentence is probation, the offender is discharged from community supervision, or the offender is pardoned, unless the pardon is granted for proof of innocence.

CRIMINAL INSTRUMENT = Anything that is normally legal but that is put to illegal use.

CRIMINAL NEGLIGENCE = A complex legal concept related to personal responsibility, determined in a court of law, covered in §6.01 through §6.04, and §8.07.

CULPABLE MENTAL STATE = An accountable state of mind. Specifically and in decreasing order of seriousness: intentionally, knowingly, recklessly or with criminal negligence, in the sense described by law.

DEADLY FORCE = Force that you know can cause death or serious physical injury.

DEADLY WEAPON = Anything made or adapted for lethal use or for inflicting serious bodily injury, including a firearm.

EXPLOSIVE WEAPON = An explosive or incendiary bomb, grenade, rocket or mine that can inflict serious bodily injury, death, substantial property damage, or a noise loud enough to cause public alarm or terror. Also included is any device for delivering or shooting an explosive weapon.

FELONY = A serious crime. An offense that carries a prison term of from six months to life. A Capital Felony (capital murder) is the most serious, and has a possible sentence of death. Texas uses lethal injection to inflict the penalty of death. A State Jail Felony is the least serious, and carries a possible sentence of six months. Felony fines may be up to $10,000 for an individual, and up to $20,000 for an enterprise.

FIREARM = A device that can (or can be readily converted to) expel a projectile through a barrel by using the energy of an explosion or burning substance. Antique or curio firearms made before 1899 and that may have an integral folding knife, are not firearms.

FIREARM SILENCER = Any device that can muffle the sound of a firearm.

GOVERNMENT = The recognized political structure within the state.

HANDGUN = A firearm designed, made or adapted for firing with one hand. Synonymous with sidearm.

HARM = Loss, disadvantage or injury to a person or someone that person is responsible for.

HOAX BOMB = A device that reasonably appears to be an explosive or incendiary device. A device that, by its design, causes alarm or reaction of any type by a public safety agency official or emergency volunteer agency is a hoax bomb.

ILLEGAL KNIFE = A knife with a blade over five and a half inches, a hand instrument designed to cut or stab by being thrown, a dagger (which includes but isn't limited to a dirk, stiletto and poniard), a bowie knife, a sword or a spear.

INDIVIDUAL = A living human being.

INTOXICATED = Having an alcohol concentration of 0.08 or more (the tolerance for truckers is zero), or being unable to function normally physically or mentally due to the use of alcohol or a controlled substance or drug or a combination of these.

KNIFE = Any bladed hand instrument that can inflict serious bodily injury or death by cutting or stabbing.

KNUCKLES = A hard substance that can be worn on a fist and can inflict serious bodily injury or death by striking.

LAW = Formal rules by which society controls itself. In Texas, the law means the Texas State Statutes, the state Constitution, the U.S. Constitution and statutes, city ordinances, county commissioners court orders, official court decisions, and rules adopted by law.

MACHINE GUN = A firearm capable of shooting more than two shots, without manually reloading, by a single pull of the trigger.

MISDEMEANOR = A crime less serious than a felony. An offense against the law that carries a sentence of imprisonment of up to 1 year. Misdemeanor fines can run up to $4,000 for an individual, and up to $10,000 for an enterprise.

PEACE OFFICER = Anyone duly appointed with legal authority to maintain public order and make arrests. Includes more than 26 categories (listed in Article 2.12 of the Code of Criminal Procedure, such as sheriffs, their deputies, an officer employed by the Texas Dept. of Health, and more.

PERSON = An individual, corporation, or association.

POSSESSION = Care, custody, control, or management.

PREMISES = Under CHL laws, *premises* includes real property and a recreational vehicle, whether it is motorized or designed to be towed, being used as temporary or permanent living quarters. In unlawful-carry law it is a building or portion of a building and omits streets, sidewalks, parking areas and more. Other laws have their own specific definitions.

PUBLIC PLACE = Anywhere the public can go.

PUBLIC SERVANT = Any officer or employee of any branch of government, either elected, appointed, or hired. Jurors, grand jurors, arbitrators, referees, attorneys or notary publics working for the government, candidates for public office, and a person performing government work under a claim of right even if not qualified.

QUALIFIED HANDGUN INSTRUCTOR = Someone certified by the Dept. of Public Safety to teach a concealed handgun course for a concealed-handgun license, and who may issue a Handgun Proficiency Certificate.

REAL PROPERTY = Land, and generally anything erected, growing on or affixed to the land.

REASONABLE BELIEF = A belief that an ordinary and prudent person would have in the same circumstances.

RECREATIONAL VEHICLE = Under CHL laws, an RV used as temporary or permanent living quarters, either motorized or designed to be towed, is a premises, and includes a travel trailer, camping trailer, truck camper, motor home and horse trailer with living quarters.

RECKLESS = Acting with an awareness of and conscious disregard for a risk so dangerous that it is a gross deviation from the standard of care that a reasonable person would follow.

SERIOUS BODILY INJURY = Injury that creates a reasonable risk of death or death itself. Also, injury that causes serious and permanent disfigurement, or loss or impairment of any bodily member or organ.

SHORT-BARREL FIREARM = A rifle with a barrel less than 16 inches, a shotgun with a barrel less than 18 inches, or any weapon made from a rifle or shotgun and less than 26 inches overall.

STUN GUN = A device that propels darts attached to wires, to deliver an electrical impulse capable of incapacitating a person.

SWITCHBLADE KNIFE = A knife with a blade that comes out of its handle automatically by centrifugal force, by gravity, or by pressing a button or other device on the handle.

UNLAWFUL = Anything that's criminal or a tort.

UNSOUND MIND = The mental condition of someone who has been judged mentally incompetent or mentally ill, who has been found not guilty of a crime by reason of insanity, or who has been diagnosed by a licensed physician as being unable to manage themselves or their personal affairs, or as suffering from depression, manic depression, or post-traumatic stress syndrome.

WATERCRAFT = Any boat, motorboat, vessel or personal watercraft, other than a seaplane on water, used or capable of being used for transportation on water.

ZIP GUN = A device not originally a firearm, which has been adapted to function like one.

APPENDIX
Crime and
Punishment Chart B

EXPLANATIONS

Type of Crime: Illegal activities are divided into these eight categories, to match the punishment to the crime. The category may be affected by how the crime is committed. Felonies are serious crimes, misdemeanors are less serious. Felonies remove the right to keep and bear arms, hold public office, vote, obtain certain types of employment and more.

Jail Term: These are the ranges for a first offense involving a gun; many crimes have special sentences. A capital felony, in addition to life imprisonment, carries a possible death penalty for first degree murder, which is administered by lethal injection.

Fines: These are maximums, which may be lowered at court discretion. Fines can be payable immediately or a court may grant permission to pay by a certain date or in installments.

Statute of Limitations: The period of time, from the discovery of an offense (or from the time when an offense should have been discovered with the exercise of reasonable diligence), within which a prosecution may begin (CCP Art. 12.01). There is no limitation on murder or manslaughter; 10 years for some kinds of theft, forgery, indecency with a child, and most forms of sexual assault; 7 years for misapplication of funds; 5 years for some kinds of theft, burglary, robbery, arson and some forms of sexual assault.

Offenses: The chart provides a partial list of offenses in each category, and exceptions often apply.

CRIME AND PUNISHMENT

Type of Crime	Max. Sent. 1st Offense	Max. Fine for Person	Max. Fine for Business	Statute of Limitation
Capital Felony	Death or Life in Jail	None	$20,000	None
Capital murder, which includes murder of a peace officer or firefighter while on duty.				
1st Degree Felony	5 Yrs.–Life	$10,000	$20,000	—
Murder, aggravated sexual assault, armed robbery, felony burglary of a habitation, shooting at a train and causing damage of $200,000 or more,				
2nd Degree Felony	2-20 Yrs.	$10,000	$20,000	—
Murder triggered by passion, manslaughter, aggravated assault, armed kidnapping, gun smuggling for profit, shooting at a train and causing damage of $100,000–$200,000.				
3rd Degree Felony	2-10 Yrs.	$10,000	$20,000	—
Deadly conduct with a firearm, unlawful possession of a firearm by a felon, carrying in a prohibited place, carrying a gun in a penal institution, most prohibited weapons offenses, taking peace officer's gun, shooting at a train causing damage of $20,000–$100,000.				
State Jail Felony	6 Mos.	$10,000	$20,000	—
Criminally negligent homicide, reckless injury to a child or an elderly or disabled person, aiding suicide where injury occurs, trying to take a gun from a peace officer, shooting at a train causing damage of $1,500–$20,000.				
Class A Misdemeanor	1 Year	$4,000	$10,000	—
Unlawful carrying of a handgun, possessing, making, transporting or selling a prohibited weapon or hoax bomb, allowing child access to a loaded firearm who causes injury or death, possession of knuckles, deliberately letting a concealed handgun show, intoxicated CHL holder while armed, CHL trespass under §30.06, CHL failure to depart if requested, causing bodily injury, unlawful discharge in a city of at least 100,000 population, shooting at a train causing damage of $500–$1500.				
Class B Misdemeanor	6 Mos.	$2,000	$10,000	—
Disorderly conduct with firearm, threatening bodily injury or provocative physical contact with a sports participant by a non-participant, shooting at train causing damage $20–$500.				
Class C Misdemeanor	None	$500	$2,000	—
Disorderly conduct, assisting suicide with no injury, reckless damage or destruction, allowing a child access to a loaded firearm, threatening bodily injury, provocative physical contact.				

THE PROPER C
AUTHORITIES

Regulations on guns and their use come from a lot of places. Listed with each authority are the addresses and phones of the nearest offices. All cities are in Texas (TX) unless indicated.

Attorney General 800-252-8011, 512-463-2100 PO Box 12548, Austin
    78711; 300 W. 15th St., Austin 78701
Bureau of Alcohol, Tobacco, Firearms and Explosives
    800-800-3855, 202-648-7777; 99 New York Ave. NE, Washington, DC
    20226
Bureau of Indian Affairs 202-208-3710, Dept. of Interior;
    1849 C St., N.W., Washington, D.C. 20240
Coastal Water Authority 713-658-9020 500 Dallas St.,
    One Allen Center, Suite 2800, Houston 77002

National Forests
Angelina National Forest , Angelina Ranger District
    936-897-1068 415 S. First St., Suite 110, Lufkin 75901
Caddo & Lyndon B. Johnson National Grasslands
    940-627-5475 1400 US 811287, Decatur 76234
Davy Crockett National Forest, Neches Ranger District
    936-655-22992 Highway 94, Apple Springs, 75926
Sabine National Forest, Yellowpine District, 409-625-1940
    201 South Palm Street, Hemphill 75948
Sam Houston National Forest Trinity Ranger District, 936-344-6205 394 FM
    1375 West, New Waverly, 77358
Rita Blanca National Grassland (in Cibola National Forest) 2113 Osuna Rd.,
    NE, Albuquerque, NM 87113
    505-346-3900

National Park and Recreational Areas
National Park Service Regional Office 505-988-6100
    PO Box 728, Santa Fe, NM 87504
National Parks, Seashore and Preserve Regional Office
    505-988-6011 National Parks Service, PO Box 728,
    Santa Fe, NM 87504-0728

Amistad Recreation Area 830-775-7491
    4121 Veterans Blvd., Del Rio 78840
Big Bend National Park 432-477-2251 PO Box 129
    Big Bend National Park, 79834
Big Thicket National Preserve 409-951-6725
    6044 FM420, Kountze 77625
Guadalupe Mountains National Park 915-828-3251
    HC 60, Box 400, Salt Flat 79847-9400
Lake Meredith Recreation Area 806-857-3151 Superintendent, National Park
    Service, Box 1460, Fritch 79036
Lyndon B. Johnson National Historical Park 830-868-7128
    PO Box 329, Johnson City 78636
Padre Island National Seashore 361-949-8068
    9405 South Padre Island Drive, Corpus Christi 78418
San Antonia Missions National Historical Park 210-534-8833 2202 Roosevelt
    Avenue, San Antonio 78210

National Rifle Association
    800-336-7402 11250 Waples Mill Rd., Fairfax, VA 22030.
    Locally, see Texas State Rifle Assoc., 512-615-4200

River Authorities:
Brazos River Authority 254-761-3100 PO Box 7555,
    Waco 76714
Central Colorado River Authority 325-625-4398
    PO Box 964, Coleman 76834
Guadalupe-Blanco River Authority 830-379-5822
    933 East Court Street PO Box 271, Seguin 78156
Lavaca-Navidad River Authority 361-782-5229
    PO Box 429, Edna 77957
Lower Colorado River Authority 512-473-3200
    PO Box 220, Austin 78767
Nueces River Authority 830-278-6810 First State Bank Building, Suite 206,
    PO Box 349, Uvalde 78802
Sabine River Authority 409-746-2192
    PO Box 579, Orange 77631
San Antonio River Authority 210-227-1373 100 East
    Guenther St., PO Box 830027 San Antonio 78204
San Jacinto River Authority 409-588-1111 PO Box 329,
    Conroe 77305
Trinity River Authority 817-467-4343 PO Box 60
    Arlington 76004
Upper Colorado River Authority 325-655-0565
    512 Orient San Angelo 76903
Upper Guadalupe River Authority 830-896-5445
    125 Lehmann Dr. Suite 100, Kerrville 78028

Secretary of State 512-463-5701 5561 State Capitol Room
    1E.8, PO Box 12697, Austin 78711
Texas Association of Concealed Carry Instructors
    877-300-5213 PO Box 55533, Houston 77255

Texas Bureau of Indian Affairs Southern Plains Division
405-247-6673 W.C.D. Office Complex PO Box 368
Anadarko, OK 73005
Alabama-Coushatta Reservation 936-563-1100
Route 3, Box 640, Livingston 77351
Kickapoo Traditional Tribe of Texas 210-773-2105
PO Box 972, Eagle Pass 78853
Tigua Ysleta del Sur Pueblo 915-859-7913
PO Box 17579, El Paso 79917

Texas Concealed Handgun Association 866-516-5117
Box 161713, Austin, Texas 78716

Texas Dept. of Public Safety Headquarters 512-424-2000
5805 N. Lamar Blvd., PO Box 4087, Austin 78773
Emergency Line 800-525-5555
CHL Licensing Section Routine Mail Address
Texas Department of Public Safety
Concealed Handgun – MSC 0245
PO Box 4087, Austin, TX 78773-0001
512-424-7293
Region 1 Dallas 214-861-2000
350 West IH 30, Garland 75043
Region 2 Houston 281-517-1200
12230 West Rd., Houston 77065
Region 3 Corpus Christi 361-698-5500
1922 S. Padre Island Dr., Box 5277, Corpus Christi 78465
Region 4 Midland 432-498-2100
2405 S. Loop 250 West, Midland 79703
Region 5: Lubbock:
1302 W. 6th St., Box 420, Lubbock 79109
Region 6 Waco 254-759-7100
1617 E. Crest Dr., Waco 76705
Texas General Land Office 512-463-5001
1700 N. Congress Ave., Austin 78701
Texas Gun Dealers Association
512-477-1991 PO Box 476, Austin 78767
Texas Parks and Wildlife Department 512-389-4800
800-792-1112 4200 Smith School Rd., Austin 78744
Hunter Education Section 512-389-4999
Operation Game Thief 800-792-GAME
Texas Roadside Assistance 800-525-5555
Texas State Rifle Association 512-615-4200
314 E. Highland Mall Blvd., Suite 300, Austin 78752
U.S. Army Corps of Engineers, SW Division 469-487-7007 1100 Commerce
Street, Suite 831, Dallas 75242
U.S. Forest Service 800-832-1355
1400 Independence Ave. SW, Washington, D.C. 20250

APPENDIX **D**
THE TEXAS GUN LAWS

On the following pages are excerpts from official firearms-related Texas Codes in alphabetical order. Fourteen separate codes are covered, including of course The Right to Carry law, enacted in 1995 as *Senate Bill 60,* which created the concealed-handgun license. This was codified initially as Texas Civil Statute 4413(29ee), and then as modifications to a number of other existing statutes. It has been amended numerous times, and is now generally codified under Government Code chapter 411.

Texas law covers a broad spectrum of subjects and fills more than 100 thick books, but **only gun laws for private citizens are included in this appendix.** A complete copy of state law is available at major libraries and online, but keep in mind that those copies are incomplete (and in many instances inaccurate) without the new material from the last legislative session, which this book includes **up to January, 2014.**

The laws reproduced here are *edited excerpts.* Only material related to keeping and bearing arms has been included. In some cases this means substantial portions of laws may have been edited. **For official legal proceedings do not rely on these excerpts**—obtain unedited texts and competent professional assistance.

In Texas, the legislature meets only during odd-numbered years. The 1997 session substantially revised one of the most common gun laws, Penal Code §46.02, by moving most of its content to §46.15, and changes like this happen continuously. **The newest laws provided here became effective Jan. 1, 2014**; offenses and events that occurred prior to that date may be governed by earlier versions of the statutes. The next legislative session won't even begin until 2015. **Links to recent officially posted gun laws in America are found at GunLaws.com.**

How State Law Is Arranged: Each numbered part of a Texas state code is called a "section," represented by a "§" sign. This makes it easy to refer to any particular statute—you just call it by its title and section numbers. For instance, Penal Code §46.02 is the section about lawful carrying of weapons. You say it like this, "Texas Penal Code, section forty six oh two," or simply, "forty six oh two." Each code appears here in alphabetical order, with its sections then listed in numerical order.

A Note About The Official Law Books
Law books can be confusing because one book can be known by several different names. For example, here is the name of the book that contained the original 1995 version of the Right-to-Carry law. If you think this is confusing, you're correct:

ON THE SPINE:
Vernon's Texas Civil Statutes

ON THE COVER:
Vernon's Civil Statutes of the State of Texas Annotated

ON THE TITLE PAGE:
Vernon's Annotated Revised Civil Statutes of the State of Texas

ON THE "CITE THIS BOOK THUS" PAGE:
Vernon's Ann.Civ.St.

IN SENATE BILL 60, THE RIGHT-TO-CARRY LAW:
Title 70, Revised Statutes

IN PENAL CODE §46.035:
Revised Statutes

ON THE DPS CHL-LAWS AFFIDAVIT:
V.C.S.

Excerpt from the
Constitution of the State of Texas

Article 1, Section 23:
RIGHT TO KEEP AND BEAR ARMS

Every citizen shall have the right to keep and bear arms
in the lawful defense of himself or the State;
but the Legislature shall have power, by law, to regulate
the wearing of arms, with a view to prevent crime.

GROWTH IN TEXAS GUN LAW

Year	Word Count	Statutes	New Words	Change
1995	38,321		—	—
1997	41,360		+2,661	+7.0%
1999	42,042		+682	+1.6%
2001	43,390		+1,348	+3.2%
2003	46,126		+2,736	+6.3%
2005	49,442	226	+3,316	+7.2%
2007	53,923	233	+4,481	+9.1%
2009	55,673	236	+1,750	+3.2%
2011	58,760	244	+3,087	+5.5%
2013	61,045	251	+2,285	+3.9%

Descriptions below are *very* abbreviated for reference only; for more thorough descriptions see Updates at gunlaws.com.

2013 Bills Affecting Texas Gun Law

HB48   GC §411.185, .188, .1881, .201, Simplified CHL renewal process
HB333   OC §2155.101, Hotel firearm guest policy posting requirements
HB485   GC §411.1951, 1952, 1991, Reduction of CHL fees for government officials
HB698   GC §411.175, Simplified procedures for CHL fingerprinting
HB1009   EC §37.0811, GC §411.1871, OC §1701.260, OC §1701.001, OC §1701.301, School
             Marshal program
HB1349   FC §231.302, No social security required for CHL licenses
HB3142   ABC §11.041, ABC §11.61, ABC §61.11, ABC §61.71, GC §411.177, GC §411.179, GC
             §411.187, GC §411.188, GC §411.1882, GC §411.199, PWC §62.082, PC §30.05,
             PC §46.15, GC §411.184, and selected repeals, Elimination of semi-auto and non-
             semi-auto handgun categories for CHL permits
SB299   PC §46.035, Unintentional display of a handgun relaxed
SB864   GC §411.185, GC §411.188, Reduction of CHL proficiency course requirements
SB987   LGC §229.001, LGC §236.002, Attorney general may enforce preemption against localities
             violating preemption protections
SB1400   LGC §229.001, LGC §235.020, LGC §235.022, LGC §235.023, LGC §236.001, LGC
             §236.002, LGC §236.003, Add air gun definition, preemption and protection
SB1857   GC §411.1901, Advanced certification process for school safety training
SB1907   GC §411.2032, CHL firearms storage in private vehicles on certain campuses

2011 Bills Affecting Texas Gun Law

HB25   PC §46.02, Carry in watercraft.
HB1080   P&WC §62.014, Vets hunter education live fire exemption
HB2127   LGC §229.004, Restrictions on municipalities regarding firearm discharge
HB2560   HRC §42.042, Foster parent carry with CHL in vehicles with foster children
SB321   LC §52.061, .062, .063, .064, GC §411-203, Public and private employers cannot stop
             employees from transporting or storing lawful firearms or ammo in locked private
             vehicles in parking space provided for employees, with conditions and exceptions;
             liability protection for employers, with limits on CHL carry and prohibited places
SB766   LGC §229.001, §236.001, .002, .003, §250.001; CPRC §128.001, §128.051, .052, .053,
             Broad shooting range protection from noise and nuisance lawsuits
             LGC §229.001, §236.001, Preemption protection against municipalities for ranges

2009 Bills Affecting Texas Gun Law

HB8   EC 37.007, Students with guns OK at approved events on or off campus
HB267   PC 46.07, Texans free to buy firearms in any state allowed by law ("contiguous" repealed)
HB1805   PWC 62.005, 62.0056, Hunter certified with impaired sight may use laser device
HB2664   PC 46.035, CHL-ban signs at "51" bars must give "effective notice"
HB2730   244-page DPS "cleanup" bill covers numerous subjects; Extensive changes to Private
           Security Act don't effect general public. PC 46.03 and 46.15 amended for changes to
           armed guards, bodyguards and similar, called "security officers," defined by new
           Texas Private Security Board (formerly Texas Commission on Private Security).
           411.1711: For CHL disqualification an expunged, pardoned, vacated, set aside, annulled,
               invalidated, voided, or sealed felony does not count.
           411.172: Disqualifiers for CHL expanded to include "equivalent offenses;" student loan
               default no longer counts; felony definition revised; no time limit on psych disqualifier
           411.174: CHL photo and proficiency certificates are now as DPS stipulates
           411.175 and 189: Repealed, and replaced by related language elsewhere
           411.179: CHL permits now indicate "status" of holder (trainer, judge, DA, etc.)
           411.181: CHLs must notify DPS within 30 days of a change of status
           411.185 (renewals) and 411.199 (national cop carry)
           411.186: A CHL must be revoked (was "may" be revoked) for material-fact errors; bounced
               payment can now be corrected by full payment plus $25 paid within 30 days
           411.187 and 205: Requirement to display CHL license and ID to officials on demand
               remains in effect but the penalty and suspension for not doing so is repealed
           411.187: CHL suspension for causes listed now mandatory (was discretionary)
           411.188: CHL instructor may submit, in writing, a recommendation against issuing a CHL
           411.1882: Sworn proficiency statement sufficient for certain "proper authorities
           411.190: Online renewal options for CHL instructors, renewal requirements reduced
           411.208: Limited instructor immunity does not cover fraud or deceptive trade practice
           CCP 17.292: A CHL shall (was "may") be suspended under emergency order of protection
           FC 85.022: A CHL shall (was "may") be suspended for commission of family violence
           PC 46.06: Amended to comply with the current definition of a felony
HB3352   GC 411.052, 411.0521, HSC 574.088, Updates to mental health disqualifications. DPS
           may only give key prohibited possessor info to NICS and such people have access to
           their own info, which is otherwise confidential; requires procedure to correct the info;
           procedure for relief from disabilities; courts must give related health info to DPS.
HB4336   PC 46.14, PC 71.02, CCP 59.01, Having, transporting, transferring a firearm obtained
           illegally is a 3rd degree felony, for three or more firearms 2nd degree felony.
HB4456   PC46.01, Certain knives designed to open easily aren't switchblades.
SB1236   CCP 14.06, Domestic-violence proceedings must warn that conviction removes RKBA
SB1742   LGC 229.003, Municipal control over certain discharges of a firearm is increased

2007 Bills Affecting Texas Gun Laws

HB8   PC 12.35, Adds offenses under PC 21.02 (continuous child sex abuse) to state jail felonies
HB8   EC 37.007, Student exhibiting weapon subject to expulsion
HB41   GC 411.179, Judges' and spouses address on CHL uses court address for protection
HB126   PC 71.02, Adds to gang activity, any offense under 37.10
HB233   GC 411.1951, Reduces CHL fee to zero for veterans' apps within 365 days of discharge
HB308   PWC 62.0055, Lasers OK for sight-impaired hunters, with conditions
HB495   PC 22.01, Assault against emergency service personnel is class 3 felony
HB638   OC 1701.357, Criminal investigators are now law-enforcement officers, defines retired
           cops eligible for national cop carry under HR 218 LEOSA (now 18 USC §926C)
HB638   GC 614.121-124, Defines ID card and eligibility for national cop carry (LEOSA)
HB872   PC 37.09, Altering evidence is a class 2 felony if a corpse is involved
HB964   PC 46.15, Changes names and cites for private investigators (now Private Security Board),
           adds law-enforcement student to exemptions for carry firearm to, from or at class
HB991   GC 411.192, Changes text to outline format, release of CHL info for official business only
HB1815   PC 46.02, Motorist Protection Act—Concealed carry on your premises or in your vehicle is
           OK. Must be concealed in vehicle, can't be committing crime or be gang member
HB1815   PC 46.15, Conforms to new 46.02, cleans language and cites for private investigators
HB1839   GC 411.185, CHL renewal class once every ten years on 3rd renewal and beyond
HB1887   PC 30.04, Penalties for vehicle burglary are increased for repeat offenders
HB1889   PC 46.15, Adds municipal attorneys and certain bailiffs to the long list of officials who are
           exempt from concealed carry laws and prohibited places list. Authorities continue to
           exempt themselves from bans placed on the general public, a disturbing trend
HB2101   OC 1702.169, 1702.206, Travel restrictions for private security officers is eased
HB2101   PC 46.15, Changes names and cites for private investigators (now Private Security Board)

HB2300	GC 411.179, Judges and related officials must be identified on their CHLs
HB2300	GC 411.181, Judges and similar who are no longer officials must have their CHL changed
HB2300	GC 411.1882, Judges and similar don't need a handgun proficiency certificate if a CHL instructor swears they demonstrated proficiency in the 12 months prior to applying
HB2300	GC 411.201, Federal judges residing in Texas are added to the list of officials who are exempt from the CHL rules the public must obey
HB2300	PC 46.035, Judges and similar are added to the list of officials who are exempt from some bans on carrying without a CHL, which the public must obey
HB2300	PC 46.15, Assistant DAs and similar are exempt from the prohibited places list
HB2884	FC 59.003, Adds sniffing fumes to juvenile offenses list
HB3167	PC 46.01, Corrects the spelling of "stiletto," ABC 61.71, Paragraph "j" is now "l" (L)
SB112	GC 418.003, The Katrina Bill—no gun grabs in emergencies; also changes GC 418.184, GC 433.002, LGC 229.001 and adds GC 433.0045 to accomplish its purpose
SB378	PC 9.01, The Castle Doctrine—Stand your ground in assault, and reasonableness defined in favor of victims, changes PC 9.31, 9.32 and CPR 83.001 to accomplish its purpose
SB535	PWC 62.082, Title is changed for clarity, and makes clear that valid CHLs are exempt from the restrictions on carry or justifiable use of a handgun in certain hunt areas
SB1709	GC 411.207, Police can disarm CHLs temporarily at non-public secure police facilities (defined), put gun in locker for duration. English and Spanish signs must be posted

2005 Bills Affecting Texas Gun Laws

Texas gun laws were affected in 2005 by 28 bills (out of 5,369 introduced, 1,388 enacted and 19 vetoed) in the 79th legislative session. The appendix and text of this book were updated to reflect these changes.

HB225	Gov Code 411.173(a), (b), Non-resident may apply for CHL; bkgrd check is NICS, III
HB225	Gov Code 411.183(b), CHL now good for five years instead of four
HB322	Gov Code 411.172(g), (h), "Arm the government" CHL for military at age 18 not 21
HB322	Gov Code 411.174(a), CHL under 21 must provide photos in profile
HB322	Gov Code 411.184(a), CHL under 21 modifying a license must provide profile photo
HB322	Gov Code 411.1951, "Arm the government" Half-price sale for CHLs for armed forces
HB505	Parks and Wildlife Code 62.0121, Shooting across property lines generally banned
HB582	Penal Code 38.14(a), (b), Stun gun defined
HB685	Gov Code 411.1881, No CHL shooting test for qualified military personnel
HB823	Penal Code 46.15, The Big Change: "Traveling" defined at last, almost, after more than 125 years, for people in private motor vehicles only. Intended to allow an otherwise innocent person to carry a firearm concealed from sight while in a vehicle, with no provision for getting to or from the vehicle
HB823	Penal Code 2.05, Statutory presumption of innocence redefined for traveling law
HB1038	Gov Code 411.195, Half-price sale for CHL renewals for seniors (over 60)
HB1132	Occ Code 1702.163(a), Security officers must qualify with handgun to Bd. standards
Various	Occ Code 1702.163 et seq, Numerous standards for armed security guards
HB1132	Penal Code 46.05, Renamed Private Security Board of the Texas DPS
HB1326	Gov Code, "Arm the government" Reduces authorization for officer to carry weapon
HB1483	Gov Code 411.181, $25 fee applies for bad payment on duplicate CHL request
HB1483	Gov Code 411.184, $25 fee applies for bad payment on a modified CHL request
HB1483	Gov Code 411.186, CHL revocable for a bad payment, $25 re-app fee applies
HB1483	Gov Code 411.196, Pay your CHL tax with cash, personal check or credit card
HB1575	Penal Code 8.07, Ability to prosecute children under 15 expanded
HB1634	Penal Code 28.02, Arson statute and penalties changed
HB1690	Civ Pract Rem Code 125 et seq, Common and public nuisance redefined
HB1813	Alcohol Bev Code 11.61, Historical reenactments w/no live ammo at liquor licensees
HB1813	Alcohol Bev Code 61.71, Historical reenactments w/no live ammo at liquor licensees
HB1813	Penal Code 46.035, Historical reenactments w/no live ammo at liquor licensees
HB1813	Penal Code 46.15, Historical reenactments w/no live ammo at liquor licensees
HB1831	Gov Code 411.171(4), 10-year-old deferred adjudication not a ban for getting CHL
HB1831	Gov Code 411.1711, Redefines "convicted" for the purpose of getting a CHL
HB2018	Penal Code 20.01, Numbering changes
HB2018	Penal Code 46.12(d), Texas Rules of "Evidence" no longer "Criminal Evidence."
HB2027	Parks/Wildlife Code 284.001, New shooting limits on rivers, streams in nine counties
HB2110	Penal Code 46.15(a), "Arm the government" Increases list of officials who are exempt from carry restrictions the public must endure, plus nation cop carry
HB2110	Penal Code 30.05, "Arm the government" Removes the armed trespass ban for specified LEOs including reciprocal states' LEOs
HB2110	Penal Code 46.15(g), Repeals the former paragraph (g)

HB2110	Occ Code 1701.357, "Arm the government" Cleans language to exempt active and retired LEOs from carry bans the public must endure, and facilitates federal national cop carry certification
HB2303	Occ Code 1702 et seq, Rules for commissioned security officers
HB3376	Penal Code 71.02(a)(10), Adds a reference to a money-fraud statute
SB9	Penal Code 30.05(b)(7), "Critical infrastructure facility" (relates to terrorism law)
SB60	Penal Code 12.31(a), (b), Capital felony life imprisonment has no parole
SB60	Penal Code 8.07(d) [was (c)], No death penalty for perp under 18
SB91	Penal Code 22.01(b), Redefine family members for assault statute
SB91	Penal Code 22.01(f), Apply the new definitions from above
SB91	Penal Code 22.02(b), Aggravated assault w/ gun on family member first degree felony
SB526	Local Government Code 118.011, CHL mental-health background check fee repealed
SB578	Penal Code 46.15(a), "Arm the government" Exempts specified LEOs from carry bans the public must endure
SB578	Penal Code 46.15(g) (from SB103 in 2003), Defined reciprocal states for police, now covered under national cop carry
SB578	Occ Code 1701.357(a-d), (i), "Arm the government" Expands the officials who are exempt from carry bans the public must endure, and national cop carry
SB734	Agri Code 251.005, City power over gunfire limited by Loc. Gov. Code 229.002.
SB734	Local Gov Code 43.002, City reg on gunfire must conform to Loc. Gov. Code 229.002
SB734	Local Gov Code 229.002, Limits city power over firing guns on agricultural land
SB1791	Penal Code 19.03, "Arm the government" Adds retaliatory killing of certain court personnel to capital murder law

For earlier listings go to gunlaws.com.

TEXAS GUN LAWS

EXCERPTS FROM VERNON'S TEXAS CODE ANNOTATED

With material from the 2013 legislative session taken directly from enacted bills.

Updates, changes and corrections may be found at GunLaws.com.

<Editorial notes appear in pointed brackets and are not part of the law.>

Warning: Official Texas statutes were not updated on the government website for nearly three years from 2007 to 2010; this led to incorrect language getting amended, amendments getting amended, numbering patterns set askew, repeals remaining on the books or being removed in a haphazard manner and other problems, so a fully accurate statement of our laws was unavailable for some time. The 2013 bills contained some irreconcilable elements as well, and are unlikely to be addressed by state officials for quite some time. An effort has been made here to reconcile the morass and to make conflicting new bills harmonize, but this is an imperfect process—you should always check the official state website, keeping in mind that it may not always provide clear resolutions. Always exercise care and look to official versions, to the extent possible, for accurate, current law.

Agriculture Code §251.005. Effect of Governmental Requirements
(c) A governmental requirement of a city does not apply to any agricultural operation situated outside the corporate boundaries of the city on the effective date of this chapter. If an agricultural operation so situated is subsequently annexed or otherwise brought within the corporate boundaries of the city, the governmental requirements of the city do not apply to the agricultural operation unless the requirement is reasonably necessary to protect persons who reside in the immediate vicinity or persons on public property in the immediate vicinity of the agricultural operation from the danger of:
(2) discharge of firearms or other weapons, subject to the restrictions in Section 229.002, Local Government Code.

Alcoholic Beverage Code §11.041. Warning Sign Required
(a) Each holder of a permit who is not otherwise required to display a sign under Section 411.204, Government Code, shall display in a prominent place on the permit holder's premises a sign giving notice that it is unlawful for a person to carry a weapon on the premises unless the weapon is a concealed handgun the person is licensed to carry under Subchapter H, Chapter 411, Government Code.
(b) The sign must be at least 6 inches high and 14 inches wide, must appear in contrasting colors, and shall be displayed in a conspicuous manner clearly visible to the public. The commission or administrator may require the permit holder to also display the sign in a language other than English if it can be observed or determined that a substantial portion of the expected customers speak the other language as their familiar language.

Alcoholic Beverage Code §11.61. Cancellation or Suspension of Permit
(e) Except as provided by Subsection (f) or (i), the commission or administrator shall cancel an original or renewal permit if it is found, after notice and hearing, that the permittee knowingly allowed a person to possess a firearm in a building on the licensed premises. This subsection does not apply to a person:
(1) who holds a security officer commission issued under Chapter 1702, Occupations Code, if:
(A) the person is engaged in the performance of the person's duties as a security officer;
(B) the person is wearing a distinctive uniform; and
(C) the weapon is in plain view;
(2) who is a peace officer; or
(3) who is a permittee or an employee of a permittee if the person is supervising the operation of the premises; or
(4) who possesses a concealed handgun the person is licensed to carry under Subchapter H, Chapter 411, Government Code, unless the person is on the premises of a business described by Section 46.035(b)(1), Penal Code.
(f) The commission may adopt a rule allowing:
(1) a gun or firearm show on the premises of a permit holder, if the premises is owned or leased by a governmental entity or a nonprofit civic, religious, charitable, fraternal, or veterans' organization;

(2) the holder of a permit for the sale of alcoholic beverages for off-premises consumption to also hold a federal firearms license; or

(3) the ceremonial display of firearms on the premises of the permit holder.

(i) The commission shall adopt rules allowing a historical reenactment on the premises of a permit holder. Rules adopted under this subsection must prohibit the use of live ammunition in a historical reenactment.

Alcoholic Beverage Code §61.11. Warning Sign Required

(a) Each holder of a license who is not otherwise required to display a sign under Section 411.204, Government Code, shall display in a prominent place on the license holder's premises a sign giving notice that it is unlawful for a person to carry a weapon on the premises unless the weapon is a concealed handgun the person is licensed to carry under Subchapter H, Chapter 411, Government Code.

(b) The sign must be at least 6 inches high and 14 inches wide, must appear in contrasting colors, and shall be displayed in a conspicuous manner clearly visible to the public. The commission or administrator may require the holder of the license to also display the sign in a language other than English if it can be observed or determined that a substantial portion of the expected customers speak the other language as their familiar language.

Alcoholic Beverage Code §61.71. Grounds for Cancellation or Suspension: Retail Dealer

(f) Except as provided by Subsection (g) or (j), the commission or administrator shall cancel an original or renewal dealer's on-premises or off-premises license if it is found, after notice and hearing, that the licensee knowingly allowed a person to possess a firearm in a building on the licensed premises. This subsection does not apply to a person:

(1) who holds a security officer commission issued under Chapter 1702, Occupations Code, if:

(A) the person is engaged in the performance of the person's duties as a security officer;

(B) the person is wearing a distinctive uniform; and

(C) the weapon is in plain view;

(2) who is a peace officer;

(3) who is a licensee or an employee of a licensee if the person is supervising the operation of the premises; or

(4) who possesses a concealed handgun the person is licensed to carry under Subchapter H, Chapter 411, Government Code, unless the person is on the premises of a business described by Section 46.035(b)(1), Penal Code.

(g) The commission may adopt a rule allowing:

(1) a gun or firearm show on the premises of a license holder, if the premises is owned or leased by a governmental entity or a nonprofit civic, religious, charitable, fraternal, or veterans' organization;

(2) the holder of a license for the sale of alcoholic beverages for off-premises consumption to also hold a federal firearms license; or

(3) the ceremonial display of firearms on the premises of the license holder.

(j) The commission shall adopt rules allowing a historical reenactment on the premises of a license holder. Rules adopted under this subsection must prohibit the use of live ammunition in a historical reenactment.

Alcoholic Beverage Code §104.06. Monitoring Of Gross Receipts

(a) On the issuance and renewal of a license or permit that allows on-premises consumption of any alcoholic beverage the commission shall determine whether the holder receives, or for the issuance of a license or permit is to receive, 51 percent or more of the gross receipts of the premises for which the license or permit is issued from the holder's sale or service of alcoholic beverages for on-premises consumption.

(b) The commission shall:

(1) adopt rules for making a determination under Subsection (a); and

(2) require a holder of a license or permit to provide any information or document that the commission needs to make a determination.

(c) If the commission makes a determination under Subsection (a) that a holder of a license or permit receives 51 percent or more of the gross receipts of the premises from the sale or service of alcoholic beverages, the holder shall comply with the requirements of Section 411.204, Government Code, and shall continue to comply with those requirements until the commission determines that the holder receives less than 51 percent of the gross receipts of the premises from the sale or service of alcoholic beverages for on-premises consumption.

Civil Practice and Remedies Code §82.006. Firearms and Ammunition

(a) In a products liability action brought against a manufacturer or seller of a firearm or ammunition that alleges a design defect in the firearm or ammunition, the burden is on the claimant to prove, in addition to any other elements that the claimant must prove, that:

(1) the actual design of the firearm or ammunition was defective, causing the firearm or ammunition not to function in a manner reasonably expected by an ordinary consumer of firearms or ammunition; and

(2) the defective design was a producing cause of the personal injury, property damage, or death.

(b) The claimant may not prove the existence of the defective design by a comparison or weighing of the benefits of the firearm or ammunition against the risk of personal injury, property damage, or death posed by its potential to cause such injury, damage, or death when discharged.

Civil Practice and Remedies Code §83.001. Civil Immunity
A defendant who uses force or deadly force that is justified under Chapter 9 Penal Code, is immune from civil liability for personal injury or death that results from the defendant's use of force or deadly force, as applicable.

Civil Practice and Remedies Code §125.001. Definitions
(1) "Common nuisance" is a nuisance described by Section 125.0015.
(2) "Public nuisance" is a nuisance described by Section 125.062 or 125.063.
(3) "Multiunit residential property" means improved real property with at least three dwelling units, including an apartment building, condominium, hotel, or motel. The term does not include a single-family home or duplex.

Civil Practice and Remedies Code §125.0015. Common Nuisance
(a) A person who maintains a place to which persons habitually go for the following purposes and who knowingly tolerates the activity and furthermore fails to make reasonable attempts to abate the activity maintains a common nuisance:
(1) discharge of a firearm in a public place as prohibited by the Penal Code;
(2) reckless discharge of a firearm as prohibited by the Penal Code;
(3) engaging in organized criminal activity as a member of a combination as prohibited by the Penal Code;
(14) unlawfully carrying a weapon as described by Section 46.02, Penal Code;
(b) A person maintains a common nuisance if the person maintains a multiunit residential property to which persons habitually go to commit acts listed in Subsection (a) and knowingly tolerates the acts and furthermore fails to make reasonable attempts to abate the acts.

Civil Practice and Remedies Code §125.004. Evidence
(a) Proof that an activity described by Section 125.0015 is frequently committed at the place involved or that the place is frequently used for an activity described by Section 125.0015 is prima facie evidence that the defendant knowingly tolerated the activity.
(b) Evidence that persons have been arrested for or convicted of offenses for an activity described by Section 125.0015 in the place involved is admissible to show knowledge on the part of the defendant with respect to the act that occurred. The originals or certified copies of the papers and judgments of those arrests or convictions are admissible in the suit for injunction, and oral evidence is admissible to show that the offense for which a person was arrested or convicted was committed at the place involved.
(c) Evidence of the general reputation of the place involved is admissible to show the existence of the nuisance.
(d) Notwithstanding Subsection (a), evidence that the defendant, the defendant's authorized representative, or another person acting at the direction of the defendant or the defendant's authorized representative requested law enforcement or emergency assistance with respect to an activity at the place where the common nuisance is allegedly maintained is not admissible for the purpose of showing the defendant tolerated the activity or failed to make reasonable attempts to abate the activity alleged to constitute the nuisance but may be admitted for other purposes, such as showing that a crime listed in Section 125.0015 occurred. Evidence that the defendant refused to cooperate with law enforcement or emergency services with respect to the activity is admissible. The posting of a sign prohibiting the activity alleged is not conclusive evidence that the owner did not tolerate the activity.

Civil Practice and Remedies Code §125.061. Definitions
In this subchapter:
(1) "Combination" and "criminal street gang" have the meanings assigned by Section 71.01, Penal Code.
(2) "Continuously or regularly" means at least five times in a period of not more than 12 months.
(3) "Gang activity" means the following types of conduct:
(A) organized criminal activity as described by Section 71.02, Penal Code;
(B) terroristic threat as described by Section 22.07, Penal Code;
(C) coercing, soliciting, or inducing gang membership as described by Section 22.015, Penal Code;
(D) criminal trespass as described by Section 30.05, Penal Code;
(E) disorderly conduct as described by Section 42.01, Penal Code;
(F) criminal mischief as described by Section 28.03, Penal Code, that causes a pecuniary loss of $500 or more;
(G) a graffiti offense in violation of Section 28.08, Penal Code, that;
(H) a weapons offense in violation of Chapter 46, Penal Code; or
(I) unlawful possession of a substance or other item in violation of Chapter 481, Health and Safety Code.

Civil Practice and Remedies Code §128.001. Limitation On Right To Bring Suit Or Recover Damages
(a) In this section:
(1) "Governmental unit" means:
(A) a political subdivision of the state, including a municipality or county; and
(B) any other agency of government whose authority is derived from the laws or constitution of this state.
(2) "Sport shooting range" has the meaning assigned by Section 250.001, Local Government Code.
(b) Except as provided by Subsections (c) and (f), a governmental unit may not bring suit against:
(1) a firearms or ammunition manufacturer, trade association, or seller for recovery of damages resulting from, or injunctive relief or abatement of a nuisance relating to, the lawful design, manufacture, marketing, or sale of firearms or ammunition to the public; or
(2) a sport shooting range, the owners or operators of a sport shooting range, or the owners of real property on which a sport shooting range is operated, for the lawful discharge of firearms on the sport shooting range.
(c) A governmental unit on behalf of the state or any other governmental unit may bring a suit described by Subsection (b) if the suit is approved in advance by the legislature in a concurrent resolution or by enactment of a law. This subsection does not create a cause of action.
(d) Nothing in this section shall prohibit a governmental unit from bringing an action against a firearms manufacturer, trade association, or seller for recovery of damages for:
(1) breach of contract or warranty as to firearms or ammunition purchased by a governmental unit;
(2) damage or harm to property owned or leased by the governmental unit caused by a defective firearm or ammunition;
(3) personal injury or death, if such action arises from a governmental unit's claim for subrogation;
(4) injunctive relief to enforce a valid ordinance, statute, or regulation; or
(5) contribution under Chapter 33, Civil Practice and Remedies Code.
(e) Nothing in this section shall prohibit the attorney general from bringing a suit described by Subsection (b) on behalf of the state or any other governmental unit. This subsection does not create a cause of action.
(f) Nothing in this section shall prohibit a governmental unit from bringing an action against a sport shooting range, the owners or operators of a sport shooting range, or the owners of real property on which a sport shooting range is operating if the sport shooting range began operation after September 1, 2011, and operates exclusively within the governmental unit's geographical limits, exclusive of the governmental unit's extraterritorial jurisdiction:
(1) for injunctive relief to enforce a valid ordinance, statute, or regulation; or
(2) to require the sport shooting range to comply with generally accepted standards followed in the sport shooting range industry in this state at the time of the sport shooting range's construction.

Civil Practice and Remedies Code §128.051. Definitions
In this subchapter:
(1) "Claim" means any relief sought in a civil action, including all forms of monetary recovery or injunctive relief.
(2) "Claimant" has the meaning assigned by Section 41.001.
(3) "Expert" means a person who is:
(A) giving opinion testimony about the appropriate standard of care for a sport shooting range, an owner or operator of a sport shooting range, or the owner of real property on which a sport shooting range is operated, or the causal relationship between the injury, harm, or damages claimed and the alleged departure from the applicable standard of care; and
(B) qualified to render opinions on the standards and causal relationship described by Paragraph (A) under the Texas Rules of Evidence.
(4) "Expert report" means a written report by an expert that provides a fair summary of the expert's opinions as of the date of the report regarding applicable standards of care for operation of a sport shooting range, the manner in which a defendant failed to meet the standards, and the causal relationship between that failure and the injury, harm, or damages claimed.
(5) "Sport shooting range" has the meaning assigned by Section 250.001, Local Government Code.

Civil Practice and Remedies Code §128.052. Limitation On Civil Action And Recovery Of Damages
(a) Except as provided by Subsection (b), a civil action may not be brought against a sport shooting range, the owner or operator of a sport shooting range, or the owner of the real property on which a sport shooting range is operated for recovery of damages resulting from, or injunctive relief or abatement of a nuisance relating to, the discharge of firearms.
(b) Nothing in this section prohibits a civil action against a sport shooting range, the owner or operator of a sport shooting range, or the owner of the real property on which a sport shooting range is operated for recovery of damages for:
(1) breach of contract for use of the real property on which a sport shooting range is located;
(2) damage or harm to private property caused by the discharge of firearms on a sport shooting range;
(3) personal injury or death caused by the discharge of a firearm on a sport shooting range; or
(4) injunctive relief to enforce a valid ordinance, statute, or regulation.

(c) Damages may be awarded, or an injunction may be obtained, in a civil action brought under this section if the claimant shows by a preponderance of the evidence, through the testimony of one or more expert witnesses, that the sport shooting range, the owner or operator of the sport shooting range, or the owner of real property on which the sport shooting range is operated deviated from the standard of care that is reasonably expected of an ordinarily prudent sport shooting range, owner or operator of a sport shooting range, or owner of real property on which a sport shooting range is operated in the same or similar circumstances.

Civil Practice and Remedies Code §128.053. Expert Report

(a) In a suit against a sport shooting range, an owner or operator of a sport shooting range, or the owner of real property on which a sport shooting range is operated, a claimant shall, not later than the 90th day after the date the original petition was filed, serve on each party or the party's attorney one or more expert reports, with a curriculum vitae of each expert listed in the report for each defendant against whom a claim is asserted. The date for serving the report may be extended by written agreement of the affected parties. Each defendant whose conduct is implicated in a report must file and serve any objection to the sufficiency of the report not later than the 21st day after the date the report is served or all objections are waived.

(b) If, as to a defendant, an expert report has not been served within the period specified by Subsection (a), the court, on the motion of the affected defendant, shall, subject to Subsection (c), enter an order that:

(1) awards to the affected defendant attorney's fees and costs of court incurred by the defendant; and

(2) dismisses the claim with prejudice with respect to the affected defendant.

(c) If an expert report has not been served within the period specified by Subsection (a) because elements of the report are found deficient, the court may grant one extension of not more than 30 days to the claimant in order to cure the deficiency. If the claimant does not receive notice of the court's ruling granting the extension until after the 90th day after the date the deadline has passed, then the 30-day extension runs from the date the plaintiff first receives the notice.

(d) Notwithstanding any other provision of this section, a claimant may satisfy any requirement of this section for serving an expert report by serving reports of separate experts regarding different defendants or regarding different issues arising from the conduct of a defendant, including issues of liability and causation. Nothing in this section shall be construed to mean that a single expert must address all liability and causation issues with respect to all defendants or with respect to both liability and causation issues for a defendant.

(e) A court shall grant a motion challenging the adequacy of an expert report only if it appears to the court, after a hearing, that the report does not represent an objective, good faith effort to comply with the requirements of an expert report.

(f) Until a claimant has served the expert report and curriculum vitae as required by Subsection (a), all discovery is stayed except that after a claim is filed all claimants, collectively, may take not more than two depositions before the expert report is served as required by Subsection (a).

Education Code §4.31. Exhibition of Firearms

(a) It shall be unlawful to interfere with the normal activities, the normal occupancy, or normal use of any building or portion of a campus, or of any school bus engaged in the transportation of children to and from school sponsored activities, of any private or public school or institution of higher education or public vocational and technical school or institute by exhibiting or using or threatening to exhibit or use a firearm.

(b) A person who violates this section is guilty of a felony and upon conviction is punishable by a fine of up to $1,000 or by imprisonment in jail for a period not to exceed six months, or by both fine and imprisonment, or by imprisonment in the state penitentiary for a period not to exceed five years.

Education Code §21.118. Firearms Safety Program

(a) A school district may, and is strongly encouraged to, provide or participate in a firearms safety program for students in grades kindergarten through 12. A school district that provides a firearms safety program shall consult with a certified firearms instructor before establishing the curriculum for the program.

(b) A school district may not require a student to participate in a firearms safety program if the district receives written notice from a parent of the student to exempt the student from the program. A school district that provides or participates in a firearms safety program may not permit a student participating in the program, while the student is on district property, to handle a readily dischargeable firearm.

(c) The firearms safety program will meet the standards of the National Rifle Association Eddie Eagle Children's Gun Safety Course.

Education Code 37.007. Expulsion For Serious Offenses

(a) Except as provided by Subsection (k), a student shall be expelled from a school if the student, on school property or while attending a school-sponsored or school-related activity on or off of school property:

(1) uses, exhibits, or possesses:

(A) a firearm as defined by Section 46.01(3), Penal Code;

(B) an illegal knife as defined by Section 46.01(6), Penal Code, or by local policy;
(C) a club as defined by Section 46.01(1), Penal Code; or
(D) a weapon listed as a prohibited weapon under Section 46.05, Penal Code;
(2) engages in conduct that contains the elements of the offense of:
(A) aggravated assault under Section 22.02, Penal Code, sexual assault under Section 22.011, Penal Code, or aggravated sexual assault under Section 22.021, Penal Code;
(C) murder under Section 19.02, Penal Code, capital murder under Section 19.03, Penal Code, or criminal attempt, under Section 15.01, Penal Code, to commit murder or capital murder;
(G) manslaughter under Section 19.04, Penal Code;
(H) criminally negligent homicide under Section 19.05, Penal Code; or
(b) A student may be expelled if the student:
(D) engages in conduct that contains the elements of the offense of deadly conduct under Section 22.05, Penal Code;
(3) subject to Subsection (d), while within 300 feet of school property, as measured from any point on the school's real property boundary line:
(A) engages in conduct specified by Subsection (a); or
(B) possesses a firearm, as defined by 18 U.S.C. §921; or
(4) engages in conduct that contains the elements of any offense listed in Subsection (a)(2)(A) or (C) or the offense of aggravated robbery under Section 29.03, Penal Code, against another student, without regard to whether the conduct occurs on or off of school property or while attending a school-sponsored or school-related activity on or off of school property.
(e) In accordance with 20 U.S.C. §7151, a local educational agency, including a school district, home-rule school district, or open-enrollment charter school, shall expel a student who brings a firearm, as defined by 18 U.S.C. §921, to school. The student must be expelled from the student's regular campus for a period of at least one year, except that:
(1) the superintendent or other chief administrative officer of the school district or of the other local educational agency, as defined by 20 U. S.C. Section 7801, may modify the length of the expulsion in the case of an individual student;
(f) A student who engages in conduct that contains the elements of the offense of criminal mischief under Section 28.03, Penal Code, may be expelled at the district's discretion if the conduct is punishable as a felony under that section. The student shall be referred to the authorized officer of the juvenile court regardless of whether the student is expelled.
(i) A student who engages in conduct described by Subsection (a) may be expelled from school by the district in which the student attends school if the student engages in that conduct:
(1) on school property of another district in this state; or
(2) while attending a school-sponsored or school-related activity of a school in another district in this state.
(k) A student may not be expelled solely on the basis of the student's use, exhibition, or possession of a firearm that occurs:
(1) at an approved target range facility that is not located on a school campus; and
(2) while participating in or preparing for a school-sponsored shooting sports competition or a shooting sports educational activity that is sponsored or supported by the Parks and Wildlife Department or a shooting sports sanctioning organization working with the department.
(l) Subsection (k) does not authorize a student to bring a firearm on school property to participate in or prepare for a school-sponsored shooting sports competition or a shooting sports educational activity described by that subsection.

Education Code §37.0811. School Marshals
(a) The board of trustees of a school district or the governing body of an open-enrollment charter school may appoint not more than one school marshal per 400 students in average daily attendance per campus.
(b) The board of trustees of a school district or the governing body of an open-enrollment charter school may select for appointment as a school marshal under this section an applicant who is an employee of the school district or open-enrollment charter school and certified as eligible for appointment under Section 1701.260, Occupations Code. The board of trustees or governing body may, but shall not be required to, reimburse the amount paid by the applicant to participate in the training program under that section.
(c) A school marshal appointed by the board of trustees of a school district or the governing body of an open-enrollment charter school may carry or possess a handgun on the physical premises of a school, but only:
(1) in the manner provided by written regulations adopted by the board of trustees or the governing body; and
(2) at a specific school as specified by the board of trustees or governing body, as applicable.
(d) Any written regulations adopted for purposes of Subsection (c) must provide that a school marshal may carry a concealed handgun as described by Subsection (c), except that if the primary duty of the school marshal involves regular, direct contact with students, the marshal may not carry a concealed handgun but may possess a handgun on the physical premises of a school in a locked and secured safe within the marshal's immediate reach when conducting the marshal's primary

duty. The written regulations must also require that a handgun carried by or within access of a school marshal may be loaded only with frangible ammunition designed to disintegrate on impact for maximum safety and minimal danger to others.

(e) A school marshal may access a handgun under this section only under circumstances that would justify the use of deadly force under Section 9.32 or 9.33, Penal Code.

(f) A school district or charter school employee's status as a school marshal becomes inactive on:

(1) expiration of the employee's school marshal license under Section 1701.260, Occupations Code;

(2) suspension or revocation of the employee's license to carry a concealed handgun issued under Subchapter H, Chapter 411, Government Code;

(3) termination of the employee's employment with the district or charter school; or

(4) notice from the board of trustees of the district or the governing body of the charter school that the employee's services as school marshal are no longer required.

(g) The identity of a school marshal appointed under this section is confidential, except as provided by Section 1701.260(j), Occupations Code, and is not subject to a request under Chapter 552, Government Code.

Education Code §37.125. Exhibition Of Firearms

(a) A person commits an offense if, in a manner intended to cause alarm or personal injury to another person or to damage school property, the person intentionally exhibits, uses, or threatens to exhibit or use a firearm:

(1) in or on any property, including a parking lot, parking garage, or other parking area, that is owned by a private or public school; or

(2) on a school bus being used to transport children to or from school-sponsored activities of a private or public school.

Family Code §53.02 Release From Detention

(b) A child taken into custody may be detained prior to hearing on the petition only if:

(6) the child's detention is required under Subsection (f).

(f) A child who is alleged to have engaged in delinquent conduct and to have used, possessed, or exhibited a firearm, as defined by Section 46.01, Penal Code, in the commission of the offense shall be detained until the child is released at the direction of the judge of the juvenile court, a substitute judge authorized by Section 51.04(f), or a referee appointed under Section 51.04(g), including an oral direction by telephone, or until a detention hearing is held as required by Section 54.01.

Family Code §54.0406. Child Placed On Probation For Conduct Involving A Handgun

(a) If a court or jury places a child on probation under Section 54.04(d) for conduct that violates a penal law that includes as an element of the offense the possession, carrying, using, or exhibiting of a handgun, as defined by Section 46.01, Penal Code, and if at the adjudication hearing the court or jury affirmatively finds that the child personally possessed, carried, used, or exhibited the handgun, the court shall require as a condition of probation that the child, not later than the 30th day after the date the court places the child on probation, notify the juvenile probation officer who is supervising the child of the manner in which the child acquired the handgun, including the date and place of and any person involved in the acquisition.

(b) On receipt of information described by Subsection (a), a juvenile probation officer shall promptly notify the appropriate local law enforcement agency of the information.

(c) Information provided by a child to a juvenile probation officer as required by Subsection (a) and any other information derived from that information may not be used as evidence against the child in any juvenile or criminal proceeding.

Family Code §59.003 Sanction Level Assignment Model

(a) Subject to Subsection (e), after a child's first commission of delinquent conduct or conduct indicating a need for supervision, the probation department or prosecuting attorney may, or the juvenile court may, in a disposition hearing under Section 54.04 or a modification hearing under Section 54.05, assign a child one of the following sanction levels according to the child's conduct:

(1) for conduct indicating a need for supervision, other than conduct described in Section 51.03(b)(4) or (5) or a Class A or B misdemeanor, the sanction level is one;

(2) for conduct indicating a need for supervision under Section 51.03(b)(4) or (5) or a Class A or B misdemeanor, other than a misdemeanor involving the use or possession of a firearm, or for delinquent conduct under Section 51.03(a)(2), the sanction level is two;

(3) for a misdemeanor involving the use or possession of a firearm or for a state jail felony or a felony of the third degree, the sanction level is three;

(4) for a felony of the second degree, the sanction level is four;

(5) for a felony of the first degree, other than a felony involving the use of a deadly weapon or causing serious bodily injury, the sanction level is five;

(6) for a felony of the first degree involving the use of a deadly weapon or causing serious bodily injury, for an aggravated controlled substance felony, or for a capital felony, the sanction level is six; or

(7) for a felony of the first degree involving the use of a deadly weapon or causing serious bodily injury, for an aggravated controlled substance felony, or for a capital felony, if the petition has

been approved by a grand jury under Section 53.045, or if a petition to transfer the child to criminal court has been filed under Section 54.02, the sanction level is seven.

Family Code §85.022. Requirements of Order Applying to Person Who Committed Family Violence
(b) In a protective order, the court may prohibit the person found to have committed family violence from:
(6) possessing a firearm, unless the person is a peace officer, as defined by Section 1.07, Penal Code, actively engaged in employment as a sworn, full-time paid employee of a state agency or political subdivision.
(d) In a protective order, the court shall suspend a license to carry a concealed handgun issued under Subchapter H, Chapter 411, Government Code, that is held by a person found to have committed family violence.
(e) In this section, "firearm" has the meaning assigned by Section 46.01, Penal Code.

Family Code §85.026. Warning On Protective Order
(a) Each protective order issued under this subtitle, including a temporary ex parte order, must contain the following prominently displayed statements in boldfaced type, capital letters, or underlined:
"A PERSON WHO VIOLATES THIS ORDER MAY BE PUNISHED FOR CONTEMPT OF COURT BY A FINE OF AS MUCH AS $500 OR BY CONFINEMENT IN JAIL FOR AS LONG AS SIX MONTHS, OR BOTH.
"NO PERSON, INCLUDING A PERSON WHO IS PROTECTED BY THIS ORDER, MAY GIVE PERMISSION TO ANYONE TO IGNORE OR VIOLATE ANY PROVISION OF THIS ORDER. DURING THE TIME IN WHICH THIS ORDER IS VALID, EVERY PROVISION OF THIS ORDER IS IN FULL FORCE AND EFFECT UNLESS A COURT CHANGES THE ORDER.
"IT IS UNLAWFUL FOR ANY PERSON, OTHER THAN A PEACE OFFICER, AS DEFINED BY SECTION 1.07, PENAL CODE, ACTIVELY ENGAGED IN EMPLOYMENT AS A SWORN, FULL-TIME PAID EMPLOYEE OF A STATE AGENCY OR POLITICAL SUBDIVISION, WHO IS SUBJECT TO A PROTECTIVE ORDER TO POSSESS A FIREARM OR AMMUNITION."

Family Code §231.302. Information To Assist In Location Of Persons Or Property
(c-1) For purposes of issuing a license to carry a concealed handgun under Subchapter H, Chapter 411, Government Code, the Department of Public Safety is not required to request, and an applicant is not required to provide, the applicant's social security number.

Government Code §76.0051. Authorization To Carry Weapon
An officer is authorized to carry a weapon while engaged in the actual discharge of the officer's duties only if:
(1) the officer possesses a certificate of firearms proficiency issued by the Texas Commission on Law Enforcement under Section 1701.257 Occupations Code; and
(2) the director of the department agrees to the authorization.

Government Code §411.042. Bureau Of Identification And Records
(b) The bureau of identification and records shall:
(3) make ballistic tests of bullets and firearms and chemical analyses of bloodstains, cloth, materials, and other substances for law enforcement officers of the state;
(5) maintain a list of all previous background checks for applicants for any position regulated under Chapter 1702, Occupations Code, who have undergone a criminal history background check under Section 411.119, if the check indicates a Class B misdemeanor or equivalent offense or a greater offense;

Government Code §411.047. Reporting Related To Concealed Handgun Incidents
(a) The department may maintain statistics on its website related to responses by law enforcement agencies to incidents in which a person licensed to carry a handgun under Subchapter H is convicted of an offense only if the offense is prohibited under Subchapter H or under Title 5, Chapter 29, Chapter 46, or Section 30.02, Penal Code.
(b) Such statistics shall be drawn and reported annually from the Department of Public Safety computerized criminal history file on persons 21 years of age and older and shall be compared in numerical and graphical format to all like offenses committed in the state for the reporting period as a percentage of the total of such reported offenses.
(c) The department by rule shall adopt procedures for local law enforcement to make reports to the department described by Subsection (a).

Government Code §411.053. Federal Firearm Reporting
(a) In this section, "federal prohibited person information" means information that identifies an individual as:
(1) a person ordered by a court to receive inpatient mental health services under Chapter 574, Health and Safety Code;
(2) a person acquitted in a criminal case by reason of insanity or lack of mental responsibility, regardless of whether the person is ordered by a court to receive inpatient treatment or residential care under Chapter 46C, Code of Criminal Procedure;

(3) a person determined to have mental retardation and committed by a court for long-term placement in a residential care facility or state developmental center under Chapter 593, Health and Safety Code;

(4) an incapacitated adult individual for whom a court has appointed a guardian of the individual under Chapter XIII, Probate Code, based on the determination that the person lacks the mental capacity to manage the person's affairs; or

(5) a person determined to be incompetent to stand trial under Chapter 46B, Code of Criminal Procedure.

(b) The department by rule shall establish a procedure to provide federal prohibited person information to the Federal Bureau of Investigation for use with the National Instant Criminal Background Check System. Except as otherwise provided by state law, the department may disseminate federal prohibited person information under this subsection only to the extent necessary to allow the Federal Bureau of Investigation to collect and maintain a list of persons who are prohibited under federal law from engaging in certain activities with respect to a firearm.

(c) The department shall grant access to federal prohibited person information to the person who is the subject of the information.

(d) Federal prohibited person information maintained by the department is confidential information for the use of the department and, except as otherwise provided by this section and other state law, may not be disseminated by the department.

(e) The department by rule shall establish a procedure to correct department records and transmit those corrected records to the Federal Bureau of Investigation when a person provides:

(1) a copy of a judicial order or finding that a person is no longer an incapacitated adult or is entitled to relief from disabilities under Section 574.088, Health and Safety Code; or

(2) proof that the person has obtained notice of relief from disabilities under 18 U.S.C. §925.

Government Code §411.0521. Report To Department Concerning Certain Persons' Access To Firearms

(a) The clerk of the court shall prepare and forward to the department the information described by Subsection (b) not later than the 30th day after the date the court:

(1) orders a person to receive inpatient mental health services under Chapter 574, Health and Safety Code;

(2) acquits a person in a criminal case by reason of insanity or lack of mental responsibility, regardless of whether the person is ordered to receive inpatient treatment or residential care under Chapter 46C, Code of Criminal Procedure;

(3) commits a person determined to have mental retardation for long-term placement in a residential care facility or state developmental center under Chapter 593, Health and Safety Code;

(4) appoints a guardian of the incapacitated adult individual under Chapter XIII, Probate Code, based on the determination that the person lacks the mental capacity to manage the person's affairs;

(5) determines a person is incompetent to stand trial under Chapter 46B, Code of Criminal Procedure; or

(6) finds a person is entitled to relief from disabilities under Section 574.088, Health and Safety Code.

(b) The clerk of the court shall prepare and forward the following information under Subsection (a):

(1) the complete name, race, and sex of the person;

(2) any known identifying number of the person, including social security number, driver's license number, or state identification number;

(3) the person's date of birth; and

(4) a copy of or an electronic transmission of information continued in:

(A) the order for inpatient mental health services;

(B) the order for inpatient treatment or residential care;

(C) the order committing the person to a residential care facility;

(D) the order appointing a guardian;

(E) the judgment specifying that the person was found not guilty of a criminal offense by reason of insanity or lack of mental responsibility;

(F) the order determining that the person is incompetent to stand trial; or

(G) the order stating that the person is no longer an incapacitated adult or is entitled to relief under Section 574.088, Health and Safety Code.

(c) If practicable, the clerk of the court shall forward to the department the information described by Subsection (b) in an electronic format prescribed by the department.

(d) If an order previously reported to the department under Subsection (a) is reversed by order of any court, the clerk shall notify the department of the reversal not later than 30 days after the clerk receives the mandate from the appellate court.

(e) The duty of a clerk to prepare and forward information under this section is not affected by:

(1) any subsequent appeal of the court order;

(2) any subsequent modification of the court order; or

(3) the expiration of the court order.

THE TEXAS RIGHT-TO-CARRY LAW

Originally enacted as "Senate Bill 60" in 1995, and amended in every session since then; originally codified as "Article 4413 (29ee) Revised Statutes" and subsequently moved to "Subchapter H, Chapter 411, Government Code." Note that some portions of the Right-to-Carry Law, as amended, are found as additions and amendments to other statutes in Texas law (e.g., PC §46.035). CHL applicants are required to read the Right-to-Carry law. Updates, changes and corrections may be found at GunLaws.com.

GOVERNMENT CODE, SUBCHAPTER H. LICENSE TO CARRY A CONCEALED HANDGUN

Government Code §411.171. Definitions
In this subchapter:
(1) <repealed 2013, formerly, definition of firearm action>
(2) "Chemically dependent person" means a person who frequently or repeatedly becomes intoxicated by excessive indulgence in alcohol or uses controlled substances or dangerous drugs so as to acquire a fixed habit and an involuntary tendency to become intoxicated or use those substances as often as the opportunity is presented.
(3) "Concealed handgun" means a handgun, the presence of which is not openly discernible to the ordinary observation of a reasonable person.
(4) "Convicted" means an adjudication of guilt or, except as provided in Section 411.1711, an order of deferred adjudication entered against a person by a court of competent jurisdiction whether or not the imposition of the sentence is subsequently probated and the person is discharged from community supervision. The term does not include an adjudication of guilt or an order of deferred adjudication that has been subsequently:
(A) expunged;
(B) pardoned under the authority of a state or federal official; or
(C) otherwise vacated, set aside, annulled, invalidated, voided, or sealed under any state or federal law.
(4-a) "Federal judge" means:
(A) a judge of a United States court of appeals;
(B) a judge of a United States district court;
(C) a judge of a United States bankruptcy court; or
(D) a magistrate judge of a United States district court.
(4-b) "State judge" means:
(A) the judge of an appellate court, a district court, or a county court at law of this state; or
(B) an associate judge appointed under Chapter 201, Family Code.
(5) "Handgun" has the meaning assigned by Section 46.01, Penal Code.
(6) "Intoxicated" has the meaning assigned by Section 49.01, Penal Code.
(7) "Qualified handgun instructor" means a person who is certified to instruct in the use of handguns by the department.

Government Code §411.1711. Certain Exemptions From Convictions
A person is not convicted, as that term is defined by Section 411.171, if an order of deferred adjudication was entered against the person on a date not less than 10 years preceding the date of the person's application for a license under this subchapter unless the order of deferred adjudication was entered against the person for:
(1) a felony [an] offense under:
(A) Title 5, Penal Code;
(B) Chapter 29, Penal Code;
(C) Section 25.07 or 25.072, Penal Code; or
(D) Section 30.02, Penal Code, if the offense is punishable under Subsection (c)(2) or (d) of that section; or
(2) an offense under the laws of another state if the offense contains elements that are substantially similar to the elements of an offense listed in Subdivision (1).

Government Code §411.172. Eligibility
(a) A person is eligible for a license to carry a concealed handgun if the person:
(1) is a legal resident of this state for the six-month period preceding the date of application under this subchapter or is otherwise eligible for a license under Section 411.173(a);
(2) is at least 21 years of age;
(3) has not been convicted of a felony;
(4) is not charged with the commission of a Class A or Class B misdemeanor or equivalent offense, or of an offense under Section 42.01, Penal Code, or equivalent offense, or of a felony under an information or indictment;

(5) is not a fugitive from justice for a felony or a Class A or Class B misdemeanor or equivalent offense;

(6) is not a chemically dependent person;

(7) is not incapable of exercising sound judgment with respect to the proper use and storage of a handgun;

(8) has not, in the five years preceding the date of application, been convicted of a Class A or Class B misdemeanor or equivalent offense or of an offense under Section 42.01, Penal Code, or equivalent offense;

(9) is fully qualified under applicable federal and state law to purchase a handgun;

(10) has not been finally determined to be delinquent in making a child support payment administered or collected by the attorney general;

(11) has not been finally determined to be delinquent in the payment of a tax or other money collected by the comptroller, the tax collector of a political subdivision of the state, or any agency or subdivision of the state;

(12) is not currently restricted under a court protective order or subject to a restraining order affecting the spousal relationship, other than a restraining order solely affecting property interests;

(13) has not, in the 10 years preceding the date of application, been adjudicated as having engaged in delinquent conduct violating a penal law of the grade of felony; and

(14) has not made any material misrepresentation, or failed to disclose any material fact, in an application submitted pursuant to Section 411.174.

(b) For the purposes of this section, an offense under the laws of this state, another state, or the United States is:

(1) except as provided by Subsection (b-1), a felony if the offense, at the time the offense is committed:

(A) is designated by a law of this state as a felony;

(B) contains all the elements of an offense designated by a law of this state as a felony; or

(C) is punishable by confinement for one year or more in a penitentiary; and

(2) a Class A misdemeanor if the offense is not a felony and confinement in a jail other than a state jail felony facility is affixed as a possible punishment.

(b-1) An offense is not considered a felony for purposes of Subsection (b) if, at the time of a person's application for a license to carry a concealed handgun, the offense:

(1) is not designated by a law of this state as a felony; and

(2) does not contain all the elements of any offense designated by a law of this state as a felony.

(c) An individual who has been convicted two times within the 10-year period preceding the date on which the person applies for a license of an offense of the grade of Class B misdemeanor or greater that involves the use of alcohol or a controlled substance as a statutory element of the offense is a chemically dependent person for purposes of this section and is not qualified to receive a license under this subchapter. This subsection does not preclude the disqualification of an individual for being a chemically dependent person if other evidence exists to show that the person is a chemically dependent person.

(d) For purposes of Subsection (a)(7), a person is incapable of exercising sound judgment with respect to the proper use and storage of a handgun if the person:

(1) has been diagnosed by a licensed physician as suffering from a psychiatric disorder or condition that causes or is likely to cause substantial impairment in judgment, mood, perception, impulse control, or intellectual ability;

(2) suffers from a psychiatric disorder or condition described by Subdivision (1) that:

(A) is in remission but is reasonably likely to redevelop at a future time; or

(B) requires continuous medical treatment to avoid redevelopment;

(3) has been diagnosed by a licensed physician, determined by a review board or similar authority, or declared by a court to be incompetent to manage the person's own affairs; or

(4) has entered in a criminal proceeding a plea of not guilty by reason of insanity.

(e) The following constitutes evidence that a person has a psychiatric disorder or condition described by Subsection (d)(1):

(1) involuntary psychiatric hospitalization;

(2) psychiatric hospitalization;

(3) inpatient or residential substance abuse treatment in the preceding five-year period;

(4) diagnosis in the preceding five-year period by a licensed physician that the person is dependent on alcohol, a controlled substance, or a similar substance; or

(5) diagnosis at any time by a licensed physician that the person suffers or has suffered from a psychiatric disorder or condition consisting of or relating to:

(A) schizophrenia or delusional disorder;

(B) bipolar disorder;

(C) chronic dementia, whether caused by illness, brain defect, or brain injury;

(D) dissociative identity disorder;

(E) intermittent explosive disorder; or

(F) antisocial personality disorder.

(f) Notwithstanding Subsection (d), a person who has previously been diagnosed as suffering from a psychiatric disorder or condition described by Subsection (d) or listed in Subsection (e) is not because of that disorder or condition incapable of exercising sound judgment with respect to the proper use and storage of a handgun if the person provides the department with a certificate from a licensed physician whose primary practice is in the field of psychiatry stating that the psychiatric disorder or condition is in remission and is not reasonably likely to develop at a future time.

(g) Notwithstanding Subsection (a)(2), a person who is at least 18 years of age but not yet 21 years of age is eligible for a license to carry a concealed handgun if the person:

(1) is a member or veteran of the United States armed forces, including a member or veteran of the reserves or national guard;

(2) was discharged under honorable conditions, if discharged from the United States armed forces, reserves, or national guard; and

(3) meets the other eligibility requirements of Subsection (a) except for the minimum age required by federal law to purchase a handgun.

(h) The issuance of a license to carry a concealed handgun to a person eligible under Subsection (g) does not affect the person's ability to purchase a handgun or ammunition under federal law.

Government Code §411.173. Nonresident License

(a) The department by rule shall establish a procedure for a person who meets the eligibility requirements of this subchapter other than the residency requirement established by Section 411.172(a)(1) to obtain a license under this subchapter if the person is a legal resident of another state or if the person relocates to this state with the intent to establish residency in this state. The procedure must include payment of a fee in an amount sufficient to recover the average cost to the department of obtaining a criminal history record check and investigation on a nonresident applicant. A license issued in accordance with the procedure established under this subsection:

(1) remains in effect until the license expires under Section 411.183; and

(2) may be renewed under Section 411.185.

(a-1) Repealed by Acts 2005, 79th Leg., ch. 915, § 4.

(b) The governor shall negotiate an agreement with any other state that provides for the issuance of a license to carry a concealed handgun under which a license issued by the other state is recognized in this state or shall issue a proclamation that a license issued by the other state is recognized in this state if the attorney general of the State of Texas determines that a background check of each applicant for a license issued by that state is initiated by state or local authorities or an agent of the state or local authorities before the license is issued. For purposes of this subsection, "background check" means a search of the National Crime Information Center database and the Interstate Identification Index maintained by the Federal Bureau of Investigation.

(c) The attorney general of the State of Texas shall annually:

(1) submit a report to the governor, lieutenant governor, and speaker of the house of representatives listing the states the attorney general has determined qualify for recognition under Subsection (b); and

(2) review the statutes of states that the attorney general has determined do not qualify for recognition under Subsection (b) to determine the changes to their statutes that are necessary to qualify for recognition under that subsection.

(d) The attorney general of the State of Texas shall submit the report required by Subsection (c)(1) not later than January 1 of each calendar year.

Government Code §411.174. Application

(a) An applicant for a license to carry a concealed handgun must submit to the director's designee described by Section 411.176:

(1) a completed application on a form provided by the department that requires only the information listed in Subsection (b);

(2) one or more photographs of the applicant that meet the requirements of the department;

(3) a certified copy of the applicant's birth certificate or certified proof of age;

(4) proof of residency in this state;

(5) two complete sets of legible and classifiable fingerprints of the applicant taken by a person appropriately trained in recording fingerprints who is employed by a law enforcement agency or by a private entity designated by a law enforcement agency as an entity qualified to take fingerprints of an applicant for a license under this subchapter;

(6) a nonrefundable application and license fee of $140 paid to the department;

(7) evidence of handgun proficiency, in the form and manner required by the department;

(8) an affidavit signed by the applicant stating that the applicant:

(A) has read and understands each provision of this subchapter that creates an offense under the laws of this state and each provision of the laws of this state related to use of deadly force; and

(B) fulfills all the eligibility requirements listed under Section 411.172; and

(9) a form executed by the applicant that authorizes the director to make an inquiry into any noncriminal history records that are necessary to determine the applicant's eligibility for a license under Section 411.172(a).

(b) An applicant must provide on the application a statement of the applicant's:

(1) full name and place and date of birth;

(2) race and sex;

(3) residence and business addresses for the preceding five years;

(4) hair and eye color;

(5) height and weight;

(6) driver's license number or identification certificate number issued by the department;

(7) criminal history record information of the type maintained by the department under this chapter, including a list of offenses for which the applicant was arrested, charged, or under an information or indictment and the disposition of the offenses; and

(8) history, if any, of treatment received by, commitment to, or residence in:

(A) a drug or alcohol treatment center licensed to provide drug or alcohol treatment under the laws of this state or another state, but only if the treatment, commitment, or residence occurred during the preceding five years; or

(B) a psychiatric hospital.

(b-1) The application must provide space for the applicant to:

(1) list any military service that may qualify the applicant to receive a license with a veteran's designation under Section 411.179(e); and

(2) include proof required by the department to determine the applicant's eligibility to receive that designation.

(c) The department shall distribute on request a copy of this subchapter and application materials.

(d) The department may not request or require an applicant to provide the applicant's social security number as part of an application under this section.

Government Code §411.175. Procedures For Submitting Fingerprints

The department shall establish procedures for the submission of legible and classifiable fingerprints by an applicant for a license under this subchapter who:

(1) is required to submit those fingerprints to the department, including an applicant under Section 411.199, 411.1991, or 411.201; and

(2) resides in a county having a population of 46,000 or less and does not reside within a 25-mile radius of a facility with the capability to process digital or electronic fingerprints.

Government Code §411.176. Review Of Application Materials

(a) On receipt of the application materials by the department at its initial Austin headquarters, the department shall conduct the appropriate criminal history record check of the applicant through its computerized criminal history system. Not later than the 30th day after the date the department receives the application materials, the department shall forward the materials to the director's designee in the geographical area of the applicant's residence so that the designee may conduct the investigation described by Subsection (b). For purposes of this section, the director's designee may be a noncommissioned employee of the department.

(b) The director's designee as needed shall conduct an additional criminal history record check of the applicant and an investigation of the applicant's local official records to verify the accuracy of the application materials. The director's designee may access any records necessary for purposes of this subsection. The scope of the record check and the investigation are at the sole discretion of the department, except that the director's designee shall complete the record check and investigation not later than the 60th day after the date the department receives the application materials. The department shall send a fingerprint card to the Federal Bureau of Investigation for a national criminal history check of the applicant. On completion of the investigation, the director's designee shall return all materials and the result of the investigation to the appropriate division of the department at its Austin headquarters.

(c) The director's designee may submit to the appropriate division of the department, at the department's Austin headquarters, along with the application materials a written recommendation for disapproval of the application, accompanied by an affidavit stating personal knowledge or naming persons with personal knowledge of a ground for denial under Section 411.172. The director's designee may also submit the application and the recommendation that the license be issued.

(d) On receipt at the department's Austin headquarters of the application materials and the result of the investigation by the director's designee, the department shall conduct any further record check or investigation the department determines is necessary if a question exists with respect to the accuracy of the application materials or the eligibility of the applicant, except that the department shall complete the record check and investigation not later than the 180th day after the date the department receives the application materials from the applicant.

Government Code §411.177. Issuance Or Denial Of License

(a) The department shall issue a license to carry a concealed handgun to an applicant if the applicant meets all the eligibility requirements and submits all the application materials. The department shall administer the licensing procedures in good faith so that any applicant who meets all the eligibility requirements and submits all the application materials shall receive a license. The department may not deny an application of the basis of a capricious or arbitrary decision by the department.

(b) The department shall, not later than the 60th day after the date of the receipt by the director's designee of the completed application materials:

(1) issue the license;

(2) notify the applicant in writing that the application was denied:
(A) on the grounds that the applicant failed to qualify under the criteria listed in Section 411.172;
(B) based on the affidavit of the director's designee submitted to the department under Section 411.176(c); or
(C) based on the affidavit of the qualified handgun instructor submitted to the department under Section 411.188(k); or
(3) notify the applicant in writing that the department is unable to make a determination regarding the issuance or denial of a license to the applicant within the 60-day period prescribed by this subsection and include in that notification an explanation of the reason for the inability and an estimation of the amount of time the department will need to make the determination.
(c) Failure of the department to issue or deny a license for a period of more than 30 days after the department is required to act under Subsection (b) constitutes denial.
(d) A license issued under this Subchapter is effective from the date of issuance.

Government Code §411.178. Notice to Local Law Enforcement
On request of a local law enforcement agency, the department shall notify the agency of the licenses that have been issued to license holders who reside in the county in which the agency is located.

Government Code §411.179. Form of License
(a) The department by rule shall adopt the form of the license. A license must include:
(1) a number assigned to the license holder by the department;
(2) a statement of the period for which the license is effective;
(3) a color photograph of the license holder;
(4) the license holder's full name, date of birth, hair and eye color, height, weight, and signature;
(5) the license holder's residence address or, as provided by Subsection (c), the street address of the courthouse in which the license holder or license holder's spouse serves as a federal judge or the license holder serves as a state judge; and
(6) the number of a driver's license or an identification certificate issued to the license holder by the department; and
(8) the designation "VETERAN" if required under Subsection (e). <sic, "(8)" SB164 2013>
(e) In this subsection, "veteran" has the meaning assigned by Section 411.1951. The department shall include the designation "VETERAN" on the face of any original, duplicate, modified, or renewed license under this subchapter or on the reverse side of the license, as determined by the department, if the license is issued to a veteran who:
(1) requests the designation;
(2) provides proof sufficient to the department of the veteran's military service and honorable discharge.
(b) <repealed in 2013; formerly, SA semi-automatic and NSA non-semi-automatic handguns>
(c) In adopting the form of the license under Subsection (a), the department shall establish a procedure for the license of a qualified handgun instructor or of a judge, justice, prosecuting attorney, or assistant prosecuting attorney, as described by Section 46.15(a)(4) or (6), Penal Code, to indicate on the license the license holder's status as a qualified handgun instructor or as a judge, justice, district attorney, criminal district attorney, or county attorney. In establishing the procedure, the department shall require sufficient documentary evidence to establish the license holder's status under this subsection.
(d) In adopting the form of the license under Subsection (a), the department shall establish a procedure for the license of a federal judge, a state judge, or the spouse of a federal judge or state judge to omit the license holder's residence address and to include, in lieu of that address, the street address of the courthouse in which the license holder or license holder's spouse serves as a federal judge or state judge. In establishing the procedure, the department shall require sufficient documentary evidence to establish the license holder's status as a federal judge, a state judge, or the spouse of a federal judge or state judge.

Government Code §411.180. Notification Of Denial, Revocation, Or Suspension Of License; Review
(a) The department shall give written notice to each applicant for a handgun license of any denial, revocation, or suspension of that license. Not later than the 30th day after the notice is received by the applicant, according to the records of the department, the applicant or license holder may request a hearing on the denial, revocation, or suspension. The applicant must make a written request for a hearing addressed to the department at its Austin address. The request for hearing must reach the department in Austin prior to the 30th day after the date of receipt of the written notice. On receipt of a request for hearing from a license holder or applicant, the department shall promptly schedule a hearing in the appropriate justice court in the county of residence of the applicant or license holder. The justice court shall conduct a hearing to review the denial, revocation, or suspension of the license. In a proceeding under this section, a justice of the peace shall act as an administrative hearing officer. A hearing under this section is not subject to Chapter 2001 (Administrative Procedure Act). A district attorney or county attorney, the attorney general, or a designated member of the department may represent the department.

(b) The department, on receipt of a request for hearing, shall file the appropriate petition in the justice court selected for the hearing and send a copy of that petition to the applicant or license holder at the address contained in departmental records. A hearing under this section must be scheduled within 30 days of receipt of the request for a hearing. The hearing shall be held expeditiously but in no event more than 60 days after the date that the applicant or license holder requested the hearing. The date of the hearing may be reset on the motion of either party, by agreement of the parties, or by the court as necessary to accommodate the court's docket.

(c) The justice court shall determine if the denial, revocation, or suspension is supported by a preponderance of the evidence. Both the applicant or license holder and the department may present evidence. The court shall affirm the denial, revocation, or suspension if the court determines that denial, revocation, or suspension is supported by a preponderance of the evidence. If the court determines that the denial, revocation, or suspension is not supported by a preponderance of the evidence, the court shall order the department to immediately issue or return the license to the applicant or license holder.

(d) A proceeding under this section is subject to Chapter 105, Civil Practice and Remedies Code, relating to fees, expenses, and attorney's fees.

(e) A party adversely affected by the court's ruling following a hearing under this section may appeal the ruling by filing within 30 days after the ruling a petition in a county court at law in the county in which the applicant or license holder resides or, if there is no county court at law in the county, in the county court of the county. A person who appeals under this section must send by certified mail a copy of the person's petition, certified by the clerk of the court in which the petition is filed, to the appropriate division of the department at its Austin headquarters. The trial on appeal shall be a trial de novo without a jury. A district or county attorney or the attorney general may represent the department.

(f) A suspension of a license may not be probated.

(g) If an applicant or a license holder does not petition the justice court, a denial becomes final and a revocation or suspension takes effect on the 30th day after receipt of written notice.

(h) The department may use and introduce into evidence certified copies of governmental records to establish the existence of certain events that could result in the denial, revocation, or suspension of a license under this subchapter, including records regarding convictions, judicial findings regarding mental competency, judicial findings regarding chemical dependency, or other matters that may be established by governmental records that have been properly authenticated.

(i) This section does not apply to a suspension of a license under Section 85.022, Family Code, or Article 17.292, Code of Criminal Procedure.

Government Code §411.181. Notice Of Change Of Address Or Name

(a) If a person who is a current license holder moves from any residence address stated on the license, if the name of the person is changed by marriage or otherwise, or if the person's status becomes inapplicable for purposes of the information required to be displayed on the license under Section 411.179, the person shall, not later than the 30th day after the date of the address, name, or status change, notify the department and provide the department with the number of the person's license and, as applicable, the person's:

(1) former and new addresses;

(2) former and new names; or

(3) former and new status.

(b) If the name of the license holder is changed by marriage or otherwise, or if the person's status becomes inapplicable as described by Subsection (a), the person shall apply for a duplicate license. The duplicate license must reflect the person's current name, residence address, and status.

(c) If a license holder moves from the address stated on the license, the person shall apply for a duplicate license.

(d) The department shall charge a license holder a fee of $25 for a duplicate license.

(e) The department shall make the forms available on request.

(f) On request of a local law enforcement agency, the department shall notify the agency of changes made under Subsection (a) by license holders who reside in the county in which the agency is located.

(g) If a license is lost, stolen, or destroyed, the license holder shall apply for a duplicate license not later than the 30th day after the date of the loss, theft, or destruction of the license.

(h) If a license holder is required under this section to apply for a duplicate license and the license expires not later than the 60th day after the date of the loss, theft, or destruction of the license, the applicant may renew the license with the modified information included on the new license. The applicant must pay only the nonrefundable renewal fee.

(i) A license holder whose application fee for a duplicate license under this section is dishonored or reversed may reapply for a duplicate license at any time, provided the application fee and a dishonored payment charge of $25 is paid by cashier's check or money order made payable to the "Texas Department of Public Safety."

Government Code §411.182. Notice
(a) For the purpose of a notice required by this subchapter, the department may assume that the address currently reported to the department by the applicant or license holder is the correct address.
(b) A written notice meets the requirements under this subchapter if the notice is sent by certified mail to the current address reported by the applicant or license holder to the department.
(c) If a notice is returned to the department because the notice is not deliverable, the department may give notice by publication once in a newspaper of general interest in the county of the applicant's or license holder's last reported address. On the 31st day after the date the notice is published, the department may take the action proposed in the notice.

Government Code §411.183. Expiration
(a) A license issued under this subchapter expires on the first birthday of the license holder occurring after the fourth anniversary of the date of issuance.
(b) A renewed license expires on the license holder's birthdate, five years after the date of the expiration of the previous license.
(c) A duplicate license expires on the date the license that was duplicated would have expired.
(d) A modified license expires on the date the license that was modified would have expired.
(e) Expired.

Government Code §411.185. License Renewal Procedure
(a) To renew a license, a license holder must, on or before the date the license expires, submit to the department by mail or, in accordance with the procedure adopted under Subsection (f), on the Internet:
(1) a renewal application on a form provided by the department;
(2) payment of a nonrefundable renewal fee as set by the department; and
(3) the informational form described by Subsection (c) signed or electronically acknowledged by the applicant.
(b) The director by rule shall adopt a renewal application form requiring an update of the information on the original completed application. The director by rule shall set the renewal fee in an amount that is sufficient to cover the actual cost to the department to:
(1) verify the information contained in the renewal application form;
(2) conduct any necessary investigation concerning the license holder's continued eligibility to hold a license; and
(3) issue the renewed license.
(c) The director by rule shall adopt an informational form that describes state law regarding the use of deadly force and the places where it is unlawful for the holder of a license issued under this subchapter to carry a concealed handgun. An applicant for a renewed license must sign and return the informational form to the department by mail or acknowledge the form electronically on the Internet according to the procedure adopted under Subsection (f).
(d) Not later than the 60th day before the expiration date of the license, the department shall mail to each license holder a written notice of the expiration of the license, a renewal application form, and the informational form described by Subsection (c).
(e) <HB48 2013> The department shall renew the license of a license holder who meets all the eligibility requirements to continue to hold a license and submits all the renewal materials described by Subsection (a). Not later than the 45th day after receipt of the renewal materials, the department shall issue the renewed license or notify the license holder in writing that the department denied the license holder's renewal application.
(e) <HB1349 2013> The department may not request or require a license holder to provide the license holder's social security number to renew a license under this section.
(f) The director by rule shall adopt a procedure by which a license holder who satisfies the eligibility requirements to continue to hold a license may submit the renewal materials described by Subsection (a) by mail or on the Internet.

Government Code §411.186. Revocation
(a) The department shall revoke a license under this section if the license holder:
(1) was not entitled to the license at the time it was issued;
(2) made a material misrepresentation or failed to disclose a material fact in an application submitted under this subchapter;
(3) subsequently becomes ineligible for a license under Section 411.172, unless the sole basis for the ineligibility is that the license holder is charged with the commission of a Class A or Class B misdemeanor or equivalent offense, or of an offense under Section 42.01, Penal Code, or equivalent offense, or of a felony under an information or indictment;
(4) is convicted of an offense under Section 46.035, Penal Code;
(5) is determined by the department to have engaged in conduct constituting a reason to suspend a license listed in Section 411.187(a) after the person's license has been previously suspended twice for the same reason; or
(6) submits an application fee that is dishonored or reversed if the applicant fails to submit a cashier's check or money order made payable to the "Department of Public Safety of the State of Texas" in

the amount of the dishonored or reversed fee, plus $25, within 30 days of being notified by the department that the fee was dishonored or reversed.

(b) If a peace officer believes a reason listed in Subsection (a) to revoke a license exists, the officer shall prepare an affidavit on a form provided by the department stating the reason for the revocation of the license and giving the department all of the information available to the officer at the time of the preparation of the form. The officer shall attach the officer's reports relating to the license holder to the form and send the form and attachments to the appropriate division of the department at its Austin headquarters not later than the fifth working day after the date the form is prepared. The officer shall send a copy of the form and the attachments to the license holder. If the license holder has not surrendered the license or the license was not seized as evidence, the license holder shall surrender the license to the appropriate division of the department not later than the 10th day after the date the license holder receives the notice of revocation from the department, unless the license holder requests a hearing from the department. The license holder may request that the justice court in the justice court precinct in which the license holder resides review the revocation as provided by Section 411.180. If a request is made for the justice court to review the revocation and hold a hearing, the license holder shall surrender the license on the date an order of revocation is entered by the justice court.

(c) A license holder whose license is revoked for a reason listed in Subsections (a)(1)-(5) may reapply as a new applicant for the issuance of a license under this subchapter after the second anniversary of the date of the revocation if the cause for revocation does not exist on the date of the second anniversary. If the cause for revocation exists on the date of the second anniversary after the date of revocation, the license holder may not apply for a new license until the cause for revocation no longer exists and has not existed for a period of two years.

(d) A license holder whose license is revoked under Subsection (a)(6) may reapply for an original or renewed license at any time, provided the application fee and a dishonored payment charge of $25 is paid by cashier's check or money order made payable to the "Texas Department of Public Safety. "

Government Code §411.187. Suspension Of License

(a) The department shall suspend a license under this section if the license holder:

(1) is charged with the commission of a Class A or Class B misdemeanor or equivalent offense, or of an offense under Section 42.01, Penal Code, or equivalent offense, or of a felony under an information or indictment;

(2) fails to notify the department of a change of address, name, or status as required by Section 411.181;

(3) commits an act of family violence and is the subject of an active protective order rendered under Title 4, Family Code; or

(4) is arrested for an offense involving family violence or an offense under Section 42.072, Penal Code, and is the subject of an order for emergency protection issued under Article 17.292, Code of Criminal Procedure.

(b) If a peace officer believes a reason listed in Subsection (a) to suspend a license exists, the officer shall prepare an affidavit on a form provided by the department stating the reason for the suspension of the license and giving the department all of the information available to the officer at the time of the preparation of the form. The officer shall attach the officer's reports relating to the license holder to the form and send the form and the attachments to the appropriate division of the department at its Austin headquarters not later than the fifth working day after the date the form is prepared. The officer shall send a copy of the form and the attachments to the license holder. If the license holder has not surrendered the license or the license was not seized as evidence, the license holder shall surrender the license to the appropriate division of the department not later than the 10th day after the date the license holder receives the notice of suspension from the department unless the license holder requests a hearing from the department. The license holder may request that the justice court in the justice court precinct in which the license holder resides review the suspension as provided by Section 411.180. If a request is made for the justice court to review the suspension and hold a hearing, the license holder shall surrender the license on the date an order of suspension is entered by the justice court.

(c) The department shall suspend a license under this section:

(1) for 30 days, if the person's license is subject to suspension for a reason listed in Subsection (a)(2), (3), or (4), except as provided by Subdivision (2);

(2) for not less than one year and not more than three years if the person's license is subject to suspension for a reason listed in Subsection (a), other than the reason listed in Subsection (a)(1), and the person's license has been previously suspended for the same reason;

(3) until dismissal of the charges, if the person's license is subject to suspension for the reason listed in Subsection (a)(1); or

(4) for the duration of or the period specified by:

(A) the protective order issued under Title 4, Family Code, if the person's license is subject to suspension for the reason listed in Subsection (a)(5); or

(B) the order for emergency protection issued under Article 17.292, Code of Criminal Procedure, if the person's license is subject to suspension for the reason listed in Subsection (a)(6).

Government Code §411.1871. Notice Of Suspension Or Revocation Of Certain Licenses
The department shall notify the Texas Commission on Law Enforcement Officer Standards and Education if the department takes any action against the license of a person identified by the commission as a person certified under Section 1701.260, Occupations Code, including suspension or revocation.

Government Code §411.188. Handgun Proficiency Requirement
(a) The director shall by rule establish minimum standards for handgun proficiency and shall develop a course to teach handgun proficiency and examinations to measure handgun proficiency. The course to teach handgun proficiency is required for each person who seeks to obtain or renew a license and must contain training sessions divided into two parts. One part of the course must be classroom instruction and the other part must be range instruction and an actual demonstration by the applicant of the applicant's ability to safely and proficiently use a handgun. An applicant must be able to demonstrate, at a minimum, the degree of proficiency that is required to effectively operate a handgun of .32 caliber or above. The department shall distribute the standards, course requirements, and examinations on request to any qualified handgun instructor.
(b) Only qualified handgun instructors may administer the classroom instruction part or the range instruction part of the handgun proficiency course. The classroom instruction part of the course must include not less than four hours and not more than six hours of instruction on:
(1) the laws that relate to weapons and to the use of deadly force;
(2) handgun use and safety;
(3) nonviolent dispute resolution; and
(4) proper storage practices for handguns with an emphasis on storage practices that eliminate the possibility of accidental injury to a child.
(c) <repealed 2013, formerly, the department's continuing education course for CHL renewals>
(d) Only a qualified handgun instructor may administer the proficiency examination to obtain a license. The proficiency examination must include:
(1) a written section on the subjects listed in Subsection (b); and
(2) a physical demonstration of proficiency in the use of one or more handguns and in handgun safety procedures.
(e) <repealed 2013, formerly, instructor category certification>
(f) The department shall develop and distribute directions and materials for course instruction, test administration, and recordkeeping. All test results shall be sent to the department, and the department shall maintain a record of the results.
(g) A person who wishes to obtain a license to carry a concealed handgun must apply in person to a qualified handgun instructor to take the appropriate course in handgun proficiency and demonstrate handgun proficiency as required by the department.
(h) <repealed 2013, formerly, instructor category qualification>
(i) A certified firearms instructor of the department may monitor any class or training presented by a qualified handgun instructor. A qualified handgun instructor shall cooperate with the department in the department's efforts to monitor the presentation of training by the qualified handgun instructor. A qualified handgun instructor shall make available for inspection to the department any and all records maintained by a qualified handgun instructor under this subchapter. The qualified handgun instructor shall keep a record of all information required by department rule.
(j) For license holders seeking to renew their licenses, the department may offer online, or allow a qualified handgun instructor to offer online, the classroom instruction part of the handgun proficiency course and the written section of the proficiency examination. <repealed, HB48 2013, but also added, SB864, 2013>
(k) A qualified handgun instructor may submit to the department a written recommendation for disapproval of the application for a license or modification of a license, accompanied by an affidavit stating personal knowledge or naming persons with personal knowledge of facts that lead the instructor to believe that an applicant does not possess the required handgun proficiency. The department may use a written recommendation submitted under this subsection as the basis for denial of a license only if the department determines that the recommendation is made in good faith and is supported by a preponderance of the evidence. The department shall make a determination under this subsection not later than the 45th day after the date the department receives the written recommendation. The 60-day period in which the department must take action under Section 411.177(b) is extended one day for each day a determination is pending under this subsection.

Government Code §411.1881. Exemption From Instruction For Certain Persons
(a) Notwithstanding any other provision of this subchapter, a person may not be required to complete the range instruction portion of a handgun proficiency course to obtain a license issued under this subchapter if the person:
(1) is currently serving in or is honorably discharged from:
(A) the army, navy, air force, coast guard, or marine corps of the United States or an auxiliary service or reserve unit of one of those branches of the armed forces; or
(B) the Texas military forces, as defined by Section 437.001; and

(2) has, within the five years preceding the date of the person's application the license, completed a course of training in handgun proficiency or familiarization as part of the person's service with the armed forces or Texas military forces.

(b) The director by rule shall adopt a procedure by which a license holder who is exempt under Subsection (a) from the range instruction portion of the handgun proficiency requirement may submit a form demonstrating the license holder's qualification for an exemption under that subsection. The form must provide sufficient information to allow the department to verify whether the license holder qualifies for the exemption.

Government Code §411.1882. Evidence Of Handgun Proficiency For Certain Persons

(a) A person who is serving in this state as a judge or justice of a federal court, as an active judicial officer, as defined by Section 411.201, or as a district attorney, assistant district attorney, criminal district attorney, assistant criminal district attorney, county attorney, or assistant county attorney may establish handgun proficiency for the purposes of this subchapter by obtaining from a handgun proficiency instructor approved by the Commission on Law Enforcement Officer Standards and Education for purposes of Section 1702.1675, Occupations Code, a sworn statement that indicates that the person, during the 12-month period preceding the date of the person's application to the department, demonstrated to the instructor proficiency in the use of handguns.

(b) The director by rule shall adopt a procedure by which a person described under Subsection (a) may submit a form demonstrating the person's qualification for an exemption under that subsection. The form must provide sufficient information to allow the department to verify whether the person qualifies for the exemption.

(c) A license issued under this section automatically expires on the six-month anniversary of the date the person's status under Subsection (a) becomes inapplicable. A license that expires under this subsection may be renewed under Section 411.185.

Government Code §411.190. Qualified Handgun Instructors

(a) The director may certify as a qualified handgun instructor a person who:
(1) is certified by the Commission on Law Enforcement Officer Standards and Education or under Chapter 1702, Occupations Code to instruct others in the use of handguns;
(2) regularly instructs others in the use of handguns and has graduated from a handgun instructor school that uses a nationally accepted course designed to train persons as handgun instructors; or
(3) is certified by the National Rifle Association of America as a handgun instructor.

(b) In addition to the qualifications described by Subsection (a), a qualified handgun instructor must be qualified to instruct persons in:
(1) the laws that relate to weapons and to the use of deadly force;
(2) handgun use, proficiency, and safety;
(3) nonviolent dispute resolution; and
(4) proper storage practices for handguns, including storage practices that eliminate the possibility of accidental injury to a child.

(c) In the manner applicable to a person who applies for a license to carry a concealed handgun, the department shall conduct a background check of a person who applies for certification as a qualified handgun instructor. If the background check indicates that the applicant for certification would not qualify to receive a handgun license, the department may not certify the applicant as a qualified handgun instructor. If the background check indicates that the applicant for certification would qualify to receive a handgun license, the department shall provide handgun instructor training to the applicant. The applicant shall pay a fee of $100 to the department for the training. The applicant must take and successfully complete the training offered by the department and pay the training fee before the department may certify the applicant as a qualified handgun instructor. The department shall issue a license to carry a concealed handgun under the authority of this subchapter to any person who is certified as a qualified handgun instructor and who pays to the department a fee of $100 in addition to the training fee. The department by rule may prorate or waive the training fee for an employee of another governmental entity.

(d) The certification of a qualified handgun instructor expires on the second anniversary after the date of certification. To renew a certification, the qualified handgun instructor must pay a fee of $100 and take and successfully complete the retraining courses required by department rule.

(d-1) The department shall ensure that an applicant may renew certification under Subsection (d) from any county in this state by using an online format to complete the required retraining courses if:
(1) the applicant is renewing certification for the first time; or
(2) the applicant completed the required retraining courses in person the previous time the applicant renewed certification.

(e) After certification, a qualified handgun instructor may conduct training for applicants for a license under this subchapter.

(f) If the department determines that a reason exists to revoke, suspend, or deny a license to carry a concealed handgun with respect to a person who is a qualified handgun instructor or an applicant for certification as a qualified handgun instructor, the department shall take that action against the person's:

(1) license to carry a concealed handgun, if the person is an applicant for or the holder of a license issued under this subchapter; and
(2) certification as a qualified handgun instructor.

Government Code §411.191. Review Of Denial, Revocation, Or Suspension Of Certification As Qualified Handgun Instructor
The procedures for the review of a denial, revocation, or suspension of a license under Section 411.180 apply to the review of a denial, revocation, or suspension of certification as a qualified handgun instructor. The notice provisions of this subchapter relating to denial, revocation, or suspension of handgun licenses apply to the proposed denial, revocation, or suspension of a certification of a qualified handgun instructor or an applicant for certification as a qualified handgun instructor.

Government Code §411.192. Confidentiality Of Records
(a) The department shall disclose to a criminal justice agency information contained in its files and records regarding whether a named individual or any individual named in a specified list is licensed under this subchapter. Information on an individual subject to disclosure under this section includes the individual's name, date of birth, gender, race, and zip code. Except as otherwise provided by this section and by Section 411.193, all other records maintained under this subchapter are confidential and are not subject to mandatory disclosure under the open records law, Chapter 552.
(b) An applicant or license holder may be furnished a copy of disclosable records regarding the applicant or license holder on request and the payment of a reasonable fee.
(c) The department shall notify a license holder of any request that is made for information relating to the license holder under this section and provide the name of the agency making the request.
(d) This section does not prohibit the department from making public and distributing to the public at no cost lists of individuals who are certified as qualified handgun instructors by the department.

Government Code §411.193. Statistical Report
The department shall make available, on request and payment of a reasonable fee to cover costs of copying, a statistical report that includes the number of licenses issued, denied, revoked, or suspended by the department during the preceding month, listed by age, gender, race, and zip code of the applicant or license holder.

Government Code §411.194. Reduction Of Fees Due To Indigency
(a) Notwithstanding any other provision of this subchapter, the department shall reduce by 50 percent any fee required for the issuance of an original, duplicate, modified, or renewed license under this subchapter if the department determines that the applicant is indigent.
(b) The department shall require an applicant requesting a reduction of a fee to submit proof of indigency with the application materials.
(c) For purposes of this section, an applicant is indigent if the applicant's income is not more than 100 percent of the applicable income level established by the federal poverty guidelines.

Government Code §411.195. Reduction Of Fees For Senior Citizens
Notwithstanding any other provision of this subchapter, the department shall reduce by 50 percent any fee required for the issuance of an original, duplicate, modified, or renewed license under this subchapter if the applicant for the license is 60 years of age or older.

Government Code §411.1951. Waiver Or Reduction Of Fees For Members Or Veterans Of United States Armed Forces
(a) In this section, "veteran" means a person who:
(1) has served in:
(A) the army, navy, air force, coast guard, or marine corps of the United States;
(B) the Texas military forces as defined by Section 437.001; or
(C) an auxiliary service of one of those branches of the armed forces; and
(2) has been honorably discharged from the branch of the service in which the person served.
(b) Notwithstanding any other provision of this subchapter, the department shall waive any fee required for the issuance of an original, duplicate, modified, or renewed license under this subchapter if the applicant for the license is:
(1) a member of the United States armed forces, including a member of the reserves, national guard, or state guard; or
(2) a veteran who, within 365 days preceding the date of the application, was honorably discharged from the branch of service in which the person served.
(c) Notwithstanding any other provision of this subchapter, the department shall reduce by 50 percent any fee required for the issuance of an original, duplicate, modified, or renewed license under this subchapter if the applicant for the license is a veteran who, more than 365 days preceding the date of the application, was honorably discharged from the branch of the service in which the person served.

Government Code §411.196. Method Of Payment
A person may pay a fee required by this subchapter by cash, credit card, personal check, cashier's check, or money order. A person who pays a fee required by this subchapter by cash must pay the fee in person. Checks or money orders must be made payable to the "Texas Department of Public Safety." A person whose payment for a fee required by this subchapter is dishonored or reversed must pay any future fees required by this subchapter by cashier's check or money order made payable to the "Texas Department of Public Safety." A fee received by the department under this subchapter is nonrefundable.

Government Code §411.197. Rules
The director shall adopt rules to administer this subchapter.

Government Code §411.198. Law Enforcement Officer Alias Handgun License
(a) On written approval of the director, the department may issue to a law enforcement officer an alias license to carry a concealed handgun to be used in supervised activities involving criminal investigations.
(b) It is a defense to prosecution under Section 46.035, Initial Penal Code, that the actor, at the time of the commission of the offense, was the holder of an alias license issued under this section.

Government Code §411.199. Honorably Retired Peace Officers
(a) A person who is licensed as a peace officer under Chapter 1701, Occupations Code, and who has been employed full-time as a peace officer by a law enforcement agency may apply for a license under this subchapter at any time after retirement.
(b) The person shall submit two complete sets of legible and classifiable fingerprints and a sworn statement from the head of the law enforcement agency employing the applicant. A head of a law enforcement agency may not refuse to issue a statement under this subsection. If the applicant alleges that the statement is untrue, the department shall investigate the validity of the statement. The statement must include:
(1) the name and rank of the applicant;
(2) the status of the applicant before retirement;
(3) whether or not the applicant was accused of misconduct at the time of the retirement;
(4) the physical and mental condition of the applicant;
(5) the type of weapons the applicant had demonstrated proficiency with during the last year of employment;
(6) whether the applicant would be eligible for reemployment with the agency, and if not, the reasons the applicant is not eligible; and
(7) a recommendation from the agency head regarding the issuance of a license under this subchapter.
(c) The department may issue a license under this subchapter to an applicant under this section if the applicant is honorably retired and physically and emotionally fit to possess a handgun. In this subsection, "honorably retired" means the applicant:
(1) did not retire in lieu of any disciplinary action;
(2) was eligible to retire from the law enforcement agency or was ineligible to retire only as a result of an injury received in the course of the applicant's employment with the agency; and
(3) is entitled to receive a pension or annuity for service as a law enforcement officer or is not entitled to receive a pension or annuity only because the law enforcement agency that employed the applicant does not offer a pension or annuity to its employees.
(d) An applicant under this section must pay a fee of $25 for a license issued under this subchapter.
(e) A retired peace officer who obtains a license under this subchapter must maintain the proficiency required for a peace officer under Section 1701.355, Occupations Code. The department or a local law enforcement agency shall allow a retired peace officer of the department or agency an opportunity to annually demonstrate the required proficiency. The proficiency shall be reported to the department on application and renewal. <repealed, HB48, 2013>
(f) A license issued under this section expires as provided by Section 411.183.
(g) A retired officer of the United States who was eligible to carry a firearm in the discharge of the officer's official duties is eligible for a license under this section. An applicant described by this subsection may submit the application at any time after retirement. The applicant shall submit with the application proper proof of retired status by presenting the following documents prepared by the agency from which the applicant retired:
(1) retirement credentials; and
(2) a letter from the agency head stating the applicant retired in good standing.

Government Code §411.1991. Peace Officers
(a) A person who is licensed as a peace officer under Chapter 1701, Occupations Code, and is employed as a peace officer by a law enforcement agency, or a member of the Texas military forces, excluding Texas State Guard members who are serving in the Texas Legislature may apply for a license under this subchapter. The person shall submit to the department two complete sets of legible and classifiable fingerprints and a sworn statement of the head of the law enforcement agency employing the applicant. A head of a law enforcement agency may not refuse to issue a

statement under this subsection. If the statement is alleged by the applicant to be untrue, the department shall investigate the validity of the statement. The statement must include:

(1) the name and rank of the applicant;

(2) whether the applicant has been accused of misconduct at any time during the applicant's period of employment with the agency and the disposition of that accusation;

(3) a description of the physical and mental condition of the applicant;

(4) a list of the types of weapons the applicant has demonstrated proficiency with during the preceding year; and

(5) a recommendation from the agency head that a license be issued to the person under this subchapter.

(b) The department may issue a license under this subchapter to an applicant under this section if the statement from the head of the law enforcement agency employing the applicant complies with Subsection (a) and indicates that the applicant is qualified and physically and mentally fit to carry a handgun.

(c) An applicant under this section shall pay a fee of $25 for a license issued under this subchapter.

(d) A license issued under this section expires as provided by Section 411.183.

Government Code §411.200. Application To Licensed Security Officers

This subchapter does not exempt a license holder who is also employed as a security officer and licensed under Chapter 1702, Occupations Code from the duty to comply with that Act or Section 46.02, Penal Code.

Government Code §411.201. Active And Retired Judicial Officers

(a) In this section:

(1) "Active judicial officer" means:

(A) a person serving as a judge or justice of the supreme court, the court of criminal appeals, a court of appeals, a district court, a criminal district court, a constitutional county court, a statutory county court, a justice court, or a municipal court; or

(B) a federal judge who is a resident of this state.

(2) "Retired judicial officer" means:

(A) a special judge appointed under Section 26.023 or 26.024; or

(B) a senior judge designated under Section 75.001, or a judicial officer as designated or defined by Section 75.001, 831.001, or 836.001.

(b) Notwithstanding any other provision of this subchapter, the department shall issue a license under this subchapter to an active or retired judicial officer who meets the requirements of this section.

(c) An active judicial officer is eligible for a license to carry a concealed handgun under the authority of this subchapter. A retired judicial officer is eligible for a license to carry a concealed handgun under the authority of this subchapter if the officer:

(1) has not been convicted of a felony;

(2) has not, in the five years preceding the date of application, been convicted of a Class A or Class B misdemeanor or equivalent offense;

(3) is not charged with the commission of a Class A or Class B misdemeanor or equivalent offense or of a felony under an information or indictment;

(4) is not a chemically dependent person; and

(5) is not a person of unsound mind.

(d) An applicant for a license who is an active or retired judicial officer must submit to the department:

(1) a completed application, including all required affidavits, on a form prescribed by the department;

(2) one or more photographs of the applicant that meet the requirements of the department;

(3) two complete sets of legible and classifiable fingerprints of the applicant, including one set taken by a person employed by a law enforcement agency who is appropriately trained in recording fingerprints;

(4) evidence of handgun proficiency, in the form and manner required by the department for an applicant under this section;

(5) a nonrefundable application and license fee set by the department in an amount reasonably designed to cover the administrative costs associated with issuance of a license to carry a concealed handgun under this subchapter; and

(6) if the applicant is a retired judicial officer, a form executed by the applicant that authorizes the department to make an inquiry into any noncriminal history records that are necessary to determine the applicant's eligibility for a license under this subchapter.

(e) On receipt of all the application materials required by this section, the department shall:

(1) if the applicant is an active judicial officer, issue a license to carry a concealed handgun under the authority of this subchapter; or

(2) if the applicant is a retired judicial officer, conduct an appropriate background investigation to determine the applicant's eligibility for the license and, if the applicant is eligible, issue a license to carry a concealed handgun under the authority of this subchapter.

(f) Except as otherwise provided by this subsection, an applicant for a license under this section must satisfy the handgun proficiency requirements of Section 411.188. The classroom instruction part of

the proficiency course for an active judicial officer is not subject to a minimum hour requirement. The instruction must include instruction only on:
(1) handgun use, proficiency, and safety; and
(2) proper storage practices for handguns with an emphasis on storage practices that eliminate the possibility of accidental injury to a child.
(g) A license issued under this section expires as provided by Section 411.183 and may be renewed in accordance with Section 411.185.
(h) The department shall issue a license to carry a concealed handgun under the authority of this subchapter to an elected attorney representing the state in the prosecution of felony cases who meets the requirements of this section for an active judicial officer. The department shall waive any fee required for the issuance of an original, duplicate, or renewed license under this subchapter for an applicant who is an attorney elected or employed to represent the state in the prosecution of felony cases.

Government Code §411.202. License A Benefit
The issuance of a license under this subchapter is a benefit to the license holder for purposes of those sections of the Penal Code to which the definition of "benefit" under Section 1.07, Penal Code, apply.

Government Code §411.203. Rights Of Employers
This subchapter does not prevent or otherwise limit the right of a public or private employer to prohibit persons who are licensed under this subchapter from carrying a concealed handgun on the premises of the business. In this section, "premises" has the meaning assigned by Section 46.035(f)(3), Penal Code.

Government Code §411.204. Notice Required On Certain Premises
(a) A business that has a permit or license issued under Chapter 25, 28, 32, 69, or 74, Alcoholic Beverage Code, and that derives 51 percent or more of its income from the sale of alcoholic beverages for on-premises consumption as determined by the Texas Alcoholic Beverage Commission under Section 104.06, Alcoholic Beverage Code, shall prominently display at each entrance to the business premises a sign that complies with the requirements of Subsection (c).
(b) A hospital licensed under Chapter 241, Health and Safety Code, or a nursing home licensed under Chapter 242, Health and Safety Code, shall prominently display at each entrance to the hospital or nursing home, as appropriate, a sign that complies with the requirements of Subsection (c) other than the requirement that the sign include on its face the number "51".
(c) The sign required under Subsections (a) and (b) must give notice in both English and Spanish that it is unlawful for a person licensed under this subchapter to carry a handgun on the premises. The sign must appear in contrasting colors with block letters at least one inch in height and must include on its face the number "51" printed in solid red at least five inches in height. The sign shall be displayed in a conspicuous manner clearly visible to the public.
(d) A business that has a permit or license issued under the Alcoholic Beverage Code and that is not required to display a sign under this section may be required to display a sign under Section 11.041 or Section 61.11, Alcoholic Beverage Code.
(e) This section does not apply to a business that has a food and beverage certificate issued under the Alcoholic Beverage Code.

Government Code §411.206. Seizure Of Handgun And License
(a) If a peace officer arrests and takes into custody a license holder who is carrying a handgun under the authority of this subchapter, the officer shall seize the license holder's handgun and license as evidence.
(b) The provisions of Article 18.19, Code of Criminal Procedure, relating to the disposition of weapons seized in connection with criminal offenses, apply to a handgun seized under this subsection.
(c) Any judgment of conviction entered by any court for an offense under Section 46.035, Penal Code, must contain the handgun license number of the convicted license holder. A certified copy of the judgment is conclusive and sufficient evidence to justify revocation of a license under Section 411.186(a)(4).

Government Code §411.207. Authority Of Peace Officer To Disarm
(a) A peace officer who is acting in the lawful discharge of the officer's official duties may disarm a license holder at any time the officer reasonably believes it is necessary for the protection of the license holder, officer, or other individual. The peace officer shall return the handgun to the license holder before discharging the license holder from the scene if the officer determines that the license holder is not a threat to the officer, license holder, or other individual, and if the license holder has not violated any provision of this subchapter, or committed any other violation that results in the arrest of the license holder.
(b) A peace officer who is acting in the lawful discharge of the officer's official duties may temporarily disarm a license holder when a license holder enters a nonpublic, secure portion of a law enforcement facility, if the law enforcement agency provides a gun locker where the peace officer can secure the license holder's handgun. The peace officer shall secure the handgun in the

locker and shall return the handgun to the license holder immediately after the license holder leaves the nonpublic, secure portion of the law enforcement facility.

(c) A law enforcement facility shall prominently display at each entrance to a nonpublic, secure portion of the facility a sign that gives notice in both English and Spanish that, under this section, a peace officer may temporarily disarm a license holder when the license holder enters the nonpublic, secure portion of the facility. The sign must appear in contrasting colors with block letters at least one inch in height. The sign shall be displayed in a clearly visible and conspicuous manner.

(d) In this section:

(1) "Law enforcement facility" means a building or a portion of a building used exclusively by a law enforcement agency that employs peace officers as described by Articles 2.12(1) and (3), Code of Criminal Procedure, and support personnel to conduct the official business of the agency. The term does not include:

(A) any portion of a building not actively used exclusively to conduct the official business of the agency; or

(B) any public or private driveway, street, sidewalk, walkway, parking lot, parking garage, or other parking area.

(2) "Nonpublic, secure portion of a law enforcement facility" means that portion of a law enforcement facility to which the general public is denied access without express permission and to which access is granted solely to conduct the official business of the law enforcement agency.

Government Code §411.208. Limitation Of Liability

(a) A court may not hold the state, an agency or subdivision of the state, an officer or employee of the state, a peace officer, or a qualified handgun instructor liable for damages caused by:

(1) an action authorized under this subchapter or failure to perform a duty imposed by this subchapter; or

(2) the actions of an applicant or license holder that occur after the applicant has received a license or been denied a license under this subchapter.

(b) A cause of action in damages may not be brought against the state, an agency or subdivision of the state, an officer or employee of the state, a peace officer, or a qualified handgun instructor for any damage caused by the actions of an applicant or license holder under this subchapter.

(c) The department is not responsible for any injury or damage inflicted on any person by an applicant or license holder arising or alleged to have arisen from an action taken by the department under this subchapter.

(d) The immunities granted under Subsections (a), (b), and (c) do not apply to an act or a failure to act by the state, an agency or subdivision of the state, an officer of the state, or a peace officer if the act or failure to act were capricious or arbitrary.

(e) The immunities granted under Subsection (a) to a qualified handgun instructor do not apply to a cause of action for fraud or a deceptive trade practice.

Government Code §411.1901. School Safety Certification For Qualified Handgun Instructors

(a) The department shall establish a process to enable qualified handgun instructors certified under Section 411.190 to obtain an additional certification in school safety. The process must include a school safety certification course that provides training in the following:

(1) the protection of students;

(2) interaction of license holders with first responders;

(3) tactics for denying an intruder entry into a classroom or school facility; and

(4) methods for increasing a license holder's accuracy with a handgun while under duress.

(b) The school safety certification course under Subsection (a) must include not less than 15 hours and not more than 20 hours of instruction.

(c) A qualified handgun instructor certified in school safety under this section may provide school safety training, including instruction in the subjects listed under Subsection (a), to employees of a school district or an open-enrollment charter school who hold a license to carry a concealed handgun issued under this subchapter.

(d) The department shall establish a fee in an amount that is sufficient to cover the costs of the school safety certification under this section.

(e) The department may adopt rules to administer this section.

Government Code §411.2032. Transportation And Storage Of Firearms And Ammunition By License Holders In Private Vehicles On Certain Campuses

(a) For purposes of this section:

(1) "Campus" means all land and buildings owned or leased by an institution of higher education or private or independent institution of higher education.

(2) "Institution of higher education" and "private or independent institution of higher education" have the meanings assigned by Section 61.003, Education Code.

(b) An institution of higher education or private or independent institution of higher education in this state may not adopt or enforce any rule, regulation, or other provision or take any other action, including posting notice under Section 30.06, Penal Code, prohibiting or placing restrictions on the storage or transportation of a firearm or ammunition in a locked, privately owned or leased motor vehicle by a person, including a student enrolled at that institution, who holds a license to carry a concealed handgun under this subchapter and lawfully possesses the firearm or ammunition:

(1) on a street or driveway located on the campus of the institution; or

(2) in a parking lot, parking garage, or other parking area located on the campus of the institution.

Government Code §418.003. Limitations

This chapter does not:

(5) except as provided by Section 418.184, authorize the seizure or confiscation of any firearm or ammunition from an individual who is lawfully carrying or possessing the firearm or ammunition;

Government Code §418.019. Restricted Sale and Transportation of Materials The governor may suspend or limit the sale, dispensing, or transportation of alcoholic beverages, firearms, explosives, and combustibles. <Applies when an official state of disaster has been declared, see Government Code §418.001 et seq.>

Government Code §431.114. Sale of Arms

The commanding officer of forces called to enforce law may order the closing of any place where arms, ammunition, or explosives are sold and forbid the sale, barter, loan, or gift of arms, ammunition, or explosives while forces are on duty in or near that place.

Government Code §418.184. Firearms

(a) A peace officer who is acting in the lawful execution of the officer's official duties during a state of disaster may disarm an individual if the officer reasonably believes it is immediately necessary for the protection of the officer or another individual.

(b) The peace officer shall return a firearm and any ammunition to an individual disarmed under Subsection (a) before ceasing to detain the individual unless the officer:

(1) arrests the individual for engaging in criminal activity; or

(2) seizes the firearm as evidence in a criminal investigation.

Government Code §433.002. Issuance Of Directives

(b) The directive may provide for:

(6) control of the sale, transportation, and use of alcoholic beverages, weapons, and ammunition, except as provided by Section 433.0045;

Government Code §433.0045. Firearms

(a) A directive issued under this chapter may not authorize the seizure or confiscation of any firearm or ammunition from an individual who is lawfully carrying or possessing the firearm or ammunition.

(b) A peace officer who is acting in the lawful execution of the officer's official duties during a state of emergency may disarm an individual if the officer reasonably believes it is immediately necessary for the protection of the officer or another individual.

(c) The peace officer shall return a firearm and any ammunition to an individual disarmed under Subsection (b) before ceasing to detain the individual unless the officer:

(1) arrests the individual for engaging in criminal activity; or

(2) seizes the firearm as evidence in a criminal investigation.

Health and Safety Code §12.092. Medical Advisory Board; Board Members

(b) The medical advisory board shall assist the Department of Public Safety of the State of Texas in determining whether:

(2) an applicant for or holder of a license to carry a concealed handgun under the authority of Subchapter H, Chapter 411, Government Code, or an applicant for or holder of a commission as a security officer under Chapter 1702, Occupations Code, is capable of exercising sound judgment with respect to the proper use and storage of a handgun.

Health and Safety Code §12.095. Board Panels; Powers and Duties

(a) If the Department of Public Safety of the State of Texas requests an opinion or recommendation from the medical advisory board as to the ability of an applicant or license holder to operate a motor vehicle safely or to exercise sound judgment with respect to the proper use and storage of a handgun, the commissioner or a person designated by the commissioner shall convene a panel to consider the case or question submitted by that department.

(c) Each panel member shall prepare an individual independent written report for the Department of Public Safety of the State of Texas that states the member's opinion as to the ability of the applicant or license holder to operate a motor vehicle safely or to exercise sound judgment with respect to the proper use and storage of a handgun, as appropriate. In the report the panel member may also make recommendations relating to that department's subsequent action.

(d) In its deliberations, a panel may examine any medical record or report that contains material that may be relevant to the ability of the applicant or license holder.

(e) The panel may require the applicant or license holder to undergo a medical or other examination at the applicant's or holder's expense. A person who conducts an examination under this subsection may be compelled to testify before the panel and in any subsequent proceedings under

Subchapter H, Chapter 411, Government Code, or Subchapter N, Chapter 521, Transportation Code, as applicable, concerning the person's observations and findings.

Health and Safety Code §161.041. Mandatory Reporting of Gunshot Wounds
A physician who attends or treats, or who is requested to attend or treat, a bullet or gunshot wound, or the administrator, superintendent, or other person in charge of a hospital, sanitarium, or other institution in which a bullet or gunshot wound is attended or treated or in which the attention or treatment is requested shall report the case at once to the law enforcement authority of the municipality or county in which the physician practices or in which the institution is located.

Health and Safety Code §161.043. Criminal Penalty
(a) A person commits an offense if the person is required to report under this subchapter and intentionally fails to report.
(b) An offense under this section is a misdemeanor punishable by confinement in jail for not more than six months or by a fine of not more than $100.

Health and Safety Code §247.065. Providers' Bill Of Rights
(a) Each assisted living facility shall post a providers' bill of rights in a prominent place in the facility.
(b) The providers' bill of rights must provide that a provider of personal care services has the right to:
(9) maintain an environment free of weapons and drugs;

Health and Safety Code §574.088. Relief From Disabilities In Mental Health Cases
(a) A person who is furloughed or discharged from court-ordered mental health services may petition the court that entered the commitment order for an order stating that the person qualifies for relief from a firearms disability.
(b) In determining whether to grant relief, the court must hear and consider evidence about:
(1) the circumstances that led to imposition of the firearms disability under 18 U.S.C. §922(g)(4);
(2) the person's mental history;
(3) the person's criminal history; and
(4) the person's reputation.
(c) A court may not grant relief unless it makes and enters in the record the following affirmative findings:
(1) the person is no longer likely to act in a manner dangerous to public safety; and
(2) removing the person's disability to purchase a firearm is in the public interest.

Health and Safety Code §756.041. Applicability
This subchapter applies only to an outdoor shooting range located in a county with a population of more than 150,000.

Health and Safety Code §756.0411. Definition
In this subchapter, "outdoor shooting range" means an outdoor shooting range, outdoor firing range, or other open property on which persons may fire a weapon for a fee or other remuneration but does not include a deer lease or other similar leases of property for the purpose of hunting or an archery range.

Health and Safety Code §756.042. Construction Standards
The owner of an outdoor shooting range shall construct and maintain the range according to standards that are at least as stringent as the standards printed in the National Rifle Association range manual.

Health and Safety Code §756.043. Civil Penalty
(a) The owner of an outdoor shooting range who fails to comply with Section 756.042 is liable within 60 days after a finding of noncompliance for a civil penalty of $50 for each day of noncompliance; the aggregate amount not to exceed $500.
(b) The attorney general or the appropriate district attorney, criminal district attorney, or county attorney shall recover the civil penalty in a suit on behalf of the state. If the attorney general brings the suit, the penalty shall be deposited in the state treasury to the credit of the general revenue fund. If another attorney brings the suit, the penalty shall be deposited in the general fund of the county in which the violation occurred.

Health and Safety Code §756.044. Criminal Penalties
(a) The owner of an outdoor shooting range commits an offense if the owner intentionally or recklessly fails to comply with Section 756.042 and that failure results in injury to another person.
(b) An offense under this section is a Class C misdemeanor, except that if it is shown on the trial of the defendant that the defendant has previously been convicted of an offense under this section, the offense is a Class A misdemeanor.

Health and Safety Code §756.045. Insurance Required
(a) The owner of an outdoor shooting range shall purchase and maintain an insurance policy that provides coverage of at least $500,000 for bodily injuries or death and another policy that provides that level of coverage for property damage resulting from firing any weapon while on the shooting range.

(b) The owner of an outdoor shooting range shall prominently display a sign at the shooting range stating that the owner has purchased insurance to cover bodily injury, death, or property damage occurring from activities at the shooting range.

Human Resources Code §42.042. Rules And Standards

(e-1) The department may not prohibit possession of lawfully permitted firearms and ammunition in a foster home of any type, including a foster group home, a foster home, an agency foster group home, and an agency foster home. Minimum standards may be adopted under this section relating to safety and proper storage of firearms and ammunition, including standards requiring firearms and ammunition to be stored separately in locked locations.

(e-2) The department may not prohibit the foster parent of a child who resides in the foster family's home from transporting the child in a vehicle where a handgun is present if the handgun is in the possession and control of the foster parent and the foster parent is licensed to carry the handgun under Subchapter H, Chapter 411, Government Code.

Human Resources Code §222.005. Carrying Of Firearms By Certain Officers Prohibited

(a) A juvenile probation, detention, or corrections officer may not carry a firearm in the course of the person's official duties.

(b) This section does not apply to:

(1) an employee of the department; or

(2) a juvenile probation officer authorized to carry a firearm under Section 142.006.

Labor Code §52.061. Restriction On Prohibiting Employee Access To Or Storage Of Firearm Or Ammunition

A public or private employer may not prohibit an employee who holds a license to carry a concealed handgun under Subchapter H, Chapter 411, Government Code, who otherwise lawfully possesses a firearm, or who lawfully possesses ammunition from transporting or storing a firearm or ammunition the employee is authorized by law to possess in a locked, privately owned motor vehicle in a parking lot, parking garage, or other parking area the employer provides for employees.

Labor Code §52.062. Exceptions

(a) Section 52.061 does not:

(1) authorize a person who holds a license to carry a concealed handgun under Subchapter H, Chapter 411, Government Code, who otherwise lawfully possesses a firearm, or who lawfully possesses ammunition to possess a firearm or ammunition on any property where the possession of a firearm or ammunition is prohibited by state or federal law; or

(2) apply to:

(A) a vehicle owned or leased by a public or private employer and used by an employee in the course and scope of the employee's employment, unless the employee is required to transport or store a firearm in the official discharge of the employee's duties;

(B) a school district;

(C) an open-enrollment charter school, as defined by Section 5.001, Education Code;

(D) a private school, as defined by Section 22.081, Education Code;

(E) property owned or controlled by a person, other than the employer, that is subject to a valid, unexpired oil, gas, or other mineral lease that contains a provision prohibiting the possession of firearms on the property; or

(F) property owned or leased by a chemical manufacturer or oil and gas refiner with an air authorization under Chapter 382, Health and Safety Code, and on which the primary business conducted is the manufacture, use, storage, or transportation of hazardous, combustible, or explosive materials, except in regard to an employee who holds a license to carry a concealed handgun under Subchapter H, Chapter 411, Government Code, and who stores a firearm or ammunition the employee is authorized by law to possess in a locked, privately owned motor vehicle in a parking lot, parking garage, or other parking area the employer provides for employees that is outside of a secured and restricted area:

(i) that contains the physical plant;

(ii) that is not open to the public; and

(iii) the ingress into which is constantly monitored by security personnel.

(b) Section 52.061 does not prohibit an employer from prohibiting an employee who holds a license to carry a concealed handgun under Subchapter H, Chapter 411, Government Code, or who otherwise lawfully possesses a firearm, from possessing a firearm the employee is otherwise authorized by law to possess on the premises of the employer's business. In this subsection, "premises" has the meaning assigned by Section 46.035(f)(3), Penal Code.

Labor Code §52.063. Immunity From Civil Liability

(a) Except in cases of gross negligence, a public or private employer, or the employer's principal, officer, director, employee, or agent, is not liable in a civil action for personal injury, death, property damage, or any other damages resulting from or arising out of an occurrence involving a firearm or ammunition that the employer is required to allow on the employer's property under this subchapter.

(b) The presence of a firearm or ammunition on an employer's property under the authority of this subchapter does not by itself constitute a failure by the employer to provide a safe workplace.

(c) For purposes of this section, a public or private employer, or the employer's principal, officer, director, employee, or agent, does not have a duty:

(1) to patrol, inspect, or secure:

(A) any parking lot, parking garage, or other parking area the employer provides for employees; or

(B) any privately owned motor vehicle located in a parking lot, parking garage, or other parking area described by Paragraph (A); or

(2) to investigate, confirm, or determine an employee's compliance with laws related to the ownership or possession of a firearm or ammunition or the transportation and storage of a firearm or ammunition.

Labor Code §52.064. Construction Of Provision Relating To Immunity From Civil Liability

Section 52.063 does not limit or alter the personal liability of:

(1) an individual who causes harm or injury by using a firearm or ammunition;

(2) an individual who aids, assists, or encourages another individual to cause harm or injury by using a firearm or ammunition; or

(3) an employee who transports or stores a firearm or ammunition on the property of the employee's employer but who fails to comply with the requirements of Section 52.061.

Local Government Code §43.002. Continuation of Land Use

(d) A regulation relating to the discharge of firearms or other weapons is subject to the restrictions in Section 229.002.

Local Government Code §85.004. Reserve Deputies

(a) The commissioners court of a county may authorize the sheriff to appoint reserve deputy sheriffs. The commissioners court may limit the number of reserve deputies that may be appointed.

(b) A reserve deputy serves at the discretion of the sheriff and may be called into service if the sheriff considers it necessary to have additional officers to preserve the peace and enforce the law. The sheriff may authorize a reserve deputy who is a peace officer as described by Article 2.12, Code of Criminal Procedure, to carry a weapon or act as a peace officer at all times, regardless of whether the reserve deputy is engaged in the actual discharge of official duties, or may limit the authority of the reserve deputy to carry a weapon or act as a peace officer to only those times during which the reserve deputy is engaged in the actual discharge of official duties. A reserve deputy who is not a peace officer as described by Article 2.12, Code of Criminal Procedure, may act as a peace officer only during the actual discharge of official duties. A reserve deputy, regardless of whether the reserve deputy is a peace officer as described by Article 2.12, Code of Criminal Procedure, is not:

(1) eligible for participation in any program provided by the county that is normally considered a financial benefit of full-time employment or for any pension fund created by statute for the benefit of full-time paid peace officers; or

(2) exempt from Chapter 1702, Occupations Code.

Local Government Code §86.012. Reserve Deputy Constables

(a) The commissioners court of a county may authorize a constable of the county to appoint reserve deputy constables. The commissioners court may limit the number of reserve deputy constables that a constable may appoint.

(b) A reserve deputy constable serves at the discretion of the constable and may be called into service at any time that the constable considers it necessary to have additional officers to preserve the peace and enforce the law. The constable may authorize a reserve deputy constable who is a peace officer as described by Article 2.12, Code of Criminal Procedure, to carry a weapon or act as a peace officer at all times, regardless of whether the reserve deputy constable is engaged in the actual discharge of official duties, or may limit the authority of the reserve deputy constable to carry a weapon or act as a peace officer to only those times during which the reserve deputy constable is engaged in the actual discharge of official duties. A reserve deputy constable who is not a peace officer as described by Article 2.12, Code of Criminal Procedure, may act as a peace officer only during the actual discharge of official duties. A reserve deputy constable, regardless of whether the reserve deputy constable is a peace officer as described by Article 2.12, Code of Criminal Procedure, is not:

(1) eligible for participation in any program provided by the county that is normally considered a financial benefit of full-time employment or for any pension fund created by statute for the benefit of full-time paid peace officers; or

(2) exempt from Chapter 1702, Occupations Code.

Local Government Code §118.0217. Mental Health Background Check

(a) The fee for a "mental health background check for license to carry a concealed weapon" is for a check, conducted by the county clerk at the request of the Texas Department of Public Safety, of the county records involving the mental condition of a person who applies for a license to carry a concealed handgun under Subchapter H, Chapter 411, Government Code. The fee, not to exceed

$2, will be paid from the application fee submitted to the Department of Public Safety according to Section 411.174(a)(6), Government Code.

Local Government Code §229.001. Firearms; Explosives
(a) Notwithstanding any other law, including Section 43.002 of this code and Chapter 251, Agriculture Code, a municipality may not adopt regulations relating to:
(1) the transfer, private ownership, keeping, transportation, licensing, or registration of firearms, air guns, ammunition, or firearm or air gun supplies; or
(2) the discharge of a firearm or air gun at a sport shooting range.
(b) Subsection (a) does not affect the authority a municipality has under another law to:
(1) require residents or public employees to be armed for personal or national defense, law enforcement, or other lawful purpose;
(2) regulate the discharge of firearms or air guns within the limits of the municipality, other than at a sport shooting range;
(3) regulate the use of property, the location of a business, or uses at a business under the municipality's fire code, zoning ordinance, or land-use regulations as long as the code, ordinance, or regulations are not used to circumvent the intent of Subsection (a) or Subdivision (5) of this subsection;
(4) regulate the use of firearms or air guns in the case of an insurrection, riot, or natural disaster if the municipality finds the regulations necessary to protect public health and safety;
(5) regulate the storage or transportation of explosives to protect public health and safety, except that 25 pounds or less of black powder for each private residence and 50 pounds or less of black powder for each retail dealer are not subject to regulation;
(6) regulate the carrying of a firearm or air guns by a person other than a person licensed to carry a concealed handgun under Subchapter H, Chapter 411, Government Code, at a:
(A) public park;
(B) public meeting of a municipality, county, or other governmental body;
(C) political rally, parade, or official political meeting; or
(D) nonfirearms-related school, college, or professional athletic event;
(7) regulate the hours of operation of a sport shooting range, except that the hours of operation may not be more limited than the least limited hours of operation of any other business in the municipality other than a business permitted or licensed to sell or serve alcoholic beverages for on-premises consumption; or
(8) regulate the carrying of an air gun by a minor on:
(A) public property; or
(B) private property without consent of the property owner.
(c) The exception provided by Subsection (b)(6) does not apply if the firearm or air gun is in or is carried to or from an area designated for use in a lawful hunting, fishing, or other sporting event and the firearm or air gun is of the type commonly used in the activity.
(d) The exception provided by Subsection (b)(4) does not authorize the seizure or confiscation of any firearm, air gun, or ammunition from an individual who is lawfully carrying or possessing the firearm, air gun, or ammunition.
(e) In this section:
(1) "Air gun"" means any gun that discharges a pellet, BB, or paintball by means of compressed air, gas propellant, or a spring.
(2) "Sport shooting range" has the meaning assigned by Section 250.001.
(f) The attorney general may bring an action in the name of the state to obtain a temporary or permanent injunction against a municipality adopting a regulation in violation of this section.

Local Government Code §229.002. Regulation Of Discharge Of Weapon
A municipality may not apply a regulation relating to the discharge of firearms or other weapons in the extraterritorial jurisdiction of the municipality or in an area annexed by the municipality after September 1, 1981, if the firearm or other weapon is:
(1) a shotgun, air rifle or pistol, BB gun, or bow and arrow discharged:
(A) on a tract of land of 10 acres or more and more than 150 feet from a residence or occupied building located on another property; and
(B) in a manner not reasonably expected to cause a projectile to cross the boundary of the tract; or
(2) a center fire or rim fire rifle or pistol of any caliber discharged:
(A) on a tract of land of 50 acres or more and more than 300 feet from a residence or occupied building located on another property; and
(B) in a manner not reasonably expected to cause a projectile to cross the boundary of the tract.

Local Government Code §229.003. Regulation Of Discharge Of Weapon By Certain Municipalities
(a) This section applies only to a municipality located wholly or partly in a county:
(1) with a population of 450,000 or more;
(2) in which all or part of a municipality with a population of one million or more is located; and
(3) that is located adjacent to a county with a population of two million or more.

(b) Notwithstanding Section 229.002, a municipality may not apply a regulation relating to the
   discharge of firearms or other weapons in the extraterritorial jurisdiction of the municipality or in
   an area annexed by the municipality after September 1, 1981, if the firearm or other weapon is:
(1) a shotgun, air rifle or pistol, BB gun, or bow and arrow discharged:
(A) on a tract of land of 10 acres or more and:
(i) more than 1,000 feet from:
(a) the property line of a public tract of land, generally accessible by the public, that is routinely used
   for organized sporting or recreational activities or that has permanent recreational facilities or
   equipment; and
(b) the property line of a school, hospital, or commercial day-care facility;
(ii) more than 600 feet from:
(a) the property line of a residential subdivision; and
(b) the property line of a multifamily residential complex; and
(iii) more than 150 feet from a residence or occupied building located on another property; and
(B) in a manner not reasonably expected to cause a projectile to cross the boundary of the tract;
(2) a center fire or rim fire rifle or pistol of any caliber discharged:
(A) on a tract of land of 50 acres or more and:
(i) more than 1,000 feet from:
(a) the property line of a public tract of land, generally accessible by the public, that is routinely used
   for organized sporting or recreational activities or that has permanent recreational facilities or
   equipment; and
(b) the property line of a school, hospital, or commercial day-care facility;
(ii) more than 600 feet from:
(a) the property line of a residential subdivision; and
(b) the property line of a multifamily residential complex; and
(iii) more than 300 feet from a residence or occupied building located on another property; and
(B) in a manner not reasonably expected to cause a projectile to cross the boundary of the tract; or
(3) discharged at a sport shooting range, as defined by Section 250.001, in a manner not reasonably
   expected to cause a projectile to cross the boundary of a tract of land.

Local Government Code §229.004. Regulation Of Discharge Of Weapon By Certain Municipalities
(a) This section applies only to a municipality located in a county in which the majority of the
   population of two or more municipalities with a population of 300,000 or more are located.
(b) Notwithstanding Section 229.002, a municipality may not apply a regulation relating to the
   discharge of firearms or other weapons in the extraterritorial jurisdiction of the municipality or in
   an area annexed by the municipality on or before September 1, 1981, if the firearm or other
   weapon is:
(1) a shotgun, air rifle or pistol, BB gun, or bow and arrow discharged:
(A) on a tract of land of 100 acres or more and more than 150 feet from a residence or occupied
   building located on another property; and
(B) in a manner not reasonably expected to cause a projectile to cross the boundary of the tract; or
(2) a center fire or rim fire rifle or pistol of any caliber discharged:
(A) on a tract of land of 100 acres or more and more than 300 feet from a residence or occupied
   building located on another property; and
(B) in a manner not reasonably expected to cause a projectile to cross the boundary of the tract.

Local Government Code §235.020. Definition
In this subchapter, "air gunÆ has the meaning assigned by Section 229.001.

Local Government Code §235.021. Subdivisions Covered By Subchapter
This subchapter applies only to a subdivision all or a part of which is located in the unincorporated
   area of a county and for which a plat is required to be prepared and filed under Chapter 232.

Local Government Code §235.022. Authority To Regulate
To promote the public safety, the commissioners court of a county by order may prohibit or
   otherwise regulate the discharge of firearms and air guns on lots that are 10 acres or smaller and
   are located in the unincorporated area of the county in a subdivision.

Local Government Code §235.023. Prohibited Regulations
This subchapter does not authorize the commissioners court to regulate the transfer, ownership,
   possession, or transportation of firearms or air guns and does not authorize the court to require the
   registration of firearms or air guns.

Local Government Code §235.025. Criminal Penalty
A person commits an offense if the person intentionally or knowingly engages in conduct that is a
   violation of a regulation adopted under this subchapter by the commissioners court. An offense
   under this section is a Class C misdemeanor. If it is shown on the trial of an offense under this
   section that the person has previously been convicted of an offense under this section, the offense
   is a Class B misdemeanor.

Local Government Code §236.001. Definitions
In this chapter:
(1) "Air gun" has the meaning assigned by Section 229.001.
(2) "Sport shooting range" has the meaning assigned by Section 250.001.

Local Government Code §236.002. Firearms; Air Guns; Sport Shooting Range
(a) Notwithstanding any other law, including Chapter 251, Agriculture Code, a county may not adopt regulations relating to:
(1) the transfer, private ownership, keeping, transportation, licensing, or registration of firearms, air guns, ammunition, or firearm or air gun supplies; or
(2) the discharge of a firearm at a sport shooting range.
(b) The attorney general may bring an action in the name of the state to obtain a temporary or permanent injunction against a county adopting a regulation, other than a regulation under Section 236.003, in violation of this section.

Local Government Code §236.003. Regulation Of Outdoor Sport Shooting Range
Notwithstanding Section 236.002, a county may regulate the discharge of a firearm or air gun at an outdoor sport shooting range as provided by Subchapter B, Chapter 235.

Local Government Code §250.001. Restriction on Regulation of Sport Shooting Ranges
(a) In this section:
(1) "Association" or "private club" means an association or private club that operates a sport shooting range at which not fewer than 20 different individuals discharge firearms each calendar year.
(2) "Sport shooting range" means a business establishment, private club, or association that operates an area for the discharge or other use of firearms for silhouette, skeet, trap, black powder, target, self defense, or similar recreational shooting.
(b) A governmental official may not seek a civil or criminal penalty against a sport shooting range or its owner or operator based on the violation of a municipal or county ordinance, order, or rule regulating noise:
(1) if the sport shooting range is in compliance with the applicable ordinance, order, or rule; or
(2) if no applicable noise ordinance, order, or rule exists.
(c) A person may not bring a nuisance or similar cause of action against a sport shooting range based on noise:
(1) if the sport shooting range is in compliance with all applicable municipal and county ordinances, orders, and rules regulating noise; or
(2) if no applicable noise ordinance, order, or rule exists.

Local Government Code §341.012 Police Reserve Force
(f) A member of a reserve force who is not a peace officer as described by Article 2.12, Code of Criminal Procedure, may act as a peace officer only during the actual discharge of official duties.
(g) An appointment to the reserve force must be approved by the governing body before the person appointed may carry a weapon or otherwise act as a peace officer. On approval of the appointment of a member who is not a peace officer as described by Article 2.12, Code of Criminal Procedure, the person appointed may carry a weapon only when authorized to do so by the chief of police and only when discharging official duties as a peace officer.
(h) Reserve police officers may act only in a supplementary capacity to the regular police force and may not assume the full-time duties of regular police officers without complying with the requirements for regular police officers. On approval of the appointment of a member who is a peace officer as described by Article 2.12, Code of Criminal Procedure, the chief of police may authorize the person appointed to carry a weapon or act as a peace officer at all times, regardless of whether the person is engaged in the actual discharge of official duties, or may limit the authority of the person to carry a weapon or act as a peace officer to only those times during which the person is engaged in the actual discharge of official duties. A reserve police officer, regardless of whether the reserve police officer is a peace officer as described by Article 2.12, Code of Criminal Procedure, is not:
(1) eligible for participation in any program provided by the governing body that is normally considered a financial benefit of full-time employment or for any pension fund created by statute for the benefit of full-time paid peace officers; or
(2) exempt from Chapter 1702, Occupations Code.

Local Government Code §342.003. Fire Regulations
(a) The governing body of the municipality may:
(8) prohibit or otherwise regulate the use of fireworks and firearms;
(9) prohibit, direct, or otherwise regulate the keeping and management of buildings within the city that are used to store gunpowder or other combustible, explosive, or dangerous materials, and regulate the keeping and conveying of those materials;
(b) Subsection (a)(8) or (9) does not authorize a municipality to adopt any prohibition or other regulation in violation of Section 229.001.

Occupation Code §1701.001. Definitions
(8) "School marshal" means a person employed and appointed by the board of trustees of a school district or the governing body of an open-enrollment charter school under Article 2.127, Code of Criminal Procedure, and in accordance with and having the rights provided by Section 37.0811, Education Code.

Occupation Code §1701.260. Training For Holders Of License To Carry Concealed Handgun; Certification Of Eligibility For Appointment As School Marshal
(a) The commission shall establish and maintain a training program open to any employee of a school district or open-enrollment charter school who holds a license to carry a concealed handgun issued under Subchapter H, Chapter 411, Government Code. The training may be conducted only by the commission staff or a provider approved by the commission.
(b) The commission shall collect from each person who participates in the training program identifying information that includes the person's name, the person's date of birth, the license number of the license issued to the person under Subchapter H, Chapter 411, Government Code, and the address of the person]'s place of employment.
(c) The training program shall include 80 hours of instruction designed to:
(1) emphasize strategies for preventing school shootings and for securing the safety of potential victims of school shootings;
(2) educate a trainee about legal issues relating to the duties of peace officers and the use of force or deadly force in the protection of others;
(3) introduce the trainee to effective law enforcement strategies and techniques;
(4) improve the trainee's proficiency with a handgun; and
(5) enable the trainee to respond to an emergency situation requiring deadly force, such as a situation involving an active shooter.
(d) The commission, in consultation with psychologists, shall devise and administer to each trainee a psychological examination to determine whether the trainee is psychologically fit to carry out the duties of a school marshal in an emergency shooting or situation involving an active shooter. The commission may license a person under this section only if the results of the examination indicate that the trainee is psychologically fit to carry out those duties.
(e) The commission shall charge each trainee a reasonable fee to cover the cost to the commission of conducting the program. The commission shall charge each person seeking renewal of a school marshal license a reasonable fee to cover the cost to the commission of renewing the person's license.
(f) The commission shall license a person who is eligible for appointment as a school marshal who:
(1) completes training under this section to the satisfaction of the commission staff; and
(2) is psychologically fit to carry out the duties of a school marshal as indicated by the results of the psychological examination under this section.
(g) A person's license under this section expires on the first birthday of the person occurring after the second anniversary of the date the commission licenses the person. A renewed school marshal license expires on the person's birth date, two years after the expiration of the previous license.
(h) A person may renew the school marshal license under this section by:
(1) successfully completing a renewal course designed and administered by the commission, which such license renewal training will not exceed 16 hours combined of classroom and simulation training;
(2) demonstrating appropriate knowledge on an examination designed and administered by the commission;
(3) demonstrating handgun proficiency to the satisfaction of the commission staff; and
(4) demonstrating psychological fitness on the examination described in Subsection (d).
(i) The commission shall revoke a person's school marshal license if the commission is notified by the Department of Public Safety that the person's license to carry a concealed handgun issued under Subchapter H, Chapter 411, Government Code, has been suspended or revoked. A person whose school marshal license is revoked may obtain recertification by:
(1) furnishing proof to the commission that the person's concealed handgun license has been reinstated; and
(2) completing the initial training under Subsection (c) to the satisfaction of the commission staff, paying the fee for the training, and demonstrating psychological fitness on the psychological examination described in Subsection (d).
(j) The commission shall submit the identifying information collected under Subsection (b) for each person licensed by the commission under this section to:
(1) the director of the Department of Public Safety;
(2) the person's employer, if the person is employed by a school district or open-enrollment charter school;
(3) the chief law enforcement officer of the local municipal law enforcement agency if the person is employed at a campus of a school district or open-enrollment charter school located within a municipality;
(4) the sheriff of the county if the person is employed at a campus of a school district or open-enrollment charter school that is not located within a municipality; and

(5) the chief administrator of any peace officer commissioned under Section 37.081, Education Code, if the person is employed at a school district that has commissioned a peace officer under that section.

(k) The commission shall immediately report the expiration or revocation of a school marshal license to the persons listed in Subsection (j).

(l) Identifying information about a person collected or submitted under this section is confidential, except as provided by Subsection (j), and is not subject to disclosure under Chapter 552, Government Code.

Occupation Code §1701.357. Weapons Proficiency For Certain Retired Peace Officers And Federal Law Enforcement Officers And For Former Reserve Law Enforcement Officers

(a) This section applies only to:

(1) a peace officer;

(2) a federal criminal investigator designated as a special investigator under Article 2.122, Code of Criminal Procedure; and

(3) a qualified retired law enforcement officer who is entitled to carry a concealed firearm under 18 U.S.C. §926C and is not otherwise described by Subdivision (1) or (2); and

(4) a former reserve law enforcement officer who served in that capacity not less than a total of 15 years with a state or local law enforcement agency.

(b) The head of a state or local law enforcement agency may allow an honorably retired peace officer an opportunity to demonstrate weapons proficiency if the retired officer provides to the agency a sworn affidavit stating that:

(1) the officer:

(A) honorably retired after not less than a total of 15 years of service as a commissioned officer with one or more state or local law enforcement agencies; or

(B) before completing 15 years of service as a commissioned officer with a state or local law enforcement agency, separated from employment with the agency or agencies and is a qualified retired law enforcement officer, as defined by 18 U.S.C. §926C;

(2) the officer's license as a commissioned officer was not revoked or suspended for any period during the officer's term of service as a commissioned officer; and

(3) the officer has no psychological or physical disability that would interfere with the officer's proper handling of a handgun.

(b-1) The head of a state or local law enforcement agency may allow a person who served as a reserve law enforcement officer as described by Subsection (a)(4) an opportunity to demonstrate weapons proficiency if the person provides to the agency a sworn affidavit stating that:

(1) the person served not less than a total of 15 years as a reserve law enforcement officer with a state or local law enforcement agency;

(2) the person's appointment as a reserve law enforcement officer was not revoked or suspended for any period during the person's term of service; and

(3) the person has no psychological or physical disability that would interfere with the person's proper handling of a handgun.

(c) The agency shall establish written procedures for the issuance or denial of a certificate of proficiency under this section. The agency shall issue the certificate to a retired officer who satisfactorily demonstrates weapons proficiency under Subsection (b), provides proof that the officer is entitled to receive a pension or annuity for service with a state or local law enforcement agency or is not entitled to receive a pension or annuity only because the law enforcement agency that employed the retired officer does not offer a pension or annuity to its retired employees, and satisfies the written procedures established by the agency. The agency shall issue the certificate to a person described by Subsection (a)(4) who satisfactorily demonstrates weapons proficiency under Subsection (b-1). The agency shall maintain records of any person who holds a certificate issued under this section.

(c-1) For purposes of Subsection (c), proof that a retired officer is entitled to receive a pension or annuity or is not entitled to receive a pension or annuity only because the agency that last employed the retired officer does not offer a pension or annuity may include a retired peace officer identification card issued under Subchapter H, Chapter 614, Government Code.

(d) A certificate issued under this section expires on the second anniversary of the date the certificate was issued. A person to whom this section applies may request an annual evaluation of weapons proficiency and issuance of a certificate of proficiency as needed to comply with applicable federal or other laws.

(e) The head of a state or local law enforcement agency may set and collect fees to recover the expenses the agency incurs in performing duties under this section.

(f) The amount of a fee set by a county law enforcement agency under Subsection (e) is subject to the approval of the commissioners court of the county. A county law enforcement agency that collects a fee under Subsection (e) shall deposit the amounts collected to the credit of the general fund of the county.

(g) A county law enforcement agency must obtain approval of the program authorized by this section from the commissioners court of the county before issuing a certificate of proficiency under this section.

(h) The head of a state law enforcement agency may allow an honorably retired federal criminal investigator or a qualified retired law enforcement officer to whom this section applies an opportunity to demonstrate weapons proficiency in the same manner as, and subject to the same requirements applicable to, an honorably retired peace officer as described by this section. The agency shall issue a certificate of proficiency to an honorably retired federal criminal investigator or a qualified retired law enforcement officer who otherwise meets the requirements of this section and shall maintain records regarding the issuance of that certificate.

(i) On request of a retired officer who holds a certificate of proficiency under this section, the head of a state or local law enforcement agency may issue to the retired officer identification that indicates that the officer retired from the agency. An identification under this subsection must include a photograph of the retired officer.

(j) On request of a person described by Subsection (a)(4) who holds a certificate of proficiency under this section, the head of the state or local law enforcement agency at which the person last served as a reserve law enforcement officer shall issue to the person identification that indicates the person's status. An identification under this subsection must include a photograph of the person.

Occupation Code §1701.603. Firearms Accident Prevention Program

(a) A peace officer who is a visiting school resource officer in a public elementary school shall at least once each school year offer to provide instruction to students in a firearms accident prevention program, as determined by the school district.

(b) A firearms accident prevention program must include the safety message, "Stop! Don't Touch. Leave the Area. Tell an Adult.", and may include instructional materials from the National Rifle Association Eddie Eagle GunSafe Program, including animated videos and activity books.

Occupations Code §1702.161. Security Officer Commission Required

(a) An individual may not accept employment as a security officer to carry a firearm in the course and scope of the individual's duties unless the individual holds a security officer commission.

(b) An individual employed as a security officer may not knowingly carry a firearm during the course of performing duties as a security officer unless the commission has issued a security officer commission to the individual.

(c) A person may not hire or employ an individual as a security officer to carry a firearm in the course and scope of the individual's duties unless the individual holds a security officer commission.

Occupations Code §1702.163. Qualifications For Security Officer Commission

(a) An applicant employed by a license holder is not eligible for a security officer commission unless the applicant submits as part of the application satisfactory evidence that the applicant has:
(1) completed the basic training course at a school or under an instructor approved by the board;
(2) met each qualification established by this chapter and administrative rule;
(3) achieved the score required by the board on the examination under Section 1702.1685; and
(4) demonstrated to the satisfaction of the firearm training instructor that the applicant has complied with other board standards for minimum marksmanship competency with a handgun.

(b) An individual is not eligible for a security officer commission if the individual:
(1) is disqualified by state or federal law from owning or possessing a firearm;
(2) is incapable of exercising sound judgment in the proper use and storage of a handgun;

(d) For purposes of Subsection (b)(2), a person is incapable of exercising sound judgment with respect to the proper use and storage of a handgun if the person:
(1) has been diagnosed by a licensed physician as suffering from a psychiatric disorder or condition that causes or is likely to cause substantial impairment in judgment, mood, perception, impulse control, or intellectual ability;
(2) suffers from a psychiatric disorder or condition described by Subdivision (1) that:
(A) is in remission but is reasonably likely to redevelop at a future time; or
(B) requires continuous medical treatment to avoid redevelopment;
(3) has been diagnosed by a licensed physician or declared by a court as incompetent to manage the person's own affairs; or
(4) has entered a plea of not guilty by reason of insanity in a criminal proceeding.

(f) Notwithstanding Subsection (d), a person who has previously been diagnosed as suffering from a psychiatric disorder or condition described by Subsection (d) or listed in Subsection (e) is not because of that disorder or condition incapable of exercising sound judgment with respect to the proper use and storage of a handgun if the person provides the department with a certificate from a licensed physician whose primary practice is in the field of psychiatry stating that the psychiatric disorder or condition is in remission and is not reasonably likely to develop at a future time.

(g) An individual's eligibility under this section is not affected by a relationship or lack of relationship between the nature of a criminal charge or conviction and the regulated occupation.

Occupations Code §1702.1675. Training Programs

(a) The commission shall establish a basic training course for commissioned security officers. The course must include, at a minimum:
(1) general security officer training issues;
(2) classroom instruction on handgun proficiency; and
(3) range instruction on handgun proficiency.

(b) The course must be offered and taught by schools and instructors approved by the commission. To receive commission approval, a school or an instructor must submit an application to the commission on a form provided by the commission.

(c) The basic training course approved by the commission must consist of a minimum of 30 hours.

(d) The general security officer training portion of the course must include instruction on:

(1) commission rules and applicable state laws;

(2) field note taking and report writing; and

(3) any other topics of security officer training curriculum the commission considers necessary.

(e) The commission shall develop a commissioned security officer training manual that contains applicable state laws and commission rules to be used in the instruction and training of commissioned security officers.

(f) The commission shall adopt rules necessary to administer the provisions of this section concerning the training requirements of this chapter.

(g) The handgun proficiency course must include at least 10 hours and not more than 15 hours of instruction on:

(1) the laws that relate to weapons and to the use of deadly force;

(2) handgun use, proficiency, and safety;

(3) nonviolent dispute resolution; and

(4) proper storage practices for handguns, with an emphasis on storage practices that eliminate the possibility of accidental injury to a child.

(h) The range instruction on handgun proficiency must include an actual demonstration by the applicant of the applicant's ability to safely and proficiently use a handgun. The applicant must demonstrate, at a minimum, the degree of proficiency that is required to effectively operate a 9-millimeter or .38-caliber handgun.

(i) The commission by rule shall establish minimum standards for handgun proficiency that are at least as stringent as the standards for handgun proficiency developed by the public safety director under Section 411.188, Government Code.

Occupations Code §1702.168. Firearm Requirements

(a) In addition to the requirements of Section 1702.163(a), the commission by rule shall establish other qualifications for individuals who are employed in positions requiring the carrying of firearms. The qualifications may include:

(1) physical and mental standards;

(2) standards of good moral character; and

(3) other requirements that relate to the competency and reliability of individuals to carry firearms.

(b) The commission shall prescribe appropriate forms and adopt rules by which evidence is presented that the requirements are fulfilled.

Occupations Code §1702.1685. Handgun Proficiency Examination

(a) The proficiency examination required to obtain or renew a security officer commission must include:

(1) a written section on the subjects listed in Section 1702.1675(g); and

(2) a physical demonstration of handgun proficiency that meets the minimum standards established under Section 1702.1675(h) or (i).

(b) Only a commission-approved instructor may administer the handgun proficiency examination.

(c) An applicant for a security officer commission must demonstrate the required proficiency within the 90-day period before the date the security officer commission is issued.

(d) The school shall maintain the records of the required proficiency and make the records available for inspection by the commission.

Occupations Code §1702.169. Firearm Restrictions

A commissioned security officer other than a person acting as a personal protection officer may not carry a firearm unless:

(1) the security officer is:

(A) engaged in the performance of duties as a security officer; or

(B) traveling to or from the place of assignment;

(2) the security officer wears a distinctive uniform indicating that the individual is a security officer; and

(3) the firearm is in plain view.

Occupations Code §1702.170. Nonapplicability Of Firearm Restrictions

Sections 1702.161, 1702.169, and 1702.206 do not apply to the holder of a temporary security officer commission who:

(1) is in uniform;

(2) possesses only one firearm; and

(3) is performing the individual's duties.

Occupations Code §1702.201. Personal Protection Officer Authorization Required

A commissioned security officer may not act as a personal protection officer unless the officer holds a personal protection officer authorization.

Occupations Code § 1702.202. Personal Protection Officer
An individual acts as a personal protection officer if the individual:
(1) has been issued a security officer commission to carry a concealed firearm; and
(2) provides to an individual personal protection from bodily harm.

Occupations Code §1702.203. Application For Personal Protection Officer Authorization
An applicant for a personal protection officer authorization must submit a written application on a
   form prescribed by the commission.

Occupations Code §1702.204. Personal Protection Officer Authorization; Qualifications
(a) An applicant for a personal protection officer authorization must be at least 21 years of age and
   must provide:
(1) a certificate of completion of the basic security officer training course;
(2) proof that the applicant:
(A) has been issued a security officer commission;
(B) is employed at the time of application by an investigations company or guard company licensed
   by the commission; and
(C) has completed the required training in nonlethal self-defense or defense of a third person; and
(3) proof of completion and the results of the Minnesota Multiphasic Personality Inventory
   psychological testing.
(b) The commission by rule shall require an applicant for a personal protection officer authorization
   to complete the Minnesota Multiphasic Personality Inventory test. The commission may use the
   results of the test to evaluate the applicant's psychological fitness.

Occupations Code §1702.205. Personal Protection Officer Training
(a) The commission shall establish a 15-hour course for a personal protection officer consisting of
   training in nonlethal self-defense or defense of a third person.
(b) The training required by this section is in addition to the basic training course for security officers.

Occupations Code §1702.206. Concealed Firearms
An individual acting as a personal protection officer may not carry a concealed firearm unless the
   officer:
(1) is either:
(A) engaged in the exclusive performance of the officer's duties as a personal protection officer for the
   employer under whom the officer's personal protection officer authorization is issued; or
(B) traveling to or from the officer's place of assignment; and
(2) carries the officer's security officer commission and personal protection officer authorization on
   the officer's person while performing the officer's duties or traveling as described by Subdivision
   (1) and presents the commission and authorization on request.

Occupations Code §2155.101. Definition
In this subchapter, "hotel" has the meaning assigned by Section 156.001, Tax Code.

Occupations Code §2155.102. Applicability Of Subchapter
This subchapter applies only to a hotel that has a policy prohibiting or restricting the possession,
   storage, or transportation of firearms by hotel guests.

Occupations Code §2155.103. Notice Regarding Firearms Policy
(a) A hotel shall include on the hotel's Internet reservation website the hotel's policy regarding the
   possession, storage, and transportation of firearms.
(b) If a hotel provides a written confirmation or a written statement of terms and conditions to a
   consumer after accepting the consumer's hotel reservation by telephone, the hotel shall include
   information specifying how the consumer may review applicable guest policies. The guest policies
   must indicate the hotel's policy regarding the possession, storage, and transportation of firearms by
   guests.
(c) A hotel owner or keeper commits an offense if the person does not comply with this section. An
   offense under this subsection is a misdemeanor punishable by a fine of not more than $100.

Parks and Wildlife Code §13.101. Authorization
The commission may promulgate regulations governing the health, safety, and protection of persons
   and property in state parks, historic sites, scientific areas, or forts under the control of the
   department, including public water within state parks, historic sites, scientific areas, and forts.

Parks and Wildlife Code §13.108. Removal From Park
(a) Any person directly or indirectly responsible for disruptive, destructive, or violent conduct which
   endangers property or the health, safety, or lives of persons or animals may be removed from a
   park, historic site, scientific area, or fort for a period not to exceed 48 hours.
(b) Prior to removal under this section, the person must be given notice of the provisions of this
   section and an opportunity to correct the conduct justifying removal.
(c) A court of competent jurisdiction may enjoin a person from reentry to the park, scientific area,
   site, or fort, on cause shown, for any period set by the court.

Parks and Wildlife Code §13.201. Authorization

The commission may make regulations prohibiting the use of firearms or certain types of firearms on state property adjacent to state parks and within 200 yards of the boundary of the state park.

Parks and Wildlife Code §13.202. Application Limited
The regulations of the commission under Section 13.201 of this code apply only to state parks located within one mile of coastal water of this state.

Parks and Wildlife Code §43.112. Confiscation and Disposition of Aircraft, Vehicles, Guns, and Other Devices; Immunity
(a) A game warden or other authorized employee of the department may seize and hold as evidence an aircraft, vehicle, gun, or other device used by a person if:
(1) the person is charged with a violation of this subchapter or a proclamation or regulation adopted under this subchapter; and
(2) The person used the aircraft, vehicle, gun, or other device in committing the violation with which the person is charged.
(b) The department may sell an aircraft, vehicle, gun, or other device seized under this section to the highest bidder if:
(1) the person who used the aircraft, vehicle, gun, or other device to commit a violation is convicted of the violation or enters a plea of nolo contendere to the violation;
(2) the department receives at least three written bids; and
(3) the highest bid is not less than the appraised value of the aircraft, vehicle, gun, or other device.
(c) The department shall release an aircraft, vehicle, gun, or other device seized under this section to the owner if the person charged with a violation is acquitted or the charge against the person is dismissed.
(d) If the department is not authorized to sell or required to release the aircraft, vehicle, gun, or other device, the department may keep and use the aircraft, vehicle, gun, or other device to protect the wildlife resources of this state.
(e) A game warden or authorized employee of the department is not liable for any damages arising from the seizure of an aircraft, vehicle, gun, or other device under this section unless the damages are caused by an act that was intentional or grossly negligent.
(f) The department shall deposit money received under this section in the state treasury to the credit of the game, fish, and water safety fund for the enforcement of fish, shrimp, and oyster laws, game laws, and laws pertaining to sand, shell, and gravel.

Parks and Wildlife Code §62.0055. Hunting With Laser Sighting Device By Legally Blind Hunter
(a) In this section, "legally blind" has the meaning assigned by Section 62.104, Government Code.
(b) A legally blind hunter may use a laser sighting device during regular hunting hours when assisted by a person who:
(1) is not legally blind;
(2) has a hunting license; and
(3) is at least 13 years of age.
(c) The legally blind hunter must carry proof of being legally blind.
(d) Section 62.014 applies to a hunter under this section.

Parks and Wildlife Code §62.0056. Hunting With Laser Sighting Device By Hunters With Certain Disabilities
(a) In this section, "physically disabled person" means a person with a documented physical disability that renders the person incapable of using a traditional firearm sighting device. A physician's statement certifying the extent of the disability is sufficient documentation.
(b) A hunter who is a physically disabled person may use a laser sighting device during regular hunting hours when assisted by a person who:
(1) is not physically disabled;
(2) has a hunting license; and
(3) is at least 13 years of age.
(c) The hunter who is a physically disabled person must carry proof of being physically disabled.
(d) Section 62.014 applies to a hunter under this section.

Parks and Wildlife Code §62.012. Written Consent To Hunt Or Target Shoot Required
(a) This section applies only to a county having a population of 3.3 million or more. This section does not apply to a person hunting or target shooting on a public or private shooting range.
(b) Except as provided by Subsection (d) of this section, no person possessing a firearm may hunt a wild animal or wild bird, or engage in target shooting on land owned by another unless the person has in his immediate possession the written consent of the owner of the land to hunt or engage in target shooting on the land.
(c) To be valid, the written consent required by Subsection (b) of this section must:
(1) contain the name of the person permitted to hunt or engage in target shooting on the land;
(2) identify the land on which hunting or target shooting is permitted;
(3) be signed by the owner of the land or by an agent, lessee, or legal representative of the owner; and
(4) show the address and phone number of the person signing the consent.

(d) The owner of the land on which hunting or target shooting occurs, the landowner's lessee, agent, or legal representative, and a person hunting or target shooting with the landowner or the landowner's lessee, agent, or legal representative are not required to have in their possession the written consent required by Subsection (b) of this section.

Parks and Wildlife Code §62.014. Hunter Education Program

(a) In this section:

(1) "Firearm" means any device designed, made, or adapted to expel a projectile through a barrel by using the energy generated by an explosion or burning substance or any device readily convertible to that use.

(b) The department may establish and administer a statewide hunter education program. The program must include but is not limited to instruction concerning:

(1) the safe handling and use of firearms, archery equipment, and crossbows;

(d) If funds are available for its implementation the commission may establish a mandatory hunter education program and may require a person to have successfully completed a training course before the person may hunt with firearms, archery equipment as defined in Subsection (a) of this section, or crossbows in Texas. If the certificate is so required, the person must possess the certificate or other evidence of completion of the program while hunting with firearms, archery equipment as defined in Subsection (a) of this section, or crossbows.

(n) The following persons are exempt from any requirement to complete the live firing portion of a hunter education course under this section:

(1) an honorably discharged veteran of the United States armed forces; or

(2) a person who is on active duty as a member of the United States military forces, the Texas Army National Guard, the Texas Air National Guard, or the Texas State Guard.

Parks and Wildlife Code §62.0121. Discharge Of Firearm Across Property Line

(a) In this section, "firearm" has the meaning assigned by Section 62.014(a).

(b) A person commits an offense if:

(1) the person, while hunting or engaging in recreational shooting, knowingly discharges a firearm; and

(2) the projectile from the firearm travels across a property line.

(c) It is a defense to prosecution under this section that the person:

(1) owns the property on both sides of each property line crossed by the projectile; or

(2) has a written agreement with any person who owns property on either side of each property line crossed by the projectile that allows the person to discharge a firearm on, over, or across the property or property line.

(d) The written agreement required under Subsection (c)(2) must:

(1) contain the name of the person allowed to hunt or engage in recreational shooting in a manner described by Subsection (b);

(2) identify the property on either side of the property line crossed by the projectile; and

(3) be signed by any person who owns the property on either side of the line crossed by the projectile.

(e) An offense under this section is a Class C Parks and Wildlife Code misdemeanor.

(f) If conduct constituting an offense under this section constitutes an offense under a section of the Penal Code, the person may be prosecuted under either section or both sections.

Parks and Wildlife Code §62.081. Weapons Prohibited

Except as provided in Section 62.082 of this code, no person may hunt with, possess, or shoot a firearm, bow, crossbow, slingshot, or any other weapon on or across the land of the Lower Colorado River Authority.

Parks and Wildlife Code §62.082. Target Ranges, Managed Hunts, And Other Exceptions; Rules

(a) The Board of Directors of the Lower Colorado River Authority may lease river authority land to be used on a nonprofit basis for a target rifle or archery range only and not for hunting.

(b) A member of the boy scouts or the girl scouts or other nonprofit public service group or organization may possess and shoot a firearm, bow, and crossbow for target or instructional purposes under the supervision of a qualified instructor registered with and approved by the Lower Colorado River Authority on ranges designated by the Lower Colorado River Authority. This subsection does not permit hunting by any person.

(c) The Board of Directors of the Lower Colorado River Authority may authorize lawful hunting on Lower Colorado River Authority lands, consistent with sound biological management practices.

(d) Section 62.081 does not apply to:

(1) an employee of the Lower Colorado River Authority;

(2) a person authorized to hunt under Subsection (c);

(3) a peace officer as defined by Article 2.12, Code of Criminal Procedure; or

(4) a person who:

(A) possesses a concealed handgun and a license issued under Subchapter H, Chapter 411, Government Code, to carry a concealed handgun; or

(B) under circumstances in which the person would be justified in the use of deadly force under Chapter 9, Penal Code, shoots a handgun the person is licensed to carry under Subchapter H, Chapter 411, Government Code.

(e) A state agency, including the department, the Department of Public Safety, and the Lower Colorado River Authority, may not adopt a rule that prohibits a person who possesses a license issued under Subchapter H, Chapter 411, Government Code, from entering or crossing the land of the Lower Colorado River Authority while:

(1) possessing a concealed handgun; or

(2) under circumstances in which the person would be justified in the use of deadly force under Chapter 9, Penal Code, shooting a handgun.

Parks and Wildlife Code §143.023. Discharge Of Firearm

(a) Except as provided in Subsections (b) and (c) of this section, no person may shoot, fire, or discharge any firearm in, on, along, or across Lake Lavon in Collin County.

(b) This section does not apply to peace officers, game wardens, or other representatives of the department in the lawful discharge of their duties.

(c) This section does not apply to a person hunting with a shotgun during an open season or when it is lawful to hunt in or on Lake Lavon.

(d) A person who violates this section is guilty of a misdemeanor and on conviction is punishable by a fine of not less than $10 nor more than $200 plus costs, or confinement in the county jail for not more than one year, or both.

Parks and Wildlife Code §284.001. Discharge Of Firearm Prohibited

(a) In this section:

(1) "Archery equipment" means a longbow, recurved bow, compound bow, or crossbow.

(2) "Firearm" has the meaning assigned by Section 62.014.

(3) "Navigable river or stream" has the meaning assigned by Section 90.001.

(b) This section applies only to a navigable river or stream located wholly or partly in Dimmit, Edwards, Frio, Kenedy, Llano, Maverick, Real, Uvalde, or Zavala County.

(c) Except as provided by Subsection (d), a person may not discharge a firearm or shoot an arrow from any kind of bow if:

(1) the person is located in or on the bed or bank of a navigable river or stream at the time the firearm is discharged or the arrow is shot from the bow; or

(2) any portion of the ammunition discharged or arrow shot could physically contact the bed or bank of a navigable river or stream.

(d) This section does not apply to:

(1) an individual acting in the scope of the individual's duties as a peace officer or department employee; or

(2) the discharge of a shotgun loaded with ammunition that releases only shot when discharged.

(e) This section does not limit the ability of a license holder to carry a concealed handgun under the authority of Subchapter H, Chapter 411, Government Code.

EXCERPTS FROM THE TEXAS PENAL CODE

CHAPTER 1 · GENERAL PROVISIONS

Penal Code §1.01. Short Title
This code shall be known and may be cited as the Penal Code.

Penal Code §1.02. Objectives Of The Code
The general purposes of this code are to establish a system of prohibitions, penalties, and correctional measures to deal with conduct that unjustifiably and inexcusably causes or threatens harm to those individual or public interests for which state protection is appropriate. To this end, the provisions of this code are intended, and shall be construed, to achieve the following objectives:

(1) to insure the public safety through:

(A) the deterrent influence of the penalties hereinafter provided;

(B) the rehabilitation of those convicted of violations of this code; and

(C) such punishment as may be necessary to prevent likely recurrence of criminal behavior;

(2) by definition and grading of offenses to give fair warning of what is prohibited and of the consequences of violation;

(3) to prescribe penalties that are proportionate to the seriousness of offenses and that permit recognition of differences in rehabilitation possibilities among individual offenders;

(4) to safeguard conduct that is without guilt from condemnation as criminal;
(5) to guide and limit the exercise of official discretion in law enforcement to prevent arbitrary or oppressive treatment of persons suspected, accused, or convicted of offenses; and
(6) to define the scope of state interest in law enforcement against specific offenses and to systematize the exercise of state criminal jurisdiction.

Penal Code §1.07. Definitions

(a) In this code:
(1) "Act" means a bodily movement, whether voluntary or involuntary, and includes speech.
(2) "Actor" means a person whose criminal responsibility is in issue in a criminal action. Whenever the term "suspect" is used in this code, it means "actor."
(3) "Agency" includes authority, board, bureau, commission, committee, council, department, district, division, and office.
(4) "Alcoholic beverage" has the meaning assigned by Section 1-04, Alcoholic Beverage Code.
(5) "Another" means a person other than the actor.
(6) "Association" means a government or governmental subdivision or agency, trust, partnership, or two or more persons having a joint or common economic interest.
(7) "Benefit" means anything reasonably regarded as economic gain or advantage, including benefit to any other person in whose welfare the beneficiary is interested.
(8) "Bodily injury" means physical pain, illness, or any impairment of physical condition.
(9) "Coercion" means a threat, however communicated:
(A) to commit an offense;
(B) to inflict bodily injury in the future on the person threatened or another;
(C) to accuse a person of any offense
(D) to expose a person to hatred, contempt, or ridicule;
(E) to harm the credit or business repute of any person; or
(F) to take or withhold action as a public servant, or to cause a public servant to take or withhold action.
(10) "Conduct" means an act or omission and its accompanying mental state.
(11) "Consent" means assent in fact, whether express or apparent.
(12) "Controlled substance" has the meaning assigned by Section 481.002, Health and Safety Code.
(13) "Corporation" includes nonprofit corporations, professional associations created pursuant to statute, and joint stock companies.
(14) "Correctional facility" means a place designated by law for the confinement of a person arrested for, charged with, or convicted of a criminal offense. The term includes:
(A) a municipal or county jail;
(B) a confinement facility operated by the Texas Department of Criminal Justice;
(C) a confinement facility operated under contract with any division of the Texas Department of Criminal Justice; and
(D) a community corrections facility operated by a community supervision and corrections department.
(15) "Criminal negligence" is defined in Section 6.03 (Culpable Mental States).
(16) "Dangerous drug" has the meaning assigned by Section 483.001, Health and Safety Code.
(17) "Deadly weapon" means:
(A) a firearm or anything manifestly designed, made, or adapted for the purpose of inflicting death or serious bodily injury; or
(B) anything that in the manner of its use or intended use is capable of causing death or serious bodily injury.
(18) "Drug" has the meaning assigned by Section 481.002, Health and Safety Code.
(19) "Effective consent" includes consent by a person legally authorized to act for the owner. Consent is not effective if:
(A) induced by force, threat, or fraud;
(B) given by a person the actor knows is not legally authorized to act for the owner;
(C) given by a person who by reason of youth, mental disease or defect, or intoxication is known by the actor to be unable to make reasonable decisions; or
(D) given solely to detect the commission of an offense.
(20) "Electric generating plant" means a facility that generates electric energy for distribution to the public.
(21) "Electric utility substation" means a facility used to switch or change voltage in connection with the transmission of electric energy for distribution to the public.
(22) "Element of offense" means:
(A) the forbidden conduct;
(B) the required culpability;
(C) any required result; and
(D) the negation of any exception to the offense.
(23) "Felony" means an offense so designated by law or punishable by death or confinement in a penitentiary.
(24) "Government" means:

(A) the state;
(B) a county, municipality, or political subdivision of the state; or
(C) any branch or agency of the state, a county, municipality, or political subdivision.
(25) "Harm" means anything reasonably regarded as loss, disadvantage, or injury. including harm to another person in whose welfare the person affected is interested.
(26) "Individual" means a human being who is alive, including an unborn child at every stage of gestation from fertilization until birth.
(27) "Institutional division" means the institutional division of the Texas Department of Criminal Justice. <repealed, SB1969 §25.144, 2009>
(28) "Intentional" is defined in Section 6.03 (Culpable Mental States).
(29) "Knowing" is defined in Section 6.03 (Culpable Mental States).
(30) "Law" means the constitution or a statute of this state or of the United States, a written opinion of a court of record, a municipal ordinance, an order of a county commissioners court, or a rule authorized by and lawfully adopted under a statute.
(31) "Misdemeanor" means an offense so designated by law or punishable by fine, by confinement in jail, or by both fine and confinement in jail.
(32) "Oath" includes affirmation.
(33) "Official proceeding" means any type of administrative, executive, legislative, or judicial proceeding that may be conducted before a public servant.
(34) "Omission" means failure to act.
(35) "Owner" means a person who:
(A) has title to the property, possession of the property, whether lawful or not, or a greater right to possession of the property than the actor; or
(B) is a holder in due course of a negotiable instrument.
(36) "Peace officer" means a person elected, employed, or appointed as a peace officer under Article 2.12, Code of Criminal Procedure, Section 51.212 or 51.214, Education Code, or other law.
(37) "Penal institution" means a place designated by law for confinement of persons arrested for, charged with, or convicted of an offense.
(38) "Person" means an individual, corporation, or association.
(39) "Possession" means actual care, custody, control, or management.
(40) "Public place" means any place to which the public or a substantial group of the public has access and includes, but is not limited to, streets, highways, and the common areas of schools, hospitals, apartment houses, office buildings, transport facilities, and shops.
(41) "Public servant" means a person elected, selected, appointed, employed, or otherwise designated as one of the following, even if he has not yet qualified for office or assumed his duties:
(A) an officer, employee, or agent of government;
(B) a juror or grand juror; or
(C) an arbitrator, referee, or other person who is authorized by law or private written agreement to hear or determine a cause or controversy; or
(D) an attorney at law or notary public when participating in the performance of a governmental function; or
(E) a candidate for nomination or election to public office; or
(F) a person who is performing a governmental function under a claim of right although he is not legally qualified to do so.
(42) "Reasonable belief" means a belief that would be held by an ordinary and prudent man in the same circumstances as the actor.
(43) "Reckless" is defined in Section 6.03 (Culpable Mental States).
(44) "Rule" includes regulation.
(45) "Secure correctional facility" means:
(A) a municipal or county jail; or
(B) a confinement facility operated by or under a contract with any division of the Texas Department of Criminal Justice.
(46) "Serious bodily injury" means bodily injury that creates a substantial risk of death or that causes death, serious permanent disfigurement, or protracted loss or impairment of the function of any bodily member or organ.
(46-a) "Sight order" means a written or electronic instruction to pay money that is authorized by the person giving the instruction and that is payable on demand or at a definite time by the person being instructed to pay. The term includes a check, an electronic debit, or an automatic bank draft.
(46-b) "Federal special investigator" means a person described by Article 2.122, Code of Criminal Procedure.
(47) "Swear" includes affirm.
(48) "Unlawful" means criminal or tortious or both and includes what would be criminal or tortious but for a defense not amounting to justification or privilege.
(49) "Death" includes, for an individual who is an unborn child, the failure to be born alive.
(b) The definition of a term in this code applies to each grammatical variation of the term.

Penal Code §1.08. Preemption
No governmental subdivision or agency may enact or enforce a law that makes any conduct covered
by this code an offense subject to a criminal penalty. This section shall apply only as long as the
law governing the conduct proscribed by this code is legally enforceable.

CHAPTER 2 · BURDEN OF PROOF

Penal Code §2.01. Proof Beyond A Reasonable Doubt
All persons are presumed to be innocent and no person may be convicted of an offense unless each
element of the offense is proved beyond a reasonable doubt. The fact that he has been arrested,
confined, or indicted for, or otherwise charged with, the offense gives rise to no inference of guilt
at his trial.

Penal Code §2.02. Exception
(a) An exception to an offense in this code is so labeled by the phrase: "It is an exception to the
application of ...."
(b) The prosecuting attorney must negate the existence of an exception in the accusation charging
commission of the offense and prove beyond a reasonable doubt that the defendant or defendant's
conduct does not fall within the exception.
(c) This section does not affect exceptions applicable to offenses enacted prior to the effective date of
this code.

Penal Code §2.03. Defense
(a) A defense to prosecution for an offense in this code is so labeled by the phrase: "It is a defense to
prosecution ...."
(b) The prosecuting attorney is not required to negate the existence of a defense in the accusation
charging commission of the offense.
(c) The issue of the existence of a defense is not submitted to the jury unless evidence is admitted
supporting the defense.
(d) If the issue of the existence of a defense is submitted to the jury, the court shall charge that a
reasonable doubt on the issue requires that the defendant be acquitted.
(e) A ground of defense in a penal law that is not plainly labeled in accordance with this chapter has
the procedural and evidentiary consequences of a defense.

Penal Code §2.04. Affirmative Defense
(a) An affirmative defense in this code Is so labeled by the phrase: "It is an affirmative defense to
prosecution ...."
(b) The prosecuting attorney is not required to negate the existence of an affirmative defense in the
accusation charging commission of the offense.
(c) The issue of the existence of an affirmative defense is not submitted to the jury unless evidence is
admitted supporting the defense.
(d) If the issue of the existence of an affirmative defense is submitted to the jury, the court shall
charge that the defendant must prove the affirmative defense by a preponderance of evidence

Penal Code §2.05. Presumption
(a) Except as provided by Subsection (b), when this code or another penal law establishes a
presumption with respect to any fact, it has the following consequences:
(1) if there is sufficient evidence of the facts that give rise to the presumption, the issue of the
existence of the presumed fact must be submitted to the jury, unless the court is satisfied that the
evidence as a whole clearly precludes a finding beyond a reasonable doubt of the presumed fact;
and
(2) if the existence of the presumed fact is submitted to the jury, the court shall charge the jury, in
terms of the presumption and the specific element to which it applies, as follows:
(A) that the facts giving rise to the presumption must be proven beyond a reasonable doubt;
(B) that if such facts are proven beyond a reasonable doubt the jury may find that the element of the
offense sought to be presumed exists, but it is not bound to so find;
(C) that even though the jury may find the existence of such element, the state must prove beyond a
reasonable doubt each of the other elements of the offense charged; and
(D) if the jury has a reasonable doubt as to the existence of a fact or facts giving rise to the
presumption, the presumption fails and the jury shall not consider the presumption for any
purpose.
(b) When this code or another penal law establishes a presumption in favor of the defendant with
respect to any fact, it has the following consequences:
(1) if there is sufficient evidence of the facts that give rise to the presumption, the issue of the
existence of the presumed fact must be submitted to the jury unless the court is satisfied that the
evidence as a whole clearly precludes a finding beyond a reasonable doubt of the presumed fact;
and
(2) if the existence of the presumed fact is submitted to the jury, the court shall charge the jury, in
terms of the presumption, that:

(A) the presumption applies unless the state proves beyond a reasonable doubt that the facts giving rise to the presumption do not exist;
(B) if the state fails to prove beyond a reasonable doubt that the facts giving rise to the presumption do not exist, the jury must find that the presumed fact exists;
(C) even though the jury may find that the presumed fact does not exist, the state must prove beyond a reasonable doubt each of the elements of the offense charged; and
(D) if the jury has a reasonable doubt as to whether the presumed fact exists, the presumption applies and the jury must consider the presumed fact to exist.

CHAPTER 6 · CULPABILITY GENERALLY

Penal Code §6.01. Requirement of Voluntary Act or Omission
(a) A person commits an offense only if he voluntarily engages in conduct, including an act, an omission, or possession.
(b) Possession is a voluntary act if the possessor knowingly obtains or receives the thing possessed or is aware of his control of the thing for a sufficient time to permit him to terminate his control.
(c) A person who omits to perform an act does not commit an offense unless a law as defined by Section 1.07 provides that the omission is an offense or otherwise provides that he has a duty to perform the act.

Penal Code §6.02. Requirement of Culpability
(a) Except as provided in Subsection (b), a person does not commit an offense unless he intentionally, knowingly, recklessly, or with criminal negligence engages in conduct as the definition of the offense requires.
(b) If the definition of an offense does not prescribe a culpable mental state, a culpable mental state is nevertheless required unless the definition plainly dispenses with any mental element.
(c) If the definition of an offense does not prescribe a culpable mental state, but one is nevertheless required under Subsection (b), intent, knowledge, or recklessness suffices to establish criminal responsibility.
(d) Culpable mental states are classified according to relative degrees, from highest to lowest, as follows:
(1) intentional;
(2) knowing;
(3) reckless;
(4) criminal negligence.
(e) Proof of a higher degree of culpability than that charged constitutes proof of the culpability charged.

Penal Code §6.03. Definitions of Culpable Mental States
(a) A person acts intentionally, or with intent, with respect to the nature of his conduct or to a result of his conduct when it is his conscious objective or desire to engage in the conduct or cause the result.
(b) A person acts knowingly, or with knowledge, with respect to the nature of his conduct or to circumstances surrounding his conduct when he is aware of the nature of his conduct or that the circumstances exist. A person acts knowingly, or with knowledge, with respect to a result of his conduct when he is aware that his conduct is reasonably certain to cause the result.
(c) A person acts recklessly, or is reckless, with respect to circumstances surrounding his conduct or the result of his conduct when he is aware of but consciously disregards a substantial and unjustifiable risk that the circumstances exist or the result will occur. The risk must be of such a nature and degree that its disregard constitutes a gross deviation from the standard of care that an ordinary person would exercise under all the circumstances as viewed from the actor's standpoint.
(d) A person acts with criminal negligence, or is criminally negligent, with respect to circumstances surrounding his conduct or the result of his conduct when he ought to be aware of a substantial and unjustifiable risk that the circumstances exist or the result will occur. The risk must be of such a nature and degree that the failure to perceive it constitutes a gross deviation from the standard of care that an ordinary person would exercise under all the circumstances as viewed from the actor's standpoint.

Penal Code §6.04. Causation: Conduct and Results
(a) A person is criminally responsible if the result would not have occurred but for his conduct, operating either alone or concurrently with another cause, unless the concurrent cause was clearly sufficient to produce the result and the conduct of the actor clearly insufficient.
(b) A person is nevertheless criminally responsible for causing a result if the only difference between what actually occurred and what he desired. contemplated, or risked is that:
(1) a different offense was committed; or
(2) a different person or property was injured, harmed, or otherwise affected.

CHAPTER 8
GENERAL DEFENSES TO CRIMINAL RESPONSIBILITY

Penal Code §8.03. Mistake of Law
(a) It is no defense to prosecution that the actor was ignorant of the provisions of any law after the law has taken effect.

Penal Code §8.07. Age Affecting Criminal Responsibility
(a) A person may not be prosecuted for or convicted of any offense that the person committed when younger than 15 years of age except:
(1) perjury and aggravated perjury when it appears by proof that the person had sufficient discretion to understand the nature and obligation of an oath;
(2) a violation of a penal statute cognizable under Chapter 729, Transportation Code, except for conduct for which the person convicted may be sentenced to imprisonment or confinement in jail;
(3) a violation of a motor vehicle traffic ordinance of an incorporated city or town in this state;
(4) a misdemeanor punishable by fine only other than public intoxication;
(5) a violation of a penal ordinance of a political subdivision;
(6) a violation of a penal statute that is, or is a lesser included offense of, a capital felony, an aggravated controlled substance felony, or a felony of the first degree for which the person is transferred to the court under Section 54.02, Family Code, for prosecution if the person committed the offense when 14 years of age or older; or
(7) a capital felony or an offense under Section 19.02 for which the person is transferred to the court under Section 54.02(j)(2)(A), Family Code.
(b) Unless the juvenile court waives jurisdiction under Section 54.02, Family Code, and certifies the individual for criminal prosecution or the juvenile court has previously waived jurisdiction under that section and certified the individual for criminal prosecution, a person may not be prosecuted for or convicted of any offense committed before reaching 17 years of age except an offense described by Subsections (a)(1)-(5).
(c) No person may, in any case, be punished by death for an offense committed while the person was younger than 18 years.

CHAPTER 9
JUSTIFICATION EXCLUDING CRIMINAL RESPONSIBILITY

SUBCHAPTER A. GENERAL PROVISIONS

Penal Code §9.01. Definitions
In this chapter:
(1) "Custody" means:
(A) under arrest by a peace officer; or
(B) under restraint by a public servant pursuant to an order of a court.
(2) "Escape" means unauthorized departure from custody or failure to return to custody following temporary leave for a specific purpose or limited period, but does not include a violation of conditions of community supervision or parole, or following leave that is part of an intermittent sentence.
(3) "Deadly force" means force that is intended or known by the actor to cause, or in the manner of its use or intended use is capable of causing, death or serious bodily injury.
(4) "Habitation" has the meaning assigned by Section 30.01.
(5) "Vehicle" has the meaning assigned by Section 30.01.

Penal Code §9.02. Justification as a Defense
It is a defense to prosecution that the conduct in question is justified under this chapter.

Penal Code §9.03. Confinement as Justifiable Force
Confinement is justified when force is justified by this chapter if the actor takes reasonable measures to terminate the confinement as soon as he knows he safely can unless the person confined has been arrested for an offense.

Penal Code §9.04. Threats as Justifiable Force
The threat of force is justified when the use of force is justified by this chapter. For purposes of this section, a threat to cause death or serious bodily injury by the production of a weapon or otherwise, as long as the actor's purpose is limited to creating an apprehension that he will use deadly force if necessary, does not constitute the use of deadly force.

Penal Code §9.05. Reckless Injury of Innocent Third Person
Even though an actor is justified under this chapter in threatening or using force or deadly force against another, if in doing so he also recklessly injures or kills an innocent third person, the justification afforded by this chapter is unavailable in a prosecution for the reckless in jury or killing of the innocent third person.

Penal Code §9.06. Civil Remedies Unaffected
The fact that conduct is justified under this chapter does not abolish or impair any remedy for the conduct that is available in a civil suit.

SUBCHAPTER B. JUSTIFICATION GENERALLY

Penal Code §9.21. Public Duty
(a) Except as qualified by Subsections (b) and (c), conduct is justified if the actor reasonably believes the conduct is required or authorized by law, by the judgment or order of a competent court or other governmental tribunal, or in the execution of legal process.
(b) The other sections of this chapter control when force is used against a person to protect persons (subchapter C), to protect property (Subchapter D), for law enforcement (Subchapter E), or by virtue of a special relationship (Subchapter F).
(c) The use of deadly force is not justified under this section unless the actor reasonably believes the deadly force is specifically required by statute or unless it occurs in the lawful conduct of war. If deadly force is so justified, there is no duty to retreat before using it.
(d) The justification afforded by this section is available if the actor reasonably believes:
(1) the court or governmental tribunal has jurisdiction or the process is lawful, even though the court or governmental tribunal lacks jurisdiction or the process is unlawful; or
(2) his conduct is required or authorized to assist a public servant in the performance of his official duty, even though the servant exceeds his lawful authority.

Penal Code §9.22. Necessity
Conduct is justified if:
(1) the actor reasonably believes the conduct is immediately necessary to avoid imminent harm;
(2) the desirability and urgency of avoiding the harm clearly outweigh, according to ordinary standards of reasonableness, the harm sought to be prevented by the law proscribing the conduct; and
(3) a legislative purpose to exclude the justification claimed for the conduct does not otherwise plainly appear.

SUBCHAPTER C. PROTECTION OF PERSONS

Penal Code §9.31. Self-Defense
(a) Except as provided in Subsection (b), a person is justified in using force against another when and to the degree the actor reasonably believes the force is immediately necessary to protect the actor against the other's use or attempted use of unlawful force. The actor's belief that the force was immediately necessary as described by this subsection is presumed to be reasonable if the actor:
(1) knew or had reason to believe that the person against whom the force was used:
(A) unlawfully and with force entered, or was attempting to enter unlawfully and with force, the actor's occupied habitation, vehicle, or place of business or employment;
(B) unlawfully and with force removed, or was attempting to remove unlawfully and with force, the actor from the actor's habitation, vehicle, or place of business or employment; or
(C) was committing or attempting to commit aggravated kidnapping, murder, sexual assault, aggravated sexual assault, robbery, or aggravated robbery;
(2) did not provoke the person against whom the force was used; and
(3) was not otherwise engaged in criminal activity, other than a Class C misdemeanor that is a violation of a law or ordinance regulating traffic at the time the force was used.
(b) The use of force against another is not justified:
(1) in response to verbal provocation alone;
(2) to resist an arrest or search that the actor knows is being made by a peace officer, or by a person acting in a peace officer's presence and at his direction, even though the arrest or search is unlawful, unless the resistance is justified under Subsection (c);
(3) if the actor consented to the exact force used or attempted by the other;
(4) if the actor provoked the other's use or attempted use of unlawful force, unless:
(A) the actor abandons the encounter, or clearly communicates to the other his intent to do so reasonably believing he cannot safely abandon the encounter; and
(B) the other nevertheless continues or attempts to use unlawful force against the actor; or
(5) if the actor sought an explanation from or discussion with the other person concerning the actor's differences with the other person while the actor was:
(A) carrying a weapon in violation of Section 46.02; or

(B) possessing or transporting a weapon in violation of Section 46.05.

(c) The use of force to resist an arrest or search is justified:

(1) if, before the actor offers any resistance, the peace officer (or person acting at his direction) uses or attempts to use greater force than necessary to make the arrest or search; and

(2) when and to the degree the actor reasonably believes the force is immediately necessary to protect himself against the peace officer's (or other person's) use or attempted use of greater force than necessary.

(d) The use of deadly force is not justified under this subchapter except as provided in Sections 9.32, 9.33, and 9.34.

(e) A person who has a right to be present at the location where the force is used, who has not provoked the person against whom the force is used, and who is not engaged in criminal activity at the time the force is used is not required to retreat before using force as described by this section.

(f) For purposes of Subsection (a), in determining whether an actor described by Subsection (e) reasonably believed that the use of force was necessary, a finder of fact may not consider whether the actor failed to retreat.

Penal Code §9.32. Deadly Force in Defense of Person

(a) A person is justified in using deadly force against another:

(1) if the actor would be justified in using force against the other under Section 9.31; and

(2) when and to the degree the actor reasonably believes the deadly force is immediately necessary:

(A) to protect the actor against the other's use or attempted use of unlawful deadly force; or

(B) to prevent the other's imminent commission of aggravated kidnapping, murder, sexual assault, aggravated sexual assault, robbery, or aggravated robbery.

(b) The actor's belief under Subsection (a)(2) that the deadly force was immediately necessary as described by that subdivision is presumed to be reasonable if the actor:

(1) knew or had reason to believe that the person against whom the deadly force was used:

(A) unlawfully and with force entered, or was attempting to enter unlawfully and with force, the actor's occupied habitation, vehicle, or place of business or employment;

(B) unlawfully and with force removed, or was attempting to remove unlawfully and with force, the actor from the actor's habitation, vehicle, or place of business or employment; or

(C) was committing or attempting to commit an offense described by Subsection (a)(2)(B);

(2) did not provoke the person against whom the force was used; and

(3) was not otherwise engaged in criminal activity, other than a Class C misdemeanor that is a violation of a law or ordinance regulating traffic at the time the force was used.

(c) A person who has a right to be present at the location where the deadly force is used, who has not provoked the person against whom the deadly force is used, and who is not engaged in criminal activity at the time the deadly force is used is not required to retreat before using deadly force as described by this section.

(d) For purposes of Subsection (a)(2), in determining whether an actor described by Subsection (c) reasonably believed that the use of deadly force was necessary, a finder of fact may not consider whether the actor failed to retreat.

Penal Code §9.33. Defense of a Third Person

A person is justified in using force or deadly force against another to protect a third person if:

(1) under the circumstances as the actor reasonably believes them to be, the actor would be justified under Section 9.31 or 9.32 in using force or deadly force to protect himself against the unlawful force or unlawful deadly force he reasonably believes to be threatening the third person he seeks to protect; and

(2) the actor reasonably believes that his intervention is immediately necessary to protect the third person.

Penal Code §9.34. Protection of Life or Health

(a) A person is justified in using force, but not deadly force, against another when and to the degree he reasonably believes the force is immediately necessary to prevent the other from committing suicide or inflicting serious bodily injury to himself.

(b) A person is justified in using both force and deadly force against another when and to the degree he reasonably believes the force or deadly force is immediately necessary to preserve the other's life in an emergency.

SUBCHAPTER D. PROTECTION OF PROPERTY

Penal Code §9.41. Protection of One's Own Property

(a) A person in lawful possession of land or tangible, movable property is justified in using force against another when and to the degree the actor reasonably believes the force is immediately necessary to prevent or terminate the other's trespass on the land or unlawful interference with the property.

(b) A person unlawfully dispossessed of land or tangible, movable property by another is justified in using force against the other when and to the degree the actor reasonably believes the force is

immediately necessary to reenter the land or recover the property if the actor uses the force
immediately or in fresh pursuit after the dispossession and:
(1) the actor reasonably believes the other had no claim of right when he dispossessed the actor; or
(2) the other accomplished the dispossession by using force, threat, or fraud against the actor.

Penal Code §9.42. Deadly Force to Protect Property
A person is justified in using deadly force against another to protect land or tangible, movable
property:
(1) if he would be justified in using force against the other under Section 9.41; and
(2) when and to the degree he reasonably believes the deadly force is immediately necessary:
(A) to prevent the other's imminent commission of arson, burglary, robbery, aggravated robbery, theft
during the nighttime, or criminal mischief during the nighttime; or
(B) to prevent the other who is fleeing immediately after committing burglary, robbery, aggravated
robbery, or theft during the nighttime from escaping with the property; and
(3) he reasonably believes that:
(A) the land or property cannot be protected or recovered by any other means; or
(B) the use of force other than deadly force to protect or recover the land or property would expose
the actor or another to a substantial risk of death or serious bodily injury.

Penal Code §9.43. Protection of Third Person's Property
A person is justified in using force or deadly force against another to protect land or tangible,
movable property of a third person if, under the circumstances as he reasonably believes them to
be, the actor would be justified under Section 9.41 or 9.42 in using force or deadly force to
protect his own land or property and:
(1) the actor reasonably believes the unlawful interference constitutes attempted or consummated
theft of or criminal mischief to the tangible, movable property; or
(2) the actor reasonably believes that:
(A) the third person has requested his protection of the land or property;
(B) he has a legal duty to protect the third person's land or property; or
(C) the third person whose land or property he uses force or deadly force to protect is the actor's
spouse, parent, or child, resides with the actor, or is under the actor's care.

Penal Code §9.44. Use of Device to Protect Property
The justification afforded by Sections 9.41 and 9.43 applies to the use of a device to protect land or
tangible, movable property if:
(1) the device is not designed to cause, or known by the actor to create a substantial risk of causing,
death or serious bodily injury; and
(2) use of the device is reasonable under all the circumstances as the actor reasonably believes them
to be when he installs the device.

SUBCHAPTER E. LAW ENFORCEMENT

Penal Code §9.51. Arrest and Search
(a) A peace officer, or a person acting in a peace officer's presence and at his direction, is justified in
using force against another when and to the degree the actor reasonably believes the force is
immediately necessary to make or assist in making an arrest or search, or to prevent or assist in
preventing escape after arrest, if:
(1) the actor reasonably believes the arrest or search is lawful or, if the arrest or search is made under
a warrant, he reasonably believes the warrant is valid; and
(2) before using force, the actor manifests his purpose to arrest or search and identifies himself as a
peace officer or as one acting at a peace officer's direction, unless he reasonably believes his
purpose and identity are already known by or cannot reasonably be made known to the person to
be arrested.
(b) A person other than a peace officer (or one acting at his direction) is justified in using force against
another when and to the degree the actor reasonably believes the force is immediately necessary
to make or assist in making a lawful arrest, or to prevent or assist in preventing escape after lawful
arrest if, before using force, the actor manifests his purpose to and the reason for the arrest or
reasonably believes his purpose and the reason are already known by or cannot reasonably be
made known to the person to be arrested.
(c) A peace officer is justified in using deadly force against another when and to the degree the peace
officer reasonably believes the deadly force is immediately necessary to make an arrest, or to
prevent escape after arrest, if the use of force would have been justified under Subsection (a) and:
(1) the actor reasonably believes the conduct for which arrest is authorized Included the use or
attempted use of deadly force; or
(2) the actor reasonably believes there is a substantial risk that the person to be arrested will cause
death or serious bodily injury to the actor or another if the arrest is delayed.
(d) A person other than a peace officer acting in a peace officer's presence and at his direction is
justified in using deadly force against another when and to the degree the person reasonably

believes the deadly force is immediately necessary to make a lawful arrest, or to prevent escape after a lawful arrest, if the use of force would have been justified under Subsection (b) and:

(1) the actor reasonably believes the felony or offense against the public peace for which arrest is authorized included the use or attempted use of deadly force: or

(2) the actor reasonably believes there is a substantial risk that the person to be arrested will cause death or serious bodily injury to another if the arrest is delayed.

(e) There is no duty to retreat before using deadly force justified by Subsection (c) or (d).

(f) Nothing in this section relating to the actor's manifestation of purpose or identity shall be construed as conflicting with any other law relating to the issuance, service, and execution of an arrest or search warrant either under the laws of this state or the United States.

(g) Deadly force may only be used under the circumstances enumerated in Subsections (c) and (d).

Penal Code §9.52. Prevention of Escape From Custody
The use of force to prevent the escape of an arrested person from custody is justifiable when the force could have been employed to effect the arrest under which the person is in custody, except that a guard employed by a correctional facility or a peace officer is justified in using any force, including deadly force, that he reasonably believes to be immediately necessary to prevent the escape of a person from the correctional facility.

Penal Code §9.53. Maintaining Security in Correctional Facility
An officer or employee of a correctional facility is justified in using force against a person in custody when and to the degree the officer or employee reasonably believes the force is necessary to maintain the security of the correctional facility, the safety or security of other persons in custody or employed by the correctional facility, or his own safety or security.

CHAPTER 12 · PUNISHMENTS

SUBCHAPTER A. GENERAL PROVISIONS

Penal Code §12.01. Punishment in Accordance with Code
(a) A person adjudged guilty of an offense under this code shall be punished in accordance with this chapter and the Code of Criminal Procedure.

(b) Penal laws enacted after the effective date of this code shall be classified for punishment purposes in accordance with this chapter.

(c) This chapter does not deprive a court of authority conferred by law to forfeit property, dissolve a corporation, suspend or cancel a license or permit, remove a person from office, cite for contempt, or impose any other civil penalty. The civil penalty may be included in the sentence.

Penal Code §12.02. Classification of Offenses
Offenses are designated as felonies or misdemeanors.

Penal Code §12.03. Classification of Misdemeanors
(a) Misdemeanors are classified according to the relative seriousness of the offense into three categories:

(1) Class A misdemeanors;

(2) Class B misdemeanors;

(3) Class C misdemeanors.

(b) An offense designated a misdemeanor in this code without specification as to punishment or category is a Class C misdemeanor.

(c) Conviction of a Class C misdemeanor does not impose any legal disability or disadvantage.

Penal Code §12.04. Classification of Felonies
(a) Felonies are classified according to the relative seriousness of the offense into five categories:

(1) capital felonies;

(2) felonies of the first degree;

(3) felonies of the second degree;

(4) felonies of the third degree; and

(5) state jail felonies.

(b) An offense designated a felony in this code without specification as to category is a state jail felony.

SUBCHAPTER B. ORDINARY MISDEMEANOR PUNISHMENTS

Penal Code §12.21. Class A Misdemeanor
An individual adjudged guilty of a Class A misdemeanor shall be punished by:

(1) a fine not to exceed $4,000;

(2) confinement in jail for a term not to exceed one year; or

(3) both such fine and confinement.

Penal Code §12.22. Class B Misdemeanor
An individual adjudged guilty of a Class B misdemeanor shall be punished by:
(1) a fine not to exceed $2,000;
(2) confinement in jail for a term not to exceed 180 days; or
(3) both such fine and confinement.

Penal Code §12.23. Class C Misdemeanor
An individual adjudged guilty of a Class C misdemeanor shall be punished by a fine not to exceed
 $500.

SUBCHAPTER C. ORDINARY FELONY PUNISHMENTS

Penal Code §12.31. Capital Felony
(a) An individual adjudged guilty of a capital felony in a case in which the state seeks the death
 penalty shall be punished by imprisonment in the institutional division for life without parole or by
 death. An individual adjudged guilty of a capital felony in a case in which the state does not seek
 the death penalty shall be punished by imprisonment in the institutional division for life without
 parole.
(b) In a capital felony trial in which the state seeks the death penalty, prospective jurors shall be
 informed that a sentence of life imprisonment without parole is mandatory on conviction
 of a capital felony. In a capital felony trial in which the state does not seek the death penalty,
 prospective jurors shall be informed that the state is not seeking the death penalty and that a
 sentence of life imprisonment without parole is mandatory on conviction of the capital felony.

Penal Code §12.32. First Degree Felony Punishment
(a) An individual adjudged guilty of a felony of the first degree shall be punished by imprisonment in
 the institutional division for life or for any term of not more than 99 years or less than 5 years.
(b) In addition to imprisonment, an individual adjudged guilty of a felony of the first degree may be
 punished by a fine not to exceed $10,000.

Penal Code §12.33. Second Degree Felony Punishment
(a) An individual adjudged guilty of a felony of the second degree shall be punished by imprisonment
 in the institutional division for any term of not more than 20 years or less than 2 years.
(b) In addition to imprisonment, an individual adjudged guilty of a felony of the second degree may
 be punished by a fine not to exceed $10,000.

Penal Code §12.34. Third Degree Felony Punishment
(a) An individual adjudged guilty of a felony of the third degree shall be punished by imprisonment in
 the institutional division for any term of not more than 10 years or less than 2 years.
(b) In addition to imprisonment, an individual adjudged guilty of a felony of the third degree may be
 punished by a fine not to exceed $10,000.

Penal Code §12.35. State Jail Felony Punishment
(a) Except as provided by Subsection (c), an individual adjudged guilty of a state jail felony shall be
 punished by confinement in a state jail for any term of not more than two years or less than 180
 days.
(b) In addition to confinement, an individual adjudged guilty of a state jail felony may be punished by
 a fine not to exceed $10,000.
(c) An individual adjudged guilty of a state jail felony shall be punished for a third degree felony if it
 is shown on the trial of the offense that:
(1) a deadly weapon as defined by Section 1.07 was used or exhibited during the commission of the
 offense or during immediate flight following the commission of the offense, and that the individual
 used or exhibited the deadly weapon or was a party to the offense and knew that a deadly weapon
 would be used or exhibited; or
(2) the individual has previously been finally convicted of any felony:
(A) under Section 20A.03 or 21.02 or listed in Section 3g(a)(1), Article 42.12, Code of Criminal
 Procedure; or
(B) for which the judgment contains an affirmative finding under Section 3g(a)(2), Article 42.12, Code
 of Criminal Procedure.

SUBCHAPTER E. CORPORATIONS AND ASSOCIATIONS

Penal Code §12.51. Authorized Punishments for Corporations and Associations
(a) If a corporation or association is adjudged guilty of an offense that provides a penalty consisting of
 a fine only, a court may sentence the corporation or association to pay a fine in an amount fixed
 by the court, not to exceed the fine provided by the offense.

(b) If a corporation or association is adjudged guilty of an offense that provides a penalty including imprisonment, or that provides no specific penalty, a court may sentence the corporation or association to pay a fine in an amount fixed by the court, not to exceed:
(1) $20,000 if the offense is a felony of any category;
(2) $10,000 if the offense is a Class A or Class B misdemeanor;
(3) $2,000 if the offense is a Class C misdemeanor; or
(4) $50,000 if, as a result of an offense classified as a felony or Class A misdemeanor, an individual suffers serious bodily injury or death.
(c) In lieu of the fines authorized by Subsections (a), (b)(1), (b)(2), and (b)(4), if a court finds that the corporation or association gained money or property or caused personal injury or death, property damage, or other loss through the commission of a felony or Class A or Class B misdemeanor, the court may sentence the corporation or association to pay a fine in an amount fixed by the court, not to exceed double the amount gained or caused by the corporation or association to be lost or damaged, whichever is greater.
(d) In addition to any sentence that may be imposed by this section, a corporation or association that has been adjudged guilty of an offense may be ordered by the court to give notice of the conviction to any person the court deems appropriate.
(e) On conviction of a corporation or association, the court shall notify the attorney general of that fact.

CHAPTER 16 · CRIMINAL INSTRUMENTS AND OFFENSES INVOLVING CERTAIN COMMUNICATIONS

Penal Code §16.01. Unlawful Use Of Criminal Instrument Or Mechanical Security Device
(a) A person commits an offense if:
(1) the person possesses a criminal instrument or mechanical security device with the intent to use the instrument or device in the commission of an offense; or
(2) with knowledge of its character and with the intent to use a criminal instrument or mechanical security device or aid or permit another to use the instrument or device in the commission of an offense, the person manufactures, adapts, sells, installs, or sets up the instrument or device.
(b) For the purpose of this section:
(1) "Criminal instrument" means anything, the possession, manufacture, or sale of which is not otherwise an offense, that is specially designed, made, or adapted for use in the commission of an offense.
(2) "Mechanical security device" means a device designed or manufactured for use by a locksmith to perform services for a customer who seeks entry to a structure, motor vehicle, or other property.
(c) An offense under Subsection (a)(1) is one category lower than the offense intended. An offense under Subsection (a)(2) is a state jail felony.

CHAPTER 19 · CRIMINAL HOMICIDE

Penal Code §19.01. Types Of Criminal Homicide
(a) A person commits criminal homicide if he intentionally, knowingly, recklessly, or with criminal negligence causes the death of an individual.
(b) Criminal homicide is murder, capital murder, manslaughter, or criminally negligent homicide.

Penal Code §19.02. Murder
(a) In this section:
(1) "Adequate cause" means cause that would commonly produce a degree of anger, rage, resentment, or terror in a person of ordinary temper, sufficient to render the mind incapable of cool reflection.
(2) "Sudden passion" means passion directly caused by and arising out of provocation by the individual killed or another acting with the person killed which passion arises at the time of the offense and is not solely the result of former provocation.
(b) A person commits an offense if he:
(1) intentionally or knowingly causes the death of an individual;
(2) Intends to cause serious bodily injury and commits an act clearly dangerous to human life that causes the death of an individual; or
(3) commits or attempts to commit a felony, other than manslaughter, and in the course of and in furtherance of the commission or attempt, or in immediate flight from the commission or attempt, he commits or attempts to commit an act clearly dangerous to human life that causes the death of an individual.
(c) Except as provided by Subsection (d), an offense under this section is a felony of the first degree.
(d) At the punishment stage of a trial, the defendant may raise the issue as to whether he caused the death under the immediate influence of sudden passion arising from an adequate cause. If the

defendant proves the issue in the affirmative by a preponderance of the evidence, the offense is a felony of the second degree.

Penal Code §19.03. Capital Murder
(a) A person commits an offense if the person commits murder as defined under Section 19.02(b)(1) and:
(1) the person murders a peace officer or fireman who is acting in the lawful discharge of an official duty and who the person knows is a peace officer or fireman;
(2) the person intentionally commits the murder in the course of committing or attempting to commit kidnapping, burglary, robbery, aggravated sexual assault, arson, obstruction or retaliation, or terroristic threat under Section 22.07(a)(1), (3), (4), (5), or (6);
(3) the person commits the murder for remuneration or the promise of remuneration or employs another to commit the murder for remuneration or the promise of remuneration;
(4) the person commits the murder while escaping or attempting to escape from a penal institution;
(5) the person, while incarcerated in a penal institution, murders another:
(A) who is employed in the operation of the penal institution; or
(B) with the intent to establish, maintain, or participate in a combination or in the profits of a combination;
(6) the person:
(A) while incarcerated for an offense under this section or Section 19.02, murders another; or
(B) while serving a sentence of life imprisonment or a term of 99 years for an offense under Section 20.04, 22.021, or 29.03, murders another;
(7) the person murders more than one person:
(A) during the same criminal transaction; or
(B) during different criminal transactions but the murders are committed pursuant to the same scheme or course of conduct;
(8) the person murders an individual under 10 years of age; or
(9) the person murders another person in retaliation for or on account of the service or status of the other person as a judge or justice of the supreme court, the court of criminal appeals, a court of appeals, a district court, a criminal district court, a constitutional county court, a statutory county court, a justice court, or a municipal court.
(b) An offense under this section is a capital felony.
(c) If the jury or, when authorized by law, the judge does not find beyond a reasonable doubt that the defendant is guilty of an offense under this section, he may be convicted of murder or of any other lesser included offense.

Penal Code §19.04. Manslaughter
(a) A person commits an offense if he recklessly causes the death of an individual.
(b) An offense under this section is a felony of the second degree.

Penal Code §19.05. Criminally Negligent Homicide
(a) A person commits an offense if he causes the death of an individual by criminal negligence.
(b) An offense under this section is a state jail felony.

CHAPTER 20 · KIDNAPPING AND FALSE IMPRISONMENT

Penal Code §20.01. Definitions
In this chapter:
(1) "Restrain" means to restrict a person's movements without consent, so as to interfere substantially with the person's liberty, by moving the person from one place to another or by confining the person) Restraint is "without consent" if it is accomplished by:
(A) force, intimidation, or deception; or
(B) any means, including acquiescence of the victim, if:
(i) the victim is a child who is less than 14 years of age or an incompetent person and the parent, guardian, or person or institution acting in loco parentis has not acquiesced in the movement or confinement; or
(ii) the victim is a child who is 14 years of age or older and younger than 17 years of age, the victim is taken outside of the state and outside a 120-mile radius from the victim's residence, and the parent, guardian, or person or institution acting in loco parentis has not acquiesced in the movement.
(2) "Abduct" means to restrain a person with intent to prevent his liberation by:
(A) secreting or holding him in a place where he is not likely to be found; or
(B) using or threatening to use deadly force.
(3) "Relative" means a parent or stepparent, ancestor, sibling, or uncle or aunt, including an adoptive relative of the same degree through marriage or adoption.
(4) "Person" means an individual, corporation, or association.
(5) Notwithstanding Section 1.07, "individual" means a human being who has been born and is alive.

Penal Code §20.02. False Imprisonment
(a) A person commits an offense if he intentionally or knowingly restrains another person.
(b) It is an affirmative defense to prosecution under this section that:
(1) the person restrained was a child younger than 14 years of age;
(2) the actor was a relative of the child; and
(3) the actor's sole intent was to assume lawful control of the child.
(c) An offense under this section is a Class A misdemeanor, except that the offense is:
(1) a state jail felony if the person restrained was a child younger than 17 years of age; or
(2) a felony of the third degree if:
(A) the actor recklessly exposes the victim to a substantial risk of serious bodily injury;
(B) the actor restrains an individual the actor knows is a public servant while the public servant is lawfully discharging an official duty or in retaliation or on account of an exercise of official power or performance of an official duty as a public servant; or
(C) the actor while in custody restrains any other person.
(d) It is no offense to detain or move another under this section when it is for the purpose of effecting a lawful arrest or detaining an individual lawfully arrested.
(e) It is an affirmative defense to prosecution under this section that:
(1) the person restrained was a child who is 14 years of age or older and younger than 17 years of age;
(2) the actor does not restrain the child by force, intimidation, or deception; and
(3) the actor is not more than three years older than the child.

Penal Code §20.03. Kidnapping
(a) A person commits an offense if he intentionally or knowingly abducts another person.
(b) It is an affirmative defense to prosecution under this section that:
(1) the abduction was not coupled with intent to use or to threaten to use deadly force;
(2) the actor was a relative of the person abducted; and
(3) the actor's sole intent was to assume lawful control of the victim.
(c) An offense under this section is a felony of the third degree, except that an offense under this section is a felony of the second degree if the actor exposed the person abducted to a risk of serious bodily injury.

Penal Code §20.04. Aggravated Kidnapping
(a) A person commits an offense if:
(1) the person intentionally or knowingly abducts another person with the intent to:
(A) hold the person abducted for ransom or reward or to coerce a third person to perform some act;
(B) use the person abducted as a shield or hostage;
(C) facilitate the commission of a felony or the flight after the attempt or commission of a felony;
(D) inflict bodily injury on the person abducted or violate or abuse the person abducted sexually;
(E) terrorize the person abducted or a third person;
(F) interfere with the performance of any governmental or political function; or
(G) hold the person abducted in a condition of involuntary servitude; or
(2) the person intentionally or knowingly abducts another person who is:
(A) younger than 17 years of age; or
(B) incompetent.
(b) A person commits an offense if the person intentionally or knowingly abducts another person and uses or exhibits a deadly weapon during the commission of the offense.
(c) Except as provided by Subsection (d), an offense under this section is a felony of the first degree.
(d) At the punishment stage of a trial, the defendant may raise the issue as to whether he voluntarily released the victim in a safe place. If the defendant proves the issue in the affirmative by a preponderance of the evidence, the offense is a felony of the second degree.

CHAPTER 22 · ASSAULTIVE OFFENSES

Penal Code §22.01. Assault
(a) A person commits an offense if the person:
(1) intentionally, knowingly, or recklessly causes bodily injury to another, including the person's spouse;
(2) intentionally or knowingly threatens another with imminent bodily injury, including the person's spouse; or
(3) intentionally or knowingly causes physical contact with another when the person knows or should reasonably believe that the other will regard the contact as offensive or provocative.
(b) An offense under Subsection (a)(1) is a Class A misdemeanor, except that the offense is a felony of the third degree if the offense is committed against:
(1) a person the actor knows is a public servant while the public servant is lawfully discharging an official duty, or in retaliation or on account of an exercise of official power or performance of an official duty as a public servant;

(2) a person whose relationship to or association with the defendant is described by Section 71.0021(b), 71.003, or 71.005, Family Code, if it is shown on the trial of the offense that the defendant has been previously convicted of an offense under this chapter, Chapter 19, or Section 20.03, 20.04, or 21.11 against a person whose relationship to or association with the defendant is described by Section 71.0021(b), 71.003, or 71.005, Family Code;

(3) a person who contracts with government to perform a service in a facility as defined by Section 1.07(a)(14), Penal Code, or Section 51.02(13) or (14), Family Code, or an employee of that person:

(A) while the person or employee is engaged in performing a service within the scope of the contract, if the actor knows the person or employee is authorized by government to provide the service; or

(B) in retaliation for or on account of the person's or employee's performance of a service within the scope of the contract;

(4) a person the actor knows is a security officer while the officer is performing a duty as a security officer; or

(5) a person the actor knows is emergency services personnel while the person is providing emergency services.

(c) An offense under Subsection (a)(2) or (3) is a Class C misdemeanor, except that the offense is:

(1) a Class A misdemeanor if the offense is committed under Subsection (a)(3) against an elderly individual or disabled individual, as those terms are defined by Section 22.04; or

(2) a Class B misdemeanor if the offense is committed by a person who is not a sports participant against a person the actor knows is a sports participant either:

(A) while the participant is performing duties or responsibilities in the participant's capacity as a sports participant; or

(B) in retaliation for or on account of the participant's performance of a duty or responsibility within the participant's capacity as a sports participant.

(d) For purposes of Subsection (b), the actor is presumed to have known the person assaulted was a public servant, a security officer, or emergency services personnel if the person was wearing a distinctive uniform or badge indicating the person's employment as a public servant or status as a security officer or emergency services personnel.

(e) In this section:

(1) "Emergency services personnel" includes firefighters, emergency medical services personnel as defined by Section 773.003, Health and Safety Code, emergency room personnel, and other individuals who, in the course and scope of employment or as a volunteer, provide services for the benefit of the general public during emergency situations.

(2) Repealed by Acts 2005, 79th Leg., ch. 788, §6.

(3) "Security officer" means a commissioned security officer as defined by Section 1702.002, Occupations Code, or a noncommissioned security officer registered under Section 1702.221, Occupations Code.

(4) "Sports participant" means a person who participates in any official capacity with respect to an interscholastic, intercollegiate, or other organized amateur or professional athletic competition and includes an athlete, referee, umpire, linesman, coach, instructor, administrator, or staff member.

(f) For the purposes of Subsection (b)(2):

(1) a defendant has been previously convicted of an offense listed in Subsection (b)(2) committed against a person whose relationship to or association with the defendant is described by Section 71.0021(b), 71.003, or 71.005, Family Code, if the defendant was adjudged guilty of the offense or entered a plea of guilty or nolo contendere in return for a grant of deferred adjudication, regardless of whether the sentence for the offense was ever imposed or whether the sentence was probated and the defendant was subsequently discharged from community supervision; and

(2) a conviction under the laws of another state for an offense containing elements that are substantially similar to the elements of an offense listed in Subsection (b)(2) is a conviction of an offense listed in Subsection (b)(2).

Penal Code §22.02. Aggravated Assault

(a) A person commits an offense if the person commits assault as defined in § 22.01 and the person:

(1) causes serious bodily injury to another, including the person's spouse; or

(2) uses or exhibits a deadly weapon during the commission of the assault.

(b) An offense under this section is a felony of the second degree, except that the offense is a felony of the first degree if:

(1) the actor uses a deadly weapon during the commission of the assault and causes serious bodily injury to a person whose relationship to or association with the defendant is described by Section 71.0021(b), 71.003, or 71.005, Family Code; or

(2) regardless of whether the offense is committed under Subsection (a)(1) or (a)(2), the offense is committed:

(A) by a public servant acting under color of the servant's office or employment;

(B) against a person the actor knows is a public servant while the public servant is lawfully discharging an official duty, or in retaliation or on account of an exercise of official power or performance of an official duty as a public servant;

(C) in retaliation against or on account of the service of another as a witness, prospective witness, informant, or person who has reported the occurrence of a crime; or

(D) against a person the actor knows is a security officer while the officer is performing a duty as a security officer.

(c) The actor is presumed to have known the person assaulted was a public servant or a security officer if the person was wearing a distinctive uniform or badge indicating the person's employment as a public servant or status as a security officer.

(d) In this section, "security officer" means a commissioned security officer as defined by Section 1702.002, Occupations Code, or a noncommissioned security officer registered under Section 1702.221, Occupations Code.

Penal Code §22.021 Aggravated Sexual Assault
(a) A person commits an offense:
(1) if the person:
(A) intentionally or knowingly:
<commits any of 8 enumerated sex-related offenses, and:>
(2) if:
(A) the person:
(iv) uses or exhibits a deadly weapon in the course of the same criminal episode;

Penal Code §22.05. Deadly Conduct
(a) A person commits an offense if he recklessly engages in conduct that places another in imminent danger of serious bodily injury.
(b) A person commits an offense if he knowingly discharges a firearm at or in the direction of:
(1) one or more individuals; or
(2) a habitation, building, or vehicle and is reckless as to whether the habitation, building, or vehicle is occupied.
(c) Recklessness and danger are presumed if the actor knowingly pointed a firearm at or in the direction of another whether or not the actor believed the firearm to be loaded.
(d) For purposes of this section, "building," "habitation," and "vehicle" have the meanings assigned those terms by Section 30.01.
(e) An offense under Subsection (a) is a Class A misdemeanor. An offense under Subsection (b) is a felony of the third degree.

Penal Code §22.08. Aiding Suicide
(a) A person commits an offense if, with intent to promote or assist the commission of suicide by another, he aids or attempts to aid the other to commit or attempt to commit suicide.
(b) An offense under this section is a Class C misdemeanor unless the actor's conduct causes suicide or attempted suicide that results in serious bodily injury, in which event the offense is a state jail felony.

Penal Code §25.07. Violation of Protective Order or Magistrate's Order
(a) A person commits an offense if, in violation of an order issued under Section 6.504 or Chapter 85, Family Code, under Article 17.292, Code of Criminal Procedure, or by another jurisdiction as provided by Chapter 88, Family Code, the person knowingly or intentionally:
(4) possesses a firearm
(b) For the purposes of this section:
(2) "Firearm" has the meaning assigned by Chapter 46.
(g) An offense under this section is a Class A misdemeanor unless it is shown on the trial of the offense that the defendant has previously been convicted under this section two or more times or has violated the protective order by committing an assault or the offense of stalking, in which event the offense is a third degree felony.

CHAPTER 28 · ARSON, CRIMINAL MISCHIEF, AND OTHER PROPERTY DAMAGE OR DESTRUCTION

Penal Code §28.01. Definitions
In this chapter:
(1) "Habitation" means a structure or vehicle that is adapted for the overnight accommodation of persons and includes:
(A) each separately secured or occupied portion of the structure or vehicle; and
(B) each structure appurtenant to or connected with the structure or vehicle.
(2) "Building" means any structure or enclosure intended for use or occupation as a habitation or for some purpose of trade, manufacture, ornament, or use.
(3) "Property" means:
(A) real property;
(B) tangible or intangible personal property, including anything severed from land; or
(C) a document, including money, that represents or embodies anything of value.

(4) "Vehicle" includes any device in, on, or by which any person or property is or may be propelled, moved, or drawn in the normal course of commerce or transportation.
(5) "Open-space land" means real property that is undeveloped for the purpose of human habitation.
(6) "Controlled burning" means the burning of unwanted vegetation with the consent of the owner of the property on which the vegetation is located and in such a manner that the fire is controlled and limited to a designated area.

Penal Code §28.02. Arson
(a) A person commits an offense if the person starts a fire, regardless of whether the fire continues after ignition, or causes an explosion with intent to destroy or damage:
(1) any vegetation, fence, or structure on open-space land; or
(2) any building, habitation, or vehicle:
(A) knowing that it is within the limits of an incorporated city or town;
(B) knowing that it is insured against damage or destruction;
(C) knowing that it is subject to a mortgage or other security interest;
(D) knowing that it is located on property belonging to another;
(E) knowing that it has located within it property belonging to another; or
(F) when the person is reckless about whether the burning or explosion will endanger the life of some individual or the safety of the property of another.
(a-1) A person commits an offense if the person recklessly starts a fire or causes an explosion while manufacturing or attempting to manufacture a controlled substance and the fire or explosion damages any building, habitation, or vehicle.
(b) It is an exception to the application of Subsection (a)(1) that the fire or explosion was a part of the controlled burning of open-space land.
(c) It is a defense to prosecution under Subsection (a)(2)(A) that prior to starting the fire or causing the explosion, the actor obtained a permit or other written authorization granted in accordance with a city ordinance, if any, regulating fires and explosions.
(d) An offense under Subsection (a) is a felony of the second degree, except that the offense is a felony of the first degree if it is shown on the trial of the offense that:
(1) bodily injury or death was suffered by any person by reason of the commission of the offense; or
(2) the property intended to be damaged or destroyed by the actor was a habitation or a place of assembly or worship.
(e) An offense under Subsection (a-1) is a state jail felony, except that the offense is a felony of the third degree if it is shown on the trial of the offense that bodily injury or death was suffered by any person by reason of the commission of the offense.
(f) It is a felony of the third degree if a person commits an offense under Subsection (a)(2) of this section and the person intentionally starts a fire in or on a building, habitation, or vehicle, with intent to damage or destroy property belonging to another, or with intent to injure any person, and in so doing, recklessly causes damage to the building, habitation, or vehicle.
(g) If conduct that constitutes an offense under Subsection (a-1) or that constitutes an offense under Subsection (f) also constitutes an offense under another subsection of this section or another section of this code, the actor may be prosecuted under Subsection (a-1) or Subsection (f), under the other subsection of this section, or under the other section of this code.

Penal Code §28.03. Criminal Mischief
(a) A person commits an offense if, without the effective consent of the owner:
(1) he intentionally or knowingly damages or destroys the tangible property of the owner;
(2) he intentionally or knowingly tampers with the tangible property of the owner and causes pecuniary loss or substantial inconvenience to the owner or a third person; or
(3) he intentionally or knowingly makes markings, including inscriptions, slogans, drawings, or paintings, on the tangible property of the owner.
(b) Except as provided by Subsections (f) and (h), an offense under this section is:
(1) a Class C misdemeanor if:
(A) the amount of pecuniary loss is less than $50; or
(B) except as provided in Subdivision (3)(A) or (3)(B), it causes substantial inconvenience to others;
(2) a Class B misdemeanor if the amount of pecuniary loss is $50 or more but less than $500;
(3) a Class A misdemeanor if:
(A) the amount of pecuniary loss is:
(i) $500 or more but less than $1,500; or
(ii) less than $1,500 and the actor causes in whole or in part impairment or interruption of public communications, public transportation, public gas or power supply, or other public service, or causes to be diverted in whole, in part, or in any manner, including installation or removal of any device for any such purpose, any public communications or public gas or power supply; or
(B) the actor causes in whole or in part impairment or interruption of any public water supply, or causes to be diverted in whole, in part, or in any manner, including installation or removal of any device for any such purpose, any public water supply, regardless of the amount of the pecuniary loss;
(4) a state jail felony if the amount of pecuniary loss is:
(A) $1,500 or more but less than $20,000;

(B) less than $1,500, if the property damaged or destroyed is a habitation and if the damage or destruction is caused by a firearm or explosive weapon; or

(C) less than $1,500, if the property was a fence used for the production or containment of:

(i) cattle, bison, horses, sheep, swine, goats, exotic livestock, or exotic poultry; or

(ii) game animals as that term is defined by Section 63.001, Parks and Wildlife Code;

(5) a felony of the third degree if the amount of the pecuniary loss is $20,000 or more but less than $100,000;

(6) a felony of the second degree if the amount of pecuniary loss is $100,000 or more but less than $200,000; or

(7) a felony of the first degree if the amount of pecuniary loss is $200,000 or more.

(d) The terms "public communication, public transportation, public gas or power supply, or other public service" and "public water supply" shall mean, refer to, and include any such services subject to regulation by the Public Utility Commission of Texas, the Railroad Commission of Texas, or the Texas Natural Resource Conservation Commission or any such services enfranchised by the State of Texas or any political subdivision thereof.

(g) In this section:

(1) "Explosive weapon" means any explosive or incendiary device that is designed, made, or adapted for the purpose of inflicting serious bodily injury, death, or substantial property damage, or for the principal purpose of causing such a loud report as to cause undue public alarm or terror, and includes:

(A) an explosive or incendiary bomb, grenade, rocket, and mine;

(B) a device designed, made, or adapted for delivering or shooting an explosive weapon; and

(C) a device designed, made, or adapted to start a fire in a time-delayed manner.

(2) "Firearm" has the meaning assigned by Section 46.01.

(3) "Institution of higher education" has the meaning assigned by Section 61.003, Education Code.

(h) An offense under this section is a state jail felony if the amount of the pecuniary loss to real property or to tangible personal property is $1,500 or more but less than $20,000 and the damage or destruction is inflicted on a public or private elementary school, secondary school, or institution of higher education.

Penal Code §28.04. Reckless Damage Or Destruction

(a) A person commits an offense if, without the effective consent of the owner, he recklessly damages or destroys property of the owner.

(b) An offense under this section is a Class C misdemeanor.

Penal Code §28.05. Actor's Interest In Property

It is no defense to prosecution under this chapter that the actor has an interest in the property damaged or destroyed if another person also has an interest that the actor is not entitled to infringe.

Penal Code §28.07. Interference With Railroad Property

(b) A person commits an offense if the person:

(1) throws an object or discharges a firearm or weapon at a train or railmounted work equipment(c) An offense under Subsection (b)(1) is a Class B misdemeanor unless the person causes bodily injury to another, in which event the offense is a felony of the third degree.

CHAPTER 29 · ROBBERY

Penal Code §29.02. Robbery

(a) A person commits an offense if, in the course of committing theft as defined in Chapter 31 and with intent to obtain or maintain control of the property, he:

(1) intentionally, knowingly, or recklessly causes bodily injury to another; or

(2) intentionally or knowingly threatens or places another in fear of imminent bodily injury or death.

(b) An offense under this section is a felony of the second degree.

Penal Code §29.03. Aggravated Robbery

(a) A person commits an offense if he commits robbery as defined in Section 29.02, and he:

(1) causes serious bodily injury to another;

(2) uses or exhibits a deadly weapon; or

(3) causes bodily injury to another person or threatens or places another person in fear of imminent bodily injury or death, if the other person is:

(A) 65 years of age or older; or

(B) a disabled person.

(b) An offense under this section is a felony of the first degree.

(c) In this section, "disabled person" means an individual with a mental, physical, or developmental disability who is substantially unable to protect himself from harm.

CHAPTER 30 · BURGLARY AND CRIMINAL TRESPASS

Penal Code §30.02. Burglary

(a) A person commits an offense if, without the effective consent of the owner, the person:

(1) enters a habitation, or a building (or any portion of a building) not then open to the public, with intent to commit a felony, theft or an assault; or

(2) remains concealed, with intent to commit a felony, theft or an assault, in a building or habitation; or

(3) enters a building or habitation and commits or attempts to commit a felony, theft or an assault.

(b) For purposes of this section, "enter" means to intrude:

(1) any part of the body; or

(2) any physical object connected with the body.

(c) Except as provided in Subsection (d), an offense under this section is a:

(1) state jail felony if committed in a building other than a habitation; or

(2) felony of the second degree if committed in a habitation.

(d) An offense under this section is a felony of the first degree if:

(1) the premises are a habitation; and

(2) any party to the offense entered the habitation with intent to commit a felony other than felony theft or committed or attempted to commit a felony other than felony theft.

Penal Code §30.04. Burglary Of Vehicles

(a) A person commits an offense if, without the effective consent of the owner, he breaks into or enters a vehicle or any part of a vehicle with intent to commit any felony or theft.

(b) For purposes of this section, "enter" means to intrude:

(1) any part of the body; or

(2) any physical object connected with the body.

(c) For purposes of this section, a container or trailer carried on a rail car is a part of the rail car.

(d) An offense under this section is a Class A misdemeanor, except that:

(1) the offense is a Class A misdemeanor with a minimum term of confinement of six months if it is shown on the trial of the offense that the defendant has been previously convicted of an offense under this section; and

(2) the offense is a state jail felony if:

(A) it is shown on the trial of the offense that the defendant has been previously convicted two or more times of an offense under this section; or

(B) the vehicle or part of the vehicle broken into or entered is a rail car.

(d-1) For the purposes of Subsection (d), a defendant has been previously convicted under this section if the defendant was adjudged guilty of the offense or entered a plea of guilty or nolo contendere in return for a grant of deferred adjudication, regardless of whether the sentence for the offense was ever imposed or whether the sentence was probated and the defendant was subsequently discharged from community supervision.

(e) It is a defense to prosecution under this section that the actor entered a rail car or any part of a rail car and was at that time an employee or a representative of employees exercising a right under the Railway Labor Act (45 U.S.C. §151 et seq.).

Penal Code §30.05. Criminal Trespass

(a) A person commits an offense if the person enters or remains on or in property of another, including residential land, agricultural land, a recreational vehicle park, a building, or an aircraft or other vehicle, without effective consent and the person:

(1) had notice that the entry was forbidden; or

(2) received notice to depart but failed to do so.

(b) For purposes of this section:

(1) "Entry" means the intrusion of the entire body.

(2) "Notice" means:

(A) oral or written communication by the owner or someone with apparent authority to act for the owner;

(B) fencing or other enclosure obviously designed to exclude intruders or to contain livestock;

(C) a sign or signs posted on the property or at the entrance to the building, reasonably likely to come to the attention of intruders, indicating that entry is forbidden;

(D) the placement of identifying purple paint marks on trees or posts on the property, provided that the marks are:

(i) vertical lines of not less than eight inches in length and not less than one inch in width;

(ii) placed so that the bottom of the mark is not less than three feet from the ground or more than five feet from the ground; and

(iii) placed at locations that are readily visible to any person approaching the property and no more than:

(a) 100 feet apart on forest land; or

(b) 1,000 feet apart on land other than forest land; or

(E) the visible presence on the property of a crop grown for human consumption that is under cultivation, in the process of being harvested, or marketable if harvested at the time of entry.

(3) "Shelter center" has the meaning assigned by Section 51.002, Human Resources Code.

(4) "Forest land" means land on which the trees are potentially valuable for timber products.

(5) "Agricultural land" has the meaning assigned by Section 75.001, Civil Practice and Remedies Code.

(6) "Superfund site" means a facility that:

(A) is on the National Priorities List established under Section 105 of the federal Comprehensive Environmental Response, Compensation, and Liability Act of 1980 (42 U.S.C. Section 9605); or

(B) is listed on the state registry established under Section 361.181, Health and Safety Code.

(7) "Critical infrastructure facility" means one of the following, if completely enclosed by a fence or other physical barrier that is obviously designed to exclude intruders:

(A) a chemical manufacturing facility;

(B) a refinery;

(C) an electrical power generating facility, substation, switching station, electrical control center, or electrical transmission or distribution facility;

(D) a water intake structure, water treatment facility, wastewater treatment plant, or pump station;

(E) a natural gas transmission compressor station;

(F) a liquid natural gas terminal or storage facility;

(G) a telecommunications central switching office;

(H) a port, railroad switching yard, trucking terminal, or other freight transportation facility;

(I) a gas processing plant, including a plant used in the processing, treatment, or fractionation of natural gas; or

(J) a transmission facility used by a federally licensed radio or television station.

(8) "Protected freshwater area" has the meaning assigned by Section 90.001, Parks and Wildlife Code.

(9) "Recognized state" means another state with which the attorney general of this state, with the approval of the governor of this state, negotiated an agreement after determining that the other state:

(A) has firearm proficiency requirements for peace officers; and

(B) fully recognizes the right of peace officers commissioned in this state to carry weapons in the other state.

(10) "Recreational vehicle park" means a tract of land that has rental spaces for two or more recreational vehicles, as defined by Section 522.004, Transportation Code.

(11) "Residential land" means real property improved by a dwelling and zoned for or otherwise authorized for single-family or multifamily use.

(c) Repealed by Acts 2009, 81st Leg., R.S., Ch. 1138, Sec. 4, eff. September 1, 2009.

(d) An offense under this section is:

(1) a Class B misdemeanor, except as provided by Subdivisions (2) and (3);

(2) a Class C misdemeanor, except as provided by Subdivision (3), if the offense is committed:

(A) on agricultural land and within 100 feet of the boundary of the land; or

(B) on residential land and within 100 feet of a protected freshwater area; and

(3) a Class A misdemeanor if:

(A) the offense is committed:

(i) in a habitation or a shelter center;

(ii) on a Superfund site; or

(iii) on or in a critical infrastructure facility; or

(B) the person carries a deadly weapon during the commission of the offense.

(e) It is a defense to prosecution under this section that the actor at the time of the offense was:

(1) a firefighter or emergency medical services personnel, as defined by Section 773.003, Health and Safety Code, acting in the lawful discharge of an official duty under exigent circumstances;

(2) a person who was:

(A) an employee or agent of:

(i) an electric utility, as defined by Section 31.002, Utilities Code;

(ii) a telecommunications provider, as defined by Section 51.002, Utilities Code;

(iii) a video service provider or cable service provider, as defined by Section 66.002, Utilities Code;

(iv) a gas utility, as defined by Section 101.003 or 121.001, Utilities Code; or

(v) a pipeline used for the transportation or sale of oil, gas, or related products; and

(B) performing a duty within the scope of that employment or agency; or

(3) a person who was:

(A) employed by or acting as agent for an entity that had, or that the person reasonably believed had, effective consent or authorization provided by law to enter the property; and

(B) performing a duty within the scope of that employment or agency.

(f) It is a defense to prosecution under this section that:

(1) the basis on which entry on the property or land or in the building was forbidden is that entry with a handgun was forbidden; and

(2) the person was carrying a concealed handgun and a license issued under Subchapter H, Chapter 411, Government Code, to carry a concealed handgun of the same category the person was carrying.

(g) It is a defense to prosecution under this section that the actor entered a railroad switching yard or any part of a railroad switching yard and was at that time an employee or a representative of employees exercising a right under the Railway Labor Act (45 U.S.C. Section 151 et seq.).

(h) At the punishment stage of a trial in which the attorney representing the state seeks the increase in punishment provided by Subsection (d)(3)(A)(iii), the defendant may raise the issue as to whether the defendant entered or remained on or in a critical infrastructure facility as part of a peaceful or lawful assembly, including an attempt to exercise rights guaranteed by state or federal labor laws. If the defendant proves the issue in the affirmative by a preponderance of the evidence, the increase in punishment provided by Subsection (d)(3)(A)(iii) does not apply.

(i) This section does not apply if:

(1) the basis on which entry on the property or land or in the building was forbidden is that entry with a handgun or other weapon was forbidden; and

(2) the actor at the time of the offense was a peace officer, including a commissioned peace officer of a recognized state, or a special investigator under Article 2.122, Code of Criminal Procedure, regardless of whether the peace officer or special investigator was engaged in the actual discharge of an official duty while carrying the weapon.

(j) Repealed by Acts 2009, 81st Leg., R.S., Ch. 1138, Sec. 4, eff. September 1, 2009.

Penal Code §30.06. Trespass By Holder Of License To Carry Concealed Handgun

(a) A license holder commits an offense if the license holder:

(1) carries a handgun under the authority of Subchapter H, Chapter 411, Government Code, on property of another without effective consent; and

(2) received notice that:

(A) entry on the property by a license holder with a concealed handgun was forbidden; or

(B) remaining on the property with a concealed handgun was forbidden and failed to depart.

(b) For purposes of this section, a person receives notice if the owner of the property or someone with apparent authority to act for the owner provides notice to the person by oral or written communication.

(c) In this section:

(1) "Entry" has the meaning assigned by Section 30.05(b).

(2) "License holder" has the meaning assigned by Section 46.035(f).

(3) "Written communication" means:

(A) a card or other document on which is written language identical to the following: "Pursuant to Section 30.06, Penal Code (trespass by holder of license to carry a concealed handgun), a person licensed under Subchapter H, Chapter 411, Government Code (concealed handgun law), may not enter this property with a concealed handgun"; or

(B) a sign posted on the property that:

(i) includes the language described by Paragraph (A) in both English and Spanish;

(ii) appears in contrasting colors with block letters at least one inch in height; and

(iii) is displayed in a conspicuous manner clearly visible to the public.

(d) An offense under this section is a Class A misdemeanor.

(e) It is an exception to the application of this section that the property on which the license holder carries a handgun is owned or leased by a governmental entity and is not a premises or other place on which the license holder is prohibited from carrying the handgun under Section 46.03 or 46.035.

CHAPTER 37 · PERJURY AND OTHER FALSIFICATION

Penal Code §37.02. Perjury

(a) A person commits an offense if, with intent to deceive and with knowledge of the statement's meaning:

(1) he makes a false statement under oath or swears to the truth of a false statement previously made and the statement is required or authorized by law to be made under oath; or

(2) he makes a false unsworn declaration under Chapter 132, Civil Practice and Remedies Code.

(b) An offense under this section is a Class A misdemeanor.

Penal Code §37.03. Aggravated Perjury

(a) A person commits an offense if he commits perjury as defined in Section 37.02, and the false statement:

(1) is made during or in connection with an official proceeding; and

(2) is material.

(b) An offense under this section Is a felony of the third degree.

Penal Code §37.08. False Report To Peace Officer, Federal Special Investigator Or Law Enforcement Employee

(a) A person commits an offense if, with intent to deceive, he knowingly makes a false statement that is material to the criminal investigation of a felony and makes the statement to:

(1) a peace officer or federal special investigator conducting the investigation; or

(2) any employee of a law enforcement agency that is authorized by the agency to conduct the investigation and that the actor knows is conducting the investigation.

(b) A person commits an offense if, with intent to deceive, he knowingly makes a false statement that is material to the criminal investigation of a misdemeanor and makes the statement to:

(1) a peace officer conducting the investigation; or

(2) any employee of a law enforcement agency that is authorized by the agency to conduct the investigation and that the actor knows is conducting the investigation.

(c) In this section, "law enforcement agency" has the meaning assigned by Article 59.01, Code of Criminal Procedure.

(d) An offense under Subsection (a) is a state jail felony. An offense under Subsection (b) is a Class B misdemeanor.

Penal Code §37.09. Tampering With Or Fabricating Physical Evidence

(a) A person commits an offense if, knowing that an investigation or official proceeding is pending or in progress, he:

(1) alters, destroys, or conceals any record, document, or thing with intent to impair its verity, legibility, or availability as evidence in the investigation or official proceeding; or

(2) makes, presents, or uses any record, document, or thing with knowledge of its falsity and with intent to affect the course or outcome of the investigation or official proceeding.

(b) This section shall not apply if the record, document, or thing concealed is privileged or is the work product of the parties to the investigation or official proceeding.

(c) An offense under Subsection (a) or Subsection (d)(1) is a felony of the third degree, unless the thing altered, destroyed, or concealed is a human corpse, in which case the offense is a felony of the second degree. An offense under Subsection (d)(2) is a Class A misdemeanor.

(d) A person commits an offense if the person:

(1) knowing that an offense has been committed, alters, destroys, or conceals any record, document, or thing with intent to impair its verity, legibility, or availability as evidence in any subsequent investigation of or official proceeding related to the offense; or

(2) observes a human corpse under circumstances in which a reasonable person would believe that an offense had been committed, knows or reasonably should know that a law enforcement agency is not aware of the existence of or location of the corpse, and fails to report the existence of and location of the corpse to a law enforcement agency.

(e) In this section, "human corpse" has the meaning assigned by Section 42.08.

Penal Code §38.03. Resisting Arrest, Search, Or Transportation

(a) A person commits an offense if he intentionally prevents or obstructs a person he knows is a peace officer or a person acting in a peace officer's presence and at his direction from effecting an arrest, search, or transportation of the actor or another by using force against the peace officer or another.

(b) It is no defense to prosecution under this section that the arrest or search was unlawful.

(c) Except as provided in Subsection (d), an offense under this section is a Class A misdemeanor.

(d) An offense under this section is a felony of the third degree if the actor uses a deadly weapon to resist the arrest or search.

Penal Code §38.06. Escape

(a) A person commits an offense if the person escapes from custody when the person is:

(1) under arrest for, lawfully detained for, charged with, or convicted of an offense; or

(2) in custody pursuant to a lawful order of a court;

(3) detained in a secure detention facility, as that term is defined by Section 51.02, Family Code; or

(4) in the custody of a juvenile probation officer for violating an order imposed by the juvenile court under Section 52.01, Family Code.

(b) Except as provided in Subsections (c), (d), and (e), an offense under this section is a Class A misdemeanor.

(c) An offense under this section is a felony of the third degree if the actor:

(1) is under arrest for, charged with, or convicted of a felony;

(2) is confined or lawfully detained in a secure correctional facility or law enforcement facility; or

(3) is committed to or lawfully detained in a secure correctional facility, as defined by Section 51.02, Family Code, other than a halfway house, operated by or under contract with the Texas Youth Commission.

(d) An offense under this section is a felony of the second degree if the actor to effect his escape causes bodily injury.

(e) An offense under this section is a felony of the first degree if to effect his escape the actor:

(1) causes serious bodily injury; or

(2) uses or threatens to use a deadly weapon.

Penal Code §38.07. Permitting Or Facilitating Escape

(a) An official or employee of a correctional facility commits an offense if he knowingly permits or facilitates the escape of a person in custody.

(b) A person commits an offense if he knowingly causes or facilitates the escape of one who is in custody pursuant to:

(1) an allegation or adjudication of delinquency; or

(2) involuntary commitment for mental illness under Subtitle C, Title 7, Health and Safety Code, or for chemical dependency under Chapter 462, Health and Safety Code.

(c) Except as provided in Subsections (d) and (e), an offense under this section is a Class A misdemeanor.

(d) An offense under this section is a felony of the third degree if the person in custody:

(1) was under arrest for, charged with, or convicted of a felony; or

(2) was confined in a correctional facility other than a secure correctional facility after conviction of a felony.

(e) An offense under this section is a felony of the second degree if:

(1) the actor or the person in custody used or threatened to use a deadly weapon to effect the escape; or

(2) the person in custody was confined in a secure correctional facility after conviction of a felony.

(f) In this section, "correctional facility" means:

(1) any place described by Section 1.07(a)(14); or

(2) a "secure correctional facility" or "secure detention facility" as those terms are defined by Section 51.02, Family Code.

Penal Code §38.09. Implements For Escape

(a) A person commits an offense if, with intent to facilitate escape, he introduces into a correctional facility, or provides a person in custody or an inmate with, a deadly weapon or anything that may be useful for escape.

(b) An offense under this section is a felony of the third degree unless the actor introduced or provided a deadly weapon, in which event the offense is a felony of the second degree.

(c) In this section, "correctional facility" means:

(1) any place described by Section 1.07(a)(14); or

(2) a "secure correctional facility" or "secure detention facility" as those terms are defined by Section 51.02, Family Code.

Penal Code §38.14. Taking Or Attempting To Take Weapon From Peace Officer, Federal Special Investigator, Employee Or Official Of Correctional Facility, Parole Officer, Community Supervision And Corrections Department Officer, Or Commissioned Security Officer.

(a) In this section:

(1) "Firearm" has the meanings assigned by §46.01.

(2) "Stun gun" means a device designed to propel darts or other projectiles attached to wires that, on contact, will deliver an electrical pulse capable of incapacitating a person.

(3) "Commissioned security officer" has the meaning assigned by §1702.002(5), Occupations Code.

(b) A person commits an offense if the person intentionally or knowingly and with force takes or attempts to take from a peace officer, federal special investigator, employee or official of a correctional facility, parole officer, community supervision and corrections department officer, or commissioned security officer the officer's, investigator's, employee's, or official's firearm, nightstick, stun gun, or personal protection chemical dispensing device with the intention of harming the officer, investigator, employee, or official or a third person.

(c) The actor is presumed to have known that the peace officer, federal special investigator, employee or official of a correctional facility, parole officer, community supervision and corrections department officer, or commissioned security officer was a peace officer, federal special investigator, employee or official of a correctional facility, parole officer, community supervision and corrections department officer, or commissioned security officer if:

(1) the officer, investigator, employee, or official was wearing a distinctive uniform or badge indicating his employment; or

(2) the officer, investigator, employee, or official identified himself as a peace officer, federal special investigator, employee or official of a correctional facility, parole officer, community supervision and corrections department officer, or commissioned security officer.

(d) It is a defense to prosecution under this section that the defendant took or attempted to take the weapon from a peace officer, federal special investigator, employee or official of a correctional facility, parole officer, community supervision and corrections department officer, or commissioned security officer who was using force against the defendant or another in excess of the amount of force permitted by law.

(e) An offense under this section is:

(1) a felony of the third degree, if the defendant took a weapon described by Subsection (b) from an officer, investigator, employee, or official described by that subsection; and

(2) a state jail felony, if the defendant attempted to take a weapon described by Subsection (b) from an officer, investigator, employee, or official described by that subsection.

Penal Code §38.15. Interference With Public Duties

(a) A person commits an offense if the person with criminal negligence interrupts, disrupts, impedes, or otherwise interferes with:

(1) a peace officer while the peace officer is performing a duty or exercising authority imposed or granted by law;

(b) An offense under this section is a Class B misdemeanor.

Penal Code §38.112. Violation of Protective Order Issued on Basis of Sexual Assault or Abuse, Stalking or Trafficking

(a) A person commits an offense if, in violation of an order issued under Chapter 7A, Code of Criminal Procedure, the person knowingly:

(3) possesses a firearm.

(c) An offense under this section is a Class A misdemeanor.

CHAPTER 42
DISORDERLY CONDUCT AND RELATED OFFENSES

Penal Code §42.01. Disorderly Conduct

(a) A person commits an offense if he intentionally or knowingly:

(1) uses abusive, indecent, profane, or vulgar language in a public place, and the language by its very utterance tends to incite an immediate breach of the peace;

(2) makes an offensive gesture or display in a public place, and the gesture or display tends to incite an immediate breach of the peace;

(3) creates, by chemical means, a noxious and unreasonable odor in a public place;

(4) abuses or threatens a person in a public place in an obviously offensive manner;

(5) makes unreasonable noise in a public place other than a sport shooting range, as defined by Section 250.001, Local Government Code, or in or near a private residence that he has no right to occupy;

(6) fights with another in a public place;

(7) discharges a firearm in a public place other than a public road or a sport shooting range, as defined by Section 250.001, Local Government Code;

(8) displays a firearm or other deadly weapon in a public place in a manner calculated to alarm;

(9) discharges a firearm on or across a public road;

(10) exposes his anus or genitals in a public place and is reckless about whether another may be present who will be offended or alarmed by his act; or

(11) for a lewd or unlawful purpose:

(A) enters on the property of another and looks into a dwelling on the property through any window or other opening in the dwelling;

(B) while on the premises of a hotel or comparable establishment, looks into a guest room not the person's own through a window or other opening in the room; or

(C) while on the premises of a public place, looks into an area such as a restroom or shower stall or changing or dressing room that is designed to provide privacy to a person using the area.

(a-1) For purposes of Subsection (a), the term "public place" includes a public school campus or the school grounds on which a public school is located.

(b) It is a defense to prosecution under Subsection (a)(4) that the actor had significant provocation for his abusive or threatening conduct.

(c) For purposes of this section:

(1) an act is deemed to occur in a public place or near a private residence if it produces its offensive or proscribed consequences in the public place or near a private residence; and

(2) a noise is presumed to be unreasonable if the noise exceeds a decibel level of 85 after the person making the noise receives notice from a magistrate or peace officer that the noise is a public nuisance.

(d) An offense under this section is a Class C misdemeanor unless committed under Subsection (a)(7) or (a)(8), in which event it is a Class B misdemeanor.

(e) It is a defense to prosecution for an offense under Subsection (a)(7) or (9) that the person who discharged the firearm had a reasonable fear of bodily injury to the person or to another by a dangerous wild animal as defined by Section 822.101, Health and Safety Code.

(f) Subsections (a)(1), (2), (3), (5), and (6) do not apply to a person who, at the time the person engaged in conduct prohibited under the applicable subdivision, was a student younger than 12 years of age, and the prohibited conduct occurred at a public school campus during regular school hours.

Penal Code §42.12. Discharge Of Firearm In Certain Municipalities

(a) A person commits an offense if the person recklessly discharges a firearm inside the corporate limits of a municipality having a population of 100,000 or more.

(b) An offense under this section is a Class A misdemeanor.

(c) If conduct constituting an offense under this section also constitutes an offense under another section of this code, the person may be prosecuted under either section.

(d) Subsection (a) does not affect the authority of a municipality to enact an ordinance which prohibits the discharge of a firearm.

CHAPTER 46 · WEAPONS

Penal Code §46.01. Definitions

In this chapter:

(1) "Club" means an instrument that is specially designed, made, or adapted for the purpose of inflicting serious bodily injury or death by striking a person with the instrument, and includes but is not limited to the following:

(A) blackjack;

(B) nightstick;

(C) mace;

(D) tomahawk.

(2) "Explosive weapon" means any explosive or incendiary bomb, grenade, rocket, or mine, that is designed, made, or adapted for the purpose of inflicting serious bodily injury, death, or substantial property damage, or for the principal purpose of causing such a loud report as to cause undue public alarm or terror, and includes a device designed, made, or adapted for delivery or shooting an explosive weapon.

(3) "Firearm" means any device designed, made, or adapted to expel a projectile through a barrel by using the energy generated by an explosion or burning substance or any device readily convertible to that use. Firearm does not include a firearm that may have, as an integral part, a folding knife blade or other characteristics of weapons made illegal by this chapter and that is:

(A) an antique or curio firearm manufactured before 1899; or

(B) a replica of an antique or curio firearm manufactured before 1899, but only if the replica does not use rim fire or center fire ammunition.

(4) "Firearm silencer" means any device designed, made, or adapted to muffle the report of a firearm.

(5) "Handgun" means any firearm that is designed, made, or adapted to be fired with one hand.

(6) "Illegal knife" means a:

(A) knife with a blade over five and one-half inches;

(B) hand instrument designed to cut or stab another by being thrown;

(C) dagger, including but not limited to a dirk, stiletto, and poniard;

(D) bowie knife;

(E) sword; or

(F) spear.

(7) "Knife" means any bladed hand instrument that is capable of inflicting serious bodily injury or death by cutting or stabbing a person with the instrument.

(8) "Knuckles" means any instrument that consists of finger rings or guards made of a hard substance and that is designed, made, or adapted for the purpose of inflicting serious bodily injury or death by striking a person with a fist enclosed in the knuckles.

(9) "Machine gun" means any firearm that is capable of shooting more than two shots automatically, without manual reloading, by a single function of the trigger.

(10) "Short-barrel firearm" means a rifle with a barrel length of less than 16 inches or a shotgun with a barrel length of less than 18 inches, or any weapon made from a shotgun or rifle if, as altered, it has an overall length of less than 26 inches.

(11) "Switchblade knife" means any knife that has a blade that folds, closes, or retracts into the handle or sheath and that opens automatically by pressure applied to a button or other device located on the handle or opens or releases a blade from the handle or sheath by the force of gravity or by the application of centrifugal force. The term does not include a knife that has a spring, detent, or other mechanism designed to create a bias toward closure and that requires exertion applied to the blade by hand, wrist, or arm to overcome resistance and open the knife.

(12) "Armor-piercing ammunition" means handgun ammunition that is designed primarily for the purpose of penetrating metal or body armor and to be used principally in pistols and revolvers.

(13) "Hoax bomb" means a device that:

(A) reasonably appears to be an explosive or incendiary device; or

(B) by its design causes alarm or reaction of any type by an official of a public safety agency or a volunteer agency organized to deal with emergencies.

(14) "Chemical dispensing device" means a device, other than a small chemical dispenser sold commercially for personal protection, that is designed, made, or adapted for the purpose of dispensing a substance capable of causing an adverse psychological or physiological effect on a human being.

(15) "Racetrack" has the meaning assigned that term by the Texas Racing Act (Article 179e, Vernon's Texas Civil Statutes).

(16) "Zip gun" means a device or combination of devices that was not originally a firearm and is adapted to expel a projectile through a smooth-bore or rifled-bore barrel by using the energy generated by an explosion or burning substance.

Penal Code §46.02. Unlawful Carrying Weapons

(a) A person commits an offense if the person intentionally, knowingly, or recklessly carries on or about his or her person a handgun, illegal knife, or club if the person is not:

(1) on the person's own premises or premises under the person's control; or

(2) inside of or directly en route to a motor vehicle or watercraft that is owned by the person or under the person's control.

(a-1) A person commits an offense if the person intentionally, knowingly, or recklessly carries on or about his or her person a handgun in a motor vehicle or watercraft that is owned by the person or under the person's control at any time in which:

(1) the handgun is in plain view; or

(2) the person is:

(A) engaged in criminal activity, other than a Class C misdemeanor that is a violation of a law or ordinance regulating traffic or boating;

(B) prohibited by law from possessing a firearm; or

(C) a member of a criminal street gang, as defined by Section 71.01.

(a-2) For purposes of this section, "premises" includes real property and a recreational vehicle that is being used as living quarters, regardless of whether that use is temporary or permanent. In this subsection, "recreational vehicle" means a motor vehicle primarily designed as temporary living quarters or a vehicle that contains temporary living quarters and is designed to be towed by a motor vehicle. The term includes a travel trailer, camping trailer, truck camper, motor home, and horse trailer with living quarters.

(b) Except as provided by Subsection (c), an offense under this section is a Class A misdemeanor.

(c) An offense under this section is a felony of the third degree if the offense is committed on any premises licensed or issued a permit by this state for the sale of alcoholic beverages.

(a-3) For purposes of this section, "watercraft" means any boat, motorboat, vessel, or personal watercraft, other than a seaplane on water, used or capable of being used for transportation on water.

Penal Code §46.03. Places Weapons Prohibited

(a) A person commits an offense if the person intentionally, knowingly, or recklessly possesses or goes with a firearm, illegal knife, club, or prohibited weapon listed in Section 46.05(a):

(1) on the physical premises of a school or educational institution, any grounds or building on which an activity sponsored by a school or educational institution is being conducted, or a passenger transportation vehicle of a school or educational institution, whether the school or educational institution is public or private, unless pursuant to written regulations or written authorization of the institution;

(2) on the premises of a polling place on the day of an election or while early voting is in progress;

(3) on the premises of any government court or offices utilized by the court, unless pursuant to written regulations or written authorization of the court;

(4) on the premises of a racetrack;

(5) in or into a secured area of an airport; or

(6) within 1,000 feet of premises the location of which is designated by the Texas Department of Criminal Justice as a place of execution under Article 43.19, Code of Criminal Procedure, on a day that a sentence of death is set to be imposed on the designated premises and the person received notice that:

(A) going within 1,000 feet of the premises with a weapon listed under this subsection was prohibited; or

(B) possessing a weapon listed under this subsection within 1,000 feet of the premises was prohibited.

(b) It is a defense to prosecution under Subsections (a)(1)-(4) that the actor possessed a firearm while in the actual discharge of his official duties as a member of the armed forces or national guard or a guard employed by a penal institution, or an officer of the court.

(c) In this section:

(1) "Premises" has the meaning assigned by Section 46.035.

(2) "Secured area" means an area of an airport terminal building to which access is controlled by the inspection of persons and property under federal law.

(d) It is a defense to prosecution under Subsection (a) that the actor possessed a firearm or club while traveling to or from the actor's place of assignment or in the actual discharge of duties as:

(1) a member of the armed forces or national guard;

(2) a guard employed by a penal institution;

(3) a security officer commissioned by the Texas Private Security Board if:

(A) the actor is wearing a distinctive uniform; and

(B) the firearm or club is in plain view; or

(4) a security officer who holds a personal protection authorization under Chapter 1702, Occupations Code, provided that the officer is either:

(A) wearing the uniform of a security officer, including any uniform or apparel described by Section 1702.323(d), Occupations Code, and carrying the officer's firearm in plain view; or

(B) not wearing the uniform of a security officer and carrying the officer's firearm in a concealed manner.

(e) It is a defense to prosecution under Subsection (a)(5) that the actor checked all firearms as baggage in accordance with federal or state law or regulations before entering a secured area.

(f) It is not a defense to prosecution under this section that the actor possessed a handgun and was licensed to carry a concealed handgun under Subchapter H, Chapter 411, Government Code.

(g) An offense under this section is a third degree felony.

(h) It is a defense to prosecution under Subsection (a)(4) that the actor possessed a firearm or club while traveling to or from the actor's place of assignment or in the actual discharge of duties as a security officer commissioned by the Texas Board of Private Investigators and Private Security Agencies, if:

(1) the actor is wearing a distinctive uniform; and

(2) the firearm or club is in plain view.

(i) It is an exception to the application of Subsection (a)(6) that the actor possessed a firearm or club:

(1) while in a vehicle being driven on a public road; or

(2) at the actor's residence or place of employment.

Penal Code §46.035. Unlawful Carrying Of Handgun By License Holder

(a) A license holder commits an offense if the license holder carries a handgun on or about the license holder's person under the authority of Subchapter H, Chapter 411, Government Code, and intentionally displays the handgun in plain view of another person in a public place.

(b) A license holder commits an offense if the license holder intentionally, knowingly, or recklessly carries a handgun under the authority of Subchapter H, Chapter 411, Government Code, regardless of whether the handgun is concealed, on or about the license holder's person:

(1) on the premises of a business that has a permit or license issued under Chapter 25, 28, 32, 69, or 74, Alcoholic Beverage Code, if the business derives 51 percent or more of its income from the sale or service of alcoholic beverages for on-premises consumption, as determined by the Texas Alcoholic Beverage Commission under Section 104.06, Alcoholic Beverage Code;

(2) on the premises where a high school, collegiate, or professional sporting event or interscholastic event is taking place, unless the license holder is a participant in the event and a handgun is used in the event;

(3) on the premises of a correctional facility;

(4) on the premises of a hospital licensed under Chapter 241, Health and Safety Code, or on the premises of a nursing home licensed under Chapter 242, Health and Safety Code, unless the license holder has written authorization of the hospital or nursing home administration, as appropriate;

(5) in an amusement park; or

(6) on the premises of a church, synagogue, or other established place of religious worship.

(c) A license holder commits an offense if the license holder intentionally, knowingly, or recklessly carries a handgun under the authority of Subchapter H, Chapter 411, Government Code, regardless of whether the handgun is concealed, at any meeting of a governmental entity.

(d) A license holder commits an offense if, while intoxicated, the license holder carries a handgun under the authority of Subchapter H, Chapter 411, Government Code, regardless of whether the handgun is concealed.

(e) A license holder who is licensed as a security officer under Chapter 1702, Occupations Code, and employed as a security officer commits an offense if, while in the course and scope of the security officer's employment, the security officer violates a provision of Subchapter H, Chapter 411, Government Code.

(f) In this section:

(1) "Amusement park" means a permanent indoor or outdoor facility or park where amusement rides are available for use by the public that is located in a county with a population of more than one million, encompasses at least 75 acres in surface area, is enclosed with access only through controlled entries, is open for operation more than 120 days in each calendar year, and has security guards on the premises at all times. The term does not include any public or private driveway, street, sidewalk or walkway, parking lot, parking garage, or other parking area.

(2) "License holder" means a person licensed to carry a handgun under Subchapter H, Chapter 411, Government Code.

(3) "Premises" means a building or a portion of a building. The term does not include any public or private driveway, street, sidewalk or walkway, parking lot, parking garage, or other parking area.

(g) An offense under Subsection (a), (b), (c), (d), or (e) is a Class A misdemeanor, unless the offense is committed under Subsection (b)(1) or (b)(3), in which event the offense is a felony of the third degree.

(h) It is a defense to prosecution under Subsection (a) that the actor, at the time of the commission of the offense, displayed the handgun under circumstances in which the actor would have been justified in the use of force or deadly force under Chapter 9.

<Text of subsec. as added by Acts 2007, 80th Leg., R.S., Ch. 1214, Sec. 2>

(h-1) It is a defense to prosecution under Subsections (b) and (c) that the actor, at the time of the commission of the offense, was:

(1) an active judicial officer, as defined by Section 411.201, Government Code; or

(2) a bailiff designated by the active judicial officer and engaged in escorting the officer.

<Text of subsec. as added by Acts 2007, 80th Leg., R.S., Ch. 1222, Sec. 5>

(h-1) It is a defense to prosecution under Subsections (b)(1), (2), and (4)-(6), and (c) that at the time of the commission of the offense, the actor was:
(1) a judge or justice of a federal court;
(2) an active judicial officer, as defined by Section 411.201, Government Code; or
(3) a district attorney, assistant district attorney, criminal district attorney, assistant criminal district attorney, county attorney, or assistant county attorney.
(i) Subsections (b)(4), (b)(5), (b)(6), and (c) do not apply if the actor was not given effective notice under Section 30.06.
(j) Subsections (a) and (b)(1) do not apply to a historical reenactment performed in compliance with the rules of the Texas Alcoholic Beverage Commission.
(k) It is a defense to prosecution under Subsection (b)(1) that the actor was not given effective notice under Section 411.204, Government Code.

Penal Code §46.04. Unlawful Possession Of Firearm
(a) A person who has been convicted of a felony commits an offense if he possesses a firearm:
(1) after conviction and before the fifth anniversary of the person's release from confinement following conviction of the felony or the person's release from supervision under community supervision, parole, or mandatory supervision, whichever date is later; or
(2) after the period described by Subdivision (1), at any location other than the premises at which the person lives.
(b) A person who has been convicted of an offense under Section 22.01, punishable as a Class A misdemeanor and involving a member of the person's family or household, commits an offense if the person possesses a firearm before the fifth anniversary of the later of:
(1) the date of the person's release from confinement following conviction of the misdemeanor; or
(2) the date of the person's release from community supervision following conviction of the misdemeanor.
(c) A person, other than a peace officer, as defined by Section 1.07, actively engaged in employment as a sworn, full-time paid employee of a state agency or political subdivision, who is subject to an order issued under Section 6.504 or Chapter 85, Family Code, under Article 17.292, Code of Criminal Procedure, or by another jurisdiction as provided by Chapter 88, Family Code, commits an offense if the person possesses a firearm after receiving notice of the order and before expiration of the order.
(d) In this section, "family," "household," and "member of a household" have the meanings assigned by Chapter 71, Family Code.
(e) An offense under Subsection (a) is a felony of the third degree. An offense under Subsection (b) or (c) is a Class A misdemeanor.
(f) For the purposes of this section , an offense under the laws of this state, another state, or the United States is, except as provided by Subsection (g), a felony if, at the time it is committed, the offense:
(1) is designated by a law of this state as a felony;
(2) contains all the elements of an offense designated by a law of this state as a felony; or
(3) is punishable by confinement for one year or more in a penitentiary.
(g) An offense is not considered a felony for purposes of Subsection (f) if, at the time the person possesses a firearm, the offense:
(1) is not designated by a law of this state as a felony; and
(2) does not contain all the elements of any offense designated by a law of this state as a felony.

Penal Code §46.041. Unlawful possession Of Metal Or Body Armor By Felon
(a) In this section, "metal or body armor" means any body covering manifestly designed, made, or adapted for the purpose of protecting a person against gunfire.
(b) A person who has been convicted of a felony commits an offense if after the conviction the person possesses metal or body armor.
(c) An offense under this section is a felony of the third degree.

Penal Code §46.05. Prohibited Weapons
(a) A person commits an offense if he intentionally or knowingly possesses, manufactures, transports, repairs, or sells:
(1) an explosive weapon;
(2) a machine gun;
(3) a short-barrel firearm;
(4) a firearm silencer;
(5) knuckles;
(6) armor-piercing ammunition;
(7) a chemical dispensing device;
(8) a zip gun; or
(9) a tire deflation device.
(b) It is a defense to prosecution under this section that the actor's conduct was incidental to the performance of official duty by the armed forces or national guard, a governmental law enforcement agency, or a correctional facility.

(c) It is a defense to prosecution under this section that the actor's possession was pursuant to registration pursuant to the National Firearms Act, as amended.

(d) It is an affirmative defense to prosecution under this section that the actor's conduct:

(1) was incidental to dealing with a short-barrel firearm or tire deflation device solely as an antique or curio; or

(2) was incidental to dealing with armor-piercing ammunition solely for the purpose of making the ammunition available to an organization, agency, or institution listed in Subsection (b).

(e) An offense under Subsection (a)(1), (2), (3), (4), (7) or (8) is a felony of the third degree. An offense under Subsection (a)(9) is a state jail felony. An offense under Subsection (a)(5) is a Class A misdemeanor.

(f) It is a defense to prosecution under this section for the possession of a chemical dispensing device that the actor is a security officer and has received training on the use of the chemical dispensing device by a training program that is:

(1) provided by the Commission on Law Enforcement Officer Standards and Education; or

(2) approved for the purposes described by this subsection by the Texas Private Security Board of the Department of Public Safety.

(g) In Subsection (f), "security officer" means a commissioned security officer as defined by Section 1702.002, Occupations Code, or a noncommissioned security officer registered under Section 1702.221, Occupations Code.

Penal Code §46.06. Unlawful Transfer Of Certain Weapons

(a) A person commits an offense if the person:

(1) sells, rents, leases, loans, or gives a handgun to any person knowing that the person to whom the handgun is to be delivered intends to use it unlawfully or in the commission of an unlawful act;

(2) intentionally or knowingly sells, rents, leases, or gives or offers to sell, rent, lease, or give to any child younger than 18 years any firearm, club, or illegal knife;

(3) intentionally, knowingly, or recklessly sells a firearm or ammunition for a firearm to any person who is intoxicated;

(4) knowingly sells a firearm or ammunition for a firearm to any person who has been convicted of a felony before the fifth anniversary of the later of the following dates:

(A) the person's release from confinement following conviction of the felony; or

(B) the person's release from supervision under community supervision, parole, or mandatory supervision following conviction of the felony; or

(5) sells, rents, leases, loans, or gives a handgun to any person knowing that an active protective order is directed to the person to whom the handgun is to be delivered.

(b) In this section:

(1) "Intoxicated" means substantial impairment of mental or physical capacity resulting from introduction of any substance into the body.

(2) "Active protective order" means a protective order issued under Title 4, Family Code, that is in effect. The term does not include a temporary protective order issued before the court holds a hearing on the matter.

(c) It is an affirmative defense to prosecution under Subsection (a)(2) that the transfer was to a minor whose parent or the person having legal custody of the minor had given written permission for the sale or, if the transfer was other than a sale, the parent or person having legal custody had given effective consent.

(d) An offense under this section is a Class A misdemeanor.

Penal Code §46.07. Interstate Purchase

A resident of this state may, if not otherwise precluded by law, purchase firearms, ammunition, reloading components, or firearm accessories in another state. This authorization is enacted in conformance with 18 U.S.C. §922(b)(3)(A).

Penal Code §46.08. Hoax Bombs

(a) A person commits an offense if the person knowingly manufactures, sells, purchases, transports, or possesses a hoax bomb with intent to use the hoax bomb to:

(1) make another believe that the hoax bomb is an explosive or incendiary device; or

(2) cause alarm or reaction of any type by an official of a public safety agency or volunteer agency organized to deal with emergencies.

(b) An offense under this section is a Class A misdemeanor.

Penal Code §46.09. Components Of Explosives

(a) A person commits an offense if the person knowingly possesses components of an explosive weapon with the intent to combine the components into an explosive weapon for use in a criminal endeavor.

(b) An offense under this section is a felony of the third degree.

Penal Code §46.10. Deadly Weapon In Penal Institution

(a) A person commits an offense if, while confined in a penal institution, he intentionally, knowingly, or recklessly:

(1) carries on or about his person a deadly weapon; or

(2) possesses or conceals a deadly weapon in the penal institution.
(b) It is an affirmative defense to prosecution under this section that at the time of the offense the actor was engaged in conduct authorized by an employee of the penal institution.
(c) A person who is subject to prosecution under both this section and another section under this chapter may be prosecuted under either section.
(d) An offense under this section is a felony of the third degree.

Penal Code §46.11. Penalty If Offense Committed Within Weapon-Free School Zone

(a) Except as provided by Subsection (b), the punishment prescribed for an offense under this chapter is increased to the punishment prescribed for the next highest category of offense if it is shown beyond a reasonable doubt on the trial of the offense that the actor committed the offense in a place that the actor knew was:
(1) within 300 feet of the premises of a school; or
(2) on premises where:
(A) an official school function is taking place; or
(B) an event sponsored or sanctioned by the University Interscholastic League is taking place.
(b) This section does not apply to an offense under Section 46.03(a)(1).
(c) In this section:
(1) "Premises" has the meaning assigned by Section 481.134, Health and Safety Code.
(2) "School" means a private or public elementary or secondary school.

Penal Code §46.12. Maps As Evidence Of Location Or Area

(a) In a prosecution of an offense for which punishment is increased under Section 46.11, a map produced or reproduced by a municipal or county engineer for the purpose of showing the location and boundaries of weapon-free zones is admissible in evidence and is prima facie evidence of the location or boundaries of those areas if the governing body of the municipality or county adopts a resolution or ordinance approving the map as an official finding and record of the location or boundaries of those areas.
(b) A municipal or county engineer may, on request of the governing body of the municipality or county, revise a map that has been approved by the governing body of the municipality or county as provided by Subsection (a).
(c) A municipal or county engineer shall file the original or a copy of every approved or revised map approved as provided by Subsection (a) with the county clerk of each county in which the area is located.
(d) This section does not prevent the prosecution from:
(1) introducing or relying on any other evidence or testimony to establish any element of an offense for which punishment is increased under Section 46.11; or
(2) using or introducing any other map or diagram otherwise admissible under the Texas Rules of Evidence.

Penal Code §46.13. Making A Firearm Accessible To A Child

(a) in this section:
(1) "Child" means a person younger than 17 years of age.
(2) "Readily dischargeable firearm" means a firearm that is loaded with ammunition, whether or not a round is in the chamber.
(3) "Secure" means to take steps that a reasonable person would take to prevent the access to a readily dischargeable firearm by a child, including but not limited to placing a firearm in a locked container or temporarily rendering the firearm inoperable by a trigger lock or other means.
(b) A person commits an offense if a child gains access to a readily dischargeable firearm and the person with criminal negligence:
(1) failed to secure the firearm; or
(2) left the firearm in a place to which the person knew or should have known the child would gain access.
(c) It is an affirmative defense to prosecution under this section that the child's access to the firearm:
(1) was supervised by a person older than 18 years of age and was for hunting, sporting, or other lawful purposes;
(2) consisted of lawful defense by the child of people or property;
(3) was gained by entering property in violation of this code; or
(4) occurred during a time when the actor was engaged in an agricultural enterprise.
(d) Except as provided by Subsection (e), an offense under this section is a Class C misdemeanor.
(e) An offense under this section is a Class A misdemeanor if the child discharges the firearm and causes death or serious bodily injury to himself or another person.
(f) A peace officer or other person may not arrest the actor before the seventh day after the date on which the offense is committed if:
(1) the actor is a member of the family, as defined by Section 71.003, Family Code, of the child who discharged the firearm; and
(2) the child in discharging the firearm caused the death of or serious injury to the child.

(g) A dealer of firearms shall post in a conspicuous position on the premises where the dealer conducts business a sign that contains the following warning in block letters not less than one inch in height:
"IT IS UNLAWFUL TO STORE, TRANSPORT, OR ABANDON AN UNSECURED FIREARM IN A PLACE WHERE CHILDREN ARE LIKELY TO BE AND CAN OBTAIN ACCESS TO THE FIREARM."

Penal Code §46.14. Firearm Smuggling

(a) A person commits an offense if the person knowingly:
(1) possesses or transports a firearm knowing that the firearm was acquired in violation of the laws of any state or of the United States; or
(2) transfers a firearm to another person knowing that the firearm was previously acquired in violation of the laws of any state or of the United States.
(b) An offense under this section is a felony of the third degree, unless it is shown on the trial of the offense that the offense was committed with respect to three or more firearms in a single criminal episode, in which event the offense is a felony of the second degree.
(c) Notwithstanding Subsection (b), the punishment prescribed for an offense under this section is increased to the punishment prescribed for the next highest category of offense if it is shown on the trial of the offense that the actor, at the time of the offense, was engaged in the business of possessing, transporting, or transferring firearms acquired in violation of the laws of any state or of the United States. For purposes of this subsection, a person is considered to have engaged in business if, on more than one occasion, the person engaged in the applicable conduct for profit or any other form of remuneration.
(d) This section does not apply to a peace officer who is engaged in the actual discharge of an official duty.
(e) If conduct that constitutes an offense under this section also constitutes an offense under any other law, the actor may be prosecuted under this section, the other law, or both.

Penal Code §46.15. Nonapplicability

(a) Sections 46.02 and 46.03 do not apply to:
(1) peace officers or special investigators under Article 2.122, Code of Criminal Procedure, and neither section prohibits a peace officer or special investigator from carrying a weapon in this state, including in an establishment in this state serving the public, regardless of whether the peace officer or special investigator is engaged in the actual discharge of the officer's or investigator's duties while carrying the weapon;
(2) parole officers and neither section prohibits an officer from carrying a weapon in this state if the officer is:
(A) engaged in the actual discharge of the officer's duties while carrying the weapon; and
(B) in compliance with policies and procedures adopted by the Texas Department of Criminal Justice regarding the possession of a weapon by an officer while on duty;
(3) community supervision and corrections department officers appointed or employed under Section 76.004, Government Code, and neither section prohibits an officer from carrying a weapon in this state if the officer is:
(A) engaged in the actual discharge of the officer's duties while carrying the weapon; and
(B) authorized to carry a weapon under Section 76.0051, Government Code;
(4) a judge or justice of a federal court, the supreme court, the court of criminal appeals, a court of appeals, a district court, a criminal district court, a constitutional county court, a statutory county court, a justice court, or a municipal court who is licensed to carry a concealed handgun under Subchapter H, Chapter 411, Government Code;
(5) an honorably retired peace officer, qualified retired law enforcement officer, federal criminal investigator, or former reserve law enforcement officer who holds a certificate of proficiency issued under Section 1701.357, Occupations Code, and is carrying a photo identification that is issued by a federal, state, or local law enforcement agency, as applicable, and that verifies that the officer is:
(A) an honorably retired peace officer;
(B) a qualified retired law enforcement officer;
(C) a federal criminal investigator; or
(D) a former reserve law enforcement officer who has served in that capacity not less than a total of 15 years with a state or local law enforcement agency;
(6) a district attorney, criminal district attorney, county attorney, or municipal attorney who is licensed to carry a concealed handgun under Subchapter H, Chapter 411, Government Code;
(7) an assistant district attorney, assistant criminal district attorney, or assistant county attorney who is licensed to carry a concealed handgun under Subchapter H, Chapter 411, Government Code;
(8) a bailiff designated by an active judicial officer as defined by Section 411.201, Government Code, who is:
(A) licensed to carry a concealed handgun under Chapter 411, Government Code; and
(B) engaged in escorting the judicial officer; or
(9) a juvenile probation officer who is authorized to carry a firearm under Section 142.006, Human Resources Code.
(b) Section 46.02 does not apply to a person who:

(1) is in the actual discharge of official duties as a member of the armed forces or Texas military forces as defined by Section 437.001, Government Code, or as a guard employed by a penal institution;

(2) is traveling;

(3) is engaging in lawful hunting, fishing, or other sporting activity on the immediate premises where the activity is conducted, or is en route between the premises and the actor's residence, motor vehicle or watercraft, if the weapon is a type commonly used in the activity;

(4) holds a security officer commission issued by the Texas Private Security Board, if the person is engaged in the performance of the person's duties as an officer commissioned under Chapter 1702, Occupations Code, or is traveling to or from the person's place of assignment and is wearing the officer's uniform and carrying the officer's weapon in plain view;

(5) acts as a personal protection officer and carries the person's security officer commission and personal protection officer authorization if the person:

(A) is engaged in the performance of the person's duties as a personal protection officer under Chapter 1702, Occupations Code, or is traveling to or from the person's place of assignment; and

(B) is either:

(i) wearing the uniform of a security officer, including any uniform or apparel described by Section 1702.323(d), Occupations Code, and carrying the officer's weapon in plain view; or

(ii) not wearing the uniform of a security officer and carrying the officer's weapon in a concealed manner;

(6) is carrying a concealed handgun and a valid license issued under Subchapter H, Chapter 411, Government Code, to carry a concealed handgun; or

(7) holds an alcoholic beverage permit or license or is an employee of a holder of an alcoholic beverage permit or license if the person is supervising the operation of the permitted or licensed premises.

(8) is a student in a law enforcement class engaging in an activity required as part of the class, if the weapon is a type commonly used in the activity and the person is:

(A) on the immediate premises where the activity is conducted; or

(B) en route between those premises and the person's residence and is carrying the weapon unloaded.

(c) The provision of Section 46.02 prohibiting the carrying of a club does not apply to a noncommissioned security guard at an institution of higher education who carries a nightstick or similar club, and who has undergone 15 hours of training in the proper use of the club, including at least seven hours of training in the use of the club for nonviolent restraint. For the purposes of this subsection, "nonviolent restraint" means the use of reasonable force, not intended and not likely to inflict bodily injury.

(d) The provisions of Section 46.02 prohibiting the carrying of a firearm or carrying of a club do not apply to a public security officer employed by the adjutant general under Section 431.029, Government Code, in performance of official duties or while traveling to or from a place of duty.

(e) The provisions of Section 46.02 prohibiting the carrying of an illegal knife do not apply to an individual carrying a bowie knife or a sword used in a historical demonstration or in a ceremony in which the knife or sword is significant to the performance of the ceremony.

(f) Section 46.03(a)(6) does not apply to a person who possesses a firearm or club while in the actual discharge of official duties as:

(1) a member of the armed forces or Texas military forces, as defined by Section 437.001, Government Code; or

(2) an employee of a penal institution.

(g) The provisions of Sections 46.02 and 46.03 prohibiting the possession or carrying of a club do not apply to an animal control officer who holds a certificate issued under Section 829.006, Health and Safety Code, and who possesses or carries an instrument used specifically for deterring the bite of an animal while the officer is in the performance of official duties under the Health and Safety Code or is traveling to or from a place of duty.

(h) Repealed by Acts 2007, 80th Leg., R.S., Ch. 693, §3(1), eff. September 1, 2007.

(i) Redesignated (j) by Acts 2007, 80th Leg., Ch. 921, §17.001(62).

(j) The provisions of Section 46.02 prohibiting the carrying of a handgun do not apply to an individual who carries a handgun as a participant in a historical reenactment performed in accordance with the rules of the Texas Alcoholic Beverage Commission.

CHAPTER 71
ORGANIZED CRIME AND CRIMINAL STREET GANGS

Penal Code §71.01. Definitions

In this chapter,

(a) "Combination" means three or more persons who collaborate in carrying on criminal activities, although:

(1) participants may not know each other's identity;

(2) membership in the combination may change from time to time; and

(3) participants may stand in a wholesaler-retailer or other arm's-length relationship in illicit distribution operations.

(b) "Conspires to commit" means that a person agrees with one or more persons that they or one or more of them engage in conduct that would constitute the offense and that person and one or more of them perform an overt act in pursuance of the agreement. An agreement constituting conspiring to commit may be inferred from the acts of the parties.

(c) "Profits" means property constituting or derived from any proceeds obtained, directly or indirectly, from an offense listed in Section 71.02.

Penal Code §71.02. Engaging In Organized Criminal Activity

(a) A person commits an offense if, with the intent to establish, maintain, or participate in a combination or in the profits of a combination or as a member of a criminal street gang, the person commits or conspires to commit one or more of the following:

(1) murder, capital murder, arson, aggravated robbery, robbery, burglary, theft, aggravated kidnapping, kidnapping, aggravated assault, aggravated sexual assault, sexual assault, forgery, deadly conduct, assault punishable as a Class A misdemeanor, burglary of a motor vehicle, or unauthorized use of a motor vehicle;

(2) any gambling offense punishable as a Class A misdemeanor;

(3) promotion of prostitution, aggravated promotion of prostitution, or compelling prostitution;

(4) unlawful manufacture, transportation, repair, or sale of firearms or prohibited weapons;

(5) unlawful manufacture, delivery, dispensation, or distribution of a controlled substance or dangerous drug, or unlawful possession of a controlled substance or dangerous drug through forgery, fraud, misrepresentation, or deception;

(5-a) causing the unlawful delivery, dispensation, or distribution of a controlled substance or dangerous drug in violation of Subtitle B, Title 3, Occupations Code;

(6) any unlawful wholesale promotion or possession of any obscene material or obscene device with the intent to wholesale promote the same;

(7) any offense under Subchapter B, Chapter 43, depicting or involving conduct by or directed toward a child younger than 18 years of age;

(8) any felony offense under Chapter 32;

(9) any offense under Chapter 36;

(10) any offense under Chapter 34, 35 or 35a;

(11) any offense under Section 37.11(a);

(12) any offense under Chapter 20A; or

(13) any offense under Section 37.10;

(14) any offense under Section 38.06, 38.07, 38.09, or 38.11;

(15) any offense under Section 42.10;

(16) any offense under Section 46.06(a)(1) or 46.14; or

(17) any offense under Section 20.05. <Ch 223 2011>

(17) any offense classified as a felony under the Tax Code. <Ch 68 2011>

(b) Except as provided in Subsections (c) and (d), an offense under this section is one category higher than the most serious offense listed in Subsection (a) that was committed, and if the most serious offense is a Class A misdemeanor, the offense is a state jail felony, except that if the most serious offense is a felony of the first degree, the offense is a felony of the first degree.

(c) Conspiring to commit an offense under this section is of the same degree as the most serious offense listed In Subsection (a) that the person conspired to commit.

(d) At the punishment stage of a trial, the defendant may raise the issue as to whether in voluntary and complete renunciation of the offense he withdrew from the combination before commission of an offense listed in Subsection (a) and made substantial effort to prevent the commission of the offense. If the defendant proves the issue in the affirmative by a preponderance of the evidence the offense is the same category of offense as the most serious offense listed in Subsection (a) that is committed, unless the defendant is convicted of conspiring to commit the offense, in which event the offense is one category lower than the most serious offense that the defendant conspired to commit.

Property Code §42.002. Personal Property Eligible for Exemption

The following personal property is eligible for the exemption:

(D) two firearms; <Relates to bankruptcy>

Transportation Code §504.631

(a) The department shall issue specialty license plates to honor the Texas State Rifle Association.

(b) After deduction of the department's administrative costs, the remainder of the fee shall be deposited to the credit of an account in the general revenue fund that may be appropriated only to the Texas Cooperative Extension of The Texas A&M University System as follows:

(1) 50 percent to supplement existing and future scholarship programs supported by the Texas State Rifle Association; and

(2) 50 percent to support the 4-H Shooting Sports Program for youth.

Civil Statutes Article 5069-51.16. Prohibited Practices
A pawnbroker shall not:
(h) Display for sale in storefront windows or sidewalk display case so that same may be viewed from the street, any pistol, dirk, dagger, blackjack, hand chain, sword cane, knuckles made of any metal or any hard substance, switchblade knife, springblade knife, or throwblade knife, or depict same on any sign or advertisement which may be viewed from the street.

Texas Code of Criminal Procedure
Note that some aspects of Texas gun law are found in "Vernon's Texas Statutes Annotated Code Of Criminal Procedure," and these are no longer included in this Appendix. They may be obtained online at gunlaws.com or other sites. Some of the categories included in the CCP are legal protections of rights, search and seizure rules, constitutional guarantees, definitions of peace officers, statutes of limitation, powers for suppression of riots, sentencing guidelines, conditions for arrest, warrants and disposition of seized items, forfeiture of contraband and more. Elimination of this section in this edition removes 6,013 words, which remain included in the word-count charts so increases in gun law are accurately represented.

House Concurrent Resolution 57 • 1999 Legislature
WHEREAS, Teaching children to act safely around firearms is a critical step in the effort to reduce the number of firearm-related accidents among our nation's young people; and
WHEREAS, The Eddie Eagle Gun Safety Program teaches the fundamentals of firearm safety to elementary school-aged children in an effective and enjoyable way, communicating to them the lifesaving message that when they see a gun they should stop, immediately leave the area, and tell an adult; and
WHEREAS, Literature and teaching materials from this nationally recognized program are widely available to schools and police departments throughout the United States; since 1988, more than 8,000 public and private schools and 2,500 law enforcement agencies have relayed the program's valuable message to 6.5 million children in America; and
WHEREAS, House Concurrent Resolution 24 adopted by the 73rd Legislature of the State of Texas encouraged the Texas Education Agency to promote the use of the National Rifle Association's Eddie Eagle Gun Safety Program in our schools, and the importance of continuing the positive efforts of this vital program cannot be overstated; now, therefore, be it
RESOLVED, That the 76th Legislature of the State of Texas hereby declare the week of October 18–22, 1999, as Children's Firearm Safety Week and encourage all citizens of the State of Texas to support the National Rifle Association's Eddie Eagle Gun Safety Program in promoting children's firearm safety in Texas.

About Alan Korwin

Alan Korwin, author of six books and co-author of eight others, is a full-time freelance writer, consultant and businessman with a twenty-five-year track record. He is a founder and two-term past president of the Arizona Book Publishing Association, which has presented him with its Visionary Leadership award, named in his honor, the Korwin Award. He has received national awards for his publicity work as a member of the Society for Technical Communication, and is a past board member of the Phoenix, Arizona chapter of the Society of Professional Journalists.

Mr. Korwin wrote the business plan that raised $5 million in venture capital and launched the in-flight catalog *SkyMall;* he did the publicity for Pulitzer Prize cartoonist Steve Benson's fourth book; working with American Express, he wrote the strategic plan that defined their worldwide telecommunications strategy for the 1990s; and he had a hand in developing ASPED, Arizona's economic strategic plan. His writing appears nationally regularly.

Korwin turned his first book, *The Arizona Gun Owner's Guide,* into a self-published best-seller, now in its 25th edition. With his wife Cheryl he operates Bloomfield Press, which has grown into the largest publisher and distributor of gun-law books in the country. Built around ten books he has written on the subject, it includes the unabridged federal guides *Gun Laws of America* and *Supreme Court Gun Cases,* a line of more than 250 books, buttons and DVDs, and more than 1,000 radio and TV appearances. He was an invited guest at the U.S. Supreme Court for oral argument in *D.C. v. Heller,* which led to his 11th book, *The Heller Case: Gun Rights Affirmed.* His 12th book, on the limits of free speech, *Bomb Jokes at Airports,* was followed by *After You Shoot: Your gun's hot. The perp's not. Now what?* His 14th book, in 2013, is *Your First Gun.*

Alan Korwin is originally from New York City, where his clients included IBM, AT&T, NYNEX and others, many with real names. He is a pretty good guitarist and singer, with a penchant for parody (his current band is The Cartridge Family). In 1986, finally married, he moved to the Valley of the Sun. It was a joyful and successful move.

About Georgene Lockwood

In her 35-year writing career, **Georgene Lockwood** has written about everything from firearms law to beadwork, auto racing, Victoriana, computers, ultrasonic welding technology and beadwork. Her internationally best-selling self-help book, *The Complete Idiot's Guide to Organizing Your Life*, has sold more than a million copies and is in its 5th edition, and she has been interviewed by Woman's Day, Redbook and numerous radio and internet hosts on the subjects of organizing, decluttering and simpler living.

Lockwood has authored 11 other books, five of them in the *Idiot's Guide* series, and is a member of the Authors Guild. She covered land use and conservation issues as a newspaper reporter and worked as a stringer for the Associated Press covering auto racing. Lockwood also owned her own marketing communications company, specializing in high-tech industries.

Originally from New York City, Georgene Lockwood currently lives on her mini-farm in Prescott, Arizona, with her husband Jim, owner of Legends in Leather and an acclaimed craftsman of replica gun belts and holsters from western movies and television. She is an avid target shooter and enjoys contributing to her community as a Master Gardener, Community Emergency Response Team volunteer, some-time musician, and lecturer on gardening, Victorian social history and crafts. She is also owner of a jewelry-making business, teaches classes in beading techniques, and has recently made a foray into the Wordpress blogging universe.

POLITICALLY CORRECTED GLOSSARY

We've all talked about losing the war of words in the struggle for our liberties.

Well here comes the cavalry—

Certain words hurt you when you talk about your rights and liberties.

People who would deny your rights have done a good job of manipulating the language so far. Without even realizing it, you're probably using terms that actually help people who want to disarm you.

THEY WIN IF YOU SAY:	YOU WIN IF YOU SAY:
pro gun	pro rights
gun control	crime control
reasonable gun-control laws	illegal infringement laws
anti-gun movement	anti-self-defense movement
semiautomatic handgun	sidearm
concealed carry	discreet carry or right to carry
assault weapon or lethal weapon	household firearms
Saturday night specials	racist gun laws
junk guns	the affordability issue
high-capacity magazines	normal-capacity magazines
Second Amendment	Bill of Rights
the powerful gun lobby	civil rights organizations
common-sense legislation	dangerous utopian ideas
anti gun	anti-gun bigotry
anti gun	anti-gun prejudice
anti gun	anti rights

WHEN THEY SAY:	YOU SAY:
Guns kill	Guns save lives
Guns cause crime	Guns stop crime
Guns are bad	Guns are why America is still free
Assault weapons are bad	Assault is a type of behavior
Guns are too dangerous to own	You should take a safety class
People shouldn't have guns	Maybe you shouldn't have one
People don't need guns	Only good people need guns
Gun owners should be registered	Bad guys first
They should take away all the guns	Bad guys first. Who is "they"?
The purpose of a gun is to kill	The purpose of a gun is to protect
We need more gun laws	Criminal activity is already banned
Do you really have a gun?	Of course, don't you?

To preserve, protect and defend your rights in the critical debate of where power should reside in America, you need effective word choices. Try out some of the ideas in this chart the next time you deal with this subject.

This is just a small part of my full Politically Corrected Glossary. *Get the rest in ready-to-print form (a PDF file) on our website. Feel free to share this with your friends, journalists, anti-gun bigots, and anyone else who needs a refreshing perspective on the liberties your personal firearms represent.*

THE LIBERTY POLL
by Attorney Michael P. Anthony, Author Alan Korwin and Syndicated Columnist Vin Suprynowicz

"Hello, politician—What's the purpose of government?" It's time to start asking tough questions the "news" media avoids, to really learn what sort of leaders we elect. Although reporters can seem like they play hardball with candidates, they almost never do.

• If you're elected to the office you seek: a) what laws will you repeal; b) what taxes will you reduce or eliminate; c) what agencies will you shrink or close?

• Can you name any areas where government might serve the public interest, but where it has no authority to act? If not, is it still accurate to say we have a "government of limited powers"? Does this matter?

• Can you name any current areas of government operations that are outside the authority delegated to government?

• Regarding jury trials, should judges be required to inform jurors they have the power, in the sanctity of the jury room, to decide whether a law in question is just, or constitutional? Should schools teach this?

• Regarding law enforcement, are you in favor of police using deadly force when absolutely necessary to protect innocent lives from criminal attack? Do you believe that people, even people with no training of any kind, have less right to defend themselves than authorities do?

• When did you last read the state and federal Constitutions?

THE ONLY QUESTION ABOUT GUN REGISTRATION by Alan Korwin

Only one thing is overlooked in the common sense proposals to register guns. How exactly would writing down my name, or your name, help arrest criminals or make you safer? The unfortunate answer is that, no matter how good it feels when the words first pass your ears, registering honest gun owners doesn't stop criminals, and in fact focuses in the opposite direction. Gun registration schemes lack a crime-prevention component.

• Registering 90 million Americans is extremely expensive. A database that big needs 24,000 changes daily, just to keep up with people who move every ten years. Floor after floor of cubicle after cubicle—it's a federal jobs program all by itself. How many criminals will register? That's right, none, and planners know that. In fact, crooks can't register—the ban on self incrimination makes it illegal to force them. All that money and time, invested on tracking the innocent.

• Americans who fail to register would become felons without harming anyone.

• Registration, if enacted, will create an underground market for guns bigger than the drug trade. The last thing you want to encourage is import programs and price supports that drug dealers enjoy, for gun runners.

• You don't really think authorities would use registration lists to confiscate guns from people, do you? Despite examples of exactly that in New York and California, and global history for the past century, this couldn't really happen, do you think?

WHY DON'T POLICE ARREST ALL THE BRADY CRIMINALS THEY FIND?
by Alan Korwin

It's well known by now, that of all the people stopped by the Brady law's FBI background check, very few are arrested—even though it's a five-year felony for them to try to buy a gun. If the goal is to stop crime, why aren't these people arrested? Here's why:

• Because the Brady law is neither designed nor intended to increase the annual number of federal prosecutions. (from BATF, FBI, White House)

• Because the last thing you want is for police to be constantly showing up at gunstores and making arrests of felons who want guns... it's too potentially dangerous for the customers. (Arizona Police Lieut.)

• Because there isn't enough time for all the arraignments, dockets would gridlock, detention cells would burst, prisons would overflow, and nobody in the system wants to even attempt it.

• Because unless we have more crime and violence we won't be able to justify taking everybody's gun away.

• Because the real purpose of the Brady law is to build a federal gun-registration infra-structure, and it has been wildly successful.

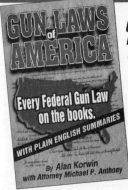
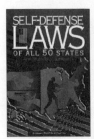
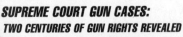

Published by
BLOOMFIELD PRESS